SURVIVING GLOBALIZATION
in Three Latin American Communities

To Bill

SURVIVING GLOBALIZATION
in Three Latin American Communities

..

Denis Lynn Daly Heyck

broadview press

NATIONAL LIBRARY OF CANADA CATALOGUING IN PUBLICATION DATA

Heyck, Denis Lynn Daly
Surviving globalization in three Latin American communities / Denis Lynn Daly Heyck.

Includes bibliographical references and index.
ISBN 1-55111-477-1

1. Globalization—Social aspects—Latin America.
2. Latin America—Commerce.
3. Rubber tappers—Brazil.
4. Guarani Indians—Bolivia.
5. Women in cooperative societies—Nicaragua.
6. Latin America—Religion.
I. Title.

HF1480.5.H49 2002   330.98   C2002-901807-2

BROADVIEW PRESS, LTD.
is an independent, international publishing house, incorporated in 1985.

North America
Post Office Box 1243,
Peterborough, Ontario, Canada K9J 7H5

3576 California Road,
Orchard Park, New York, USA 14127
TEL (705) 743-8990; FAX (705) 743-8353

www.broadviewpress.com
customerservice@broadviewpress.com

United Kingdom and Europe
Plymbridge North (Thomas Lyster Ltd.) Units
3 & 4a Ormskirk Industrial Park,
Old Boundary Way, Burscough Rd, Ormskirk,
Lancashire L39 2YW
TEL (1695) 575112; FAX (1695) 570120; E-MAIL
books@tlyster.co.uk

Australia
UNIREPS University of New South Wales
Sydney, NSW 2052
TEL 61 2 9664099; FAX 61 2 9664520
infopress@unsw.edu.au

Broadview Press gratefully acknowledges the support of the Ministry of Canadian Heritage through the Book Publishing Industry Development Program.

Cover design by Zack Taylor.
Typeset by Liz Broes, Black Eye Design.

Printed in Canada

10 9 8 7 6 5 4 3 2 1

CONTENTS

PART III NICARAGUA

ACKNOWLEDGMENTS

The purpose of this book is to give voice to traditional peoples in Latin America who are experiencing profound and wrenching cultural and economic changes—in some cases, the threat of extinction of their communities—as a result of globalization and development. *Surviving Globalization* is the work of many people in both Latin America and the US to whom I am deeply grateful. First, I am indebted to all those who gave so freely of their time and themselves in the interviews. They are acknowledged in the bibliography. In particular, I would like to express my gratitude to the people of Xapuri and Rio Branco, Brazil, for their warmth and openness, to the villagers of Ñaurenda and neighboring Guaraní pueblos in Bolivia for their heartfelt welcome and hospitality, and to the women of Malpaisillo and Guanacastillo in Nicaragua for their good humor and enthusiasm. The humility and strength of spirit of members of every community were, at times, overwhelming. I am thankful to the people in all three locales for demonstrating in their daily lives the importance of never giving in to despair, always believing that there must be a better way, and celebrating the gift of life even amid great hardship and hunger. The agency, consciousness, creativity, and organizational skills they exhibit as they hammer out concrete survival strategies remind us of the rich wisdom, experiences, and cultural and human values instructive to the modern world that are to be found at the grassroots level.

I would like to thank those who extended themselves specially through introductions, on-site assistance, and other support, logistical and moral. In Brazil, Dom Moacyr Grechi, former Bishop of the Diocese of Rio Branco and the Upper Purús and now Archbishop of Rondônia, and his former assistant, Maria Ronizia Gonçalves Pereira, former Communication Director of the Diocese, without knowing me or anything about me, immediately expressed their faith in the project and put me in touch with wonderful people in nearly inaccessible places. In Bolivia, Sr. Maura McCarthy, PBVM, again without knowing me or my work, and motivated by her faith in the project, generously shared with me her love for and knowledge of the Guaraní people, took me to remote places to meet fascinating villagers, and offered me her friendship. In Nicaragua, Licda. Miriam Lazo Laguna, a legend among that country's poor and a friend of many years, whose selfless work on behalf of destitute campesinos, impoverished women, prostitutes, and orphaned, abandoned, and drug-addicted children in Nicaragua has earned the respect and admiration of national and international organizations, quietly directed me to the remarkable campesinas who tell their stories here. This book would not have been possible without the steadfast support, advice, and assistance of these four individuals. Thanks also to the Sisters of Xapuri, Brazil, for their hospitality and to Irmã Mavy for introducing me to Terra Alta. Also in Brazil, I am indebted to Soraya Pereira da Silva and Ana Ramos for their kind help in obtaining permissions. Warm appreciation goes to Sr. Therese Marie Hawes, PBVM, of Entre Ríos for enlightening conversations on the history and work of the Rural Pastorate in Tarija.

In the US, thanks to Paolo Giordano, Chair of the Department of Modern Languages and Literatures, Loyola University Chicago, for his ongoing support of the project; to the Office of Research Services, Loyola University Chicago, for much-needed travel assistance; to former Academic Dean Kathleen McCourt, formerly of Loyola University Chicago, for the faculty leave of absence, fall 1997, that allowed me to launch the project, and to my colleagues in Spanish for shouldering additional responsibilities that semester; to the Center for Ethics, Loyola University Chicago, and its Director David Ozar, for the fellowship in the spring of 1997 that helped me establish the project's ethical bases; and to the Gannon Center for Women and Leadership, Loyola University Chicago, the Center's Director Sr. Carolyn Farrell, BVM, Archivist Valerie Browne, and Director of Women's Studies Pamela Caughie, for the fellowship in the spring of 2000 that provided the time, space, and warmly supportive atmosphere in which to begin writing.

Thanks go also to the efficient and helpful inter-library loan staff at Loyola University Chicago and Northwestern University, Evanston, Illinois. The maps were downloaded from <http://www.lib.utexas.edu/maps> and are used courtesy of The General Libraries, The University of Texas at Austin, with thanks.

I must thank my husband, Bill Heyck, for sharing the outlines of my project with Mical Moser of Broadview Press, and to Mical for her friendly, open manner and quick work in introducing me to Michael Harrison, Vice-President of Broadview Press, and Suzanne Hancock, former Assistant to the Vice-President, who were positive, helpful, and extremely prompt from the start and a delight to work with at every stage. Production Editor Barbara Conolly, Assistant Production Editor Judith Earnshaw, and Copy Editor Betsy Struthers merit warm appreciation for their careful work and highly professional assistance.

Special thanks go to Hunter Crowther-Heyck for helping to clarify the relationship between cultural survival and globalization.

The manuscript was strengthened by the insightful comments made by readers for Broadview Press, and vastly improved by the valuable suggestions made by Herman E. Daly, to whom I am deeply grateful.

Most of all, I would like to thank my husband, who has listened endlessly, read and reread countless drafts, offered constructive criticism at every juncture, and who has been all along the most enthusiastic supporter of, and ardent believer in, *Surviving Globalization.*

All errors, including those in translation, are my own.

INTRODUCTION

"Never doubt that a small group of thoughtful, committed citizens can change the world. Indeed, it is the only thing that ever has."
—MARGARET MEAD.

This book describes and compares the survival strategies of three very different Latin American cultural, linguistic, and ethnic groups as they deal with the forces of globalization and modernization. It is based on extensive field work and interviews; the main body of the manuscript presents the words of the people themselves. The three groups are the *caboclo* [mixed African, Indian, and European] Portuguese-speaking rubber tappers of the far western Brazilian Amazon; the Spanish and Guaraní-speaking Guaraní Indians of the southernmost toe of the Bolivian Chaco; and the Spanish-speaking mestizo country women of agricultural and savings cooperatives in northern and western Nicaragua. However diverse the cultures, each is located in a poor rural area with virtually no infrastructure; endemic diseases such as malaria, Chagas, and rabies; and a single export commodity in the process of being replaced by logging, ranching, or large-scale farming for export.

Of course, poverty existed long before globalization, but currently it seems that most local and national efforts to fight poverty are undercut by that process. Since poverty and its new global guardian are immediate dangers to the survival of these peoples, their cultures, and their livelihoods, they, unlike some intellectual observers, do not have the luxury of regarding globalization as simply a trend whose consequences can be described but probably not fundamentally altered. The people who tell their stories here must react in order to survive. They have no choice but to take action. They must at least alter the consequences, if not the trend itself. This book is mainly about their concrete strategies and actions, their motivating faith and vision. To set the stage for understanding their heroism (no other word suffices), extreme hardships, and accomplishments, we have to describe briefly the forces of globalization to which they are reacting. That is the purpose of this introduction.

Much recent research confirms that globalization and development are having an enormous impact even in the most remote corners of Latin America, and that their effects are destructive of traditional communities and cultures.[1] However, my research has also found that rural populations are not merely passive victims of an inexorable process; rather, they are active agents on their own behalf. For example, villagers in each setting relate the ways in which their locales have both adapted to powerful outside influences and attempted to refashion them to accommodate local realities and values. Community members detail their own efforts to develop a political, economic, and environmental awareness; to organize at the grassroots level; to form coalitions; and to raise up local leaders with the assistance of religious workers, popular education programs, and NGOs (nongovernmental organizations). In other words, while some aspects of globalization have been extremely destructive, in each case analyzed here global agencies are helping the people to cope.

Two powerful constants underlie local strategies in all three locales: attitudes toward the land—tenure, ownership, and one's relationship to it—and religious faith—both institutional and popular. But the main story varies from place to place. In Brazil, the interviews highlight the extraordinary efforts of the progressive wing of the Catholic church to protect, organize, and raise the consciousness of the population, often at great personal risk and in the face of death threats and assassinations of base community and union members. Indeed, the rubber tappers' inspirational leader Chico Mendes was assassinated by ranchers in 1988. However, neither his work nor that of the church officials with whom he collaborated in the early years was in vain, for today the movers of both the union and the cooperative were forged in the leadership training courses at the heart of base community activities in the Amazon.

In Bolivia, the story is that of the painstaking efforts of foreign missionaries working with local Guaraní to revive the degraded Guaraní culture, helping to save their language and rescue from near extinction traditional indigenous values of community and assembly, including above all a town hall type of democracy. The Guaraní themselves have placed these values in the balance as counterweights to the corruption, racism, and rigid class stratification that characterize Bolivia's political system, debilitating its ecclesiastical hierarchy and afflicting their own traditional culture. Not surprisingly, the missionaries and the Guaraní have at times provoked the displeasure of these national institutions.

In Nicaragua, the central story is the stubborn resistance by a number of campesinas, or rural women, to the erasure of certain features of the Nicaraguan revolution, particularly, their feminist consciousness in sustaining their cooperatives and their tenacity in defending their rights, at a time when the official Catholic church, like the national government, has metamorphosed from revolutionary to reactionary. In Nicaragua, there is also the related story of relative ecumenical solidarity at the grassroots level, an unusual phenomenon in Latin America and another striking legacy of the Sandinista revolution of 1979.

In each case, then, there is a unique, central story, but there is also a common one among the three: a basic conflict over land rights. This clash arises from diametrically opposed value systems. One system—capitalist, growth-oriented, and embedded in globalizing imperatives—sees human beings as economic creatures driven by self-interest. Society is a collection of self-interested individuals, who occasionally come into conflict; for this reason, outside controls, such as government or law, are required to keep random encounters from restricting individual rights. In this view, nature is an inert object, and humankind is its master. It is the entrepreneur's right and duty to make the land productive—that is, to produce economic growth—through development by logging, cutting the forest, setting up cattle ranches, drilling for oil, and promoting export agriculture. The bigger the technology applied, the better. By this vision, destruction of habitats and cultures is an unfortunate but necessary price to pay for economic growth that will one day improve the country or region as a whole. After all, it is argued, a rising tide lifts all boats.[2]

The other approach to the land, that of these particular communities, is long term and relational. It sees human activity as part of, and dependent on, the natural world. It is at bottom a traditional, not a capitalistic—much less a global—attitude. It is not primarily profit-oriented but, rather, is based on the idea of sufficiency. The notion of sufficiency implies an interrelatedness with nature, a recognition of human dependence on the natural world, and a future ethic, the sense that one must consider future generations in the economic and cultural choices made today. In the relational view, the scale of economic activity must be contained within the natural recuperative boundaries of the ecosystem. The tappers learn as children how to cut the bark correctly so that the tree keeps producing; the Guaraní restrict the gathering of palm fronds for basket-weaving when the supply gets low; and the Nicaraguan women find that organic agriculture improves their yield without harming the land. The technology applied is appropriate in scale and expense, what E.F. Schumacher called "appropriate technology."[3]

The capitalist-growth and traditional-communitarian views conflict sharply, especially when placed within the broader context of rapidly accelerating economic globalization. Currently the former is in the ascendancy in all three countries of this study, but in each case there are growing pockets of resistance where communities have organized to create what they hope will be workable alternatives, breathing spaces allowing them to survive long enough to adapt. This book focuses on three locales, chosen for their different ethnic, linguistic, and cultural histories and for their similar responses to globalization. In a broad sense, they are representative of diverse rural communities all across Latin America.

Before proceeding, it is important to clarify certain key terms that will appear throughout the book.

What is Development?

The development era in the "third world" began after World War II and continues today. The basic concept of development is that the more prosperous, or "first world," countries should assist those of the less prosperous "third world" in becoming more "advanced." By this concept, western societies constitute the model that the rest of the world should strive to attain. That standard is scientific and technical, measuring progress by the growth of a nation's GNP (Gross National Product – total sum of economic activity generated by the national economy both domestically and internationally). In his inaugural address in 1949, Harry Truman voiced development philosophy as he offered a "fair deal" for the "underdeveloped" world:

> I believe that we should make available to peace-loving peoples the benefits of our store of technical knowledge in order to help them realize their aspirations for a better life.... What we envisage is a program of development based on the concepts of democratic fair dealing.... Greater production is the key to prosperity and peace. And the key to greater production is a wider and more vigorous application of modern scientific and technical knowledge.[4]

In areas where technology and infrastructure are rudimentary, implementation of the Truman doctrine amounts to a sweeping transformation and modernization of entire cultures and societies. A United Nations statement on development spoke to the wrenching effects of such drastic change, but regarded them as regrettable by-products of an inexorable process:

> There is a sense in which rapid economic progress is impossible without painful adjustments. Ancient philosophies have to be scrapped; old social institutions have to disintegrate; bonds of caste, creed and race have to burst; and large numbers of persons who cannot keep up with progress have to have their expectations of a comfortable life frustrated.[5]

Thus, proponents of development proposed to make two-thirds of the world esteem material and technical progress as their prime goal. Development was to replicate worldwide the features of the developed countries: "high levels of industrialization and urbanization, technicalization of agriculture, rapid growth of material production and living standards, and the widespread adoption of modern education and cultural values."[6]

This vision is prevalent today among advocates of development, including international agencies like the World Bank and IMF (International Monetary Fund), whose well-intentioned plans are sometimes conceived in naiveté or arrogance. As a result, development projects often pay scant attention to their long-term cultural, environmental, and economic consequences, and they often lack meaningful consultation with the affected peoples. Lately, however, as a result of criticism, development organizations have begun to pay closer attention to local needs as articulated by residents themselves. The United Nations Development Program's Human Development Index, for example, is a measure of social and economic well-being intended to make development projects more reflective of local needs. It is part of the effort by development organizations to "enlarge people's choices" rather than impose paradigms. Even so, considerations crucial to a community's well-being, such as environmental health, are absent from the HDI, nor does the index "incorporate cultural values as an aspect of choice, for communities may value cultural survival even at the expense of certain development plans."[7]

What is Globalization?

The term globalization usually refers to the process of worldwide economic integration and may be viewed as an outcome, a carrier, and a feature of development. Globalization brings with it transnational integration of markets, products, and communications networks with social, political, and environmental systems to a degree previously unknown and unimagined.

At the most abstract level, globalization connotes the vast, constant movement of capital, goods, and jobs across borders, usually under decisions made by multinational corporations and lending institutions. This system was set in motion by the information revolution of the late twentieth century, which has overcome once insurmountable distances, bridged once unbridgeable gaps, and drawn practically all peoples into ever closer contact with once distant others. Amazonian rubber tappers, for example, are now in instant communication with suburban environmentalists in the US. The new possibilities have so rapidly and fundamentally altered our world that we are only beginning to discern their meretricious effects as well as their beneficial features. Economic integration made possible by the communications revolution offers exciting possibilities, such as new markets, new discoveries, cheaper consumer goods, and more widely available healthcare services and education, but it also brings with it dangerous consequences that threaten cultural diversity, national sovereignty, and freedom of choice and that exacerbate existing economic and social injustices.[8]

Globalization, at the macro level, also includes a new awareness of our interdependence. It places upon all humankind a shared, if unsought, responsibility for the world's future. The burning of rainforests in the Amazon and Indonesia affects air quality in North America. Industrial pollution in the US destroys forests in Canada. Financial crises in South Korea or Japan affect not only those countries' economies, but also the viability of the entire international financial system. Likewise, political oppression in Haiti, violence in Rwanda, and economic inequality in Mexico create political and economic refugees who must be relocated. As development scholar David Korten explains, in a world in which one country's destiny is so tightly interwoven with another's, any state that fails to address the issue of balancing its population with its environmental resources will generate "welfare" problems that will spill over to other countries.[9]

Our economic interdependence became painfully apparent in the powerful aftershocks of the September 11, 2001 terrorist attacks on New York City and Washington, DC, which we now realize have their roots in the poverty and inequality in much of the Islamic world, and which have caused dramatic increases in security budgets as well as drastic reductions in business activity and in all modes of travel around the globe, from Riyadh to Rio. We now know that the long arm of the global economy reaches us all. The developed world has been slow to grasp the relationship between development, globalization, and loss of local control. To traditional communities, however, the connection has been clear for some time.

To understand this relationship it is important to draw the distinction between import-substitution and export-led development. The former provided the development strategy for third-world countries from the 1940s through the 1960s and had as its basic principle that nations should begin producing themselves the products they currently imported, thus "substituting" locally produced matches, for example, for imported ones. Nascent local industries were protected by their governments, and demand for locally made goods increased as World War II limited the availability of imports. Though this strategy had its shortcomings, import substitution stimulated national economies, allowed developing countries a degree of autonomy, and offered them the freedom to trade, or not, with whomever they wished.

During the 1970s, however, this model was discarded, by the World Bank and the IMF in particular, in favor of a new mantra that governs today: export-led growth. By this concept, countries should maximize their competitive advantage, that is, what they possess in abundance and can supply cheaply, such as, for Latin America, natural resources and labor. These can be sold to the developed countries, and earnings from these sales can be used to import, say, to Nicaragua, the matches produced more efficiently and cheaply in the US, whose competitive advantage lies in efficient, mass manufacture. According to this reasoning, Nicaragua should never attempt to make its own matches, much less anything as technically challenging as computers, for Nicaragua's advantage (to say nothing of that of the developed manufacturing economies) lies elsewhere. It is not hard to see how this line of thinking increases dependency and decreases freedom of choice in trade as the world moves toward a single global economy in which separate national economies are no longer viable hubs, but rather are reduced in status to mere spokes leading only to and from a sole, central hub.

Export-led development and free capital mobility also promote the aims of multinational corporations at the expense of national or regional economies. The movement of transnational corporations to developing countries, like Nicaragua, allows their branches to make matches more cheaply than in the metropolitan center and have access to the local market as well. The match industry may even begin exporting from Nicaragua back to the US, thereby bringing US and Nicaraguan workers into competition, perhaps closing US plants, in a race to the bottom in terms of wages and working conditions. Small national firms, no longer regulated or protected by national governments, as well as workers in both Nicaragua and the US, are sacrificed at the altar of efficiency, as they lose out to large multinationals who now control match production.

Lending institutions, such as the World Bank, favor export projects such as this because they directly earn the foreign exchange necessary to pay back loans, and they hold producers to world-class standards of efficiency, as opposed to the protection governments once offered their inefficient native producers. Big corporations benefit from World Bank loans because they become the suppliers for the project. Regardless of the merit of the project it finances, the World Bank will never lose because the country's international credit rating requires that the bank will be paid back, usually first. One may ask, how does the World Bank recoup its loan if the project is a loss? The answer is simple. The borrower—the national government—increases taxes and cuts domestic spending, pushing the country's impoverished populations, including those of this study, ever deeper into the black hole of poverty.

The point to remember is that export-led development is the theoretical policy thrust behind globalization, and that globalization depends on the replacement of import-substitution by export-led development as the favored development strategy of international lending institutions and national governments. That strategy does not promote mutually beneficial trade because it is not voluntary. For trade to be voluntary, a country must be free not to trade. In order to be free not to trade, a nation must have a degree of self-sufficiency denied under globalization.

One can see how the export-led strategy leads to a single, cookie-cutter model of what constitutes development in a globalized economy and of what nations must do to achieve it. At the next step down from the macro level, globalization means, much more specifically, decisions by particular institutions that actively seek to promote global economic development exclusively along the single pattern described above. International lending institutions provide one set of solutions for a variety of complex needs and problems occurring in widely differing countries as they seek the incorporation of all regional economies into one massive global system. The net is cast widely, but it is the same net for all peoples. At this level, globalization begets what have come to be known as "neoliberal" policies in each of the states of the world including Brazil, Bolivia, and Nicaragua.

The term "neoliberal" refers to a set of market-based structural adjustment reforms mandated by international financial institutions such as the IMF, World Bank, and Inter-American Development Bank. They are intended to bring about economic stabilization, reduce inflation, and promote growth. Main features of neoliberal packages require drastic cuts in a nation's public spending, including not only spending for public employees and services such as infrastructure and fire and police protection, but also for health and educational services; privatization of the economy through massive reduction in the state's role in the economy (in Nicaragua, for example, even the public school bus system has been privatized); and liberalization, that is, reducing or eliminating tariffs on imports and removing other restrictions on the unfettered movement of capital. According to political scientist Richard Stahler-Sholk, the idea behind neoliberalism is that the market, operating freely and unencumbered by regulations, will allocate resources more efficiently than can the state and that this will ultimately benefit everyone, including the poor. However, such often has not been the case, for neoliberal packages have been imposed by international funding institutions with the consent (sometimes reluctant) of local ruling elites and without popular participation in the decision-making process. The poor, as well as the middle class, have been hit hard by neoliberal policies, which have dramatically increased unemployment, promoted mechanized agro-export crops, made credit unavailable to medium and small producers, placed vital health and educational resources beyond the reach of the poor, and eliminated funding for improvements to deteriorating and woefully inadequate infrastructure. Neoliberal policies have, unintentionally, widened the gap between rich and poor in Latin America. They constitute a major means by which globalization comes to traditional communities.[10]

What are Traditional Communities?

The groups in this study come from several different geographic communities in each of three separate countries. They are not "traditional" in the strictest anthropological sense of the term. They might be more properly termed "modernizing," except that denotation is even more problematic and misleading. The "traditional" usage, broadly construed, serves the purposes of this study well because it accurately conveys the principal, if not all, features of each community under consideration.

Traditional communities typically have little or no capital accumulation or demand for wage labor even though their production is at least partially for the market. Economically, traditional cultures are based on intensive use of labor and/or renewable natural resources. Small-scale activities like fishing, fruit or nut-harvesting, agriculture, and handicrafts are characteristic enterprises. Of course, today small-scale traditional communities no longer exist in total isolation, but are almost always mixed with capitalist structures and practices which are part, at least indirectly, of economic globalization. For traditional communities, this fundamental economic shift typically leads not only to transformations of human economic activity, but also to an alteration in the relationship between humans and nature. In this change, small-scale workers become dependent on cash for consumption and on wages; this dependency causes them to increase their exploitation of the environment, which in turn leads to environmental degradation and ultimately to migration to the city. This common scenario converts once-independent producers into economic and environmental refugees.[11]

The communities represented here are resisting this pattern of change, for their members know that it means the extinction of their way of life. Yet, they do not reject modernity by any means. These communities desire the telephones, televisions, computers, consumer goods, transportation, and educational and health improvements that are part of the modern world. However, they are unwilling to sacrifice their basic cultural values and environmental practices in order to attain them.

How Does Globalization Come to Traditional Communities?

Why do these people not simply join in the global economy, welcome development, and become more modern? Their reluctance lies in how globalization comes to them. It almost always has an abusive and culturally destructive local face—that of the logger, the cattle rancher, or the neoliberal functionary.

For traditional peoples, globalization may, though not necessarily will, mean higher wages for some, but it also usually brings environmental degradation, geographical and cultural dislocation, and economic exploitation. The poor rarely want to leave their land and their customary way of life to become day laborers on the boss's estate or factory workers in urban slums, or, worst of all, part of the "reserve army" of unemployed urban poor. In short, they do not want to lose their culture. They are not primarily profit-motivated and might ask the capitalist to "cut down the forest of your greed," for they seek not fortune but survival, and what the Buddhists term a "right livelihood" that prizes harmony and interrelatedness.[12]

More specifically, how are the traditional communities and the individuals represented affected by globalization? How are the lives of the rubber tappers, the Guaraní, and the Nicaraguan women related to the vast abstraction that is globalization? Each group represents a disenfranchised segment of the population of a nation characterized by gross and increasing social and economic inequalities, by the inability to feed itself, by dependence on imports from and exports to global markets, and by exclusion from participation in setting the terms of trade. The people who speak to us from these pages represent impoverished sectors of three countries which, despite their indebtedness, are eligible for ever larger loans from international lending institutions. As environmental economist Herman E. Daly and theologian John Cobb, Jr. point out in *For the Common Good*, more international loans mean the repayment of ever larger debts by countries increasingly unable to pay them. National debts affect traditional communities because debts are serviced by accelerated destruction of habitats, which destroys livelihoods and increases migration; removal of land from agriculture, which increases hunger; and rapid expansion of industries, which feed not the poor, but the debt.[13] This is how the forest peoples, the Guaraní, and the Nicaraguan women are affected by globalization.

One can hardly blame poverty on globalization, for the poor have always been hard pressed to satisfy their basic human needs. What is different today is the scale and intensity of the hardships confronted daily by the embattled poor and the erosion of local cultures and national autonomy, as debtor nations mortgage their sovereignty to remote policy-makers responsible to no national institution or group, least of all to *caboclos* [Brazilians of Indian or mixed origin], Indians, or country women.

What are these communities doing about the problem? They are developing alternatives to dependency, helplessness, irresponsibility, and corruption. They are practicing what David Korten terms economic "localization," working to empower themselves, that is, to regain some degree of choice, through local control of local resources for local benefit.[14] The communities are making rational, ethical choices for a sustainable future, choices based on widespread participation, control of their own assets, and alliances with like-minded groups, local, national, and international. This does not mean that their choices are always wise, but that they are their own.

The questions for these communities are how to organize themselves most effectively and how to retain their most cherished values while incorporating selected attributes of globalization. In other words, how to live with the 900-pound globalization gorilla? The communities presented here, like many others in the developing world, are practicing specific strategies that have thus far enabled them to survive, although with great difficulty. These strategies constitute both an adaptation to, and a critique of, globalization. It is these strategies, their adoption in desperate and sometimes violent circumstances, that comprise the heart of this study.

Strategies for Dealing with Globalization

There are many effective strategies for dealing with globalization, including economic and political organizing at the local level; forming labor unions; promoting health and educational initiatives; and working with activist religious, environmental, and feminist groups and NGOs that defend and give voice to the communities' needs. These strategies, addressed in the sections that follow, highlight the formation of cooperatives as the core that connects all the others. The cooperatives in this study have been created with assistance from not-for-profit governmental and non-governmental organizations, secular and religious, that help the *comunitarios* [community members] build what has been described as a kind of "shelter" constructed on the foundational values of the NGO.[15]

The three communities in this study have come to accept that they have only two alternatives—to work together to help construct this shelter or be swept away. They have been brought to cooperation through necessity. Even so, only a small percentage of the population in each community has adopted the cooperative strategy. All face huge obstacles. First, there is the logistical obstacle: most forest gatherers, Guaraní Indians, and Nicaraguan campesinos are geographically too distant from each other to organize their entire populations. But even where they are in some reasonable proximity, many individuals still prefer to go it alone, perhaps not trusting others, perhaps unaware of alternatives, perhaps telling themselves that things will get better. In any event, it is a minority that we are concerned with in each case, but a minority whose chances of surviving with their culture relatively intact are greater than those of their unorganized and isolated counterparts.

What this study shows is that globalization also includes efforts by transnational institutions such as Christian churches and countless NGOs—secular, religious, feminist, environmental—to provide technical assistance and raise environmental and gender consciousness in developing areas. To argue that these transnational helping institutions impose their values on traditional peoples misunderstands the agency that these traditional communities exercise on their own behalf.[16] Although some NGOs unconsciously attempt to impose their own paradigms, communities are rarely steamrollered into submission. A principal theme concerns how traditional communities in Latin America seek to use some aspects and institutions of globalization against others in order to survive and to preserve some degree of cultural autonomy and choice. Thus, a major contention of this book is that local communities are not acquiescing in the face of their own destruction, or instruction, but, rather, that they are active agents of their own transformation. They are seeking an eclectic adaptation that will allow them to survive, to maintain their cultural integrity and their dignity. At the same time, they are also offering a critique of the values underlying economic globalization, in a kind of "structural adjustment" of their own.

There have been many studies of traditional peoples undergoing modernization. What this book attempts to do is to see the experience through the eyes of the people themselves, at the grassroots level, and enable them to speak to readers in their own voice. Why should the study of these communities matter to us in the developed world? Both the hardships and the initiatives of these threatened communities, as relayed by the participants themselves, offer us valuable lessons in cooperation, adaptability, perseverance, and creative conflict resolution; by giving a human face to globalization, they alert us to its dangers. They also make us aware of our interrelatedness, for what we do in the US or Canada or Europe reverberates even in tiny hamlets in Brazil, Bolivia, and Nicaragua, and vice versa. Finally, these voices remind us that, as sociologist Manuel Castells argues in *The Power of Identity*, local communities and agents of civil society do have the power to challenge the new global order.[17]

NOTES

1. See for example: Jason Clay, *Indigenous Peoples and Tropical Rainforests: Models of Land Use and Management from Latin America*, Cultural Survival Report No. 27 (Cambridge, MA: Cultural Survival, Inc., 1988). For more, see Shelton Davis, *Victims of the Miracle: Development and the Indians of Brazil* (New York: Cambridge University Press, 1977). For further information, see Andrew Revkin, *The Burning Season: The Murder of Chico Mendes and the Fight for the Amazon Rain Forest* (New York: Penguin, 1990). For more

on the rubber tappers, see Steven Schwartzman, "Seringueiros Defend the Rainforest in Amazônia," *Cultural Survival Quarterly*, 10.2 (1986): 41-43. See also Robert Goodland, *Race to Save the Tropics: Ecology and Economics for a Sustainable Future* (Washington, DC, and Covelo, CA: Island Press, 1990).

2. For a criticism of the capitalist-growth approach, see Herman E. Daly and John B. Cobb, Jr. , "From Individualism to Person-in-Community," *For the Common Good: Redirecting the Economy toward Community, the Environment, and a Sustainable Future*, 2nd ed. (Boston: Beacon Press, 1994) 159-75. See also Herman E. Daly, *Beyond Growth, The Economics of Sustainable Growth* (Boston: Beacon Press, 1996); and David C. Korten, *When Corporations Rule the World* (West Hartford, CT: Kumarian Press, Inc., and San Francisco: Berrett-Koehler Publishers, Inc. 1995). For more, see Bruce Rich, *Mortgaging the Earth: The World Bank, Environmental Impoverishment, and the Crisis of Development* (Boston: Beacon Press, 1994).

3. E.F. Schumacher, *Small is Beautiful: Economics as if People Mattered* (New York: Harper and Row, 1973). See also, John B. Cobb Jr., *Sustainability: Economics, Ecology, and Justice* (Maryknoll, NY: Orbis Press, 1992).

4. Quoted in Arturo Escobar, *Encountering Development: The Making and Unmaking of the Third World* (Princeton, NJ: Princeton University Press, 1995) 3.

5. Escobar 4.

6. Escobar.

7. From Mahbub ul Haq, *Reflections on Human Development* (Oxford: Oxford University Press, 1995). Quoted in Shannon D. Heyck-Williams, "The UNDP's Human Development Index: An Incomplete Measurement of Human Well-Being," MA thesis, Yale University, 2000: 2, 3.

8. For more on globalization, see Jerry Mander and Edward Goldsmith, eds., *The Case Against the Global Economy and for a Turn Toward the Local* (San Francisco: Sierra Club Books, 1996). For a more favorable view, see Thomas L. Friedman, *The Lexus and the Olive Tree* (New York: Farrar, Straus, Giroux, 1999).

9. David C. Korten, *Getting to the 21st Century: Voluntary Action and the Global Agenda* (West Hartford, CT: Kumarian Press, 1990) 160-61.

10. Richard Stahler-Sholk, "Structural Adjustment and Resistance: The Political Economy of Nicaragua Under Chamorro," *The Undermining of the Sandinista Revolution*, ed. Gary Prevost and Harry E. Vanden (London: Macmillan Press, and New York: St. Martin's Press, 1999) 74-113. See also Sharon Hostetler, JoAnn Lynen, Tim Welsh, and Hyward Wilkirson, *Bitter Medicine: Structural Adjustment in Nicaragua* (Washington, DC: Witness for Peace, 1995).

11. Dharam Ghai and Jessica M. Vivian, eds., *Grassroots Environmental Action: People's Participation in Sustainable Development* (London and New York: Routledge, 1992) 142, 143.

12. Daly 217; and Helena Norberg-Hodge, "Buddhism in the Global Economy," *Resurgence* 181 (March/April 1997): 18-22.

13. See Daly and Cobb, Chapter 8, "From Individualism to Person-in-Community" 159-75, and Chapter 11, "Free Trade versus Community" 209-35. See also Alys Willman, with Sharon Hostetler and Steve Bennett, *A Bankrupt Future: The Human Cost of Nicaragua's Debt* (Washington, DC: Witness for Peace, 2000).

14. Korten, *When Corporations Rule the World*, 320-23.

15. See Korten, *Getting to the 21st Century*.

16. See for example, Escobar, Chapter 5, "Power and Visibility: Tales of Peasants, Women, and the Environment" 154-211.

17. Manuel Castells, *The Power of Identity*, Volume 2 of *The Information Age: Economy, Society and Culture* (Malden, MA, and Oxford, UK: Blackwell Publishers, 1997).

PART ONE

Brazil

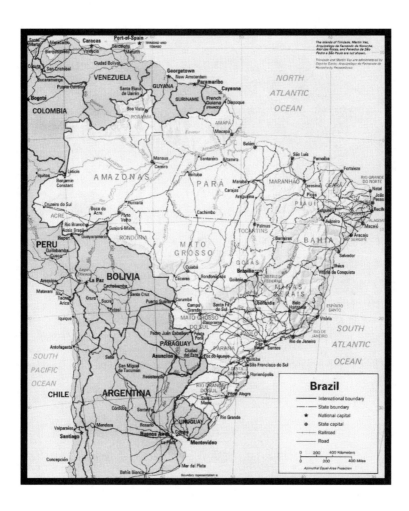

Introduction

The rubber tappers of Acre—the *seringueiros*—give voice to one of the most dramatic responses to globalization and development in Latin America because their habitat and their culture have been threatened with extinction. The tappers' story begins in the 1870s when migrants from the parched northeast of Brazil began arriving in Acre. They came fleeing the northeast's cyclic droughts, lured by stories of fabulous riches to be gained from the rubber boom. The *nordestinos* [northeasterners] who eagerly boarded the groaning, unseaworthy vessels for their arduous journey upriver to the vast green land of the rainforest had no idea what awaited them. But had they possessed psychic powers, they still could not have envisioned the depths of deception and exploitation that they and their descendants would experience, nor the determination and adaptability they would be required to exhibit.

The far western state of Acre borders Peru to the west, Bolivia to the south, and the Brazilian states of Amazônia and Rondônia to the north and east. Acre is very sparsely populated, with only about 483,726 inhabitants in its 153,149.9 square miles. Tropical rainforests cover 93 per cent of its territory, providing for a forest economy traditionally based on extractive activities such as gathering nuts, berries, and latex and supplemented by hunting and fishing.[1] The tiny, butterfly-shaped state is the largest rubber producer in Brazil, contributing the highest grade of latex, the prized *Acre fina*. The basins of the Purús, Juruá, and Madeira rivers are the sites of the richest concentration of *seringueiras*, or rubber trees.

In 1876, British traveler Henry Wickham took many thousands of *hevea brasiliensis* seeds from Acre back to Kew Gardens for the first successful cultivation experiment. The domestication of the hevea made possible the development of large-scale rubber plantations in Britain's Asian colonies of Malaya and Ceylon. From about 1912, Asian rubber began to displace Amazon rubber, leading to the eventual collapse of the Amazon rubber boom (1880-1920). During the heyday of the boom, however, Brazilian rubber barons sent their laundry to Europe, sported large diamond pinky rings and stickpins, dressed in the latest European fashions, and dined at luxurious French restaurants in Manaus, the province's major city. The opulent opera house, the Teatro Amazonas, was constructed from materials imported from Europe, and Italian opera stars arrived without first having to pass through "backward" Rio de Janeiro. Manaus boasted the country's first electric streetcars and streetlights.

Despite the collapse of the boom and of the later World War II boomlet brought about by the closing of the Asian markets and the Allies' need for rubber, extractive activities, including latex collection, still form the backbone of Acre's economy today. There are currently underway, however, many promising experiments in economic diversification that are sustainable and that respect the forest dwellers' traditional way of life.

The population of Acre is largely *caboclo*, of Indian or mixed origin. The indigenous population numbers about 8,414, and includes tribes such as the Kaxinawá, Kampa, Jaminawa, Arara, and the Ipurinã, whose term Uwákuru, transcribed by explorers as "Aquiri," gives the state its name. Nearly one-half of the state's residents now live in the capital city of Rio Branco (population 228,990), the result of increasing migration begun in the 1960s. From 1960-70, the population of Rio Branco nearly doubled, rising from 18,000 to 35,000. Between 1970-80, the population more than doubled, reaching 87,646, with much of the growth occurring in the periphery of the city. Acre's official illiteracy rate is an unrealistic 16 per cent; in the *seringais*, or rubber estates, at least until the advent of the Projeto Seringueiro literacy program in the 1980s, it was close to 100 per cent. The elevated infant mortality rate is 29 per 1,000 live births, while the fertility rate, during 1960-1970 was 9.5, the highest in the nation.[2]

Acre was a remote Bolivian outpost populated by Indians and Portuguese-speaking Brazilians in 1902 when the Bolivian government began to finalize its plan to lease thousands of square miles to a North American conglomerate that included J. Pierpoint Morgan, the Vanderbilts, and relatives of US President Teddy Roosevelt. The so-called "Bolivian syndicate" would exercise political and economic authority over what would soon become the leading rubber producing area in the world. There had been earlier hostilities between Brazilians and Bolivians, including a republican rebellion led by patriot Plácido de Castro in 1899, but the prospect of a US colony in the Amazon spurred the Brazilian government to claim Acre from Bolivia, which was unable to defend the remote area. By the Treaty of Petrópolis in 1903, Bolivia ceded Acre to Brazil. After minor border disputes with Peru were resolved, Acre became a Brazilian territory in 1909. Governors appointed by the president administered Acre from 1920-62, when the territory finally became a state. Acre today is the nation's least populous, least prosperous, and, in terms of political clout, least important state, although it became Brazil's most famous state during the 1980s for the forest peoples' resistance to the burning of the Amazon.

Back in the 1870s, when the first northeasterners arrived, Acre was a frontier area with no established political or legal institutions. All authority lay with the *patrões*, or rubber estate owners. Upon their arrival in Manaus, the northeasterners would be met by the patrão who would accompany them on the remainder of the journey downriver to Acre. There, he would provide them with the necessary tools—including *lámina* [cutting instrument], *faca* [knife], *poronga* [helmet with lamp], *espingarda* [shotgun]—and supplies—rice, beans, coffee, lard, *farinha* [ground manioc meal], and kerosene—all of which he would deduct from their pay accounts. Thus the *brabo* [untamed] recent arrival began his new life in debt; credit and debt formed the basis of the rubber economy. The worker owed the patrão, who owed the *aviador* [owner of the large supply house], and the aviador owed the foreign commercial interests. The seringueiro occupied the unenviable bottom rung in a ladder of indebtedness. Journalist Euclides da Cunha, writing at the dawn of the twentieth century, decried the debt peonage of the *sertanejo* [northeasterner], describing him as "a quasi serf, at the mercy of the discretionary empire of the bosses."[3]

To make matters worse for the newly-arrived workers, it was common practice for estate owners to send the unsuspecting sertanejos out in raiding parties, called *correrias*, either to clear the Indians from the forest or to capture them to work on the estates, which suffered from a chronic labor shortage. The decline of the Indian population was dramatic, with many deaths resulting from unfamiliar diseases such as measles and influenza, as well as from the correrias. Surviving Indians retreated deep into the jungle, leaving behind the seringueiras from which they had extracted latex and made rubber-coated implements and footwear for centuries before the arrival of the sertanejo and the patrão.

Da Cunha refers to humans as "impertinent intruders in the Amazon, whose arrival was neither expected nor desired."[4] Partly because of the natural limits imposed upon the intruders' activity in the Amazon and partly because of the decline in production occasioned by Asian competition, little has changed over the past century or so either in the technology of latex collection in the Amazon or in the geographic constraints on its marketing. Thus, a typical day for the seringueiro today is very similar to that of the first brabos from the northeast.

The seringueiro would arise at about 3:00 a.m., consume a large breakfast consisting of meat, rice, beans, farinha, and coffee. He would then go forth to cut an *estrada*, a looping trail connecting from one to 200 heveas. He would affix a bowl-shaped gourd to each tree to collect the raw "milk," and then continue on the elliptical trail which began and ended at his home. This circuit took several hours because the trees were dispersed and not concentrated in one spot. The seringueiro would eat lunch and rest during the hottest part of the day, going forth in the afternoon to tap a second estrada. After collecting the *borracha* [latex], he was ready for the *defumaça* [smoking], which he carried out just as the Indians before him had done, basting and turning the latex on a wooden spit over an open fire until it coagulated. At irregular intervals, perhaps twice a month, the seringueiro would carry the balls of black-coated rubber, or *pelles*, by land and water, foot and canoe to the designated *barracão* [trading post], a "company store" owned by the patrão. There, he would exchange his product for supplies which he was allowed to purchase only from the barracão. The tapper provided additional food for his family by hunting small game with his espingarda or by fishing in nearby rivers.

CORTANDO SERINGA

The seringueiro's wife might herself be a rubber tapper, a *mulher seringueira*, and she might also share in the hunting, though these activities were not the norm for women. Many seringueiros came to Acre and the western Amazon as single men because the patrão wanted workers unencumbered by the burdens and distractions of a family, though the northeasterners often took Indian wives.

Conditions on the estates were oppressive, with intense heat, debilitating illnesses, poor nutrition, and constant loneliness. Many observers have commented on the overwhelming loneliness the seringueiro experienced on the vast Acre estates. The nearest *colocação* [family settlement] could easily be three hours away, requiring too much time taken from work for easy sociability. Novelist Cláudio de Araújo Lima went so far as to describe Acre as "a small branch of hell," where the newcomer found "only malign fevers, backwardness, and loneliness. Principally loneliness."[5]

Regarding the appalling state of public health in Acre, the director of a medical commission in 1912-13 declared that he had never seen such an "intense," "generalized" morbidity rate from malaria as in Acre, where the "annihilation of human life has attained exceptional proportions."[6] Infant mortality has always been high; it is still common for parents to refer to their "living children." For example, Rio Branco immigrant Dona Geralda Alves de Morais, formerly of the Macuã seringal, has three living children out of 12; the others all perished from *doença que dava em criança* [childhood illnesses].[7] Even today medical care in the seringal is rudimentary to nonexistent. Another immigrant to Rio Branco, Dona Ivonilde Menezes, formerly of the Niterói *seringal* [rubber estate] on the Muru river, recalls that in the 1960s her patrão had only one *melhoral*, an aspirin-like analgesic, to offer her for her malaria, and this after she had traveled three hours by boat and was "as yellow as a chicken." Her husband, Dom Valdir, remembers taking his aged and infirm mother to the city to see a doctor for the first time and finding himself at a loss to explain to her what a doctor was, for he had no idea.[8]

In the seringal, the women were responsible for cooking, caring for the children and the household, and tending the subsistence plot, if the family was allowed to cultivate one. Women did the washing, but soap was often lacking in the barracão, so they learned to make use of the tibaúba bush, which produces a soap-like substance. Women often spent a good part of the day traveling to secure food for their children. Dona Ivonilde, for example, had to travel one entire day to the nearest colocação to trade for milk with a seringueiro who owned a cow. Most often, she fed her children sugar water and *angorré*, a kind of soft dough made from manioc flour and sugar water.[9] In the traditional household, children owed absolute obedience to their parents, especially to their father whose word was law. The wife was also expected to submit to her husband's authority.[10]

Both men and women adopted indigenous healing practices for snake bites, stomach ailments, and the "evil eye," or malicious spells cast by persons believed to possess special powers. Seringueiros typically made their own rubber shoes at home, drying them on wooden molds. When the shoes were new, seringueiros like Dona Ivonilde and Dom Valdir would dance in them and proudly leave them on when they slept in their hammocks.[11] The family was the economic unit, and children began cutting seringa as soon as they could, from about age 12. They began even younger, at age eight or nine, helping in the *roçado* [field]. Some patrões allowed their tappers to cultivate vegetables and to own a few pigs and chickens, while others did not, because they wanted workers to remain exclusively dependent on the expensive imports of sour manioc flour and canned goods from the barracão.[12]

The seringueiros rarely had cash; they lived by *troca* [barter], trading with each other for sugar, lard, coffee, kerosene, and eggs. The patrão never paid the worker in cash, and he himself rarely had cash because he, too, was in debt, to the aviador for supplies for his barracão. The patrão did not want his workers buying supplies from anyone else, for the provision of supplies was often as lucrative for him as was the actual sale of rubber. Everyone was always short of liquid assets.[13] To this day, in the seringais as opposed to the cities, barter is the preferred mode of transacting business among neighbors. Ricardo Hiroyuki Shibata of the CTA [*Centro dos Trabalhadores da Amazônia*, Amazonian Workers Center] comments, "In the seringal it is very rare to use money, generally they just use money when they go to the city. In the seringal, they exchange for everything, for example, a chicken for a kilo of manioc flour, and it is good because when you barter you make friendships."[14]

In the late nineteenth century, missionary priests began their laborious rounds of visits, known as *desobrigas*, entering the seringais at the pleasure of the patrões in order to baptize, marry, and give communion. This was a major social event for the seringueiro, as a religious emissary came only every few years, and his visit was eagerly anticipated from the time it was announced six months in advance. Beginning in 1920, the pope regularly sent priests and bishops from the Italian order of the Servants of Mary to serve the prelacy of Acre and the Upper Purús.

Even though the bishop was a figure of great authority, his power was always subordinate to that of the patrão and *coronel de barranco*, or riverbank colonel, as the more powerful patrões were known, who could forbid entry altogether or refuse to gather "his" seringueiros if he so chose. Relations between the colonels and the padres were sometimes strained because of priests' complaints about the treatment of workers. In addition to the delicate relations between colonel and bishop, the work of the missionaries was hampered also because some areas were so isolated that the desobrigas never reached them; in such places, the remote seringueiro gradually forgot much of his religious tradition. In other areas, however, the desobrigas built on the northeastern popular heritage of festivals, prayers, pilgrimages, promises, and miracles, with overlays of Indian beliefs. Because no one could read or write, the bishop would try to find elderly persons who remembered at least portions of prayers from their northeastern childhood to serve as leaders in his absence. Failing this, the bishop would teach memorization of a few prayers and hope that they would not be forgotten before his next visit.

Despite the exigencies of a harsh existence, parties were a regular, if infrequent, feature of life in the seringal. Weddings, birthdays, baptisms, and house-raisings were celebrated with a *forró*, a type of up-tempo country music and dancing somewhat reminiscent of Cajun zydeco. Verses were both memorized and improvised to the accompaniment of fiddle, accordion, and triangle. Rubber tapper Francisco Celestino da Cruz of Xapuri recalls that sometimes seringueiros managed to entertain themselves with only a "tambourine and two spoons."[15] Seringueiros would travel all day to help raise a house, for example; spend all night dancing forró and drinking *cachaça* [a cane liquor]; partake of strong, hot coffee and warm rice cake around 5:00 a.m.; and then begin the long trek home.

The difference between boom and bust for the seringueiro was not as dramatic as for the patrão. The seringueiro had traditionally varied his food and income sources through agriculture, hunting, and fishing, even though some patrões forbade such activities. Although he remained hopelessly in debt whether times were lean or flush for the regional economy, the tapper could at least survive from the forest.

The patrão's situation was different, because he formed part not only of the precapitalist world of the local estate, but also of the national and international capitalist system, which financed his rubber enterprise. When international lending agencies began to call in loans to *aviadores* [suppliers] around the beginning of World War I, which coincided with the eclipse of Amazon rubber on the international market by its Asian competitors, the aviadores began pressing for payment of their loans to the *seringalistas* [rubber estate owners], and the squeeze was on. The rubber business was highly speculative, operating on short-term credit, which meant that the seller could not afford to withhold his product until it might fetch a better price; thus, the Amazon merchants became the helpless victims of price fluctuations. Because rubber production remained a regional rather than a national enterprise, exporters enjoyed no federal subsidies to help them weather the storm; price supports came much later, after World War II. This was a seri-

SERINGUEIRO HOE-DOWN (FORRÓ)

ous drawback, because, in developing economies, support from the federal government is essential for bringing about economic transformation, which was what was needed in order for the Amazon to compete. The Amazon traders were at a serious disadvantage when compared to the highly capitalized export houses, which were owned and operated by Europeans and North Americans whose interests often ran counter to those of the regional elite.[16]

Moreover, now that the technological advance of plantation-grown heveas had become a reality, foreigners found that Britain's Asian plantations gave altogether a higher and more reliable return on their investments. For one thing, they did not face the same geographical and labor constraints as in the Amazon. In addition, as historian Warren Dean maintains, although many factors combined to bring about the defeat of the rubber industry, chief among them were environmental considerations.[17] Investing in the Asian plantations also freed the entrepreneur from the Amazon aviador system, the link between the feudal world of the rubber estate and the capitalist world of the modern businessman. The aviador structure inhibited the development of an internal market by tying the seringueiro to local traders, whose overpriced goods pushed the tapper further toward subsistence agriculture. Since the aviador himself was in debt, he was in no position to invest in the production of goods to develop a local market. This meant that all finished goods that entered the interior were expensive imports from outside the area, which the seringueiro had no cash to buy, a situation that deepened his indebtedness and further stymied the creation of an internal market. According to historian Barbara Weinstein, the shortage of labor and capital were serious problems in the system, but the basic flaw was "the aviamento network itself, which circumscribed internal demand and effectively stunted the growth of agriculture as well as industry."[18]

The effects of the decline in the demand for rubber for the seringueiros were blunted by the increase in subsistence production and in other extractive activities, such as Brazil nuts. As for the patrões, some remained on their seringais, while others moved to regional towns to engage in commerce, become bureaucrats, or participate in the Brazil nut industry, attempting whatever was required to hold on to their privileged positions.[19] The Amazon rubber industry continued to stagnate until the World War II boomlet, when the US looked to Brazil to supply wartime latex once the Japanese had blocked access to the Asian supply source. In 1943, President Getúlio Vargas, an admirer of Italy's Mussolini and supplier of rubber to Nazi Germany until 1942, reluctantly bowed to pressure from the US, declared for the Allies, and sent troops to Italy.[20] Vargas encouraged those who remained at home to serve their country by enlisting as *soldados da borracha*—rubber soldiers. Drought-plagued northeasterners were amenable to this message and to the dazzling propaganda campaign that accompanied it. Colorful posters, songs, jingles, and enthusiastic government representatives promoted the attractions of the Amazon, where "you can gather money like leaves."[21] Catchy songs romanticizing the seringueiro and valuing his role in the nation's life and in the war effort became popular. The "Hymn to the Seringueiro," for example, praised the workers as heroes who made tires for airplanes and bicycles and who supplied rubber for pressure cookers. This particular song has been revived in recent years by seringueiros themselves as a symbol of cultural pride. Those who signed up for a tour of duty in Acre were promised free transportation, supplies, and a pension. The second riverborne migration of northeasterners took place in 1943. Some 55,000, mostly men, responded to the appeal; of these, 30,000 were from Ceará.[22] Conditions on board were just as unhealthy and hazardous as those experienced by the migrants' forebearers some 60 or so years earlier.

Geralda Alves de Morais, an *arigó* [newly arrived northeasterner] from Fortaleza, Ceará, who fled the drought in 1944 recalls her journey: "Many children died, including all those ailing children who had been smuggled aboard by their parents so that they would not have to stay interned in the hospital. Many Cearenses came here and many died. The year we arrived, there was no one to give water to the other, so many of us had malaria."[23]

Rio Branco resident Francisca das Chagas Araújo remembers the arigós' bitter disappointment at the disparity between their high expectations and the harsh reality that greeted them: "The arigós complained a great deal because they brought with them contracts promising them cleared paths, a house, and a *defumado*r [rubber curing apparatus] on arrival. They came and found nothing, nothing except malaria, and many died."[24]

The rubber boomlet benefited a fortunate few, while most of the wealth, along with the latex, flowed out of the area. Government pensions were delayed for some 50 years, but the remaining rubber soldiers now proudly wear their veteran's tee shirt, collect their pensions, recall how good it felt to be part of a common effort, and express their undying gratitude to President Vargas for making it all possible.[25]

After the wartime boomlet, rubber resumed its decline, though estate owners managed to secure federal subsidies during the 1950s and 1960s. However, with the added competition from new plantations in central and southern Brazil as well as those in Malaysia and with the growth of synthetics, there was little future for wild rubber estates.

With the advent of the military government (1964-85), life changed drastically for most Brazilians, not least the seringueiro. Eager to secure Brazil's vast unpopulated borders and to modernize the country, the military pursued an aggressive development policy for the Amazon. Their plan built on Vargas's earlier notion of the Amazon as an empty space waiting to be filled. It is worth pointing out that governments have consistently behaved as if the Amazon were empty, ignoring completely the presence of Indians and caboclos whose existence has been simply disregarded. Government officials hoped that settlement of the Amazon would relieve chronic poverty in the northeast and increasing land pressures in the south, where many workers were being pushed off their lands because of the modernization of agriculture. Modernization has involved substituting export crops, such as soy and orange juice, for food crops in a pattern typical of global economic integration. The problem is that small farmers, now unable to feed themselves, join the swelling ranks of the landless. Poor southerners took hope from government propaganda that proclaimed the Amazon as "a land for people, for a people without land." The government agency INCRA [*Instituto Nacional de Colonização e Reforma Agrária*, National Colonization and Agrarian Reform Institute] was created to oversee land distribution to arriving colonists. New roads made possible the influx of destitute migrants, while fabulous government incentives made investment irresistible to financiers in the south. Investors jumped at the subsidized loans, corporate income tax exemptions, and tax credits that the government dangled before them.[26] Not only would the Amazon offer a place to live for the poor, but it would also offer opportunities for even greater riches for the already wealthy.

Forests in the Amazon began to succumb to the chainsaw and tractor in the 1960s with the first road projects, which created a swath of destruction and unleashed an uncontrolled flood of migration that escalated massively during the 1970s and 1980s. Successive waves of settlers followed the new roads to Mato Grosso, Goiás, Pará, and Rondônia, which by the early 1970s had become completely overwhelmed, spurring desperate travelers to continue along BR-364 from Rondônia to Acre. The clearing and burning of the rainforest left the poor soil exposed and dry. In between the smoldering remains of trees, settlers tried to eke out a living, but with each year the barren soil yielded less, forcing families to move on, repeating the cycle.

However meretricious its effects, uncontrolled immigration did not cause the worst destruction; it was cattle ranching, which arrived in the 1970s. This was especially true in Acre, where the majority of the invaders were not the landless but

DEFORESTATION

large landholders and speculators.[27] Indebted former rubber barons were only too happy to accommodate aspiring ranchers and rid themselves of their unprofitable estates. Seeking relief from their bank creditors, they sold out at low prices. Many rushed to obtain belated legal title to lands they, their fathers, or grandfathers had taken by force, while others did not bother to secure a piece of paper that had never before been of value in Acre. Beginning in the early 1970s, land sales were aggressively promoted by the state's governor, Wanderley Dantas, a passionate advocate of cattle ranching. Desiring to attract investors, Dantas portrayed Acre as "the northeast without drought and the south without frost." He urged *paulistas*, southerners from São Paulo state, to "produce in Acre, invest in Acre, export to the Pacific." By 1975, after Dantas's term of office, one-third of Acre's territory belonged to *sulistas* [southerners]. Dantas almost literally gave land and titles away. In 1970, for example, one hectare (2.471 acres) sold for the price of a banana, or two *cruzeiros* in Brazil's former currency. Land speculators rushed to take advantage of the giveaway, holding on to their purchases until prices soared, then selling, without ever intending to develop the land. By 1977, prices had skyrocketed, with one hectare selling for 2,000 cruzeiros.[28] By 1978, 80 per cent of Acre's land was in the hands of large landholders and conglomerates, national and international.[29]

It is important to note here that there are at least two Brazils: the developed south and the impoverished north. Under the generals' rule (1964-85), the push for modernization became a form of internal colonialism with the rich south extracting natural wealth from the poor north. The internal colonialists—military officers, businessmen, and politicians—who benefited from the rapid development of the Amazon were in some sense akin to the former aviadores; that is, they were powerful locally, but up to their necks in debt to global lending institutions and to transnational businesses looking to facilitate the export of coveted Amazon hardwood to lucrative markets in the US, Europe, and Japan.

At first glance one might be tempted to think that integration into the global market is the only hope for survival for the seringueiros against the local forces of "development." However, on closer inspection, one sees that the enabling factor behind the Amazonian development program has been transnational capital and, from the early 1980s, conditions placed by the IMF that reinforced the export-oriented tendencies of the 1960s and 1970s. Thus, in Brazil, development and globalization have gone hand in hand.

The *fazendeiros* [ranchers] cleared the forests of Acre of millions of tons of valuable hardwood, such as mahogany and cedar. These were either exported by logging concerns or simply left to burn. Ranchers sometimes used toxic herbicides containing Agent Orange to burn brush and grasses. After defoliating the *fazenda* [ranch], they would plant grass seed for pasture.[30] In their drive to accumulate vast estates, ranchers and loggers alike were often ruthless, hiring *pistoleiros* to help them expel tappers and farmers, eliminating those who resisted.

Capital penetration in Acre did not occur in so-called empty areas, but in locales that had been occupied continuously for many generations by seringueiros who lived from extractive activities and agriculture. Acre historian Luis Antônio Pinto de Oliveira emphasizes the rootedness of this culture, stating that seringueiros, small farmers, and squatters had, since the rubber crisis of 1913, developed close ties to the land and a strong identification with the syncretic culture that they were creating. The interests that motivated the businessmen, speculators, loggers, and ranchers from the south were naturally alien to the needs and social organization of the forest peoples. The invaders were not interested in the extraction of borracha, and they were even less interested in the seringueiros, farmers, and squatters residing on newly-purchased lands to which they held title. The former seringais were rapidly transformed into pastures, clashes over the possession of land became aggravated, and the migratory flux from country to city increased with the substitution of cattle for people.[31]

The conflicts between the paulistas and the Amazonian workers were sharpened by the fact that the land buyers would do whatever was necessary to "clear" the land, that is, to remove the resident families. Padre Paolino Baldassari of Sena Madureira recalls the words of one entrepreneur who was determined to carry out the *limpeza* [cleansing] of the former seringal "either by bonbons, deception, threats, or death."[32] By the logic of the speculators, it was necessary to expel the resident labor force so that the land would not depreciate; it was also necessary in order to guarantee the ranchers' de facto ownership and remove claims of *posse* [squatters' rights]. Moreover, cattle-raising activities require few work hands, so the fazendeiro could also rationalize expulsions on pragmatic grounds. Pinto de Oliveira points out the psychological and cultural significance of the expulsions, speaking of the intense trauma the seringueiros experienced on witnessing the progressive occupation, dismemberment, and burning of the seringal, including their own home, colocação, and way of life.[33] The seringueiros' way of life had evolved over a century or so in a process of successive eclectic accommodations to changing social and economic realities. The new clash, between modern concepts of labor and land usage on the one hand and traditional work relations and views of nature on the other was harsh, abrupt, and traumatic, and it produced severe psychological and cultural dislocations.

The contradictions between the two diametrically opposed ways of life set in motion enormous demographic dislocations for the seringueiro, particularly during the 1970s. Of course, many workers remained in the forest, and some found employment as peons or ranch hands, operating chain saws and tractors on the fazendas. But thousands of others accustomed to life in the forest began to migrate to the cities, most often to Rio Branco, which, with its unmanageable traffic, pollution, and noise, represented a severe culture shock for those who regarded a cluster of four or five houses as a large metropolis.[34] Even so, the city offered the hope of a job, and, as Dona Ivonilde expressed, "at least the water was not hot and filled with ashes."[35] A government and university sponsored survey of heads of household in Rio Branco in 1978 revealed that only 13.3 per cent were actually from Rio Branco. Of that same sample, 45.5 per cent had arrived within the previous ten years.[36]

Also during the 1970s, the seringueiros, *posseiros* [squatters], and agricultural workers began to organize and defend their right to the land. During this period the CEBs [*Comunidades Eclesiais de Base*, Christian Base Communities] and the trade unions were both gaining in strength. As a result of their efforts and those of the CPT (*Comissão Pastoral da Terra*, Pastoral Land Commission], some land was in fact returned to squatters or defended from expropriation, and some evicted

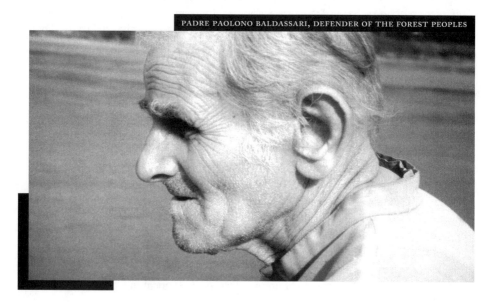

PADRE PAOLONO BALDASSARI, DEFENDER OF THE FOREST PEOPLES

seringueiros received financial compensation. At the same time, like the aviadores before them, large ranchers and loggers began to experience difficulty in obtaining further credit and special incentives because of high inflation resulting from the economic "miracle" of the 1960s. Further, ranchers and loggers were frustrated by the deteriorating or nonexistent infrastructure, such as roads and communications, which the government could not afford to maintain or provide.[37]

While the situation was becoming less than ideal for the rancher and logger, it was becoming intolerable for the seringueiro, who either had to fight back or give up. Thus, the local face of globalization, that of the rancher and the logger, represented larger faceless forces—an authoritarian national elite, transnational corporations, and the unfettered flow of capital across national boundaries. For those who favored the economic integration of Acre into the worldwide market for lumber and, to a lesser extent, cattle, human rights violations and environmental depredation were an unfortunate, but unavoidable, price to pay.

The forces arrayed against the forest peoples were formidable. Yet, they organized, raised up local leaders, fought for their rights, acquired a political consciousness, revitalized dormant cultural values, and began to seek political alliances. They worked to diversify their economic base, form cooperatives, value education, and seek incorporation into the modern world on their own terms. They came to understand that the terms set by the globalization process carry with them cultural and economic extinction.

The seringueiros have thus far survived globalization because of the complementary, simultaneous, and effective work of numerous groups and individuals, none of which has been more important than the Catholic church. From the early 1960s, the church in Acre began to reach out to the poor in a concerted effort by priests and nuns to visit the seringais, bringing a message of hope and solidarity, and laying the groundwork for the Christian base communities [CEBs]. In base communities, neighbors met in small groups to discuss Bible readings and how to apply these lessons to their own lives and social situation. CEBs were the key to creating a critical social conscience among the seringueiros and raising up local leadership to represent and defend the community. They grew like wildfire during the 1970s. The number of monitors (group leaders) increased from 34 in 1971 to 800 in 1978.[38] The CEBs and the church's popular radio program *Todos Somos Irmãos* [We are all Brothers and Sisters], begun in 1973, worked hand in hand, and between them, they reached practically every forest community in Acre.

The most discussed topics on the radio program were work, land rights, the syndicate, the problem of the Indian, the situation of women, and human rights. These themes constituted the social word, *fala social*, of the program. In both the base communities and the radio program, the sacred word, *fala sagrada*, centered on Bible passages relative to the captivity in Egypt (Exodus), the exile in Babylon (Isaiah), the organization of the first Christians (Acts), and the message of personal liberation contained in the Gospels. The sacred word legitimated the social in that it linked the Word to a worldview. *Todos Somos Irmãos* and the CEBs alike endeavored to replace religious and social passivity with active participation in the church and in society, so that the seringueiro could become a "subject," rather than an "object" in the historical process.[39] The radio program, the bishop's regular radio broadcasts, and the CEB meetings took on special importance because there were no other means for making uncensored information available to the people of Acre. Thus, early on, the church in Acre adopted an adversarial stance *vis à vis* the federal and local governments.

The driving force behind the church's courageous leadership role during this period was Dom Moacyr Grechi, Bishop of the Prelacy of Acre and the Upper Purús, 1972-98, whose interview appears later in this chapter. Under Dom Moacyr's intellectual and spiritual direction, the church nurtured and protected the seringueiros, while at the same time it worked assiduously to help them develop local leadership. As a result of the bishop's example, the message of the CEBs, the broadcasts, and the intense effort to train monitors, a sense of empowerment gradually began to replace the seringueiros' incapacitating passivity and sense of helplessness.

Ordinary individuals went to great lengths to become monitors for their communities. Matilde Ribeiro da Silva, a great-grandmother and former rubber tapper who lives in Riozinho, reflects on the sacrifices and benefits involved in becoming a monitor:

> [To get to meetings] I had to travel on foot eight hours carrying one child and dragging the other. Fortunately, I just had two at the time. But they were always hungry and tired, and we would always arrive late and exhausted, everyone would, because traveling was so difficult. But once we started singing and talking, praying, reading the Gospel and sharing experiences our tiredness went away, and we returned home with a sense of mission to our communities.[40]

It is hard to overestimate the work of the church in building local leadership and creating a sense of community. Francisco das Chagas, who tells his story later in this chapter, was an illiterate rubber tapper until padres Paolino Baldassari and Heitor Turrini began a base community in his seringal. The experience so transformed him that he vowed to study to become a priest and return to work in his home seringal. The examples of Matilde Ribeiro da Silva and Francisco das Chagas illustrate the power of the CEBs to motivate individuals to assume responsibility in their communities, do things for themselves, and overcome the defeatist legacy of dependency that popular educator Paulo Freire had decried. Indeed, the base communities themselves utilized methods advocated by Freire to encourage pupils to *tomar consciência*, raise consciousness. Brazil is unusual in Latin America for the virtual unanimity of support for the option for the poor put into practice by local clergy and church hierarchy alike and for the sustained period of exemplary leadership provided by the CNBB [*Conselho Nacional de Bispos Brasileiros*, National Council of Brazilian Bishops].

In Acre, in addition to the base communities and the fostering of local leadership, the Church offered sanctuary for seringueiros fleeing persecution, protected the fledgling unions (called syndicates), denounced publicly the perpetrators of violence and the system that harbored them, recorded and reported human rights violations, sponsored the creation of a human rights commission, and offered legal assistance through the offices of the Pastoral Land Commission (CPT), established in 1984 under Dom Moacyr's direction. The CPT is most often associated with the nationwide MST [*Movimento dos Sem Terra*, Landless Movement], but it has been very effective in protecting land rights for the seringueiro as well.

In the beginning, the church and the syndicate were completely identified. As one seringueiro recalled, "The syndicate in Sena Madureira began in the church with Padre Paolino." It was in the CEBs that the syndicates first arose; they were the "womb of the syndicates." By conservative estimate, 70 per cent of the unions were organized from the beginning with the help of the CEBs.[41] Gradually, the unions became autonomous, but they still have a close relationship with the church.

The Xapuri Rural Workers' Syndicate was founded in 1975 by Chico Mendes, the leading figure and international symbol of the seringueiros' resistance movement. His murder in 1988 galvanized worldwide opinion and forced the Brazilian government to honor its commitment to the creation of extractive reserves, protected areas where forest dwellers can continue their traditional way of life in peace. This was what Mendes had ardently desired, but it cost him his life. Mendes was a simple, intelligent, honest man who was instinctively trusted by others. He was a rubber tapper who had grown up in the Cachoeira seringal in Xapuri where his father had settled after coming to Acre from the northeast as a rubber soldier. He learned to read and write as a young adult from old newspapers provided him by socialist Euclides Fernandes Távora. A recluse who sought anonymity in the forest, Távora in his youth had joined the famed Prêstes column, which, inspired by the Russian Revolution, in the 1920s traveled into the interior of Brazil exhorting the masses to rebellion. Távora imparted to Mendes a sense of class struggle and of the need for workers to unite. This message was reinforced by the church-sponsored leadership classes that Mendes attended, where themes of brotherhood and solidarity strengthened his innate sense of justice.

Mendes dedicated himself completely to the cause of the seringueiros. A personal letter written in 1987 to Dom Moacyr reveals the depths of Mendes's commitment:

> For 14 years I have dedicated myself body and soul to the workers' struggle, making at the beginning a secret vow to God and to myself that I would maintain this ideal until my strength gave out or death arrived. I have renounced all personal and financial interests in order to engage body and soul in this struggle; there have been difficult moments, even today, there is persecution, exhaustion, hunger, but I am always nourished by the faith

> and the ideal and the will to win, to dream about the future, to dream
> about better days for our brothers and sisters....[42]

Mendes quickly developed both the skills and coherent political consciousness necessary to assume a larger role. He worked closely with fellow union organizer Wilson Pinheiro, who was murdered in 1980 at the union office in Brasiléia. Afterwards, when local authorities proved unwilling to prosecute the rancher responsible, Nilo Sérgio de Oliveira, a group of seringueiros took matters into their own hands and murdered the rancher. Subsequently, violent repression of the seringueiros increased exponentially. Pinheiro is credited with having begun the strategy of the *empate* [non-violent standoff] during the 1970s. Mendes and others refined the empate until it became the most dramatic and effective means of uniting public opinion behind the seringueiros. Other local leaders who took up the struggle after Pinheiro's death include Júlio Barbosa, later mayor of Xapuri; Marina Silva, later federal deputy; and Raimundo de Barros, later city councilman of Xapuri; their interviews follow.

Intimately connected to the union movement was Projeto Seringueiro, a joint educational effort of a number of individuals, including British activist Tony Gross, anthropologist Mary Helena Allegretti (later a key figure in the development of the Extractive Reserves), and ex-seminarian Manoel Estébio Cavalcante da Cunha, whose interview also appears in this section. Projeto Seringueiro began in Xapuri in 1981 as an adult literacy program based on the participatory pedagogy of Paulo Freire and intended to develop a political consciousness in the seringueiros so that they would organize to defend their rights and their way of life. Moreover, the nascent union, the base communities, and the tottering cooperative desperately needed literate leaders. Though Projeto Seringueiro was designed for adult learners, it soon became a program for youngsters instead, for parents were eager to take advantage of this unprecedented opportunity for their children.[43] Projeto Seringueiro's widely respected education and consciousness-raising effort holds as its core philosophy the inherent value of the seringueiros and their forest culture. According to Ricardo Shibata of the CTA, the coordinating agency for Projeto Seringueiro created in 1983, the project's mission is: "to make citizens and preserve the forest culture of the seringueiro."[44] Founding documents describe Projeto Seringueiro as having begun together with the syndicate in Xapuri to mobilize civil society and bring schools to the interior of the forest. Twenty-five schools now provide instruction in grades one through four for nearly 660 children in the municipality of Xapuri alone.[45]

The work of Projeto Seringueiro continues to inspire young teachers like Eliana Ribeiro da Silva of Riozinho, who describes the affirming quality of the workshops that she regularly attends:

> The workshops are so good because you produce something you can come
> back and use in the classroom and community. For example, geography. I

knew that we live in the state of Acre, which is the Amazon region, but I didn't
know what geography was, that is, the concept of geography and why it is
so important. That is something concrete I brought back to the community,
because even people who live on the rivers and in the forests don't know what
geography is. So, as soon as I learned, I brought it back here. That was very
exciting to share back home.[46]

Since Projeto Seringueiro and the syndicate grew up together, it is not surprising that it would be deeply involved in promoting the empates that the union
organized. In an empate, men, women, and children would link arms or lie down
in the path of chainsaws and tractors, beseeching operators, often ex-seringueiros
like themselves, to cease and sometimes offering to pay their salary. The
seringueiros were non-violent, but they were often met with force, as the fazendeiros would typically call out the police as well as their own armed guards.
Tensions mounted, and reprisals were fierce as seringueiros escalated the intensity of their empates during the 1980s at the Nazaré, Filipinas, and Equador
seringais, and the Bordon fazenda, among others. Between 1975 and 1989, the tappers of Brasiléia and Xapuri carried out 45 empates. They won 15 and lost 30; however, according to Mendes, the effort was worth it because "our resistance saved
more than 1,200,000 hectares of forest."[47] Mendes described the empates as
"born of necessity," something "that we created together, from our own heads,"
and modified "day by day." Commenting on the success of the empates, anthropologist and long-standing seringueiro advocate, Mauro Almeida, says, "The movement is very successful and has called the attention of the authorities to the
problem of the seringueiros who live from rubber extraction and Brazil nut collection, who live with the forest and conserve it, and because of this they are fighting
against the destruction of their means of survival."[48]

As repression from the fazendeiros increased during the 1970s, seringueiros
needed a mechanism for further protecting themselves from violence. Mendes,
his cousin and confidante Raimundo de Barros, and political activist Jorge Maia,
among others, determined that it would strengthen the seringueiros' organization if they joined the new Workers Party [*Partido Trabalhista*, PT]. In a letter
to Wilson Pinheiro, shortly before Pinheiro's murder, Mendes describes the
urgency of the situation: "... things in Xapuri are really hot.... the ranchers had
a meeting and they are saying that the only way out for them is to kill the president of the syndicate, the delegate from CONTAG [rural labor federation], Chico
Mendes, the padres, and other syndicate delegates." Mendes and his allies moved
quickly to create the Acre branch of the Workers Party in 1981 to link themselves
to a national political structure. The first meetings of the PT in Xapuri took
place in the syndicate headquarters, in members' homes, and in the parish hall.[49]

The Workers Party, like the union, became a spokesman for the seringueiros,
helping them run for elections and forge coalitions with larger constituencies. At
the same time, Projeto Seringueiro was raising political awareness with its forest-

based curriculum, and the base communities were fostering solidarity and a scripturally grounded critical consciousness.

The cause of the seringueiros received a huge boost in 1985 at the first *Encontro Nacional de Seringueiros da Amazônia* [National Encounter of Amazonian Rubber Tappers] held in Brasília. The meeting was the brainchild of several individuals, including Chico Mendes, Mary Allegretti, and OXFAM's Terry Gross, who encouraged the seringueiros to link their plight to that of the rainforest itself. Thus, they would join with environmentalists, human rights advocates, Indian rights activists, and ordinary citizens worldwide who were alarmed at the ever-increasing burning of the forest. At the Encontro, the tappers themselves first put forward the idea of extractive reserves as an alternative to deforestation. One hundred and fifty tappers attended the meeting as did representatives from the Ministries of Industry and Commerce, Education, Health, Agriculture, Agrarian Reform and Culture, and members of the National Congress. The tappers demanded "a development policy for Amazônia that meets the interests of rubber tappers and respects our rights. We do not accept an Amazon development policy that favours large enterprises which exploit and massacre rural workers and destroy nature." The document went on to explain: "We are not opposed to technology, provided that it is at our service and does not ignore our wisdom, our experience, our interests and our rights."[50]

The results of the Encontro were far-reaching. First, the CNS [*Conselho Nacional do Seringueiro*, National Rubber Tappers' Council] was created the same year. The CNS has been in the forefront of the cause ever since, defending the rights of the seringueiro and putting forward proposals for a sustainable future. The CNS has also been instrumental in bringing about a historic rapprochement between seringueiros and Indians, beginning with the first meeting of the Forest Peoples' Alliance in 1986.

Meanwhile, the ranchers, infuriated by all the talk of agrarian reform and the attention the seringueiros were receiving from the national government, formed their own organization, the UDR, the Rural Democratic Union. With its rallying cry of "Tradition, Family, and Property," ranchers agitated against agrarian reform, which, in their view, would only give land to farmers who were too ignorant to make it productive. Though the UDR claimed to be merely a cattleman's association, it clearly behaved as a political lobby. Moreover, funds from UDR barbecues and cattle auctions were frequently used to purchase arms. From about 1985 Mendes and the seringueiros began working closely with foreign allies, including North American environmentalists and lobbyists critical of international lending institutions for failing to take into account the environmental and social impact of the projects they funded.[51] The most flagrant example in the Amazon was *Polonoroeste*, the road-building project which, ironically, was intended to avoid negative impact problems by controlling the flood of immigrants pouring into Rondônia, encouraging the planting of sustainable crops, building small access roads, and paving BR 364 from Cuiabá to Porto Velho.

WATERING HOLE, CACHOEIRA

In 1981 the World Bank, against the advice of its own consultants, paid the Brazilian government the first instalment of the loan for Polonoroeste, the terms of which required Brazil to set aside reserves for Indians and to put environmental safeguards into place. But as soon as the loan was announced, the landless began streaming into the area, with 65,000 settlers arriving between 1981 and 1983. Thousands of busses, overflowing with desperate migrants clutching their cardboard boxes, continued to arrive through 1984. However, malaria, yellow fever, exhausted soil, and an asphyxiating shroud of smoke from the burning forests forced them to sell out to cattle ranchers who were waiting in the wings. By 1985, when the meeting of the seringueiros in Brasília took place, the Indians and the rainforests of Rondônia were on the verge of extinction.[52]

US environmentalists, who were pressing Congress to stop funding development projects like Polonoroeste, welcomed the alliance with the rubber tappers, because they needed to demonstrate that there were people actually living in the rainforest and whose lives and culture were being destroyed. For their part, the seringueiros needed the international influence of outside organizations to wake up Brazilians and their government. As Mendes remarks:

> Our biggest assets are the international environment lobby and the international press. I'm afraid we have had more support from abroad than from people in Brazil, and the opposite should be the case. It was only after international recognition and pressure that we started to get support from the rest of Brazil.[53]

Meanwhile, the situation in Acre was becoming more dangerous. In 1988, two young seringueiros were shot and wounded during the empate at the Equador estate, and prominent seringueiro leader Ivair Higino was brutally murdered. The federal government, fearing further hostilities, agreed in 1988 to establish the first three extractive reserves, among them the bitterly contested Cachoeira reserve, Mendes's home seringal. This was a great triumph for Chico Mendes and his collaborators, who had for several years been putting forward the case for the reserves. Mendes describes the reserves as the idea of "a group of companions committed to faith and idealism."[54] It was also a victory for the North American, European, and Brazilian allies who had been advising and assisting in the struggle. According to one of them, Mary Allegretti, the great accomplishment of the reserves is their combination of development with environmental protection. The principal objectives, outlined at the 1985 Encontro, included, in addition to allowing seringueiros to live undisturbed in the forest, agrarian reform, the introduction of new technologies to improve production, and the establishment of adequate educational and health systems.[55] There are currently 13 extractive reserves in Acre alone, the largest of which is the Chico Mendes Extractive Reserve, covering 976,570 hectares.

Two months after his victory, Mendes was cut down in his own home by an assassin's bullet. His murder was deplored throughout the world, and the Brazilian government acted quickly to bring charges against those responsible, rancher Darli Alves da Silva, the former owner of the Cachoeira seringal, and his son Darci, who were tried and convicted of murder. They have served time off and on since their convictions. Allegretti points out that Mendes's assassination had the effect of revealing to outsiders an important aspect of the environmental question in the Amazon—the conflict over land rights. His death highlighted the character of the struggle for the defense of the environment in countries like Brazil, where it is bound up with the "concomitant quest for social equity." Allegretti observes that, with the creation of the extractive reserves, sustainable and socially just development became established as the goal, not just for Brazil, but for all developing countries.[56]

The rubber tappers' cooperative, which had first been attempted in the early 1980s, was reborn under the aegis of the CNS after the proposal to create extractive reserves had gained momentum. The cooperative was seen as a way to try to improve the economic condition of the rubber tappers.[57] The idea was for tappers to work together to market their rubber and Brazil nuts and to buy goods in bulk at wholesale prices. Seringueiros hoped to increase production by planting more palm and other trees in order to decrease their dependence on rubber. Proponents of the cooperative encouraged potential members by explaining that, in exchange for a nominal monthly fee for services rendered, the cooperative would enable tappers to increase their income, live sustainably, and preserve the forest.

Brazilian economist and state deputy Roland Polanco, along with Brazilian and foreign advisors and supporters from Projeto Seringueiro, worked hard to help the Xapuri cooperative get on its feet. After nearly two years of conversations with seringueiros to convince them of the benefits of cooperativism, the concept gradually took hold; today, there are cooperatives in Brasiléia, Sena Madureira, and numerous other municipalities. Seringueiro Sebastião Mendes Teixeira, a cousin of Chico Mendes and resident of the Cachoeira reserve, comments on the benefits of membership: "In our cooperative, sometimes things go well and sometimes they go badly, but we are living, I think, 90 per cent better than in the time of the patrão.... We form work groups, then we go in one day for rice, bread, Brazil nuts. We don't all go, just four or five of us. We trade off days. We share, that's it, and *ninguém passa fôme não*" [no one goes hungry]. The most important benefit to this seringueiro is that now: "We are our own masters" [*Somos donos da nossa pessoa*].[58]

For Polanco, the overall objective of the cooperative was to "bring the isolated seringueiro into the market."[59] Of course, now that they are somewhat integrated, seringueiros are still dependent on the international market. Thus, the 300 to 350 members of the Xapuri cooperative have begun to diversify, cultivating native plants such as *pupunha*, *guaraná*, and *cupuaçu* to vary their production. Only a minority of Xapuri's seringueiros have joined the cooperative, perhaps 30 per cent, and Polanco has urged public officials to encourage more seringueiros to join. It would certainly help with expenses if numbers increased, but the main problem the cooperative faces is the lack of trained managers and administrators who can communicate with clients, such as the São Paulo suppliers of machine parts. Polanco attributes the situation in part to the "21 years of dictatorship, during which we lost a whole generation of leaders. Fear silenced everyone. This ruptured our entire social and cultural development. But we are recovering."[60] The seringueiro now goes back and forth between barter and the global economy, inserting himself into the latter insofar as possible only on conditions that favor his survival.

National and international organizations, both governmental and nongovernmental, such as OXFAM, the World Wildlife Federation, Amnesty International,

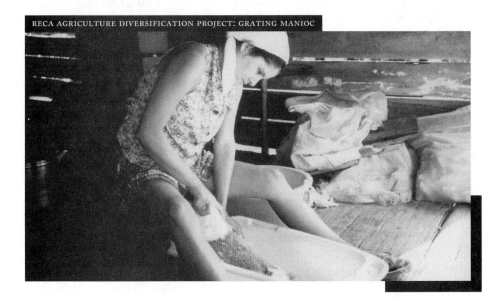

RECA AGRICULTURE DIVERSIFICATION PROJECT: GRATING MANIOC

Cultural Survival, Environmental Defense, RECA [*Reflorestamento, Econômico, Consorciado, Adensado,* or Economical reforestation that relies on cultivating a variety of species and on planting trees close together], PESACRE [*Grupo de Pesquisa e Extensão em Sistemas Agroflorestais do Acre,* Research Extension Group in Agroforestry Systems of Acre], EMBRAPA [*Empresa Brasileira de Pesquisa Agropecuária,* Brazilian Agricultural Research Enterprise], and others too numerous to mention, have assisted the seringueiros and native populations in living sustainably and diversifying their production. RECA, for example, demonstrates the benefits of national and international collaboration in producing alternative crops such as coffee, pupunha, cupuaçu, and native fruits such as *açai* for local consumption and for marketing. Similarly PESACRE, a joint Brazilian and University of Florida venture, promotes sustainable agriculture and gender equity within the programs that it sponsors for seringueiros, Indians, and *colonos* [subsistence farmers]. EMBRAPA, an agricultural research and development arm of the Brazilian government, has carried out interesting work in developing new crops, such as the *pimenta longa* [red pepper plant], which can be produced for export and enjoys great popularity in Japan. Although NGOs and government organizations sometimes compete, practice "assistentialism" [the provision of services in a way that exacerbates dependency] rather than self-help, insist on doing things their own way, duplicate efforts, and even occasionally refuse to share information, on the whole, they have been a lifesaver for the forest peoples. They have helped traditional populations adjust to a new economic reality while preserving their way of life.

The seringueiro has fought not only economic extinction but also cultural annihilation. Thus, it is especially significant that tapper Sebastião Mendes proclaims with pride, "I was born in the forest and I have remained in the forest; it is a pleasure to say that I live here."[61] Manoel Estébio Cavalcante da Cunha emphasizes the essential role that cultural concerns play in Projeto Seringueiro and in other CNS projects, which insist on maintaining a sustainable forest-based economy as the only appropriate system for a forest-based culture. Dom Moacyr and others speak of the cultural rescue efforts encouraged by the church and NGOs and of the poetry and song that have begun to flourish as the seringueiros rediscover their roots. The intimate relationship between the seringueiro and nature comes through clearly in "I Sketch a Song," by Amazonian poet Assis Pereira:

> I sketch a song
> that may be sung
> by all the organs of my body,
> that may be known
> by all who are solitary.
>
> A song that speaks of the perfume of the flowers
> that expresses the beauty of existence
> that explains the two sides of life.

A song
that transforms into dust all my mud
that has the harmony
of the songbirds and
that is like nature: always beautiful.

a song that overcomes the barrier of distance
between cultures and beliefs.

A song that is eternal.
If I can't sing it
at least I can sketch it.[62]

The interconnectedness of environment and culture finds more direct expression in the "Declaration of the Peoples of the Forest," from 1989:

> The traditional peoples who today trace on the Amazonian sky the rainbow of the Alliance of the Peoples of the Forest declare their wish to see their regions preserved. They know that the development of the potential of their people and of the regions they inhabit is to be found in the future economy of their communities, and must be preserved for the whole Brazilian nation as part of its identity and self-esteem. This Alliance of the Peoples of the Forest, bringing together Indians, rubber tappers, and riverbank communities, and founded here in Acre, embraces all efforts to protect and preserve this immense, but fragile life-system that involves our forests, lakes, rivers and springs, the source of our wealth and the basis of our cultures and traditions.[63]

The struggle of the seringueiros is by no means over. But after more than 130 years, one sees clearly that the story of the northeastern immigrant, who, displaced by poverty and drought, came and displaced the Indian, and who was himself subsequently displaced by immigrants from the south, has begun a new chapter, the theme of which is resistance. Each displacement involved an economic motive, a violation of human rights, and a cultural loss. In each case, one finds a basic dispute over land use, concepts of ownership, and views of nature itself. Basically, the conflict today is between those who view nature as an inert object to be exploited for short-term gain, and those who regard it as a living web that includes and sustains human life.

The seringueiro's trajectory offers important observations on how threatened communities can produce local leaders, become politically aware, learn to organize, collaborate with helping organizations, and act on their own behalf to fight for their way of life and for control of their own resources.

NOTES

1. Instituto Brasileiro de Geografia e Estatística (IBGE). Website: www.ibge.gov.br
2. IBGE 1992; Luiz Antônio Pinto de Oliveira, *O Sertanejo, o Brabo e o Posseiro* (*Os cem anos de andanças da população acreana*) (Rio Branco: Universidade Federal do Acre [UFAC], 1985) 33, 35, 84.
3. Euclides da Cunha, "Impressões Gerais," *Um Paraíso Perdido. Reunião dos Ensaios Amazônicos* (Petropólis: Vozes, 1976) 97. The Portuguese reads: "um quase servo, à mercê do império discricionário dos patrões."
4. da Cunha 99. The Portuguese reads: "o homem, ... é ainda um intruso impertinente. Chegou sem ser esperado nem querido...."
5. Cláudio Araújo Lima, *Coronel de Barranco* (São Paulo: Gráfica Urupês, 1970) 48.
6. de Oliveira 86. The Portuguese reads: "o aniquilamento da vida humana atinge proporções excepcionais."
7. Ana Ramos and Josenira Oliveira, "O Seringueiro Conta a sua História," BA thesis, UFAC, 1996: 33.
8. Ivonilde and Valdir Menezes, personal interview, Rio Branco, 31 May 1999.
9. Ivonilde Menezes interview.
10. Maria do Perpétuo Socorro Silva, José Rodrigues Arimatéia, Frankcinato da Silva Batista, *Seringueiros, Memória, História e Identidade*, Vol. I (Rio Branco: UFAC, Centro de Documentação e Informação Histórica, CIDH, 1997) 180-82.
11. Ivonilde Menezes interview.
12. Mauro William Barbosa de Almeida, "Rubber Tappers of the Upper Juruá River, Brazil," diss., University of Cambridge, England, 1992: 40.
13. Barbara Weinstein, *The Amazon Rubber Boom 1850-1920* (Stanford, CA: Stanford University Press, 1983) 23-24.
14. Ricardo Hiroyuki Shibata, personal interview, Rio Branco, 1 June 1999.
15. Amós D'Avila de Paulo, Angela Maria Gomes Alves, Caticilene Rodrigues, Rosilene da Silva, Valcidene Soares Menezes. "Soldados da Borracha de Xapuri: Memórias de um Viver," *Xapurys* I (Rio Branco: UFAC/DH, 1995): 14.
16. Weinstein 263-64.
17. Almeida 59.
18. Weinstein 265.
19. Weinstein 267.
20. Almeida 47.
21. de Paulo, et al. 9.
22. Almeida 47-48.
23. Ramos and Oliveira 31-32. The Portuguese reads: "Morria criança, aquelas crianças doentes que traziam escondido pra não ficar internado no hospital....Veio muito cearenses pra cá e morreram muitos. No ano que nós chegamos, não tinha nem quem desse água uns aos outros, com malária...."
24. Ramos and Oliveira 23. The Portuguese reads: "Os arigós reclamavam muito, porque quando êles vieram, êles traziam um contato que era pra receber as estradas brocadas, uma casinha e um defumador feito. Eles chegaram e não encontraram nada ... encontraram muito foi sezão, que morreram foi muitos."
25. de Paulo et al. 15.
26. Andrew Revkin, *The Burning Season: The Murder of Chico Mendes and the Fight for the Amazon Rain Forest* (New York: Penguin, 1990) 105.
27. de Oliveira 50-51.

28. Aldenir Rodrigues Mota, Alzenite de Araújo Verçosa, Cosmo Araújo e Araújo, Rosineide Rodrigues Lopes, Zairinéia Soares de Lima, Zilah Carvalho Mastub de Oliveira, "Empate pela Vida e Defesa da Floresta em Xapuri," *Xapurys* 2 (Rio Branco: UFAC, 1996): 7.
29. de Oliveira 52-53.
30. Revkin 106.
31. de Oliveira 56-57.
32. Padre Paolino Baldassari, personal interview, Sena Madureira, 31 July 1996. The Portuguese reads: "Ou com bombom, ou com engano, ou com ameaça, ou com morte."
33. de Oliveira 57, 38.
34. Shibata interview.
35. Ivonilde Menezes interview.
36. de Oliveira 38.
37. de Oliveira 94.
38. Maria Ronizia Pereira Gonçalves, "A Fala Sagrada e Social do 'Todo Somos Irmãos' de 1976 a 1982," BA thesis, UFAC, 1997: 35.
39. Gonçalves 75, 86.
40. Matilde Ribeiro da Silva, personal interview, Riozinho, 7 June 1999.
41. Gonçalves 32, 37.
42. Personal letter from Chico Mendes to Dom Moacyr Grechi, dated 29 July 1987.
43. "Projeto Político-Pedagógico para as Escolas Orientadas pelo Projeto Seringueiro (CTA-Acre)," CTA document, Rio Branco, 1 June 1999.
44. Shibata interview.
45. *Resumo do Programa*, CTA document, Rio Branco, 29 July 1997; CTA document, Rio Branco, 1 June 1999.
46. Eliana Ribeiro da Silva, personal interview, Riozinho, 7 June 1999.
47. Chico Mendes, *Fight for the Forest: Chico Mendes in His Own Words*, trans. Chris Whitehouse, additional material Tony Gross, ed. Duncan Green (London: Latin American Bureau, 1989) 79. Adapted from *O Testamento da Floresta*, ed. Cândido Grabowski (Rio de Janeiro: FASE, 1989).
48. Mota et al., "Empate ..." 10, 15.
49. Aldenir Rodrigues Mota, Alzenite de Araújo Verçosa, Cosmo Araújo e Araújo, Maria Mavy Dourado de Souza, Rosineide Rodrigues Lopes, Zairnéia Soares de Lima, Zilah Carvalho Mastub de Oliveira, "A Formação do Partido dos Trabalhadores em Xapuri: Os 15 Anos do PT," *Xapurys* 1 (1995): 21-22, 23.
50. Mendes 37.
51. Revkin 180-81, 184, 188-89. For more on the environmentalists' efforts, see Pat Aufderheide and Bruce Rich, "Environmental Reform and the Multilateral Banks," *World Policy Journal* (Spring 1988). See also David Price, *Before the Bulldozer: The Nambiquara Indians and the World Bank* (Cabin John, MD: Seven Locks Press, 1989).
52. Revkin 188-89.
53. Mendes 51.
54. Letter to Dom Moacyr Grechi, see note 42.
55. Mary Helena Allegretti, "Reservas Extrativistas: Parâmetros para uma Política de Desenvolvimento Sustentável na Amazônia," *O Destino da Floresta, Reservas extrativistas e desenvolvimento sustentável na Amazônia*, ed. Ricardo Arnt (Rio de Janeiro: Dumará Distribuidora de Publicações Ltda. Co-published by Instituto de Estudos Amazônicos e Ambientais, Fundação Konrad Adenauer, 1994) 18, 24. In this same volume, see also Stephan Schwartzman's article, "Mercados para Produtos Extrativistas da Amazônia

Brasileira" 247-59. For more on extractive reserves, see Mary Allegretti and Stephan Schwartzman, *Extractive Production in the Amazon and the Rubber Tappers' Movement* (Washington, DC: Environmental Defense Fund, 1987). See also Philip M. Fearnside, *Extractive Reserves in Brazilian Amazonia: An Opportunity to Maintain Tropical Rain Forest Under Sustainable Use* (Manaus: National Institute of Amazon Research, October, 1988).

56. Allegretti 18.

57. Mendes 72.

58. Sebastião Teixeira de Mendes, personal interview, Cachoeira Extractive Reserve, 2 August 1996.

59. Roland Polanco, personal interview, Rio Branco, 28 August 1997.

60. Polanco interview.

61. de Mendes interview.

62. Assis Pereira, *Versos Amazônicos* (Rio Branco: Fundação Garibaldi, Brasil, 1996) 25. Translation by Denis Heyck.

63. Mendes 85.

Interviews

Júlio Barbosa

Seringueiro, close ally of Chico Mendes, leader of the Xapuri syndicate, empate veteran, cooperative advocate, Workers Party [PT] activist, and mayor of Xapuri, the dynamic Barbosa has worked consistently and effectively to improve the quality of life for the people of Xapuri. In the interview that follows, Barbosa describes what life was like for the typical seringueiro in the past and what it was like for him growing up as a seringueiro. In so doing, he recalls customs and practices representative of the culture. He also contrasts the well-being of seringueiros who are members of the Xapuri cooperative with that of those who are not. This energetic politician concludes by sharing his enthusiastic vision for the future, as he outlines a modernization program based on cultural and environmental realities.

I am a seringueiro and one of 13 children. I was born in the Cachoeira seringal, but when I was five years old my father moved us closer to the city of Xapuri. We were still in the same colocação, but since we were closer to town I could attend elementary school as it was just a six kilometre walk. Later, my father had to move deeper into the forest again because he was unable to make a living near the city. The family was growing, and when we returned to the seringal I began to work as a tapper. I was 13 and continued tapping for 21 years straight. In 1988, with the assassination of Chico Mendes, I left the forest in order to come to the office in Xapuri where I had been the director of the syndicate along with Chico. So, from the end of 1988 on, I was no longer engaged in tapping rubber.

I think it is interesting to learn about the history of the seringueiro. Each seringal may have from 20 to 100 *colocações* [area occupied and worked by rubber tapper family]. It varies quite a bit. When I was a child, it was truly a system of slavery, there was no freedom at all. The tapper was obliged to collect rubber for the patrão. At that time, the seringueiro was totally dependent on the patrão, who brought supplies to the barracão, picked up the rubber, and carried it back to his house. At that time, many seringueiros not only produced rubber, they also raised animals, chickens, pigs, capote, a kind of hen, and ducks. Many engaged in subsistence agriculture also, growing rice, beans, farinha, and corn. However, at least as many seringueiros made their living from rubber alone.

When I was little, I remember the excitement of seeing my father come home laden with supplies. It was a big event. He would bring beef, *xacre, piralucú*, a type of fish, and farinha. All this arrived by *paneiro* [small boat] from Pará. Oh, we also had condensed milk; at that time we didn't consume powdered milk. The seringueiro would buy two boxes of condensed milk. The patrão would purchase all the provisions initially and then take them to the seringueiro who bought according to the quantity of latex that he had produced. If he had not produced much, then he couldn't purchase many supplies.

A week before the convoy would enter the seringal with the supplies, an employee of the patrão would visit the colocações, he was called a *noteiro* [notetaker]. He came with a pen and a small notebook, going from colocação to colocação taking note of what was needed, how many kilos of sugar, salt, how many tins of *banha de porco* [pork lard], because at that time we didn't use oil. He made all his notes, including how much borracha [latex] each seringueiro had. Then he would return to the storehouse where he would turn in his figures to the patrão's manager, who would examine them and figure out who would get what based on their productivity. The patrão usually tried to work it out so that the amount the seringueiro produced covered his need for basic supplies. At that time, the patrão system was fair in that sense; it's just that it allowed absolutely no freedom to the seringueiro.

Usually the seringueiros were northeasterners and the patrões also. The history of Acre is the history of *coronelismo*, or rule by powerful men called colonels, and these colonels were not about to liberate anyone. What was a colonel like? Well, he was not rich. What he was was courageous, a brave northeasterner, a type of *cangaceiro* [gunman], and often ruthless. So, what did he do? Well, now this was real early, the last few decades of the nineteenth century, when there was a huge amount of propaganda to get people to come out here to settle and exploit the rubber. So people came fleeing the drought in the northeast and hoping to strike it rich. They came to Belém and outfitted themselves for the journey to Amazonas, Acre, Pará, Rondônia, or Mato Grosso.

The colonel would gather a large group of men together to make the trip with him. In Belém there was a big supply house called Cangré de Comércio de Belém, which furnished all their supplies. They would come down the river and disembark where there looked to be many rubber trees scattered through the forest. Then they would climb up the steep riverbanks and set up camp there. From that base, they would enter the forest with the *mateiro* [woodsman], whose job it was to identify the flora, especially the seringas, open the forest, and clear the pathways. The estradas formed a circuit that the seringueiro would walk usually in a day's work of tapping trees and then returning to collect the latex. In all of this they used the Indians and depended on their knowledge.

But first they waged war against the Indians. The arms they used were 44 calibre rifles. A large part of the supplies the colonels brought with them consisted of arms and bullets, lots of bullets. You see, to occupy an area was like starting a war. They would go in there and kill the Indians or drive them out and take over the forest. The colonel who commanded the "batalion" was not really a soldier, much less a colonel, he was just a northeasterner with a rifle. Not too many of them died in battle because they had an effective attack strategy and superior arms, and so they began to settle in the seringal. Since it was on the riverbanks that these men first set foot, the name of "riverbank colonels" stuck. All the rubber forests of Acre, Amazonas, Mato Grosso, Rondônia, and Pará were opened by the riverbank colonels.

Now, what was it like in a seringal back then? Well, the colonel "owned" the seringal, the men, the supply center, and a group of *jagunços*, which at that time were called *capangas* [bodyguards], but today we say *jagunço* [gunmen]. They were known by this identity: "I am the capanga of the colonel." This is the history of Xapuri, pure coronelismo. What would happen whenever the seringueiro would do something that the coronel didn't like, the capangas would go out and get the seringueiro and tie him to a tree. Sometimes he would spend a week tied to the tree with just farinha and water, maybe a little salt. Or they would tie a *jamaxim* branch to his back: the jamaxim is the tree traditionally used to make the buckets for carrying water. Well, they would tie this to his back and pour *sernambí*, or impure latex, onto the wood and set it on fire, incinerating the seringueiro. These punishments were very common here in Xapuri.

This was all around 1880, through the 1890s and the beginning of the twentieth century. When they came in those early years, the northeasterners from Ceará, Rio Grande do Norte, Paraíba, they usually brought only men, no women. So, there was a scarcity of women and the patrão, if he wanted to reward a seringueiro, would say: "You're a good seringueiro, I'm going to give you So-and-So's woman." Then the capangas would go and get the woman and take her away. My grandfather, my father's father, would tell me all these stories because he was a capanga.

When they first came here to settle, the seringueiros would arrive in Xapuri by river and then go out to clear their colocação and work for a year. Then they would make the long journey back here, by foot and by river, to where the boat docked in order to deliver their goods and obtain supplies. They would work all year with barely enough to eat, just waiting for that day. It was very common for the colonel to accept their produce and then send his men out to kill the seringueiros. That's the history, and that doesn't even include the Indians, whom the seringueiros fought at the colonel's command. For reluctant seringueiros, there was always the tree trunk torture.

Coronelismo began dying out in the 1920s. When the colonel died out, the seringalista replaced him. You could say that the seringalista was a descendant of the colonel, but he was not the same thing. He was more modern in the sense that he didn't use arms anymore, he used the police. In a big seringal like Iracema, the police became the latter-day capangas of the seringalista. You know the seringueiro was not allowed to sell anything to anyone except to his own patrão. If he sold to another patrão, the police would pick him up and take him to jail.

If he was lucky, they would allow him to clear out, taking only his family and the clothes on his back.

I remember my father and my older brothers used to sell borracha under cover of night. I also remember that they could not buy a cigarette, a bullet, anything, without "burning the paper" as we called it. You had to burn the receipts because you did not want any record of any transaction.

The only thing that counted in those days was rubber; they called it "white gold" because its value was that of gold. I was born in 1954 and during the 1960s rubber was still doing well, but it began a steady decline around 1972. The wealth of Xapuri, it never stayed here, but was always carried away to other regions, and Xapuri was left poor and abandoned. But, during the heyday, there were incentives for the seringueiro. Sometimes the patrão would give prizes for the most productive seringueiro, good prizes, such as a horse. The one who produced the least, he would get a skirt as a present. Yes! That's the way it was in the seringal, and everyone worked day and night in order not to win the skirt! This was up until around 1968 or 1969, very recent.

That's about when everything changed here. Until then, rubber at least still had some value, but around 1969 was when cattle ranching began, something we had never before experienced in the region. From about 1970 all the seringalistas began to leave. I had a colocação in what is now the Reserve, and I stayed on there as did other seringueiros. When the seringalistas left, the *marreteiro* [middleman] replaced him as the one who bought rubber and supplied the goods. He would come by launch or jeep. He didn't take the place of the seringalista, he just took over his function with regard to the marketing of the rubber. During that time, the seringueiro could sell to whichever marreteiro he wished.

With the failure of rubber, in some measure because of the competition with Malaysia, there was no more incentive. The only incentives were for cattle raising. The federal government was pushing it, but the biggest push came with the opening of the Transamazonian highway and other federal highways. Road construction began about 1964 with the dictatorship, which was looking for new ways of producing and exporting, and they were eager to exploit this region. That's really when the whole process of disequilibrium for the seringueiro began. It's important to remember with regard to the highway, that up until that point the seringueiro had a very strong culture.

The seringueiro always had a deep faith; he was very religious. His faith consisted of believing in the saints, São Francisco, São Sebastião, São José: everything had to do with the saints. They also had the tradition of festivals for godparents, compadres, cousins; such celebrations forged strong cultural and family bonds. Up until then in the seringal there were many *terços* [prayers] lead by someone who had learned them by memory, usually an elderly woman. There were also many novenas and procession days. And the terços were always accompanied by a party with forró music, dancing, and big banquets. For example, there was the feast day of São Lázaro, who is the patron saint of dogs. That's right, dogs! I remember very well the tradition of having a big festival with a banquet for all the dogs. They would cook up the best meals you could imagine, gather all the dogs together, and honor them with the feast. In this festival, the people ate the leftovers, but only after the dogs had had their fill!

As rubber came to be less important to the economy and the politics of the government, the cultural unity of the seringueiro began to unravel. This was also the time when new populations, new cultures from other areas, began to come here, and that also began to destabilize our own culture. You have to consider the impact of migration. Today we have here a mixture of paulistas, whom we call Italians, and people from Capixaba, Mato Grosso, even gauchos from Rio Grande do Sul a few thousand miles away. Today, you run into all these people in the same area. So, big economic and political changes, and the mixing with other peoples, all this began to erode that culture that had been so strong. It had been vigorous because the Acrean root is northeastern and has a very direct connection to Ceará and to Padre Cícero from early in the twentieth century, who is still believed by many seringueiros to have worked miracles. But these things have declined recently. I think the biggest change is that a person used to believe in himself more and treat others with more respect. These things have definitely declined as a result of the changes.

I believe it is these factors that give rise to the somewhat negative image that people have of the seringueiro today. Previously, the image was of one who had his land, his rubber, his biscuit, his tin of milk; he was poor, but he was not hungry. The seringueiro who didn't produce barely made it, but the one who produced had all he needed to live. Now, he didn't have the freedom to walk down the street in the city if the patrão hadn't authorized it. But he ate very well. Our elders all were raised on condensed milk; they called it "strong milk."

With that cultural destabilization everything began to decline. You have the increasing social and physical isolation of the seringueiro, and many are now experiencing real hunger with no one to help them. It's very sad.

But if you go to Cachoeira you will see that there the seringueiro is not hungry. Why is that? Because he is closer to the city, that is Xapuri, he has the cooperative, he is much more politically aware, and he knows much more about planning. They plan a lot in order to make the best use of their work force and to increase their income so that they will not go hungry. But if you take a look around, in and outside the Reserve, you see that the large majority are living in a situation of great need because they make their living only from rubber. They do not cultivate rice or beans, and they don't have even one chicken or pig. When rubber falls, they do too.

Some such seringueiros go to the city. But when they arrive, it is difficult there. The seringueiro, when he leaves the forest for the city, the first thing that enters his head is that he is going to set up a little business. But when he arrives, he learns that that little business will never be. He has no profession suited to the city; his profession is that of rubber tapper. What happens to him, his wife, and kids in the city is that first he leaves his wife to become a peon on some nearby estate, doing day jobs. The daughters, the tendency is for them to go into prostitution, often the mother of the family as well. The sons become part of the "marginal" life, that is, they get involved with drugs, theft, assault. This is what happens when you leave the forest for the city. It's not 100 per cent, but it's 80 per cent of the time. So that's the situation of the seringueiro today, if he does not live somewhere like Cachoeira.

The tappers usually don't return to the forest because there it is also very difficult to make a living. Before, when the seringueiro would go to set up his colocação, the patrão would transport his goods for him and pay for the construction of his *barraca* [house], his defumador, the utensils he needed for tapping, even his shotgun. The patrão paid for or provided all of these. Of course, he put them all on the seringueiro's account, but at least it was part of an incentive system. Now, everything depends on the seringueiro himself, and that's too hard.

That's more or less the history of the seringueiro, how it used to be and how it is today.

You may wonder why all of the seringueiros don't come here to Cachoeira to join the cooperative. To give you an idea of why they do not, there are seringueiros here in Xapuri for whom to leave the city—yes, we call this small town a city—and go back to their homes is a four- or five-day journey. Very distant. Because the transport system is so precarious, they go either on foot or by burro. It's just not possible for the cooperative to reach someone who lives four or five days away.

Who does go out to those distant places where the seringueiros live is the *madereiro* [lumber merchant]. Many seringueiros have abandoned rubber tapping because there is no market for the rubber, and they have taken up felling trees instead. They exchange valuable wood for a mere kilo of sugar, a litre of oil, a can of milk, a piece of soap. When you go to one of their houses, you feel pain. The children are naked, and the wife stays hidden because she has only rags to wear. This is the situation for those who live so far away.

I think it's essential for the cooperative to ask the government for a transportation project for such areas. The Reserve needs paths, roads that are passable in a pickup truck in order to reach these families. The other problem is that the seringueiros live far from each other. The nearest colocação would be, at the minimum, a half-hour's walk. This also makes it difficult to invest in infrastructure. One thing the government should think about is how to group more families around production poles, a sort of agricultural village system. That way it would be easier for the government to put in electricity, a health post, a school.

The government should be thinking about the development of the communities, but they are not. However, if I win the mayoral election here in Xapuri, I will have that as a priority—the person in the countryside. We need productive communities because the seringais are very dispersed. The government needs to be more committed to the people, to try harder to improve their lot. In the Reserve, for example, I think that if we had a little path, not asphalted, just a small path so that any time of the year a vehicle could enter to make pick-ups and deliveries, it would improve the quality of life a great deal. Another thing that would help our area is ecotourism, but you can't attract tourists if you don't even have a road.

When I'm elected, the first thing I'm going to do is pay the salaries of the village employees. Salaries are paid about six months late, and sometimes they never arrive. Why? Because paying employees' salaries is not a priority of the government. You can imagine the chaos that creates. If I'm elected I will try to develop the people, everyone from the neighborhood resident to the country person. There are many activities to be developed in the Reserve, and I hope to gain the assistance of the World Bank, and IBAMA, the Brazilian environmental agency, for example, encouraging them to invest in the reserve. It will all work out.

Xapuri has a very strong identity because of the whole issue of the rubber tapper, extractivism, and any municipal government needs the extractivists' support. Agriculture and cattle ranching are also important, but agriculture has been abandoned in Xapuri. The key is the question of extractivism, how to reinforce it and how to attract ecotourism. There's a tree called the *samaúma*, if you cut it down and sell it, you get a certain price for it. But if you preserve it, then you can "sell" it without cutting it down because you sell it to the tourist who pays to come, to stay in a hotel, and buy meals. If you "sell" the tree in this way, 100 years from now, tourists will still be coming here to take photographs of that same tree. The income is much greater than if you had cut it down. I think we should set aside a certain percentage of hectares of the flora and fauna of the Reserve just for tourism.

The thing is that, if you talk about environmentalism, in the minds of the government that just means backwardness. They don't understand because their minds are turned toward another economic system, which is a personal one for themselves and the groups they belong to; it doesn't have anything to do with social issues. For them, it means nothing to see a picture of my marginalized companion appear in the newspaper with the caption "assailant." They see the economic question much more as one of personal benefit, personal gain. What they do is they use the economy to marginalize certain sectors that are important to society as a whole, for example, health. They use their economic control to marginalize health, education, the national ecosystem, and hygiene in the city. You know our economy needs to be linked to a good program of health and education. The ecological issue for the majority of politicians in our region, they see it as backward because economic development via the strengthening of the environment is something that benefits the entire society. They are not interested in that, but rather, in having riches for themselves. If I win the mayor's race here in Xapuri, it will be a great opportunity to provide the first effort in a new direction. Just wait, when Jorge Viana is elected governor of Acre in 1998 [Viana was elected], we'll see a big change in the economic vision of the state. All our efforts will be integrated.

Cattle raising also needs to be modernized in our state. In the mind of the cattle rancher, everything has to be burned. Ridiculous! Ninety per cent of the population of the state suffers from respiratory problems that come from smoke, from the burnings. The rancher also thinks that he needs to have one cow per hectare.

So if he has 1,000 head of cattle, he needs 1,000 hectares of pasture. It's absurd! We have to think in a more modern manner.

Also, for the politicians in our state, extractivism consists only of rubber or Brazil nuts. But in my mind it's very different. Extractivism for me includes all the renewable resources. But just to mention rubber tapping, that needs to be modernized at least as much as the cattle raising. Within Brazil, the production of rubber has increased greatly in the center-east and in the southeast. Today a hectare of planted seringal after ten years produces one tonne and a half of rubber a year. The seringueiro in Mato Grosso or São Paulo is producing about 100 kilos of rubber a day. That's a lot of rubber!

Now, the tapper in the Amazon in a native, not a planted, seringal produces only about ten kilos of rubber because the trees are dispersed. A tapper here in our region collects per year about 600 kilos of rubber. In my opinion, extractivism in the native seringal has to be supplemented by large extensions of planted rubber trees. And we have to modernize in the following way: if the seringal in the south is capable of producing enough rubber to supply consumption, then the native seringal should be utilized for another type of production. This could be for surgical and hospital materials, pharmaceuticals, and the production of other types of products, such as *couro vegetal*, a kind of waterproof covering, which is becoming popular. Also, Mercedes Benz is interested in purchasing the couro vegetal for the trim on its trucks. So, I think that modernizing extractivism here is not going to make us produce 100 kilos of rubber a day, but it is going to take advantage of the type of production and consumption that I've just described. We need to invest in this area. The Extractive Reserve is important to the country, and it guarantees our own future.

Now, other issues, like lumber. Often the seringueiro will gain a litre of oil or a kilo of sugar in exchange for a mahogany tree. That mahogany tree goes to the lumber mill, and from there it is sold and goes to Santa Catarina do Paraná. When it leaves here, it is worth $150 per square meter. After it has been processed in Paraná, it is worth $700-$900 per square meter. It leaves unfinished and goes directly to the furniture factories in England, Canada, Holland, France, Italy, Denmark, and Portugal.

Now, what I want to do is get some of that work for our people. I would like for the mayor to make an agreement with the mayor of Milan, Italy, which is a furniture-making center in Europe. We hope to receive from them technological assistance, the training of our workers so that we will be able to turn out finished products. Thus you generate employment, you value the product you create, you economize, and you use only a few trees. We have a project, I don't know if Fr. Luis Ceppi has told you about it yet, but we have a project with Italy if I win the mayor's race. Two Italian craftsmen are coming here to visit, to demonstrate their craft to us, and we are going to try to set up an apprentice's workshop here. Soon after that, we hope to create a small lumber mill and furniture store for the community of Xapuri.

Then there is the case of the Brazil nut. We should add it to the school lunch, like they do in Rio Branco. We should value our local products in that way. For example, the government of the state of Amapá, with the support of the Secretary of Education, what they did was prioritize the use of regional products in their school lunches. And do you know how much they are paying for a kilo of Brazil nuts processed locally? Six *reais*! That's $6.00! That's a huge support, because a kilo of Brazil nuts ready for delivery to the port of Manaus, or Paranaguá, or Rio de Janeiro, or São Paulo, goes for three reais, or $3.50. The government of Amapá is paying six reais per kilo! If we do something like that, use our products in school lunches, we can increase the market for the cooperative and the members will all benefit from it. All of this is what I mean by modernization of the region. Great opportunities await Xapuri.

Xapuri, 2 August 1996.

NOTE

As of the date of publication, Júlio Barbosa had served two terms as mayor of Xapuri.

Raimundo Mendes de Barros

Seringueiro, cousin and confidante of Chico Mendes, veteran of numerous empates, Barros was a founder of the Xapuri syndicate, the Workers Party [PT] in Xapuri, a participant in the first Encontro Nacional de Seringueiros, and an early proponent of extractive reserves and cooperatives. He has been elected to several terms as vereador [city councilman] by the people of Xapuri.

In the following interview, Barros recalls his life as a tapper, his experiences in the city, and the role of the syndicate, the empates, the reserves, and the cooperative in the seringueiros' struggle. He also expresses support for the new ventures projected for his community. He speaks with the warmth and sincerity that have endeared him to fellow seringueiros and made him a trusted leader.

My father was from Alto Acre, from the Patagonia seringal, and my mother was from the northeast, coming here when she was five years old, and leaving as her legacy a family of eight children. She died six years ago, and my father, eight. I was born and raised in the seringal with my brothers and sisters. The first activity I remember is going into the forest with my family and tapping rubber. Where we were born there was no school, and, of course, nothing like television or any means of communication except, to a very limited extent, radio. By eight years of age, I was going out regularly to tap trees.

The term we use most is *cortar seringa* [to cut rubber trees]. You see, the trees are scattered through the forest and we have paths called *estradas* that we clear in order to link one tree to another. There can be anywhere from 150 to 200 rubber trees along a single estrada. So we go along the estrada and cut the tree; that is, we make a v-shaped incision with a kind of knife that we call a *lámina*. We make the cuts early in the morning, and then we retrace the route in the afternoon to gather the borracha that collects in a gourd. Then we return home and smoke the latex, converting it into a ball of rubber, which we then market.

That's what a seringueiro does, and that's what I grew up doing every day. I have vivid childhood memories of all the animals that shared the forest with us, the tiger, the tapir, the deer, the boar, the paca, which is a kind of large rodent; there was such abundance. As a very young boy, I became intimately familiar with the life of the forest, always accompanied by my parents. Many women dedicate themselves to tapping too, and my mother was one such woman who spent a great many years tapping. She was also the hunter in our household; not all the women do that either, but a considerable number, like my mother, did.

Such was my life until I was about 22 years old, when I left the forest for the first time to go to the city. I went to serve my country, two brothers and myself, we volunteered for a year of military service. Then we returned to the forest and resumed our work as seringueiros. I was 23 when I returned to the seringal. At age 25, I left again, this time to work for SUCAMA, a federal government agency, in an anti-malaria project. I was tired of tapping trees and, you know, you'd hear of life in the city, of new and exciting things, and I had already had a brief urban experience, so I went back.

Some seringueiros, when they see the city, they get used to life there and never return to the countryside. Others no, they may enjoy some of the city's attractions, but they never forget the conviviality of life in the forest, that it is a very peaceful, healthful life, and the city is all tumult. I stayed on for nine years working for SUCAMA, a lot of that time in the interior. Afterwards, I returned to the seringal again. That's because I am a son of the forest, the region, and the way of life that I had lived with my brothers and sisters and my friends in the forest. It's all part of me.

By the time I returned home things were really bad in the rubber forests. You almost had to be here to believe those years of violence that we went through beginning about 1970. That's when the *latifúndio*, the huge cattle ranches, came to Acre, and by 1975 the conflict here had become extremely intense. The patrão system was gone, rubber had fallen in price, and the federal government was promoting cattle ranching for the Amazon region in order to replace rubber. Malaysia and the Japanese were now producing many tons of rubber, as were São Paulo and Bahia, so there was no market for ours.

When I worked for SUCAMA I traveled a lot in the interior, in the rubber forests, so I never lost contact with the people. I always carried them with me in my mind wherever I went. I would be absent three, six months, but afterwards I would always get together with them, I was always in close relationship with them. In this way, I began not only to see, but also to feel and to live the violence that the latifúndio was bringing upon our people.

As a matter of conscience, I left my employment and returned to the Floresta seringal to live, and to my colocação, "Rio Branco." On my return, I began to talk with the people about the goals of the union movement, with which I had become quite familiar by then. I wanted to help guide them, and prevent more companions from leaving the forest and swelling the cordons of poverty and misery in the city. The rural exodus is a big reason for the growth of the *favelas* [slums], misery, violence, prostitution, and marginality in the big city. At that time, I made the very important connection between the seringueiro's flight from the country and his disintegration in the city. Not just for the parents, but also for the children, the young children, and that was why I returned to the forest.

Chico Mendes at that time was secretary of the syndicate in Brasiléia, and he was traveling back and forth to Xapuri and meeting with us, together with Osmar Facundo de Oliveira, Chico Ramal, Pedro Telhes, all rubber tapper companions from here and from the region. We began to work together in earnest on the syndicate, which we established here in Xapuri in 1977. Both in town and in the seringal, I worked hard explaining why it was crucial to join the union, mobilize our people, and carry out the empates.

What is an *empate*? Well, it's gathering together a group of seringueiros, farmhands, and small farmers to go to where the peons were deforesting and peacefully resist their destruction. We would place ourselves in front of the chain saws and tractors, all of us, men, women, and children, trusting that they would stop. Most of the time they would, because the peons were ex-seringueiros like ourselves. Problems arose when *jagunços*, gunmen hired by the landowners to guard the workers, also appeared on the scene. But we were non-violent, and we would not be frightened away. There were empates that ended us up in jail, where companions were threatened and beaten. It was also a heavy burden to lose days and days of work because we were not gathering latex, and our families suffered as a result. We even lost lives. As you know, our companion Wilson Pinheiro, who was the president of the syndicate in Brasiléia, was murdered at the headquarters in 1981; the jagunço shot him right there where he had been working. And of course, we lost Ivair Higinio and Zé Ribeiro, who were also cut down in cold blood. Later, in 1988, came the terrible blow of Chico's assassination, but we couldn't let that defeat us. Those were dangerous times. I was prisoner here at the police station in Xapuri, and I was threatened with death by many people many times. You had to be so careful, extremely cautious in everything you said and did, or they would murder you, just like that.

We learned so much from those years of struggle and sacrifice, they were like a great school for us. You know, when we began our resistance, we didn't understand, we didn't even know about this business called ecology. We were always good ecologists without knowing it. I attribute this to our having been born and raised in the forest. Another thing we learned, in part from the experience of the avalanches and avalanches of people from the south who migrated here, is that going from the countryside to the city does not improve one's life. On the contrary, it just makes things worse. That was a big lesson for me. We understand also that we must maintain the forest and all its riches because that is our life-support system. We've learned that we must guarantee environmental equilibrium, because if the balance is tipped too much, this immense forest will be lost and there will be no retrieving it. It will be an irreparable catastrophe. This is true to such an extent that I feel not only embarrassment, but also profound worry about the ignorance and brutality of our governments and the policies that they, certainly with the help of other governments of other countries, have directed in our region. These policies destroy the forest and threaten us with genocide.

However, we will keep on resisting. In 1988 I became a city councilman. It's not a big position, but at least it's a way to keep in close contact with the city while living in the country, continuing always to organize through the syndicate. I've been re-elected twice, the first time in 1992, and then again in 1996.

The syndicate has been crucial to our struggle. I would also like to point out that the Catholic church from the beginning of the struggle played a critical role as well.

They were the first ones to inform us of our rights under the law, including the *Estatuto da Terra* [Land Statute] #4,154, which says that the one who works the land for a year and a day and who has no other land can only be ousted with just indemnization. The church helped us develop community leaders through the base communities, they encouraged us in the syndicate, they provided us with a place to meet, they offered us sanctuary in the church, they reported human rights violations, and they helped us with legal advice. From that day to this, the church has been at the side of the seringueiro doing everything possible not just to guide and instruct us, but to be there in solidarity with us in times of great difficulty and violence.

With regard to foreign assistance, in addition to offering advice and solidarity, foreign groups sometimes made financial contributions which our adversaries turned into propaganda, claiming it was bribery. They also used their demagogic instruments to accuse us of selling the Amazon to the US. They especially accused Chico Mendes of this. Some people believed that, including Darlí, who said in an interview in *Veja* magazine (17 July 1996) that Chico had been selling Brazil to foreign countries. Can you believe that he's still saying that! He repeated his ridiculous claim that Chico was a subversive. Darlí is the father of Darcí, the one who actually murdered Chico.

It's hard to say how large the seringueiro population is because of the difficulties involved in taking a census. I think that here in Acre we have about 15,000 to 20,000 seringueiros. It is a very high percentage of the state's population. The majority still live in areas that are not in the reserves. The population in the reserves is about 10,000. We don't have more reserves because of the lack of political will on the part of the federal and state governments. A part of our platform, that of the PT, the Workers Party, is that the extractive reserves should be for all our rubber tapper companions. Further, they should also have access to education, health, and transportation, and a just price for their product. Today you have seringueiros who have to travel on foot carrying the rubber on their backs, or by burro, ox, or horseback if they are fortunate enough to have an animal. They have to travel that distance just to reach a local market where they can sell their product and pick up supplies.

Those seringueiros who live on a reserve, the land they live on is the property of the federal government, and they are secure. The reserves comprise a total of 976,000 hectares, and we have the right of usufruct [use] within them. But for those who live outside a reserve, life is very precarious because the land is private, it still belongs to the latifundistas. Many of those who live outside want to move, but the reserves cannot withstand an influx of people because almost all the colocações, or sites, are occupied. Nor can they move to a reserve in order to farm, because this destroys the forest. The solution is for the government to set aside more areas, but the current government is not interested.

Let me tell you a little about the cooperative. In a given community, sometimes you have two, three, or four who are members of the cooperative, but you have five, six, or eight who are not. Everyone participates in clearing a road, or in bringing a school, or a health post, but many are still not interested in participating in the cooperative. Those who do not participate often have more difficulty than those who do because they have to sell their product to another merchant who pays them less than the cooperative does, no? They always experience some financial loss. The seringueiros are in great solidarity with each other and cooperate on a number of projects; however, when it comes to taking something out of their own pockets to invest in something else, they pull back. It will take time.

The percentage of residents in the Chico Mendes Extractive Reserve who are members of the cooperative is about 20-30 per cent, which I consider low. Perhaps it is owing to the difficulty of transportation within the Reserve. If we just had small paths within the forest, it would give them more of a chance to get to the cooperative. We are now opening the first branch, or pathway. It is very difficult, but we are struggling. It is going to be about 37-40 km long, going from the Floresta seringal to the São Francisco do Espalhe grove. It will be small, just dirt, no asphalt, inside the forest, and it will not be excavated in order to avoid erosion.

Members of the cooperative are also members of the syndicate, there is a mixture, a kind of family relationship. But the director of the cooperative cannot also be director of the syndicate at the same time. Since everyone is a rubber tapper, everyone gets along well, not just at the personal level, but also at the level of political organizations.

The problem is not that we need to work together better, or improve the syndicate, although one can always improve. The problem is survival. This is our great challenge, for the forest population is dependent upon forest products and on learning how to improve the quality of those products. That's precisely what we're working on, improving quality, looking for a better way of processing our Brazil nuts and rubber so that they will generate more income. But what collides with our efforts is this thing called globalization, that makes it hard for small producers to survive. Even so, our people are not giving up, we are keeping on, and we are still here.

The *Lei da Borracha* [Rubber Law] is a subsidy for rubber, and it is also a capital investment both for the cooperative and for the neighborhood associations— an example would be the improvement of our *usinas* [processing machines]. So that offers us some assistance. Meanwhile, we are trying new initiatives, new kinds of extractivism that we hope will serve the needs of our people for survival and also keep them here in the forest. Our big objectives have been to guarantee survival here and not to be forced to go to the city and see our families disintegrate. We have obtained a guarantee of permanence for our people in the forest and now with alternative production such as pupunha fruit and Brazil nuts in processed form, and now the Lei da Borracha, which gives hope to the rubber economy, perhaps for a short time we can keep going until we can make these alternatives work.

We have recently begun a furniture-making school here in the municipality of Xapuri; this is with the assistance of the governor of Acre, Jorge Viana, the Catholic church, and the Italian community of Milan. It is a good alternative because Italian craftsmen will teach us how to finish wood here before it is exported. We are going to take advantage only of fallen trees. What's clear is that we are not going to engage in any predatory work. If we do that, then we fall into the fatal contradiction of killing off that which sustains our way of life. The furniture-making school will also assist destitute families who have migrated from the seringais to Xapuri and who are, of course, unemployed. Our dream is to have a national and then an international market for our furniture. Of course, we are going to need basic infrastructure first, without a doubt.

I think that the small surge of rubber production through this new rubber law is another thing that will help keep us afloat until other initiatives can take hold. The rubber law is a project of our own senator Marina Silva. That, plus the incentive for Brazil nuts, the idea of the furniture-school, the diversification of cultivation with pupunha and coffee are all very positive. As we pursue these, we will also begin discovering other products that may also generate income and help guarantee the survival of our people.

The thing that worries me most is that there are administrators in our country who could give technical, financial help, who could promote good relationships with the communities, with the people, and with foreign groups that are helping the environment. But the administrators we have now are completely against these initiatives because they represent the old, backward way of thinking of the elite, of coronelismo, of the fazendeiros. They are the backward ones, not the seringueiro. Jorge Viana is our great hope in this state. It's just that our adversaries are very powerful and our state is miserably poor, the majority of the population is unemployed or underemployed. Here it is still possible to buy people's votes because they are so desperate.

Our Brazil nut processing plant is at a standstill now because we don't have the money to buy the raw material, the nuts. Our success depends on the income generated by a fairly large market that covers our expenses. But the market is currently depressed, and we don't have the money to buy the Brazil nuts.

Our rubber processing plant is working, but we are having a problem with the machine. It is a machine that depends on other machines. You see, the usina consists of three interdependent machines, and if one enters into "panic," or distress, the other two stop, and production is immobilized.

In the cooperative our usina has been a problem for some time. The thing is the low level of awareness of our members; they just don't have the preparation to produce a cleaner product. The product is somewhat dirty. Another problem is with regard to the purchase of supplies. Sometimes they buy without having the money to purchase supplies. They buy and then pay back, but that doesn't help us to invest in other supplies.

The most serious problem has been the equipment in our rubber usina which is not appropriate for the type of rubber that comes from our region. It is appropriate for the rubber that comes from the cultivated rubber plantations, not from native forests. What is the difference? Well, in the plantations everything is close together, and the rubber is still soft when it gets to the usina, which is right there close by. But with native rubber, it's all far away, one, two, three, four days journey. The seringueiro brings that rubber here, and sometimes a month or two have gone by before he can get here to Xapuri with it. By then it's all hard and dried out, and the machines can't handle it.

We discovered these things last year and ordered a second machine, because one alone is not enough. We need to produce more rubber to make the process economical, to cover the expense of operations in terms of energy, water, and transportation. We are running a deficit of about 5,000 reais a month on our usina. We are now obtaining new machines, and we are going to reequip ourselves so that we can renew our processing operations. The machinery comes all the way from São Paulo.

Another problem is lack of operating skill. We finally got a professional, someone with 25 years in that profession to come out and teach us. Up until now we have always just come up with an amateur. Now, through an initiative of our current governor Jorge Viana, and through the office of Deputy Roland Polanco who helped us organize the cooperative in the first place, we are getting a professional advisor.

Another good thing that has just happened is that the state has created an incentive, which is a subsidy of 40 cents. That is, if rubber goes on the market for 80 cents a kilo, then the seringueiro receives 120 per kilo. The subsidy is for all seringueiros who are organized in cooperatives, in associations, because the idea is to motivate them to organize themselves. This will also make it possible for the seringueiro to purchase more supplies. They hope to keep him in the forest in his colocação, not deforesting in order to raise cattle, not cutting down trees, not going to the periphery of the cities. He will stay in the forest, or return there from the city because the price of rubber will be higher. Some are actually returning. Right here in Xapuri, I've seen it, and this is a small city, but you see it too in Rio Branco. They are returning to unoccupied sites to resume work as rubber tappers.

Another incentive that is one of Jorge's efforts is the creation of more agroforestry poles, which are near, but not in, the cities. These are four to five hectares each, with electricity, schools, and health posts. It's an incentive for families to learn agriculture, subsistence farming, and, hopefully, to produce enough to sell in the market.

The seringueiros are accepting all these ideas. They like them. I know five people who have returned from the city to live in one of these agricultural centers. They have brought me *cará* [a kind of yam] which is delicious, *macaxeira* [manioc], *pimenta* [pepper], banana, and *gandinha*, which have all been produced locally, just across the river in Sibéria.

I guess you could say that the Chico Mendes Reserve is in the process of becoming a model, at least we are working for that to be the case. When all the alternatives that we are working on become successful, then it will be a model.

I think that the question of how to market our products is indispensable to that success. We need technical assistance in order to learn how to make things work more efficiently. We have meetings all the time, every week, monthly too, we also have a *mutirão* [community workgroup], adjuncts, everything. We're trying.

We also need to continue our education efforts. Take the burnings, for example. The locals burn in order to clear the land for planting. It is part of our people's culture that you burn and then you plant your manioc, beans, corn. It's a process that's very slow, getting them to plant without burning. We are trying to educate where we are building our pathway now in the Reserve. One young man planted without burning, but that is a small step. I want very much for our companions to learn, and they want to learn too.

The problem is that you have to clear the land really well, get rid of all the undergrowth, cut everything, and then allow time for the vegetation to decay. Large trees have to be cut and removed, and the seringueiro has little time to do this. He can clear without burning, but just very small areas. That's the biggest difficulty, that it takes so much time to clear without burning. I think it will happen in the future, but it will be slow.

Things change, for example we now have filters for the water in Cachoeira, and there is a privy, neither of which were part of the culture. So, I think the habit of burning can change too. When people understood that privies help reduce disease, they took to the idea. Another thing they are doing is adding vegetables to their diet. Today, many seringueiros are cultivating their own vegetable gardens. In Cachoeira, for example, they plant cabbage, onion, lettuce, and tomatoes. Technicians have come to teach us, many times. They are teaching us to fence and to keep the chickens away from the house. This project is with CNPT [*Centro Nacional das Populações Tradicionais da Amazônia*, National Center for Traditional Amazonian Populations]. They also have a health post now in Cachoeira. We all benefit from these kinds of changes, and we wish to see them extended to other communities in the rubber forests.

Xapuri, 30 July 1996; 31 August 1997.

Marina Silva

Widely regarded as the most important leader since Chico Mendes, Marina Silva is a former rubber tapper who is currently a federal senator from Acre. Her trajectory from the remote Bagaço seringal to the ultramodern city of Brasília suggests a personal story that combines the accident of fate that brought her to Rio Branco for medical treatment, with the influence of the church, the power of literacy programs, and the determination never to give up no matter what. Silva was a close friend and colleague of Chico Mendes, with whom she participated in numerous empates and co-founded the CUT [Workers Central Union]. Silva is best known for her steadfast defense of the environment, which she aims to preserve while also using it as a bargaining chip to obtain needed training and technology for Amazonians. Silva proposes imaginative, concrete plans that will use resources to improve lives. The faith, courage, and optimism of this much-admired leader come through in the interview that follows.

I'm from a family of eight living children. My father is a northeasterner, from Ceará, like the majority of people who occupy the state of Acre. He came here in 1945, married, and my mother had 11 children. Three died, an older brother and my two younger sisters who died of malaria. My mother died six months later, when she was 36, very young. My oldest sister got married right after my mother's death. I stayed with my father, helping to care for the other children and working with him in the clearing and planting. One begins to work at a very young age in the forest. I was born in 1958 and by 1968 I was working in the seringal.

Once, when my mother was still alive, we left Acre and went to Manaus, where we stayed about five months, and from there to Belém, where we remained for a year and eight months. My father was hoping that we would have a better life there, but it did not work out; we couldn't make a go of it. Then my father asked my mother to go back with him to his former patrão, the owner of the seringal where we had lived earlier. That was a big defeat, but he really had no other choice. The patrão sent us the tickets back to the same seringal, Bagaço, where we returned, now badly in debt. What's worse, we were a very large family, with eight children, my mother, my grandmother, an aunt, a grandfather, a lot of people, but not a lot of working people.

One problem was that the culture of the seringal values one who has sons more than one who has daughters. So my father was considered *um infeliz* [an unlucky man], so many daughters and no one to help him. My mother was a very strong matriarch. One day she gathered me and my other sisters together and told us that we had to prove the people wrong, that we were not a burden to our father. Then we began to help do accounts and *cortar seringa* [cut (tap) rubber trees]; that's what we learned how to do from about the age of ten. Within a year's time, with all of us working, we were able to pay the bills and get our father out of debt. We worked like crazy. For example, seringueiros usually cut one estrada a day, that is, they tap the area included in one circular path. But with me working we cut two a day, my father would work one, my sister and I would work another. Later, we began to cut *three* estradas a day: my father, one; two sisters, another; and myself and another sister, a third. Not too long after that, my mother died. Some time later, I became ill with malaria and hepatitis and couldn't work any more.

I began to feel, I don't know, very *angustiada* [anguished]. There was a religious sister in our area, and ever since I had been a very young child I had loved the sisters. I admired this sister, and I thought that I wanted to become a nun, which would mean studying in the city. Since I was ill, I had to go to the city anyway to get well. So I began to ask my father for permission to leave in order to recuperate and study. But to leave the seringal, leave my family behind, and go to the city alone, that was something that just wasn't done. My older sister had already married, and I was the oldest one at home. I knew my father needed me, but, somehow, he gave his permission, I don't know if it was because I was so ill or what. At any rate, I left, though both my father and grandfather were very fearful because of all the stories they had heard about what happens to young girls alone in the city.

So, I came here to Rio Branco because I wanted to get well and I wanted to study to become a nun. Soon I began to work in the home of a cousin, taking care of his children and then I studied with MOBRAL at night. MOBRAL is the literacy program for adults begun under the famous educator Paulo Freire. I already knew a little math, which was unusual; in the seringal, one may learn how to read and write a little, but hardly anyone knows math. And my father needed it whenever he would sell rubber, in order not to be cheated. So, when I still lived in the seringal, he gave me the responsibility for learning the four operations: addition, subtraction, multiplication and division, so I could help him out.

Rubber is sold with a certain percentage of the weight discounted because of the water content of the latex. When the water evaporates, the rubber weighs less. So, when the patrão goes to buy rubber, he always takes 17 per cent off the price. When the seringueiro doesn't know how to do sums, the patrão takes advantage of him saying that *a quebra* [the water content] is much greater than it really is. My father put me in charge of selling because, as I knew some math, we wouldn't be cheated, or at least not as badly as others were.

But the truth is that I knew very little and I basically could not read at all. I could identify some isolated words, and when I was 13 I learned to tell time and read a clock. However, all that changed as soon as I started school, for I learned very rapidly. In fact, I learned so quickly that they thought I was wasting my time in the regular program, so they moved me to a course of study called *educação integrada* [integrated education], which was the equivalent of four years of elementary school in one. I arrived in Rio Branco in September, recovered from my illness, and began the accelerated program in December. There were 46 students in the class and, at the end of the academic year, only three passed. I was one of the three. My grade was just five and a half, barely enough to get by, but I made it. I also did the *ginásio*, or high school in the same compressed fashion, through MOBRAL, completing four years in one. I completed the *segundo grau*, or middle school, in the same way. It was all very intense, but I was determined to succeed. Normally, high school is four years, middle school is three, and elementary school is four.

In 1979, I was planning to continue studying at the university, but I contracted hepatitis again. Dom Moacyr, the Bishop of Acre, helped me greatly. It was a big setback both physically and emotionally to be interned in the hospital again, in addition to which I was very ill and weak. I have chronic hepatitis and my health is rather fragile as a result. After that, I spent two and a half years as a postulant in the Madre Ilesa home. That's when I discovered that mine was not a religious vocation, even though I was passionate about liberation theology. I left my religious training behind, and, a year later, in 1980, I married.

In 1981 I entered the university and began studying to become a high school history teacher. I also began to do some work with the base communities of the Cristo Resuscitado parish in a nearby neighborhood where I remained for two years. I did community work, helping the residents obtain basic city services, such as water, electricity, and street lights. At the same time, at the university, I began to participate in the student movement, which in that decade was very militant and deeply involved in the political struggle.

In 1984, I helped found CUT [*Central Unica dos Trabalhadores*, Workers Central Union] with Chico Mendes. I had known Chico ever since I had lived with the sisters. I remember he took a course from the CPT [Pastoral Land Commission] on the formation of rural leadership. It was controversial and some of the sisters I was living with were sharply critical of the liberation theology it espoused. I was too in the beginning because I thought it went too far in mixing religion and politics. But then I began discussing it with Chico, and I came to understand that relationship much better and to see how important it is to put your faith into practice. Chico was already known as a militant leftist, at least that was his reputation, but he also had his own faith. We became close friends during the process of founding CUT. He was elected president here in Acre, and I was elected vice-president. Thus, we began to work together, above all in the empates, or stand-offs; many people in Xapuri know those stories because they were there as participants too.

In 1985, I joined the PT, the Workers Party, because it was the party that was working for justice. Chico and I were among the founders in this area. Not Lula, he was in the south. The PT was founded in 1980, and I was a sympathizer, but not a member, until 1985. In 1986 I became a PT candidate at the federal level and Chico at the state level. We were both unsuccessful the first time. Chico was elected by Xapuri as councilman in 1988. In 1990, I was elected councilwoman and, in 1994, federal deputy.

My service and activities all have to do with social issues, with my strongest ties being to the seringueiros. This commitment stems from my own background, my faith, and the work that I carried out with Chico during a very tense and dangerous time, that of the empates.

What was really difficult for me was the stand-off at the Bordon fazenda, because it was my first experience. All of a sudden there you are walking with about 85 or 90 other people, a six-hour walk, three there and three back. When we arrived at the ranch, the peons were all cutting down trees. So Chico, Raimundo de Barros, Júlio Barbosa, and I all started talking with the foreman. Everyone spread out, men, women, children, placing themselves wherever workers were cutting. We did this to oblige them to put down their chainsaws. I was terrified that they wouldn't do it, and then I didn't know what would happen next, but, thank God, they stopped, and we were successful.

The empate was very well organized. You see, you don't just go out somewhere and block deforestation. We coordinated it carefully so that at the very moment that we were at our destination, Dom Moacyr, the syndicate members in Rio Branco and Brasília, the federal capital, and lawyers who knew of the illegality of the deforestation would also be spreading the news of the destruction and of the empate. Their job was to inform people of what deforestation means for the traditional populations and for all of us. Empates were events that had to have great repercussions in order to be effective; you couldn't just have an isolated empate and get anywhere. There followed about ten days of protests and marches, with many of our companions carried off to jail.

Another difficult empate was at Cachoeira, where we had media coverage so people could see the destruction and where there were many heavily armed police, even though the seringueiros had no arms at all and were engaged in peaceful resistance. We were there nine days, and it was tense, but we were victorious there too. The cost was very great though, because Darlí, the rancher who claimed ownership of the Cachoeira area, harbored such hatred toward us all, but especially toward Chico who had defied him and won, that, one year later, he had his son, Darcí, murder Chico. The loss of Chico had a devastating impact on us, our movement, and on that of the seringueiros and forest peoples in every state of the Amazon region. But we kept going, we couldn't give up.

I have worked very, very hard for my people. Early in 1995 we began forming another group, the GTA [*Grupo de Trabalho Amazônico*, the Amazonian Work Group], a coalition of various entities here in the Amazon which are linked to three causes: economic improvement for forest peoples, social justice, and the preservation of the environment.

For third-world countries, the only way to develop ourselves is through our resources of biodiversity. We have to "deal," to trade. We have the resources, but we need technology and training. We need to protect our resources and use them to bargain for what we need. I'm part of a network of people who are discussing this topic, and we are planning legislation that compensates us for the use of our resources. The powerful landowners and loggers and ranchers have strong representation in Congress, so it is very difficult to pass anything that protects the environment, but there are also many senators who are interested in cooperating with our groups.

The problem is that we need a law of access to resources to protect them. The very things that the seringueiros have, live, and know, sometimes they don't perceive that these, too, are a treasure, the plants, the insects, the animals. We have the greatest part of the world's biodiversity. For example, we have 30 per cent of the world's fresh water. That means that we have a huge responsibility toward humanity and the planet, but that responsibility cannot be ours alone. It must be shared, and the care of the environment must be shared. One way to care for this responsibility is to discover ways in which our resources can also provide the means for improving our lives. It is a long-term project, but the strategy has to be laid now; if it is not, we will miss our chance for the future because there will be no future.

I believe that the seringueiro can continue diversifying production. For a long time it was just rubber and Brazil nuts. But today we are working with the idea of agroforestry systems as well, with new ways to utilize the forest. For example, we have *vilhas de alta densidade* [high density villages]. These are settlements that are close in, not scattered and remote, where we have planted, say, two hectares of rubber trees, and people there are living much better than before. Our idea is to improve the living conditions of the forest populations.

We have to have social investment too, in order to improve the quality of life. We need schools and health posts so that people can have access to the rights of citizenship that they do not have now. The few schools and health posts that we do have in the rubber groves of Xapuri are the result of the efforts of the CTA [*Centro dos Trabalhadores da Amazônia*, Amazonian Workers Center]. The CTA provides education and schools in the jungle through Projeto Seringueiro. They produce their own books, posters, and other teaching materials, and they train their own teachers. Their work is extremely interesting; their pedagogy, like that of MOBRAL, is inspired by Paulo Freire.

I think that the seringueiro, with help, will be able to modernize. We are entering a new phase of extractive activity, what we are calling agroextractivism, or agroforestry. If we have education, technology, and research, then we will be able to go forward, and we will be able to do so without making a sharp break with tradition. Our tradition is one of preserving the forest. There will be no Amazon if people destroy the forest. That is the lesson that we have to bring home to everyone. Acre is still one of the more preserved areas. Rondônia has already lost about 20 per cent of its forest. We have lost about 8 per cent. There would have been more lost except for our struggle, our resistance, our history, and our people's suffering because they stood up to the destruction. I remember how painful it was to be the target of a ferocious defamation campaign accusing me of being against progress, of wanting to keep our people and our country backward and ignorant. It still continues, but now we know what the opponents' "progress" looks like!

We are currently looking into better ways to extract wood without causing devastation; we are promoting sustainable harvesting. Our idea is to divide a rubber forest of, say, 300 hectares, into three parts, or *estradas de manejo* [management paths]. For example, for ten years you would exploit one "lot," extracting a certain percentage of mature wood. In a forest, about 5 per cent of the vegetation dies annually. So you identify these mature trees and harvest them. It takes about 30 years for a hardwood tree to mature, cedar or mahogany for example, not rubber. So, over the next ten years you would exploit another lot, and then, by the time you return to the original one, the trees you replaced 30 years ago are mature, and so on, sustainably.

The INPA [*Instituto de Pesquisa da Amazônia*, Amazonian Research Institute], the CTA, EMBRAPA, a national agricultural and environmental research organization, and others are researching this topic as a model for the Amazon. We have only some demonstration projects now, but I think it will take hold throughout the Amazon region because people will see that it really works. This is just one way we can demonstrate to people that there are alternatives to the unsustainable and wasteful way that things have been done, to show them that we don't have to tear everything down, and then be left with nothing.

The logger and the rancher are not in agreement with this approach, but they would have to comply if it were law. And if we had a system for certifying the origin of wood for export, they would have to abide by that too. If lumber without a designated seal of approval could not be exported, then loggers would be obliged to comply with certain standards in order to sell their lumber. We would have to bring public pressure to bear, have a rigorous system of enforcement, and we would have to enlist the cooperation of the wood importing countries not to buy "dirty" wood. That way only "clean," certified lumber that had been harvested sustainably would be sold. This big change is already under way.

By the way, the estrada de manejo that I mentioned earlier would be a dirt one, it would not be paved. It would just be a *varadouro* [small trail], large enough for a family to haul lumber using oxen, for example. And they would not just harvest wood; they would be engaged in multiple harvesting activities: rubber, Brazil nuts, honey, fish farming, and pupunha too. We have pilot projects going now, but soon we want to extend these ideas about forest management throughout the reserves themselves.

The Conselho Nacional de Seringueiros [National Rubber Tappers' Council] and the Ministério da Reforma Agraria [Ministry of Agrarian Reform] have been busy working together on proposals for creating projects for extractive settlements that would provide all the investment necessary to assist forest peoples in making their lives economically viable. This is especially important for those populations that are isolated. You see, what we want to do above all is maintain the forest, and to do so, we need to show people ways to make a living without harming the environment. That is always our main concern.

In our forest management plan, we have various colocações and a central nucleus that would have a health post, a school, and some kind of small agroindustry for processing wood and making furniture. The nucleus would have a church, small businesses, and a system of radio communication. It would be like

73

a village. There would be paths leading to this nucleus, and a central varadouro which would be a little larger. It would be wide enough to pull a cart, or maybe for a small tractor to pull a wagon, but it would not be a road, just a wide path with the dirt packed down hard. It would be in the shade because walking in the sun is miserable, whereas it's cool and pleasurable in the shade. You see, if it were a road, and, worse still, if it were a paved road, it would cause deforestation, and generally speaking, once there is a road, more deforestation follows. Not to mention that a paved road in the forest would look very strange.

We also need to utilize our rivers better. It would be a big help if the government would clean the rivers of branches, if they would have boats that would attend the riverine populations, boats with doctors, boats to transport goods, medicines, and people. The government should not see this as charity work, no, but rather as doing something significant for the future and something that is strategically important for the government.

I am a hopeful person, and I have faith in God. I do not believe that it is right that this magnificent patrimony that God gave us be destroyed. So I believe that I have to do something, and I have to believe that it is possible to do something. The government has made some positive efforts at crucial junctures when documents were discussed for the defense of the Amazon. Nobody can any longer just come in and do whatever they want here, not today. The problem is that many times one is not understood by the very people whose programs one is benefiting; many times these very people think that progress means cutting down the forest. Some people just take care of their own personal interest and are content with that, but I believe that you can not just sit around and do nothing about the world around you, I think that everyone has to do something, even if it brings you problems.

For example, many hurtful and false accusations have been made against me, that I am a subversive, and so on. But the one that always hurt the most is that I was neglecting my children, that I did not love them because, if I did, I wouldn't be involved in politics. I remember a sentence from my religious studies that has been very helpful to me in this situation and which I continue to read to this day: "Love for a person that isn't accompanied by a deep love for humanity may be many things, but it is not love." If you love people, your children, you have to love humanity too; if not, then what you feel for your children is not love, because love does not exist in a vacuum.

It's not easy, because in this journey you find those who don't merely disagree with you, but who persist in trying to destroy you. It is painful to have terrible lies told about you or to be subjected to intimidation and threats. You suffer, but you also must stand up for what you believe. I sometimes think that we women want everything to be decided by consensus because when you have to fight, to face down your very adversary in the street, whether it's a powerful person or an immoral one, or both, you suffer. But you have to face them nevertheless. At the same time, you also have to remember that your adversaries have families, children, and that it is wrong to dehumanize them.

This is a very interesting time that we are living in—globalization, for example, which frightens us but which has some positive features too. Nothing is completely bad, right? I think that we can, to some extent, make it work for us. For example, take social exclusion, it is a worldwide problem with billions of human beings marginalized and excluded from their societies. It's as if there existed one culture of human beings, and another culture of those who are not quite human, and this is a terrible perversion of justice. Before, we would all place our hopes in a particular leader, a political party, or in something similar that we thought was powerful. But now I think that the way out of injustice and exclusion will be more systemic and horizontal. Power will no longer lie just with one individual, one figure; it will be spread out among groups of citizens everywhere, at least I think it can be if we work in that direction. I have always said that power needs to be shared [*o poder precisa ser dividido*], and maybe that will be more possible now than in the past.

I learned so much from Chico. He was a systemic leader. What I mean by that is that he shared power, authority, and responsibility with everyone, seringueiros, researchers, our own people, foreigners, and with me. For our work to be effective, that's what we must do. That's why I say that you, as a researcher, can help me, and I also can help you. We are all arrows and we are all bows. Sometimes I am the bow that propels the arrow and sometime you are, but there is no such thing as a good bow without a good arrow, and vice versa. We need each other.

There is a Brazilian poet who has a song that goes "Narcissus finds ugly everything that is not a mirror" [*Narciso acha feio o que não é espelho*]. Narcissus, the god from Greek mythology, found beauty only in his own image; what's more, he regarded everything else as ugly. Perhaps the biggest challenge for humankind may be to look for those who do not represent our self image, to seek difference, outside perspectives. Maybe we should look for the one who will complement and transform us, opening up new possibilities for improving our life. That's why it's so important to share power, information, ideas, and cultures, like we are doing here.

Rio Branco, 7 August 1996.

Francisco das Chagas

Former rubber tapper Francisco das Chagas's story is also that of the CEBs and of the economic and social transformations that swept through his remote seringal with the arrival of the first road in the 1960s. As Chagas recollects his own experiences, he comments on traditional seringueiro values, now in jeopardy, and how they can be strengthened. Chagas urges that schools be established in every seringal as the best survival tool for seringueiros, for he regards education as the most effective antidote to the crippling dependence that has historically afflicted forest peoples. This gentle, reflective seringueiro-priest, whose ordination in 1999 represented a personal and collective triumph, offers an honest and sensitive portrayal of the life of the rubber tapper, then and now.

I was born in Rio Taruacá, in the municipality of Taruacá, as were my parents. My grandparents are from Ceará. We moved to Feijó when I was very young, and that's where I grew up. I worked in the rubber groves from the time I was ten years old. We are ten children, six brothers and four sisters, and we all worked in the seringal, as did our parents.

In order to be a tapper, one first has to walk long distances in the jungle locating the rubber trees. Then you make a *pique* [a cut]; next, you do the *rapado*[scraping]. You continue cutting until the latex starts to come, and then you place a gourd at each tree. When you make your rounds later, you collect the latex. You can cut anywhere from 80 to 140 trees in one day. But you have to get up before dawn; some leave at 5:00 a.m., but most, as early as 3:00 a.m. If you leave as late as 6:00 a.m., you run the risk of gathering very little "milk." The earlier you cut, the more you collect. Just one tree gives milk for many years longer than a seringueiro's lifetime.

The best time to collect is at night, except for the danger of rain. I say danger because the rain can put out your *lamparina* [lantern]. The other problem is the *onça* [the jaguar] and the *cobra* [snake], many of which are poisonous. There used to be more in the forest, but there are still enough to be a real danger. I once killed a jaguar in the jungle. I don't know where he came from; I just looked up, and there he was right in front of me. I was by myself, the seringueiro works alone. When you're really young, your parents or brothers and sisters go along with you into the forest, but by the time you're 12, people consider you a man, and you're on your own. When I was about 12 or 13, I began to go out by myself and carry a shotgun. It happened that one day I was cutting, and my brother was working nearby. Suddenly, out of nowhere, the jaguar appeared; we were forehead to forehead. I fired the shotgun without thinking and then took off running home as fast as my legs would carry me. I didn't even look back to see if I had killed him. I was very small and the jaguar was huge, as big as my 18-year-old brother, who brought it home for us to see. This was not the *onça pintada*, [spotted jaguar] but the other kind that's just one color. I also killed a *pico de xá*, one of the most poisonous snakes here in the Amazon.

It takes a certain kind of temperament for one to be a seringueiro because he works alone deep in the forest. Daily he runs the risk of losing everything, not to mention that he is obliged to turn everything over to his boss. In that line of work, if he works ten hours straight and then the rain starts, he loses everything because it comes down so fast and hard that he doesn't have time to save his work. If you lose a day of work, that's a day you go without eating. Nor is the seringueiro paid for the month or two out of the year that he is not tapping, either because he is waiting for the season, or because he is transporting his rubber in order to sell it.

The time of year for tapping is from March to December; during January and February you don't cut. After February you begin to clear your path in the forest again because after two months it will be overgrown. When you clear, you have to be cautious. For example, there's a tree in the jungle called *Tacoca*, which has sharp thorns that can tear your hands if you're not careful.

Originally, the seringueiros learned from the Indians. The two lived very closely together in my area because when the forest was first opened, the Cearenses came fleeing the drought in the northeast, and all they found here were Indians. Later, the Indians came to be considered as dangerous animals that had to be eliminated. When further waves of immigrants came, the patrões put the northeasterners to work immediately killing Indians. They had the seringueiro open estradas into the forest, and, of course, the Indians would rob them and carry away supplies; they would kill too. Indians such as the Kashinoá and the Colim killed the intruders, but they didn't have arms, just arrows. They still exist today, but they no longer work in the rubber groves. They have moved into even more remote areas of the forest where they live by hunting and fishing.

The seringueiro's medicine comes from the forest itself. For example, for snakebite if you eat a certain kind of potato with a certain kind of tea, you are well at once. There's also a tree, the *jarina*, which cures snakebites. Another tree, called *maravilha*, cures scorpion stings. It contains a *seiva* [sap] that they also use to kill fish. I don't know of a cure for malaria, or *cesão* as they used to call it. Unfortunately, I have had it many times. It is very common, and people start coming down with it when the first rains arrive.

Most people in the seringal still believe in spells and in protective prayers. For example, belief in the *quebranto* [evil eye] is widespread. People think it can cause a child to get a fever, diarrhoea, and die if a person with very strong vision targets them. They also believe in the *vento* [wind], which affects the stomach and is accompanied by a high fever. It is very common for a child to develop *susto* [fright or shock] and go into a kind of trance. When a person with the gift of prayer prays, the child recovers. These are the seringueiros' own remedies; there are certain people who have the gift of healing. Nowadays in the city you find them too. I believe in it because it is something that comes from my roots, and also the person who does the prayers speaks in the name of God and all the saints, even though it is not a Christian rite. For example, to remove a bone that has become lodged in the throat, one prays to São Brais, the saint that protects against throat illnesses. These are not *ipajés* [shamans], or padres either; they are normal, everyday people. It's just that they have this special gift. They don't charge anyone anything. If it's necessary to spend the night, they stay in that person's home and continue praying. The prayers are not accompanied by a tea or drug or herb, they're just pure prayers, nothing else. I think this comes from the indigenous influence and is part of the whole subject of remedies, which comes from Indian cultures.

I worked in the seringal until I was 33 years old. It was the only life that my family knew. My parents remained in the forest until they were too old to work, and then they moved into town. I stayed in the forest for so long because I wanted to follow my parents' wishes. Why did I leave then? Well, perhaps that will be easier to understand if I tell you more about growing up in the seringal and the changes that have come to the way of life of the seringueiro.

One thing I want to point out is how important mutual sharing is in the seringal. For example, if a rubber tapper kills some game, a deer, or a boar, he always gives a portion to others. This sharing has always existed. If you find that you have no more *farinha* [ground manioc flour], you go over to a neighbor and he will rummage around until he finds some to give you. Farinha is the basis of the diet. You can have rice, beans, and even meat, but if you lack farinha, then you have nothing. There is always someone to share their farinha when supplies are low.

With regard to religion, I would say that the seringueiro is a religious person, but his is a natural religion, *bem natural mesmo* [very natural indeed]. The custom of sharing and helping was the basis of the first Christian communities, and it is essential to us today. As you know, it usually takes three days or more to get from the seringal to the city. The closest city for us was Manoel Urbano. Well, when a person is gravely ill, they put him in a hammock, and eight or ten people carry him all the way to the city. Of course, they don't charge anything, nothing at all. They just do it because it is part of their culture; I see it as a Christian aspect. I did it for an acquaintance who lived far away and was ill. My brother also, when I was in the seminary, he carried someone in a hammock for several days. My sister as well, you usually do like she did, walk for two or three days in the mud up to your knees. It's a big sacrifice. Most of the time, the people recover their health in the hospital.

Though I was born in Rio Taruacá, I was brought up in Rio Jurupari in a seringal on the Rio Purús called Porto Brasil. In Porto Brasil we suffered a lot. We lived there with my aunt's family; we were ten brothers and sisters, and they were 11. Of these 21 people, they all became ill except the father. He had to take care of the two families and hunt. We lived deep in the forest, in a place very far from the river. If he didn't bring home any game, we didn't eat, and there were many times that he came home empty-handed. The first three years that we lived in that colocação we didn't know if we would survive. I remember how delicious it was when my mother and my sister would grate the manioc, dry it in the clay oven, and pat it in their hands before we ate it. But we only had manioc when our plot would produce, and that was not often.

We moved to another seringal because we couldn't feed ourselves. Besides not having an estrada for everyone to work, in that first colocação there was very little milk to collect either. We were always looking for more rubber, so we finally left and went to the São Miguel seringal, where we managed to get a little balance back in our lives. It was closer to Manoel Urbano. These three seringais, Porto Brasil, Sardinha, where I worked for a long time, and São Miguel all are very close to each other.

I knew that there was an available path in São Miguel because my father in that period was working as a *fiscal de seringa* [rubber overseer], whose job was to determine whether the seringueiros were cutting too deeply in the tree. You know that you are just supposed to cut the bark without injuring the wood. If you wound the tree, when it heals a scar forms, and then it is ruined for the next person who wants to cut. It also happens that, if you cut too deeply, insects can infest the tree with the first rains. If my father found a seringueiro who was cutting too deeply, he would speak with him, and he was obliged to report it to the patrão. My father couldn't make a living as an overseer because he was not paid. Who was going to pay him?

My father left that job and went to work in a different colocação, that's when everyone's life improved some. My mother stopped cutting, and only one of my sisters cut, but then she stopped in order to plant a little crop of tobacco and beans to sell. She sold her produce and lived more or less well. Actually, in my family no one gathers latex anymore. My father is now living near Sena Madureira on the banks of the Rio Purús. My brothers and sisters, one lives just off the road from Sena to Rio Branco, another works in Rio Branco, another lives with my parents in Sena, two others live in Brasiléia, another in Manoel Urbano, and so on. We are scattered about the area, but no one lives in the seringal anymore.

I was the first one to leave. I came to Rio Branco to study, and I stayed for eight years. When I arrived, I didn't like anything about it. I wanted to turn around and go back to the forest. The seminary was totally different from anything I had known. It was, well, at home, everyone would arrive and be greeted by everyone else with great attention. But when you arrived at the seminary, you were treated with indifference, at least that's how it seemed to me. I mean, in my house, that is something that people would never ever do because the first thing that the seringueiro does when someone comes to his home is ask him if he's already had breakfast, lunch, or dinner. And then he finds a hammock for the guest, while the family then sleeps two or three in their hammock or bed. I felt absolutely forlorn because of the indifference I experienced here.

Another thing is the different type of food. It, too, was a big adjustment. I was used to farinha, to getting up at two or three in the morning, and taking my breakfast, which was my main meal of the day. It consisted of coffee with meat, rice, farinha, everything, and then I would go out to work. When I went to the city, at the padre's house they had meat, which was familiar, but it was for dinner. At lunch they had soup; I had never eaten soup before, and I spilled as much as I actually consumed. I didn't say anything, but I was at a complete loss. Further, I had never been apart from my family, except once for 20 days, in my whole life. To be cut off suddenly like that was like losing an arm.

After a while I became accustomed to the ambience at the seminary in Rio Branco, but first I had to learn different table manners. In the seringal, as you ate your last mouthful you got up and left. In Rio Branco, however, you waited and waited until all the others had finished; you just sat there, waiting. That was the first time in my life I had ever done that. The other seminarians were all from the peripheral areas of the city, not the seringal, and they had some urban experience. I was the only one from the forest. But I learned. I also learned about city life from working as a street cleaner and a hospital nurse's aide to help support myself.

Before arriving, I had learned to read a little bit with my father, how to write my name. When I first began to read, it wasn't the Bible but the alphabet, the ABCs. A little later, I began reading *romances de cordel, historinhas* [popular stories from history], like the story of Lampião, the bandit hero from the northeast. Later, when my father gave a Bible to my brother, I began to do a few Bible readings. All of my brothers and sisters were interested, but I resisted. I was self taught, insofar as I was educated at all. My father had learned to read because he lived for a time with an aunt in the city of Tarauacá where he studied. Later, he left school and returned to the seringal to work with his father. My father thought it important that we learn to read, but he would get very angry with me because I didn't know how to write, even today I do not write well. I would read, but I didn't know what I was reading.

With regard to religion, all I knew were the feasts of São Francisco, São João, São Pedro, Christmas, things like that. As far as attending mass, no, just once every two or three years maybe, when a padre would come to the seringal. When a padre would visit, it was to baptize and marry people without any instruction. Whoever was 15 years old would be baptized, just like cattle, without preparation, or they would be married, also without preparation. No one had any idea what it all meant. The padre worked with the patrão; he stayed only in the house of the patrão, and he did not go out and visit the seringueiros' houses in the seringal. The padre identified with the patrão because that's who he saw and where he stayed. That was before 1975.

In 1975, everything began to change. That's when Padre Heitor, he lives in Sena Madureira, began coming out to see us; he came right into the midst of our community. That's how I met him. Then, other padres came. I met Padre Paolino, for example, and after a while there were a number of padres. Padre Heitor began the base community where we lived. From then on, I began to learn more about the church. At the beginning, I didn't want to know anything, I didn't want my sister to tell me, I just wanted to stay home.

You see, the first one to be interested in religion was not me, it was my sister. I just wanted to play ball, I didn't want to learn about faith at all. Little by little my sister began to help me *tomar consciência* [raise consciousness]. She was chosen because she could read some. The informal base community conversations began in our house because my parents were very hospitable. Little by little, and without wanting to, I became interested. The crucial step in this journey was when I was baptized there in the seringal. Dom Moacyr spoke of the importance of the sacrament of baptism and of not abandoning the journey. Gradually, I realized that I wanted to study to become a priest.

Some time after that I received the invitation to go live in the seminary. It was like a dream that could not come true because I didn't want to leave my parents. So I stayed. Then came another invitation, this time with transportation to the city. Finally, I decided to leave. My parents understood and supported me, even though it was hard for them.

For me, the city was a complete shock. I had left everyone I knew, everything I was familiar with, and everything I knew how to do, to come live in the city. What's more, I had had very little religious training. From 1975 to 1986, I had taken only very small steps, and in 1986 when I went to the seminary my only experience had been as a *monitor* [lay catechist]. I knew practically nothing.

It was only when I began classes in Rio Branco that I discovered how weak my reading skills were. I studied hard to try to improve them, but I was a poor student. It was a constant battle to retain information. I had never been inside a school before, and here I was beginning classes in Rio Branco with elementary school children. I studied the fifth, sixth, and seventh *série* in Rio Branco at the Colégio Meta. After those three years, I went on to the *segundo grau*, at the Colégio Mateo Maia, also in Rio Branco. I was, of course, the oldest student in the Colégio Meta, all the other students were children, but in the Colégio Maia, no, because I studied at night.

In the Colégio Meta when I arrived I felt like a lost ship because school had been in session for a month, so I was already behind. They were conversing about things I did not understand, I had no idea of, and I sat there at the desk completely adrift, without any point of reference. I was so lost that when recess time came and I saw that everyone got up and left, I picked up my backpack and started walking home. Then a little girl tapped me on the shoulder and said that there was class after recess.

One thing I found in the midst of these children was a very great goodness. For example, the subject of drawing, I didn't know where to begin, and a little girl took my notebook, did all the drawings, and then taught me how. They all still greet me when we pass each other on the street. I studied drawing, history, Portuguese, math, and I was lost in every subject. If they hadn't helped me, I don't know where I'd be today. You see, I failed every subject my first year, and I had to go to what they call *recuperação* [intensive remedial classes] to try to catch up. The next year I failed three subjects, then two, improving each year. But, I tell you, in the beginning, my self esteem was completely broken. I had no idea of what Brazil was, the president, the government. I had listened to the radio, but as far as any understanding of history, nothing; that Brazil at one time belonged to Portugal, no.

Because of my own experience, I believe that education is of prime importance for the seringueiro. I think that the life of the seringueiro will change with education because in the seringal he is deceived frequently with regard to the weight of his product and his own purchases. For example, if the seringueiro buys two cans of milk, if he can't read, if the patrão or *atravessador* [middleman] wants to mark down three, he does so, and the seringueiro has to pay.

Another benefit of education is in the religious area. It is very important because we have many seringueiros who wish to work in the community but they do not know how to read, how to explain. You know, the seringueiro can talk about his life, his experiences, tell jokes, be very interesting and entertaining. But to pick up a book and read, and afterwards to explain what he had read, he can't do that at all [*não da não*]. This is very, very common in the seringal. We need teachers and schools in every community.

There are other ways in which education will help the seringueiro. It will enable him to choose what is good from modernity, and that is very important. I think that the entire process of cultural and economic change that we are undergoing all began with the first road. That's when the exchange of cultures began, that of the forest and that of the city. That's when the automobile came, the first machines, which were a novelty. The road I'm referring to is the one from Rio Branco to Cruzeiro do Sul, in the area where I used to live. On Sundays we would all go out to the road to watch the machines working. That was our first contact with change, positive and negative. It was negative in that period because many girls ran away with the workers, soldiers, and peons; they just disappeared, went to the city where they were abandoned. This happened to many families. But there was also a lot of conversation between the soldiers and the local families. The soldiers wanted to know about life in the seringais, and they would tell us about the city, that it had *movimento* [movement, activity]. There were soldiers who on Sundays would come out to our homes to converse with us. They would also go hunting with us. They would exchange the meals that they had brought, usually beans, for game from the forest. There was a pleasant conviviality. Until then, we had a very negative opinion of the army, but with these experiences it changed some.

Another result of the first road, an extremely negative one, was the entry of the fazendeiros. That marked the beginning of a period of violence and fear. First, they destroyed the forest. The poor seringueiro who lived near the road lost everything, completely. Then came the disorder and brutality. They would beat and even kill people at will. I saw this violence. Once, I was going to work the colocação with my brother, and we passed by the house of a family that had been torn to pieces. They had lassoed the owner, tied him up, and were beating him with a whip. Another seringueiro, they had put a bullet in his head and left him lying there on the ground while they returned to the city. They were fazendeiros.

A positive result of the road is that people now had a way to get to the city. The seringueiro would walk along the road, carrying his rubber, which he could now sell to anyone, not just the patrão, and he would meet people on the road, buy, sell, and learn more about the world. In a way, you could say that the road brought independence for the seringueiro who lived more or less close to the city, in that he could now walk there to sell his rubber and to purchase supplies. He no longer had to pay the high price the middlemen charged who came out to the seringal.

Before, it wasn't like that, because I remember until I was 18 or so, I couldn't take out one kilo of borracha to sell, not even to another patrão. You either sold to your own patrão or you risked death; you depended totally on the patrão, who could kill with impunity. I witnessed such things during my teenage years in the seringal. The poor seringueiro! He would bring his rubber to the barracão of the patrão, where he would pay off his debt and receive whatever pay the patrão gave him. Then he would put on his hat, pick up his things and leave, except that the *capanga* [gunman] of the patrão was there on the riverbank waiting for him. I also remember a fight between two patrões, the patrão of our seringal, Porto Brasil, and the one of the Sardinha seringal. In that feud many people died. When the patrões had a feud, they "played" the seringueiro, that is, they put his life on the line, but not theirs.

In the big change from patrão to fazendeiro, the seringueiro found that the fazendeiro only wanted to raise cattle, cut down trees, and evict rubber tappers. Many times the peon who cut down the forest was an ex-seringueiro. What else was he to do? He didn't want to leave his forest home. The fazendeiro would hire a *gato* ["cat," contractor] whose job it was to recruit seringueiros to cut down trees. He didn't want peons from the city because there are many *malandros* [thieves] there, but seringueiros from the forest who were honest and hard-working. So they always tried to contract people from the forest itself, the very places they were cutting down. Many, many seringueiros left for the city because their entire way of life disappeared with the destruction of the forest. They went to the city with empty hands, without their colocação, the security of a place to call their own, a place to work, without anything.

The padres began coming to the forest and started the base communities a little before the exodus to the city began. It was when the first road was built that Padre Heitor entered, a little before the entry of the ranchers. It was the road that made possible the padres' entry. So you see, the road has brought good and evil.

The seringueiro's culture has changed drastically in the past 30 years or so because those basic values of assistance, the sense of sharing, a religious sense of life, all those things began to decline with the patrão, the fazendeiro, and the marreteiro. The sense of mutual assistance is being replaced by a sense of exploitation. For example, if the seringueiro buys a kilo of coffee in the city for five or six reais, he arrives back at the seringal and wants to sell it for ten or twelve. Before it wasn't like that, now it is.

Why? Because of the capitalist sense of profit. The seringueiro observes this kind of behavior in his struggle to survive, and a child growing up in such an atmosphere learns to be mistrustful and to take advantage of the other. That's what's happening in the seringal, they've had the example of the patrão, the fazendeiro, the army, and above all, that of the marreteiro, the merchant who cheats at every opportunity.

Sharing and trust have declined, but the relationship between husband and wife, I don't think that has changed much. The woman tends the family agriculture, makes lunch and so forth; whatever has to do with the house is the woman's job, they don't have the habit of mutual help. The woman cares for the children too, educating them; some fathers participate in this, but not all. Religious activities are also more for women than men. They do not share chores. Rare is the man who helps the woman in the house. The woman helps the man with the crops; she always, always, is in the kitchen or working the plot of land. The man, he is in the rubber grove or tending the plot, but never in the house. The man's specialty is hunting to bring home something to eat. He brings it home, and the rest is the woman's job. Gathering latex is also a man's job; although some women do it, it's mostly for men.

Both men and women seem content with this situation. The bad thing in my opinion is that the woman thinks that the man is right, that this is the way it should be. That attitude begins to be imparted early to young children. The male child, his job is to carry water, but nothing of housework or cooking, because that is all for girls to do. The mother brings the children up that way. School is for both, but schools in the seringal are few. Where I worked, they had a school, but the teacher knew very little, and besides, she was not at all interested in teaching. She was only interested in the money.

You have married couples who converse at night, the chores finished, seated together. But many couples don't talk just to be talking to each other. It is more common not to converse. They communicate in silence. But to speak of business, no. Men never discuss business with women. Business is for men; you don't have to inform the wife of anything. You either discuss it with a friend or make decisions on your own, but you don't consult a woman. And women converse with other women, but not with their husbands. Some do, there are some couples who always consult each other, but generally it's the other way. One thing that has changed some is that now couples are beginning to show their affection more openly, to embrace for example, and to express affection toward their children more openly too, but before, no. Discipline of the children, that is for the father, he punishes. Some fathers show affection, but others, only authority.

We were raised during the regime of authority. My father would sit down and remain silent and no one could say a word. Heaven help us if anyone dared to say a thing! It was such that even today, in spite of having left home and studied, it's still difficult to sit down and start a conversation. You talk at the dinner table, that's about it. This is also true when I visit my brother and his family. First we chat a little, and then we fall silent. Just being together, just seeing each other seems to be enough. That's a lovely kind of friendship—thanks be to God that we are a close family—but still, dialog is very strained because that's the way we were brought up. I think it would be much better if we did communicate more, had more dialog. Then we would know each other's problems, which is important because people suffer a lot.

For example, the suffering that I kept inside when I came here; I didn't know how to communicate it to anyone. I didn't even know what was happening. I thought that I knew how to resolve my problems myself, but I didn't. Later, I began to talk about my feelings, and the one who helped me was a nun who was a teacher. She noticed my sad face and began to converse with me about my difficulties, and, gradually, I began to express the sorrow that was inside me. From there, I went forward, and my sadness lifted.

After I left Rio Branco, I went to Guajaramerim, in Rondônia where I studied philosophy, and I also had a psychology class. That's when I began to learn, I saw that many things have to change. I began to work on myself, to know myself, to wake myself up. I developed an awareness of my own personality, my strengths, and my limitations. I learned that it's all up to me, that someone is not going to come along and solve my problems for me. That realization was crucial because I began to take responsibility for my own life.

I think that is something the seringueiro needs to do, because as it stands now, it is the father who has the responsibility for everything. He's the one who goes to the city, does the shopping, buys clothes for the children, everything, and you feel a total sense of dependence on him. When I arrived in Rio Branco, I had no idea how completely dependent I was for everything. For example, if I had to go to the doctor, someone would have to go with me. The rector helped me for a while, but there came a point when he told me, "No, you are a man, you have to go by yourself." At first I was very angry because I thought that he didn't want to help me, but later I saw that he was helping me. I suffered for many years learning that lesson, that's why I say that dependence is horrible.

When I left Rio Branco I began to study philosophy, as I said, two years in Guajaramerim, and then I went to Maringa in Paraná, where I did my last year of philosophy. From there I came here to Manaus. I have to finish this year here and then stay until June of the following year, almost two years more. My plan is to return at the end of the year to Rio Branco to take some courses, to try to shorten my time in Manaus. I like Rio Branco better because I have more friends there and that's where I began. After I finish, my dream is to return to the seringal as a priest and to work with the seringueiro and the Indian.

It is those things that we are talking about that I hope to say and do with them. That's how I think their lives can have a deeper religious sense, that's how we can recover the *partilha* [sharing] and forget a little bit this business about making a profit at the other's expense. Sharing continues, I don't mean it doesn't; you arrive at someone's home, and they always have lunch or dinner for you, but you also see the desire to take advantage of the other person.

Sometimes I get to thinking about the way life used to be in the seringal and the way it is today. I even go out and ask people what things used to be like, when I have vacations from classes. But the seringais are all practically abandoned, everyone has come to the city where they live on the periphery. A very important job for a priest is to help people stay in the seringal.

So, why did I leave the seringal? Because life was too difficult there and because I wanted to become a priest. Also because my life, too, is part of all the changes I have described that have taken place over the past several decades. Why do I intend to return? Because a way must be found to keep the seringueiro in the forest, to help him make a living, and to restore threatened cultural values such as sharing, mutual assistance, and trust. How to begin? Perhaps with another cooperative. Who tried to get a cooperative going near us was Padre Paolino, in the Purús region he tried. But it seems to me that it failed because he couldn't stay there the whole time. He had to leave and visit other sites. He began to organize people, but when he left them, no one took responsibility. Now, however, even though the illiteracy rate is still about 100 per cent, I know that some people are becoming literate in the seringal, and I believe that in the future it will be easier to work with them. In order for a cooperative to work, you have to educate, prepare people, raise consciousness, be there with the people, and all that takes a long time. But it is a good place to start.

Rio Branco, 30 July 1996; Manaus, 8 September 1997.

Manoel Estébio Cavalcante da Cunha

Currently serving as coordinator of the award-winning educational program Projeto Seringueiro, da Cunha has been a seminarian, empate participant, syndicate supporter, and participant in devising sustainable economic alternatives for forest peoples. In every activity, da Cunha has stressed the importance of education for the seringueiros, and the need for Projeto Seringueiro's materials and programs to reflect the forest base of the seringueiros' culture.

In his recollections, da Cunha shows the intimate relationship that existed between the CEBs, the syndicate, and Projeto Seringueiro in the beginning; sets out the educational philosophy of Projeto Seringueiro; and describes NGO projects to improve economic conditions in the extractive reserves. Throughout, da Cunha expresses his deep respect for the seringueiros' culture and reveals his firm grasp of the interrelatedness of environmental, economic, and cultural concerns.

I came to Rio Branco from Ceará in 1980 as a novitiate in the order of the Servants of Mary. In 1981, I went to live in Xapuri where I became involved with the syndicate, which had become very active by that time, as had Projeto Seringueiro, the educational project born of the syndicate's struggle. Raimundo de Barros was the one who facilitated my move and helped me get my classes started. In Xapuri, I worked in the areas of education, health, cooperativism, and unionism.

Under the dictatorship [1964-85], unions were very tightly controlled by the state. For one thing, the union had to petition the Ministry of Work for legal status, and they would either grant it or not, but it was arbitrary and there was no recourse. Another effective control was a literacy requirement that served to block popular leadership from assuming the presidency of the syndicate. This meant that our most effective leaders, the ones who were directing the mobilization efforts and carrying out all the empates, the ones who did everything, when it came to union elections, they were excluded. They represented our union de facto, but de jure they were closed out.

The union struggle was in full force when I moved to Xapuri. Also in 1981, we created the very first popular education experience in the state. It was in the Nazaré and nearby seringais; they were all under the control of the Bordon ranch. At that time, their influence was so great that if the Bordon fazenda cut down forests in Xapuri, then everyone else did likewise in Acre and Boca do Acre, which is in the neighboring state of Amazonas. Well, the seringueiros from those places began to organize themselves to resist deforestation in an effort to maintain their livelihood and their culture. The fazendeiros were a grave threat because they were destroying the environment, on which both the economy and the culture of the seringueiro depend. If you deforest, then there is no way to reproduce the culture of the seringal. Another culture is imposed, one that does not support pluralism; it is the hegemony of the supposedly superior culture.

The situation was that the state was doing nothing. They were not building roads, schools, health posts; they were providing no technical assistance, nothing. The fazendeiros, however, even though they had obtained the land illegally, had been given every advantage and benefit from the state, such as money and loans. Further, when families resisted being thrown off their land, police from the city would come out and help the fazendeiros expel them.

One thing became perfectly clear to us in this critical situation: the people had to become educated in order to defend themselves. The church was already doing a very good job in this area with the base communities. The people involved in social service work, mobilizations, the syndicate, and civil organizations were all linked to the base communities. They were *monitores*, leaders of evangelization groups, pastoral agents who read the Bible, reflected with the people, and encouraged them to become more literate, more reflective, and more aware. The church helped the syndicate in everything, including educational matters, because the syndicate didn't have the resources to educate, and, of course, the state wasn't going to do it.

Projeto Seringueiro needed funding to get off the ground. The church was helping in a number of ways, but we needed financing to carry out our plans. Mary Allegretti, the principal founder of Projeto Seringueiro, helped us secure monetary assistance from Oxfam. After that, we were given a line of credit from the Ministry of Education from their *Projeto Saber Comúm* [Project Common Knowledge], a federal program that sponsored educational projects with local cultures. Through that avenue we were able to obtain the resources necessary to establish the first school. This was during the Figueiredo government, still in the period of the dictatorship, but, curiously, the military was, in a way, more representative than later governments. They wanted to work with the different cultures in the country through education. It was a very progressive program. With this support we had a modicum of local control, which was essential because the local mayor was a powerful ally of the fazendeiros, as was the governor of the state of Acre during that period. Also that was precisely the time when a number of our people were in jail, including Raimundo de Barros, and many of those who were working with Projeto Seringueiro.

All those powerful people saw us as their enemies, and on May 1, 1982, when we organized an empate at the Nova Esperança ranch, they used their power against us. Nova Esperança was an area where many seringueiros lived, and the fazendeiros were planning to destroy all their settlements. The seringueiros decided to stand up against this destruction, and they staged an empate with the participation of more than 100 men, women, and children. We went there to help with the mobilization. When we arrived, the police were already beating people up, but there were only three that they were interested in arresting: Raimundo, myself, and Ronaldo, who was also one of the founders of Projeto Seringueiro and who is now working at FUNAI, the Indian protection agency. They accused us of having incited the seringueiros, of having caused the trouble. All of our *companheiros* came to the jail to keep vigil and to show their support, but in the middle of the night when everyone was tired and sleepy, the police transferred us individually

PROJETO SERINGUEIRO SCHOOL, RIOZINHO

and interrogated us. They exerted strong psychological pressure and tried to frighten us with their threats, but they did not beat us.

The lesson we drew from the empates was that we were on the right track, we were making an impact, and we had to continue educating people about their rights as citizens and human beings. We had to do this through the work of the syndicate, the association, community organization, or the church, and we definitely had to intensify the work of the school. Another important realization for us was that it was the children, not their parents, who were coming to school. We had prepared ourselves with adult education in mind, so we had to shift our focus and retrain our team of teachers as *agentes multiplicadores* [multiplying agents] who would dedicate themselves to educating the children of the seringueiros. We also began to collaborate more with the syndicate because, as time went on, the base communities declined in influence while the syndicate became stronger. The syndicate was first formed by the rural workers in Acre, which, at that time, were mostly seringueiros. Today, the majority in some locales are not seringueiros.

In 1985, the Encontro Nacional de Seringueiros [National Encounter of Rubber Tappers] had as its purpose the redress of grievances against the rubber tappers. It was there that the proposal for the extractive reserves came up, at the Encontro. But it didn't develop overnight. Earlier, in 1983 and 1984, in preparation for the national encounter, a group of us from Xapuri had made visits to municipalities in Acre and Amazonas to hold conversations on this topic. For example, I traveled with Chico Mendes to Cruzeiro do Sul and to Lacá. I went by myself to Boca do Acre; Chico also went to Rondônia, while others went to Sena Madureira and to Brasiléia.

The government's idea was to turn the forest peoples into farmers, but that was alien to their culture. I remember we discussed this with the rubber tappers from Arequense, with the Association of Rubber Soldiers of Arequense, those "veterans" of World War II who had earned government pensions because of their work providing rubber during the war effort. Next to Arequense there was an Indian reserve, and we pointed out to the residents of Arequense, "Look, they have an Indian reserve next door. We are extractivists, why don't we have an extractive reserve?" The spirit and general idea of what the reserve would be like was something we had talked about and heard about for some time in Xapuri, and it was catching on.

What would this reserve be like? First, it would allow the seringueiro to have his home in his traditional colocação in the forest. Second, it would return recognition to his culture. Third, the seringueiro would receive right of usufruct, not ownership, and if he decided to leave, he would pass his land on to another extractivist; the land had to be used for extractive purposes only. And that is, in fact, how the reserves are set up today.

Unfortunately, the state never provided education, health services, technical assistance, or financing. To the extent that these exist at all, they are the creation of NGOs: the cooperative, the syndicate, the CTA, Pesacre, which is a development NGO, the CPT [Pastoral Land Commission], these are all NGOs that have acted to fill the vacuum. But their power of investment is very limited. From the very beginning, what we have wanted to see realized is an economy with a forest base. But this has not happened yet. The federal government has simply continued to open more frontiers to imports, and with this has come an incentive for cultivating plantation rubber trees in the center east and center west, but very little has been invested here in Acre. It is unfair when people say, "Oh, those extractive reserves didn't work!" Well, it's not automatic. In order to work, the founding document was very important, but it did not establish a health post or technical and production assistance. Basically, nothing was done to create even the most minimal conditions for a forest-based economy.

When rubber declined, it lost its market, but the seringueiro was more than ever at the mercy of the market. From 1990 until today it has been that way, trade barriers have been completely removed, and rubber is imported from Malaysia and Ceylon for one-tenth of the price of that produced here. What happens is that the government has been uninterested in researching through the university, IBAMA, and even EMBRAPA how to produce forest products that will find acceptance in the market. Common sense tells us that the Amazon region represents the greatest biodiversity on the planet. Meanwhile, here in Acre, the traditional populations continue to depend only on home-grown rubber and Brazil nuts, which are not viable.

The CTA has become an institution with various projects: education, health, and forest management, for example. We want to take advantage of the forest, not just rubber and Brazil nuts, and invest also in other products, such as roots, leaves, fruits, and wood for artisans. The CTA has two small offices for processing hand-made products on the reserve and for producing cleaning products and medicinal oils. We are also working on a project for producing wood. Here in Acre, exploitation of wood has been extremely predatory, without any standards or controls; loggers have taken whatever they consider valuable with impunity. The project that we are elaborating in Porto Dias is a small *serraria* [sawmill] in the seringal itself where we are going to employ seringueiros. The idea is to produce wood exclusively from a managed system. We are taking an inventory of about 100 hectares to see which trees grow in each hectare. We will extract a designated amount of wood per year and only return to an area 30 years later. It is completely balanced.

Yes, this is a lot like what they're doing in Xapuri. Unfortunately, it can't be done in the Chico Mendes Extractive Reserve yet. The problem is that in the *Plan de Manejo* [Management Plan] of the Reserva Chico Mendes there is a prohibition against managed extraction, and that reserve is the largest of all, with about 4 million hectares. Most reserves have as their executor IBAMA [Brazilian Environmental Institute], while the Reserva Cachoeira, which is an extractivist settlement of about 20,000 hectares, has as its legal executor INCRA, the land reform agency, which permits managed extraction. The reserve in Porto Dias is administered like Cachoeira, so they, too, can process lumber.

A big topic of discussion in Xapuri, which is the heart of the forest sustainability effort, is how Brasiléia, Sena Madureira, Capixaba, Assis Brasil—these four municipalities which are part of the Reserva Chico Mendes—how they can make the statute more flexible. In each locale there exists an *Amoré*, the residents' association. They have been meeting in assemblies to consider the issue, because it doesn't make sense that at this moment we have only two products with economic potential—rubber and Brazil nuts—and the seringueiro cannot survive on these. The restriction is above all on the part of IBAMA and some people linked to the ecological movement, because they confuse rational management with predatory exploitation.

Here in Acre we import wood products from other states, wood of very poor quality. It's crazy! We buy junk from the outside and export our treasures. Can you believe we even import charcoal for grilling! We import the material this table is made from, formica, when we could provide employment using local wood. This is a non-renewable product because it is derived from petroleum, it's plastic. In Rio Branco we use plastic for everything, but we could easily be using our forest rationally and improving the lives of our people.

The seringueiros are very much in favor of rational use. Before, they knew only predatory exploitation, and some of their leaders still think this is the only way. But there are many who have a different vision. They see that rational use of the forest can be controlled by the seringueiro himself and that the value generated can benefit the community and stay within the seringal. Communities such as Porto Dias and São Luiz do Remanso are accepting these suggestions.

We, that is the CTA, also have non-wood products that we are promoting as part of a forest-based economy. Some seringueiros from Remanso last year when we had the *Expôr Amazônia* [Amazon Exposition], brought all the handcrafts they had made from seeds, shells, nuts, berries, and other forest products. The fair was supposed to last for four days, but they sold out of everything the first day. We have another interesting project; it is a management plan the CTA has created for the Axinica Indians, who live in the area that borders Peru, for them to exploit *coto murmurú*, which is a kind of wild almond you can use for food and shampoo. We are also trying to carry out a project with *jarina*, whose seeds are used to make beautiful jewelry; it's also called *marfim vegetal* [vegetable "marble"]. The US imports jarina from Ecuador and Peru, and we would like to participate in that market. These are the sort of things that the CTA is offering so that people do not remain dependent only on borracha and *castanha* [Brazil nuts] IBAMA didn't pay attention to these needs when the reserves were created; they didn't think about the need for an alternative, sustainable, forest-based economy. What they were advocating was raising sheep, pigs, chickens, and creating a farinha factory. Such activities exert a strong impact on the forest, unlike rational management.

We talk about these kinds of things in our classes and our teacher training too. The basis of our education in Projeto Seringueiro is the *mundo sensível* [sensory world] of the seringueiro. So, if we are doing social studies, we start from the seringueiros' own social reality. If we are studying science, we do not begin with abstractions, but with the living laboratory here. The CTA's curriculum is based on the daily life of the extractivist populations. Paulo Freire is our inspiration. We have been recognized internationally for our efforts. We received an award in New York, as well as a prize during Amazon Week there in 1995. Also in 1995, we received an honorable mention from UNICEF. In 1997 we won a prize in the field of teacher training, again from UNICEF. In 1998 we received the national Paulo Freire prize. Even so, education in the seringais is viable only where the CTA is active. If you were to go to some place in Xapuri or the surrounding area where the CTA is not active, you would not find any work being done in education.

I would like to give you these materials [texts]. Many things in here were proposed by the teachers themselves, in math, Portuguese, and science, but you will see that the disciplines are integrated in the text. For example, this is a math book, but the content of the math problems is scientific and cultural, and, of course, indirectly, it also teaches the Portuguese language. We have lots of workshops; we try to offer them every few months. The teachers enjoy them immensely, and so do I. We go out to them, to the communities for the workshops. I am responsible for coordinating these sessions and for overseeing Projeto Seringueiro generally.

I love creating educational materials. It's really what I feel called to do. I began the university as a novitiate with the Servants of Mary, studying philosophy, theology, and sociology. When I decided that my vocation was not the priesthood, I continued my academic studies and received a postgraduate degree in social sciences at the UFAC [Federal University of Acre]. I wanted to write texts about teaching and to create new paths in the area of teacher training.

The biggest problem we face in our work is economic, because the resources for our projects are very scarce. Before, there was more funding for social activities, now it is minimal. There was Oxfam, the Ministry of Education, Miseriore [a church organization], Bread for the World. Today, the CTA has resources only from UNICEF. Last year we had only our prize money, which was 25 reais, not enough to prepare my teacher assistance course.

You see, in addition to the workshops, once a year I give this course during the academic break between December and June, the rainy season in the Amazon region. So I take advantage of that period to provide teacher training. Everyone comes to the course. In my visits during the academic year, I go to the schools, and I learn what kinds of things teachers need, what type of pedagogical and personal support should be provided. That work is absolutely fundamental to the success of the program. Then, I give this course during the break to help the teachers—it comes directly from their expressed needs and my visits to them. State education doesn't work this way because they just hire teachers and never visit classes, and sometimes teachers have problems with the community that they can't solve alone. My presence is very important to help teachers overcome whatever tensions they are experiencing in the community. Since the state functions only to hire and pay teachers, they are unaware of the problems that teachers have to deal with.

Fortunately, this situation is beginning to change with our governor, Jorge Viana, who is a strong supporter of our educational work. I am now collaborating with the Secretary of Education because they want to expand what has been successful. The few state schools that do exist in the forest are now adopting our methodology, and we go to those areas to prepare the teachers. Where there are no schools, the idea is for the state to establish them, again using the methodology of the Projeto Seringueiro.

This is the plan for the city as well. It's part of Viana's vision for educating the population of our state generally speaking. The governor has come up with a forest-based development plan for Acre. The idea is to develop without causing environmental harm: *fazer sem agredir* [doing without harming], that's the motto. In order to carry out the plan, it is essential to educate youth from the seringal to the university to work toward that common goal. If the base is going to be the forest, if development is going to be sustainable, then the citizens who are educated in Acre—the professor, the administrator, the civil engineer, the dentist—all have to reflect a forest perspective.

Our mission in the CTA is very much along the same lines. We want to do what we can to make the extractive reserves become an economic and ecological model with a forest base. All previous projects have rejected extractivism for extensive cattle ranching, agriculture, or wood extraction. That is to deny all the experience of the Indian and the seringueiro cultures. So, our idea is that the forests and the peoples who live in them should be our teachers. To develop the ability to work and live without being predators and destroyers, that is what we have to learn. The classroom itself incorporates such lessons taught by the traditional Amazonian communities. The more we work with them, the more we learn from the wisdom of the hunters, fishermen, and herbalists, these are the forest specialists.

Of course, other people have a different perspective. They insist that cattle ranching is an economically productive activity. During the 1970s, millions and millions of dollars poured in here as incentives for cattle raising, but no amount of money can make it productive. For example, there is a fazenda on the road from Boca do Acre that has 10,000 head of cattle. Well, how many jobs does that generate? What is the social return? It is insignificant! The idea of converting huge amounts of land into pasture for cattle makes no sense, because it gives no social return. The reserve, on the other hand, does, because it settles families and brings more families to make their living from the forest. But for these people to succeed, there has to be assistance, and the only assistance has come from NGOs. The projects that the government has developed are mistaken. Huge ranches have devastated thousands and thousands of hectares of forest that today are so completely degraded they can't even support cattle. That's to say, there have been three disasters: economic, social, and ecological. Those who were living here in equilibrium before, are now living precariously on the periphery of the city.

Our governor is doing what he can to change that unsustainable situation. For one thing, he established the office of the Secretary of Extractivism and Forests, which proposed a subsidy of 40 cents for a *quintal* [100 pounds] of borracha. The proposal was approved and has been in effect since March of 1999. Already, many seringueiros who live on the outskirts of Sena Madureira, Xapuri, and Assis Brasil are beginning to return to the seringais.

The way it works is that the seringueiro cuts seringa and the government guarantees the purchase of his production. He has to belong to a cooperative, or if there is no cooperative, to an association, or if there is no association or cooperative, to a syndicate. The idea is to create solidarity and not to be individualistic. It is really intended for the seringueiro who lives in the seringal. But what is happening is that the seringal today, demographically, is depleted since so many have had to come to the city. As a result of this policy, people are beginning to return, but the project was not specifically designed for them. Either way, we will be there for them when they return, to welcome them with schools and teachers.

Rio Branco, 10 June 1999

Dom Moacyr Grechi

Dom Moacyr served as Bishop of the Prelacy of Acre and the Upper Purús from 1972-98, where he was revered by the poor as one who actively intervened on their behalf in the cause of justice, despite great risk to his own life. Dom Moacyr's arrival in Acre coincided with the influx of land grabbers, speculators, loggers, and ranchers, the burning of the rainforest, and the expulsion of seringueiros from their homes. In his interview, Dom Moacyr describes how his eyes were opened to the situation, how the church became a vocal critic of the government, how the base communities spread the social gospel, and how the church protected the rural workers' union. He also comments on his warm friendship with Chico Mendes.

Dom Moacyr links the problems of the seringueiro to the broader concern of the divorce of economic activity from an ethical base. He stresses the importance of the community in the development of the individual, and expresses his belief that the way out of the moral crisis is an evangelical world view—that is, one based on the Gospel. Dom Moacyr was named Archbishop of Rondônia in 1999.

In general, in the social realm, the church serves to unite, give continuity, and provide a critical perspective. This is significant because the communications media, for the most part, are bought, sold, or silenced through fear. Broadly speaking, the church in Brazil is a critical voice, and, as a whole, it holds to a clear position that I believe corresponds to the truth.

What helped us a great deal was the *golpe de estado*, the 1964 coup, because it forced the church to take a stand from then on. We have also had a long period of excellent church leadership. In the CNBB [*Conselho Nacional de Bispos Brasileiros*, Brazilian National Bishops' Council], we had Aluísio Lorscheider who was secretary twice and president twice. Later, his cousin, who was secretary twice and then president twice. That's eight years right there. Then came Dom Luciano Mendes, Dom Celso, they were excellent and balanced coordinators of the conference. At the same time, we had bishops who were socially committed in many areas, such as Dom Paulo Evaristo Arns, Dom Pedro Casaldáliga—there are more than 50 I could name.

After 1964 we were no longer economically dependent on the government. Argentina is still dependent, and the church has difficulties as a result. In Chile you had the admirable figure of the Cardinal, very expressive, but at the same time you had a group connected to Pinochet. Brazil has been different. Here the church has maintained its unity and a remarkable continuity for more than 30 years. Unity is its main direction; of course, we have divisions, but the great majority have expressed and continue to express a clear and consistent social position. Further, our theologians, the good ones like Clodovis Boff, have been men of the church. The option we express is profoundly evangelical; it carries with it a consequence, which is justice.

When I came here as Bishop in 1972, the worst problem I faced from a social point of view was the arrival of the land grabbers. That put a severe strain on the whole social fabric, and various issues threatened to erupt all at once: the problem of the corrupt, bought police; the total inefficiency of the local government; and the opinion of middle-class bureaucrats that deforestation was the road to progress. With extreme difficulty the syndicates became organized. Practically all of them were born in the church, not only from the point of view of the church as people, but also as a physical construction, because we offered asylum to all those who were persecuted. The church was the only institution that was more or less protected. Even so, we were invaded by both the army and the police. In Xapuri, for example, they confiscated materials, recordings, and publications.

So, the problems for a long time were violence and corruption, land-grabbing, and dispossession of the residents. Alarm over the ecological havoc came a few years later. With the rise to prominence of Chico Mendes there began to be more contact with the outside world, which defended not only the permanence of the seringueiros, but also the preservation of the forest. Later still came a rapprochement and alliance between the Indian and the seringueiro who both depend on the forest.

The root, the driving force, behind the popular resistance of the 1970s and 1980s were the ecclesial base communities, consisting of the word of God, prayer, and fellowship. From the beginning, we distinguished the base community from the syndicate, and later, from the party. Thus, in the base community all are Catholics; in the syndicate, however, everyone may and should participate in the party as well. The one should not be confused with the other. We have made a tremendous effort to keep them separate. They are not confused.

However, in the beginning, the syndicates of the rural workers were totally dependent on the church, because the ferocity of the repression forced them to take refuge in the church for their meetings. I was always the one who took a public position, leaving the workers' names aside because the risks for them were very great. The government had nothing to gain by being seen as anti-church, especially as everything that happened here had widespread repercussions throughout Brazil and Europe. So, it was a negative incentive for the governor to persecute the church. Since the church sheltered the syndicates, at the beginning all the union leaders were also church leaders. For them to say the Lord's Prayer in a syndicate meeting or to pray together before an empate was perfectly normal. The influence of the church was very great.

Little by little, though, they became autonomous and took the step of collaborating with other people and groups who were working for the same goals. The church is in solidarity in the hour of conflict, in the hour of prison, in the hour of a service the CPT [Pastoral Land Commission] can provide. Then the church is a sister, a companion on the journey, but they must have the autonomy to elect their own officials and to put forward their own proposals, which they do. When they want the explicit collaboration of the church, they request it.

The same thing for the PT [Workers Party]. Although I have expressly forbidden the participation of the padres and the *irmãs* [sisters] in political campaigns, you will occasionally see some who are very close to the people who, in practice, work for the party and feel that is their obligation. It is difficult to maintain total autonomy, but there exists near total autonomy from the church in the syndicate, the parties, and the neighborhood associations.

In the neighborhood associations, our influence has always been minimal. Gradually, most of them became co-opted by the political parties. With rare exceptions, neighborhood associations have become instruments of parties that buy and sell, that are assistentialist and whose political chiefs view the association as an instrument for them to use. In this instance, I would have to say that autonomy has not been so good. Even so, the best prepared leaders do win neighborhood elections from time to time and create a different climate. The rural syndicates have held firm to their quality because they created a different thing than the associations; their authenticity is beyond question.

For us in the church, the social agent was always the person in the base community; that is, the person of faith who believes in the word of God, who prays, who wishes to attain eternal life. This person endeavors to live a life of love and justice outside the base community. Such a person may get together with others and decide to establish a school or form a community association. Later, they may perceive that they need to organize as a class. This is the way it happens. The Catholic who prays and listens to the Gospel feels motivated to be a good citizen and perhaps a good leader of the syndicate. But he does not confuse the two things. Here, on the inside, he is a person of faith; there, in the outside world, he is a unionist. When it turned out that the syndicate and the association were not enough, the party became necessary as well. Thus, the individual who is inspired by the Gospel, nourished by life in the community, goes forth to participate in the party, guided by evangelical values. Sometimes there are crossed currents, but not confusion of organizations. The syndicate, the party, and the base community are all separate entities. I would accentuate that aspect, that stemming from a faith base, our strongest desire from the beginning was that the organizations would become autonomous.

During the 1970s and 1980s we saw a great deal of valuing of the poor, not merely as those who receive, but as those who can become subjects. It was also a time of friendship among the community leaders, the bases, the sisters. The leaders did not consider themselves as superior, or possessors of truth; rather, there was a genuine climate of dialog, of valuing what the other represented, and of co-responsibility. We were working to overcome that condition that Paulo Freire identified of people internalizing the view of the oppressor. The people considered themselves inferior. The attitude was: "You, sir, are the one who knows, who are we?" Therein lay the struggle, to which both the clergy and the people responded;

they were at great risk, but they were united, there was mutual respect and solidarity in the political struggle. The numerous *encontros* [encounters], the *cursos* [courses], and *palestra*s [talks] were a very important part of the process.

Where the base communities were victorious, it was because they had the support of the bishops, the padres, and the local leadership, even if it created conflict with other groups. That support facilitated the success of the communities. Where there was resistance from these groups, it was almost impossible for a community to succeed. Where the base community is created in contestatory circumstances, the climate becomes very unhealthy within the church itself.

Political organization and consciousness are slow to develop, but we are very fortunate to have two wonderful leaders now who absolutely represent the interests of the people. It is most unusual. The current governor of Acre and former mayor of Rio Branco, Jorge Viana, has already done a great deal for the people of Acre, as has our federal deputy Marina Silva. After Chico Mendes, Senadora Marina is the great leader of the people. She was born and raised in a seringal about an hour away by boat on the Rio Acre, the Bagaço seringal. Some years ago she went to the United States to receive an ecological prize which had a $75,000 award, of which she donated $40,000 to our leprosarium here because she knew we were out of funds. She is poor and her brothers and sisters are very poor; she lives austerely, unlike other politicians. She worked very closely with Chico Mendes in the empates.

Chico Mendes began to participate in the early leadership training programs that the base communities sponsored. He never was much for participating in the church per se, but he was a very active participant in the things that interested him. He was extremely close to the padres in Xapuri, many times staying in the parish house. During the decades of the land problems, evictions, and violence, when I served as the seringueiros' intermediary with the authorities and the press, I traveled many, many times with Chico, and we developed a deep friendship.

Chico was a good man, honest and flexible; he possessed not an ounce of extremism, he was not a communist. He was able to dialog with practically everyone; he was very open, and he never, ever became corrupt. He died poor. Chico valued the base communities and the leaders who were born of those communities. He didn't move much in those circles, but he was complemented by them. I mean that he had an important part to play, the seringueiros had another, and the church, still another. These elements all complemented each other.

Chico was not the only leader, though he was powerful, with a wonderful ability to express himself through words and gestures. Before Chico there was another, Wilson Pinheiro; his was the first murder in the struggle. Wilson was the one who began the strategy of the empate. At first the seringueiros' empates were without shotguns; then shotguns without ammunition; then, with ammunition but without firing. There was never violence on the part of the seringueiros in the empates. Chico was always afraid of violence because the repression was extremely brutal.

I think that one of the most difficult moments was when they assassinated Wilson Pinheiro. At that time, the secretary of security was of the extreme right, with a fascist view of humankind. The authorities took absolutely no steps to resolve the death of Wilson Pinheiro, and because of that, a group of seringueiros killed the rancher whom everyone considered the assassin. After that, the fury of the repression became almost indescribable. If it hadn't been for the church, they would have exterminated, exterminated, all of the seringueiros. For example, the army, the police, all supported by the secretary of security, arrested eight citizens who had absolutely nothing to do with anything and brutally tortured them for days. When I saw them, they still had splinters under their fingernails. The terror was so great that even doctors who were in my confidence became weak, afraid, and kept silent.

At that time, the president of the Pontifical Commission was Cândido Mendes, a highly educated, very well-known, and respected person. I asked him for help, explaining that the situation was grave. He responded beautifully. People can achieve many things if only one prestigious person takes up their struggle. He came here with *TV Globo* and newspaper reporters from the *Jornal do Brasil*. They arrived at night but didn't have a driver, and though I am a terrible driver, I got us to Brasiléia. Since Cândido Mendes was a recognized authority, they opened the prison. They interviewed the prisoners and recorded with the *Globo*, filming the crushed hands, bruises, and lacerations. The *Jornal do Brasil* ran many entire pages of exceptional journalistic quality, and the *Globo* broadcast the interviews on TV. It is a moment I will never forget because the shameful torture of those innocent people became a national scandal and our salvation. If they had not exposed the torture, the oppressors would have massacred the entire movement. There is absolutely no doubt about it whatsoever.

This was still during the time of the dictatorship, it was under Geisel. The governor of Acre was making all kinds of wild accusations about peasants mobilizing, getting ready to invade the town of Brasiléia en masse. I told them they were talking nonsense, but I was obliged to call another padre in the early hours of the morning and ask him please to get a jeep and drive some 20 kilometres to see if there were people mobilizing with arms. Of course, there were none. It was a dangerous time.

Things have changed a lot since then. Now the problem is not violence but corruption, which complicates and debilitates everything. The law doesn't work, authorities are bought, people disobey the law with impunity; it is a period of amoralism, without ethics. I believe that this, too, is a result of the long period of dictatorship.

The police authorities still cannot be trusted because the version of events they put out is almost always false. They are conditioned by the kind of life that they lead, on the margin. I don't mean marginalized like the poor, but on the margin of society because they are criminals. Many of them come from the very world of violence, drugs, and vice that they are supposed to combat as policemen. We had a Secretary of Security here who was a very good person, a general; he was president of the land reform agency, INCRA, for a long time too, and he helped me many, many times. One day he came to me in desperation and said, "Dom Moacyr, tomorrow I am resigning. Look here, the names of 50 new civil policemen, all are without qualifications and most are criminals. I'm leaving."

There is no ethic that guides our politics or our economy, the only criterion is a quick profit. This is obvious in the widespread deforestation which brings immediate and fabulous profits. You cut down one tree here and get five dollars for it. When it arrives in Belém it is already worth thousands, and by the time it arrives in the US or Europe it is worth a fortune, $25,000.

Part of the problem is the lack of an ethical base and part is the historic isolation of our region. For example, the territory of the diocese is vast, 120,000 square kilometres, almost all without roads. I travel by plane, boat, horse, jeep, and foot. I know from experience the geographical isolation of the seringueiros. In addition, they were socially isolated by the patrão. He wanted their settlements to be distant from each other because he did not like any conglomerations where the workers would waste time, drink, and have parties.

Their isolation also meant that they were almost completely without religious assistance. Clergy would visit just once a year at best under the old system of *desobrigas* [dispensations, exemptions]. It was a profound abandonment. There are even some communities which, because of isolation and illiteracy, no longer know how to pray the "Our Father" or the "Hail Mary." Over three or four generations they have lost all religious references, including those that form part of the culture itself. These are limited, remote, areas I am referring to, but the point is to illustrate the effects of isolation.

Over time, the seringueiros acquired aspects of indigenous culture, knowledge of the jungle, of hunting, of survival in the forest, but they lost many things from their northeastern heritage. The family used to be more structured, for example. Work involved more agriculture; they had the cultural tradition of songs and festivals. Here, especially in the distant areas, they lost practically everything. They became a people almost without their own cultural expressions.

Now that they have a chance, they are recovering their poetry and song because they themselves are beginning to write. With the base communities there sprang up many songs and much poetry that expressed the new reality, the new vision of the Evangelho, of hope, of struggle. They are beginning to produce literature and theater, some even published in bulletin form. This has happened in practically all regions; the church through its base communities has helped people rescue their culture. You also have a series of expressions of solidarity, fraternity, of *acolhida* [hospitality] that they have not lost. That quality is infused with Christian faith, with seeing the other as one's brother, the Christ who comes. The reception of others and solidarity can even reach extremes of heroism.

For example, solidarity in the hour of pain and suffering. To take a pregnant woman in a hammock, eight or ten men travel 20 hours in the jungle, the rain, the mud in order to arrive at the riverbank and then take her in a boat to where she can be attended. It is a scene of such sacrifice that it frightens me because they are exhausted, their legs are covered with mud, yet they are in complete solidarity.

The faith of the seringueiro is very strong; it is rooted in popular religion. If São Francisco were in a procession, you would have 10,000 people here in Rio Branco, because the seringueiros absolutely see him as an intermediary with God. Francisco, in the hour of pain, of injustice, attends them. He is part of their lives; he represents Christ, though sometimes I think he takes Christ's place, at least in practice. Jesus is more important in that he is the one who saves, but the Saint helps!

Padre Paolino told me a lovely story of faith. When the ranchers invaded the territory in the Iaco area, they made a landing strip. As a plane was about to land, a seringueiro who had been robbed of his forest home knelt down in the middle of the runway and cried out, "I am certain that Saint Francis will not abandon me!" [*Tenho certeza que o Senhor São Francisco não me abandonará!*] It was an act of faith, desperation actually, and he was heard. By this I mean that he and his neighbors were able to organize and overcome the invaders. This is an important aspect of the seringueiros' religious culture: they do not despair. God is great, God is good, and it is impossible that God would make a mistake.

The example of the seringueiro is instructive, because what we are witnessing on a broader scale is the waning of a life based on morality, and the divorce of economic activity from morality. I think it was Dom Helder Câmara who said that the two extremes, extreme abundance and extreme misery, both deform the human being. This is what we are seeing. Economic activity now prescinds from ethics completely, it has nothing to do with ethics. We also see here how technology, instead of being at the service of the common good, is at the service of accumulation.

Take, for example, the corruption of values. What happens is that, precisely as a result of this amoral economic activity, the seringueiro is forced to migrate to the city where he becomes corrupted. Last Sunday I was at the hospital, they called me to attend a youth who had been hit by a car. There were 37 patients in the hospital, all poor, who had been admitted between Friday and Sunday. Of these, only three were there for natural illnesses, all the others had either knife or gunshot wounds. The *convivência* [sociability] among the poor is disastrous; they have only drugs, alcohol, and extreme poverty for companions. The nurse was telling me that she attended one poor family with seven children. The parents had fought, gone their separate ways, and left the children on their own. The oldest turned to selling drugs in order to support his younger siblings. After the police picked him up, his brothers and sisters were left with nothing to eat. So, you see, one thing is linked to another, and it's hard to know where to begin.

There are ways in which life in the city is better than in the forest. For one thing, the city has schools. There is a new ideal that all the families have that their children should learn to read and write, that they should not be like their parents. And, the city has schools, however bad they may be. They have emergency medical assistance, maternity care is free, there is first aid; again, however unsatisfactory they are, at least they exist. The husband can sell bananas, the wife can wash clothes. In other ways, however, the city is diabolical—unemployment, drugs, violence, poor schools, no environment for a healthy community.

I think that the only way to reverse the situation is through constant work at the base, at the level of the individual, of small communities, where it is possible to effect a regeneration of values. We must invest in the civic formation of the citizen, and we have to do it from the ground up, so that we will have good city councils and responsible mayors. From the ecclesial point of view, I believe that we have to make an effort to recover Catholics we have lost. Those who don't practice, who are the large majority, I would say that in Brazil it is about 50 per cent of all adults. They were baptized, but they were never initiated into the faith. I believe that there will be a great effort on the part of the church to have Catholics actually live their faith, participate in the sacraments, have a fraternal life, and from that, extrapolate for justice. That's where it all begins.

You may not realize that for many years I was completely unaware of the crisis of our times. My experiences in Acre forced me to open my eyes. I was born in Santa Catarina, where I received my primary and secondary education. I studied philosophy in São Paulo, at the Seminário de São Paulo, both in the city and in the interior of São Paulo state, and I studied theology in Rome. I studied philosophy and theology from 1956 to 1961. In 1961 I became a priest. I spent a long period completely, totally alienated from the world. My preoccupations were wholly internal. I studied a great deal, read practically all the time, but I only awoke to the social, popular dimension here in Acre. In 1972 I was forced by the people to wake up.

As you know, I came here just when the speculators and ranchers were arriving. They needed workers to clear the forests, so they would round up fathers and sons and violently take them away to the seringal, where they treated them like slaves and paid them nothing. Families would come and talk with me, begging me to do something, but I didn't believe them. I thought that people here were just lazy. I shared the prejudices of the Italians, that is, of those from the southern part of our country.

Then came a concrete case that I will never forget. I had been outside talking with the authorities and the land purchasers who were telling me, "You are from the south, you don't know what these people are like; here, no one wants to work." Then this old man who had overheard the conversation, he must have been about 80, came here to the Bishop's Palace and said to me, "If I was your age, I'd already be out there." He caused me such shame that the next day I went to see for myself.

I went in the boat of the patrão. When I arrived near Xapuri, in the interior, the patrão was already waiting for me, with a security guard and a soldier. The next morning, the four of us went on horseback into the forest where they were cutting down the trees. When I arrived, I began asking people, "Did you call for me?" I asked some youths kicking a soccer ball, "Do you want to speak with me? Is there a problem?"

They all answered, "No, sir. Everything is just fine." Then the patrão said, "You heard for yourself; I was once a seminarian, and I am sensitive. These people don't want anything." Then we went on back to the house, and that night I went out to visit some nearby houses. As I was walking down the path, some men grabbed me and pulled me into the forest. There, waiting for me, were more than 40 seringueiros who had gathered to tell me their stories of how they had been beaten and enslaved. It was tragic, tragic, heartbreaking. I asked them to repeat everything to the Secretary of Security, which they did on condition that I stay there with them, which I did. I had believed only what the authorities said. I began to wake up. If I wanted to know the truth, I would have to listen closely to the people.

This event marked a profound change in my life: I began to mistrust the rich and trust the poor and to try to work with both. Before, I had not been a feeling or caring person; I was too cerebral, and this experience rescued me. After that, the Gospel came to offer another vision for me. I began to use theology to defend and not to oppress. Later, I found strong support from the padres here, they are all excellent. Also at that time, the Conference of Bishops was at its apogee. There was a series of factors that helped me open my eyes and commit myself ever more, even to the point of death, because that's when the death threats began. It's all part of the commitment.

To give you an idea of the faith, love, and suffering that are integral parts of the seringueiro's life, have I told you about Terto? It's a splendid and moving story. Terto used to live way in the interior, ten days from here by boat, in lower Amazonas. At that time he lived well, poor but not miserable, he had plenty to eat, he lived with his family, seven or eight children working in the seringal and producing garden crops and a little rice to eat.

Then, one evening, he discovered the base community, and from then on he and his family began to participate regularly in the gospel readings, the songs, the fraternal life. Then tragedy struck. One of his children came down with the black fever, a virulent form of hepatitis which then swept through the family carrying off everyone under 21 years of age. He lost five children and his wife. With that illness death is foretold. The love of the community surrounded Terto and supported him in the hour of so much death. His daughter, who was 12, asked them to read the Gospel to her. Then she asked her father to sing for her a song of Our Lady. It goes like this: "In heaven, in heaven, with my mother I will be." [*No céu, no céu, com minha mãe estarei.*] It's a traditional song. Terto sang and cried, and the daughter, who had seen four brothers and sisters and her mother die, said to her father, "Dear father, don't cry. We will meet again in heaven." It was a touching scene.

Terto's last daughter, a tiny thing, died here in the hospital. I was there with her and with the doctor, who did all she could and then turned to me and asked, "Will you provide the coffin for this one too?" I had just provided the coffin for another child who had died. About three in the morning, I went to the morgue to see what the situation was, and there I found the small coffin of the daughter, Nazaret, with Terto asleep beside it. There are pathetic examples of deep suffering and love that sometimes are hard to express. But Terto never gave up hope. He has now remarried and has two children. His life is one of a faith lived daily, whether in the depths of the forest or in the city. He is nostalgic for the forest; the only reason he does not return is that the doctors fear for his health. They had to burn his house, clothes, everything he came into contact with; it was terrible. This sort of thing is very common in that region of the Purús; it is what people have to live with.

I think that you have perceived that the work of the church is varied and far-reaching. But whatever we do, our actions and our perspective are always founded in faith. The church acts in the social realm, but its reason always stems from the Gospel message that tells me that God is our father and that Jesus Christ desires the full liberation of all people. If I embrace that message, then I have to engage myself in the social as well; that is, the Gospel can not be restricted just to worship, to catechism, and to that which is constitutive of the church strictly speaking. There has to be activity, ferment, in all areas.

The work of the church in the Amazon region has historically been one of sacramentalism; now, however, we are in a period of evangelism. For a long time, all along the rivers, people were baptized, married, and confessed, but there was virtually no evangelization and very little catechism. Above all, there was a dependence on the patrões. The former bishops would note in their diaries, "We have no freedom. We are dependent on the patrão." [*Não temos liberdade. Somos dependentes do patrão.*] Some bishops have written, "If we were to criticize the patrões, they would not even let us enter." [*Se criticaramos os patrões não nos deixaram siquer entrar.*] If the patrão forbade the Bishop from entering, then that entire population would remain without the sacraments. When they allowed the padres to enter, the patrões would call the seringueiros; then they would celebrate mass, have all the sacraments, and the padre would stay in the house of the patrão. Later, the patrão would debit the seringueiro's account for whatever he provided for each sacrament. Those early priests were men of great moral grandeur; they carried a heavy burden because at that time there were no religious communities anywhere to assist them or carry on their work. After the sacraments, there was only emptiness and loneliness; everyone would return to his place. At best, they would celebrate the festival of São Francisco and, perhaps, Holy Week.

After Medellín, the effort to evangelize began, but we never separated ourselves from the sacraments. We always looked for a synthesis because the Gospel should play a large role in the community. If the community gathers to listen to the gospel, to pray, to create a climate of fraternity, if it gathers regularly, then you have present the minimal conditions for the sacraments. After Medellín, we changed our emphasis from the sacraments to the communities. For a long period we were extremely rigorous. I would say that we were actually inhuman because, for the forest peoples, baptism is not just a sacrament: it is almost constitutive of identity. The child who is not baptized is regarded as an animal. It's part of their culture. So what happens when you deny people the sacraments because they are not prepared? You create an enemy. We were too rigid, and we hurt many people. On the other hand, that practice produced many enlightened people who are now the community leaders. But such harshness was unnecessary; we could have been much more evangelical, human, flexible, but it did not happen that way. With time we softened, but always with the risk of reverting to the sacramentalism of the past.

For example, I recently went to do baptisms. I entered the jungle, several hours by jeep, and the people began to arrive on foot. I baptized 70 people. For the most part, it was very lovely. They were people who live in the community, and they were more or less prepared, but the important thing is that they participate in the community; that they pray, sing, desire what is good for each other. Then, one feels good about giving the sacrament; it has meaning. It is the Holy Spirit which is given so that they may live in community and become missionaries to others.

Now, in that same group, I had cases of people who were not prepared. For example, a young woman of about 20 who came up to me and said, "I am coming to confess for the first time." Well, what do you do? If I deny her the sacrament, I may not get back there for another six years. So, I try to see if she can say the Lord's Prayer at least. "Yes." Can you say the "Ave Maria?" "Yes." "Do you participate in the community?" "I participate, not always, but some." "Do you intend to do better from here on out?" "Yes." Then, "*Em nome do Pãi, do Filho e do Espírito Santo, Amém.*" [In the name of the Father, the Son, and the Holy Spirit, Amen.]

In some cases, really, sacramentalism is perpetuated. Sometimes you give the sacrament simply because they come asking for it. Then you try to teach a few basic things in order to create a following for people to carry on, to facilitate evangelization, to pass on their understanding of the purpose of Jesus. I would say that we have in the sacraments the seat of the community; the community is born from hearing the word, from prayer and brotherhood. Then the sacraments become part of the process of growth. In other cases, the community is weak and the sacraments go along the earlier lines, and people believe that the sacraments do the work on their own. The center of attention for us is the community; it is within the community that the individual grows as a person, because he relates to, pardons, and helps the other.

The CEBs continue, but they have changed their emphasis. What's in crisis now are the small groups. The strength of the communities for well over 20 years was the 12, 20, 30 small groups that would meet during the week. We are trying to see how we can discover new paths for new groups, now that the situation has changed. The CEBs have to change direction and method, because before we didn't have the middle class. Today, we have at least 900 couples who took the *Encontro de Casais com Cristo* [Married Couples' Encounter with Christ] course, and they are the dynamic force in our church. They have another way of thinking than the traditional base communities; for example, they were never part of an evangelization group. So, we have a big challenge to keep the church centered in the large fundamental options of the Gospel and at the same time make room for the charismatics, the married couples, and so on. We must do all this, but without ever leaving behind the option for the poor. That option we all have to assume, because if we do not, there is no more Gospel.

I would say that we need to cultivate an evangelical view of life. That force, when authentic, moves and transforms. I am convinced that we only realize ourselves as individuals to the extent that we open up to the community. To the degree that we do that, we grow as persons. There is no contrast between the two, individual and community, but rather, a reciprocity. Recently, we have been trying to emphasize this reciprocity, showing how the Gospel leads necessarily to citizenship, to valuing each person, to believing in equality, and to working in solidarity. This, I think, is how we return ethics to our personal lives, to economics, and politics.

Rio Branco, 7 August 1996; 26 August 1997;
1 September 1997; 31 May 1999.

Conclusion

The rubber tappers have told different stories, but each one contains several recurring themes. Perhaps the most surprising, considering the isolation in which seringueiros have lived until recently, is the sharp awareness of how local events form part of the global picture. Seringueiros see their situation as connected to the larger world.

We also observe in the tappers a clear grasp of the importance of political power. Their political consciousness was raised over a very short period of time, as workers quickly learned, for example, that only those with political power can call out the police. Seringueiros have organized, formed alliances, and learned to work within a political party.

Forest workers know that it is suicide to destroy the forest on which they depend. A keen awareness of their dependence on the environment pervades nearly every interview and has been heightened in recent years by the seringueiros' association with numerous environmental groups.

Partly as a result of their view of nature as a web that supports and connects all life, the seringueiros hold a different view of property rights than do the fazendeiros or loggers. For the tappers, individual ownership is not the important thing. What is essential are use rights which allow them access to resources, not in order to amass wealth but to earn a living. The right of usufruct [use] was the land arrangement the seringueiros requested when proposing the extractive reserves.

Seringueiros by no means wish to turn their backs on the modern world. On the contrary, as we have seen, they ardently desire the health benefits, social services, basic infrastructure, and education for their children that are features of modern life everywhere. Nor do they seek isolation from the global market, but entry on their own terms, and not at the cost of economic and cultural extinction.

The seringueiros believe that viable alternatives can be found that will enable them to live sustainably and remain in the forest. A number of NGOs are providing valuable assistance with research projects and pilot programs in economic diversification.

The NGOs, however, have not built in a vacuum, but on solid community efforts first undertaken by dynamic, effective local leaders, such as Wilson

Pinheiro and Chico Mendes. In fact, the key to understanding events in Acre lies in comprehending the critical importance of local leadership. But there would be no local leaders if there were no hope that things could be different and that the workers themselves were capable of effecting the desired change. Hope is a difficult candle to light in a people who have long been regarded by others as mere objects and who, as Freire has observed, tend to internalize the view of their oppressor, that is, to regard themselves as nothing.

How did the seringueiros move from hopelessness to hope, the precondition for any kind of fruitful action? Many factors contributed to this change, such as the indomitable spirit, tenacity, and organizing ability of leaders like Pinheiro and Mendes and the survival skills tappers have acquired as a result of the unremittingly harsh conditions they have endured for generations. But the biggest push came from the Catholic church of Acre and the Upper Purús, its spiritual leader Dom Moacyr Grechi, and the egalitarian message of the local base communities over more than three decades. Padres and *irmãs* [sisters] have demonstrated in their daily lives that they value the forest people, and they have helped raise up local leaders who believe in social justice and in the responsibility of each person to help bring it about.

Most important, the seringueiros have been the principal actors in their own drama. They have been awakened by the CEBs and their local leaders, they have created their own union, joined the national Workers Party, established the National Rubber Tappers Council, formed their own cooperative, and collaborated with environmental and other NGOs when this has suited their purpose. The seringueiros themselves have been active agents in defending their way of life.

As we shall soon see, the lived experiences of these seringueiros of Acre share some important features with those of the Guaraní Indians of the Bolivian Chaco. We will also observe the special circumstances that have shaped conflicts over land, tradition, and modernity in that remote desert region and that inform the voices we are about to hear.

PART TWO

Bolivia

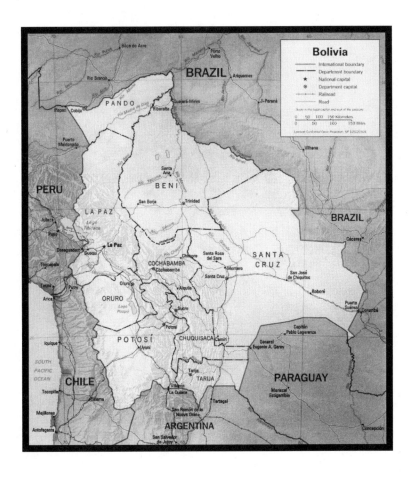

Introduction

The Guaraní of Bolivia are part of the Tupí-Guaraní people, who migrated from Brazil and Paraguay to Bolivia in various waves sometime before the arrival of the Spanish conquistadores. Most likely, they left Brazil and Paraguay because of an economic crisis caused by demographic growth and reduction in food supply. Perhaps their migration was spurred also by stories of a fertile land of happiness and plenty, rich in metals, with houses of stone—the "land without evil" [*tierra sin ma*l] of Guaraní mythology.[1]

The Guaraní are famed for having resisted subjugation by Spanish soldiers and missionaries longer and more effectively than most other indigenous groups. Likewise, they fiercely defended themselves against persecution by successive Bolivian regimes. From their arrival, they subdued other tribes, especially the sedentary, agricultural, Arawak-speaking Chané Indians, with whom they then mixed. In fact, the Inca term for the Guaraní, *chiriguano*, means mestizo and was used pejoratively. In recent years, chiriguano has come to replace the less specific term Guaraní among many scholars, though not necessarily among Guaraní advocates. The back of Guaraní resistance was broken at the bloody battle of Kurukuy in 1892, in which the Bolivian army suffered four dead, while an estimated 900 Guaraní lost their lives.[2]

The Guaraní today make up a small minority of Bolivia's 8 million people; indeed, the 3 million speakers of Guaraní are divided among Bolivia, Brazil, Paraguay, and Argentina. The Quechua comprise about 30 per cent of Bolivia's total population; the Aymara, 25 per cent; mestizos, perhaps 25 to 30 per cent; Europeans, roughly 5 to 15 per cent; and the Guaraní, 1 per cent. Spanish, Quechua, Aymara, and Guaraní are all official languages. Most of Bolivia's 80,000 Guaraní live in the arid, inhospitable Chaco region of the southeast. Though a small portion of the Chaco in the department of Tarija lies in a tropical zone, most of it is desiccated and dotted with thorny scrub vegetation, a desert briefly transformed into a verdant oasis with the arrival of life-giving seasonal rains. The sparsely populated Chaco, which comprises Santa Cruz, Cordillera, Chuquisaca, and Tarija departments and borders Paraguay and Argentina, is

GONZALO SEGUNDO

home to the 2,500 Guaraní of O'Connor province in Tarija, the site of this study, where they survive by growing corn and working on neighboring ranches.[3]

A local census carried out in 1989 showed that illiteracy among the Guaraní of O'Connor province stood at 95 per cent.[4] In this they are not unusual, for education has been slow in coming to all of Bolivia's indigenous peoples. Generous Bolivian government statistics proclaim a national literacy rate of 78 per cent, but a less inflated estimate would be more credible. Indeed, illiteracy is widespread among large segments of Bolivia's indigenous population.

The Roman Catholic church has never been as strong in Bolivia as in most other Latin American countries. In the Chaco, Dominicans, Franciscans, and Jesuits avidly sought to convert and protect the recalcitrant Guaraní, who, viewing the missions as a threat to their communal life and traditions, engaged in periodic rebellions. The story of the missions, or *reducciones* [reductions] in the frontier areas, for example, is one of hardship, deprivation, frustration, and constant danger, for many a priest fell victim to hostile arrows and to the intrigues of suspicious *hacendados* [owners of large cattle estates]. The Guaraní also resisted enclosure in the confined space of the missions, because they were accustomed to open areas and frequent migrations. Missions required chores and strict discipline; in particular, it meant that parents had to send their children to mission school. To the Guaraní, this practice amounted to a renunciation of their own way of initiating children into communal life. Further, the missionary model was a planned, urban community, whereas Guaraní settlements were spontaneous and varied. Forms of authority were different from Guaraní structures of government in which the village assembly decided all important matters.[5] On the other hand, the missions offered security and protection, food, and, for some, a chance to become like the Spanish, to use tools, and to tend cattle.

Even today, some Guaraní continue to repel or subvert attempts to "civilize" or Christianize them. For this reason, it is extraordinary that, since the early 1970s, a handful of quiet, hardworking North American missionary nuns have become respected neighbors of the Guaraní communities of O'Connor province. The sisters live out the "option for the poor" in their "accompaniment" of the Guaraní and neighboring mestizo populations—that is, through living with them on a daily basis and experiencing the world through their eyes. We will return to the Sisters of the Presentation later, but for now it is important to point out that, for the most part, the Guaraní have regarded agents of civilization, white missionaries, the military, and other authorities, as unwelcome *karai*, the descriptive Guaraní word for foreigners, which literally means lice.[6] To make their attitude even clearer, many Guaraní today still use the terms *cristiano* and karai interchangeably.

The Guaraní of the Chaco for most of the twentieth century lived in almost total isolation, with little or no government services. Yet, they have been profoundly, if indirectly, affected by national political and economic conditions. This crucial but often overlooked point must be appreciated if their situation is to be understood.

Bolivia is nominally a democratic republic; however, it is notorious for its political instability and economic dependency. From independence in 1825 to the end of the first regime of General Hugo Banzer in 1978, Bolivians endured 189 *golpes* [coups]. As the poorest, weakest, most unstable country in South America, and the one that has been most plagued by musical-chair military coups, Bolivia has been the caboose on the South American train. Its history is one of government by white oligarchs and dictators and of ever-growing dependence on foreign capital, even to conduct day-to-day affairs of state. Its governments have rested on a rigid caste system intended to exclude the overwhelming majority of the population—Indians and *cholos* [urban Indians or mestizos]—from participation in national life. Moreover, Bolivian governments have typically neglected agriculture, transportation, education, and public health, and, except for the 1952 revolution, have exhibited a blind faith in laissez-faire capitalism that has backfired tragically. These arrangements have kept the Indian majority, including the Guaraní, impoverished and disenfranchised, and the country bankrupt.

During the first half of the twentieth century, the Guaraní teetered on the brink of extinction. The battle of Kurukuy in 1892 had shattered their resistance to government authority, and there appeared to be little hope for their future. In some Guaraní communities, as much as 80 per cent of the population emigrated to Argentina to work in the sugar cane harvests or on haciendas. Historian Alfred Metraux called the diminution of the population "chilling" and lamented that the causes were always the same: "the injustices and oppressions of the mestizo and white landowners and the shameful misery that comes as a consequence."[7]

Those Guaraní who became *zafreros* [harvesters] in northern Argentina worked in the sugar cane fields for months or years at a time, and sometimes they moved on to haciendas of patrones [large land owners] in the Bolivian Chaco. Rapidly modernizing Argentina was the preferred locale, because the Guaraní generally received better treatment there and could obtain tools and clothing. Noted ethnologist Francisco Pifarré estimates that 26,000 Guaraní emigrated to Argentina in the early decades of the twentieth century, while perhaps 80,000 Guaraní and mestizos, with armed escort, were sent to the northern jungles to work on Bolivia's rubber plantations, never to return.[8]

With the disastrous Chaco War (1932-35), the Guaraní dispersed even more, either to escape military service or to assist the Guaraní of Paraguay against the Bolivian army. This war was provoked by the Bolivian government in an attempt to distract attention from its miserable response to popular unrest brought on by massive layoffs, strikes, and mine closings during the Great Depression. Some 25 per cent of Bolivian combatants were killed, deserted, or died in captivity. The army was organized according to caste, with the whites as officers, the cholos as sub-officials, and the Indians as combatants, or more accurately, cannon fodder.[9] Many succumbed to thirst and starvation in the forbidding Chaco, while others gave their lives in ill-planned encounters executed by incompetent leaders, many of whom themselves deserted. All in all, about 15,000 Guaraní were lost to Argentina, Paraguay, the interior of Bolivia, or to death by diverse causes during the Chaco War.[10] A haunting scene of bloodshed and death is recalled by a Guaraní witness:

> I don't know why there was a war. Blood was flowing, the trees were cut to pieces.... Many, many skeletons. The *collas* [Bolivians] and the *pilas* [Paraguayans], many, many dead. The trees were slashed by Bolivians who wore gold rings on their hands. People didn't want to die; but they cut the poor person's head off. Ugly, ugly. The poor boys who entered the war, they cut their heads off. Ugly, ugly.[11]

The few remaining Guaraní were rapidly absorbed by haciendas suffering from an acute labor shortage due to the mass exodus of workers to Argentina. That country, however, was no longer importing beef from the Bolivian Cordillera province, a market loss that caused the backward hacienda system to stagnate even further, a state of affairs which persists today.

On the national level, the disaffected "Chaco generation" sought to deliver Bolivia from the twin evils of an antiquated hacienda system and outside control of national affairs. The MNR (*Movimiento Nacional Revolucionario*, National Revolutionary Movement), an uneasy coalition of rightist and leftist interests, both workers and middle-class supporters, came to power in 1952 after issuing arms to the populace at large and overwhelming the Bolivian army. The MNR's populist and nationalist platform enjoyed widespread support. It seemed to offer a hopeful alternative to the elitism, racism, incompetence, corruption, and dependence on foreign capital that had characterized previous governments. MNR president Víctor Paz Estenssoro immediately abolished the literacy requirement for voting and established universal suffrage, thereby enfranchising the majority of Bolivians for the first time, including virtually 100 per cent of the indigenous population. Paz Estenssoro also drastically reduced the bloated military, supported the creation of a national labor union, the COB (Central Obrera Boliviana, Bolivian Workers Central), and nationalized the mines.

Land reform came the following year, in 1953. It was intended to free the indigenous and mestizo campesinos from centuries-old oppression under Bolivia's classic *latifundia* system: large inefficient estates run by predominantly absentee landlords and worked by Indians and mestizos under serf-like conditions. The MNR's Agrarian Reform Act of 1953 abolished the latifundia system and obligatory work service. The reform was carried out in those areas where Indians and campesinos had been most organized and politically active, notably in the Aymara and Quechua communities whose members belonged to unions, or syndicates, the entities selected to administer the MNR's reform. Lands were granted to the rural populations with the stipulation that they could not be individually sold; the intent was to create a new type of community-conscious peasantry.[12]

Unfortunately, the Guaraní, who already were very community-conscious but who belonged to no such syndicates, were bypassed in the distribution of land and titles. The Guaraní of the provinces of the Chaco, Hernando Siles, Luis Calvo, and Cordillera were especially unlucky. There, the hacendados had actively supported the MNR, which meant that white and mestizo landholders were rewarded by being granted titles to their land. Thus, the Guaraní, ironically, found themselves worse off because of agrarian reform. For example, Francisco Pifarré points out that even today in the area of Río Grande, part of the Cordillera province, only 6.71 per cent of lands are in the hands of Guaraní communities; the rest of the arable lands, 93.3 per cent, are in the hands of *hacendados latifundistas* [owners of extremely large holdings] who scarcely utilize them for cultivation.[13]

The Guaraní never accepted the redistribution of land they regarded as theirs. Today they await the legalization of their claims to title under the new Agrarian Reform Act of 1996, by which surveys carried out by the National Institute of Agrarian Reform (INRA) will determine the parameters of a proposed Guaraní Territory in the Chaco. The government has agreed to grant the Guaraní usufruct—use of the land—but they will not be able to sell or divide it. This arrangement is like that of the Extractive Reserves in the Amazon, where tappers and other traditional peoples enjoy use rights, but it is different in some major respects. For one thing, title will eventually be held by the Guaraní people as a whole, rather than by the national government, as is the case in Brazil.

Meanwhile, difficulties besides the 1953 Agrarian Reform Act affected the Guaraní. Despite its every effort, the revolutionary government of 1952 almost immediately became overwhelmed by insurmountable economic problems to the extent that it simply could not afford to finance its own reforms or feed the nation. Despite its nationalist posture, the government was forced to knuckle under and seek US capital, just as previous oligarchic governments had done. Bolivia was the first Latin

American country to receive a food export grant from the US, and, by 1960, it was the largest recipient of US foreign aid in Latin America and the highest per capita in the world. Moreover, Bolivia depended on the US to provide directly one-third of its operating budget. This dependency exacted the harsh price of permitting US private corporations to invest in Bolivian oil once again, though memories of Standard Oil's betrayal of Bolivia by secretly selling oil to Paraguay during the Chaco War were painfully fresh. Further, the US insisted on resumption of payments on previous loans, which forced Bolivia to accept an IMF monetary stabilization program that brought spending on social and economic programs to a sudden halt.[14] The MNR presidency of Paz Estenssoro's successor, Siles Zuazo (1956-60), accepted the IMF's 1957 dictates because survival was impossible without US patronage.

As Bolivia's dependency increased, so, too, did the economic and political hardships borne by the poor, including the Guaraní. As protests, strikes, and hunger marches gave popular expression to the growing desperation of Bolivia's impoverished majority, the military moved in to take control of the country. The military interregnum from 1964-82, with some ephemeral exceptions, may be summed up in three words: repression, hyperinflation, and dependency. Dictatorship and the illegal cocaine trade, in which the army became deeply involved, further weakened Bolivia's already feeble national institutions and autonomy.

Given these circumstances, there was no national institution strong enough to stand up to the dictatorship. Labor unions and religious groups were singled out by terrorist squads. The COB syndicate described the lonely position of the vulnerable population in 1980: "the people have been absolutely orphaned of any institution that might care for their economic interests or human rights."[15]

Religious workers, human rights advocates, proponents of syndicates such as the *Movimiento Campesinos en Marcha* [Movement of Campesinos on the March, MCM], indeed anyone who worked with the poor—who are predominantly Indian—became targets of intimidation, arrest, and "disappearance" by hooded, paramilitary terrorists. Widespread persecution took place during the Brazilian dictatorship (1964-85) as well, but the Brazilian church is a much stronger national institution, occupying a position of great moral authority. It provided a powerful and consistent defense of the human rights of all Brazilians. In Acre, for example, the church protected the Indians and rubber tappers and stood as a counterforce not to be taken lightly by military governments. This was not the case with the Bolivian church either nationally or in the Chaco.

By 1983, the foreign debt represented 80 per cent of Bolivia's gross domestic product, a brief tin boom was over, and the country spiraled into hyperinflation, with the government of Siles Zuazo (1982-85) printing more money until inflation hit 8,170 per cent in 1985.[16] Paz Estenssoro (1985-89) took office again, and in 1985 adopted the draconian New Economic Plan (NEP), also known as Decree #21060, which squeezed the poor in its vise-like provisions. Termed a free-market "shock treatment" by Paz Estenssoro, the decree deregulated prices, eliminated subsidies and price supports, devalued the currency, and suspended foreign debt payments.[17] The impact was immediate, with a 20 per cent rise in urban unemployment, massive migration of "relocated" workers as tin mines were closed, and more hunger in both the city and the countryside.

In rural areas of the department of Tarija the situation had been critical for some time. The Sisters of the Presentation in a 1982 newsletter expressed alarm at the helplessness of the campesinos of Tarija who could not afford to feed their families, and they criticized the Bolivian government for its abject dependency on foreign aid. In a 1989 issue of *El Catequista*, the Sisters called for the repeal of Decree 21060, citing the extensive hunger and suffering it had caused the poor. The Bolivian people, according to one expert, were already "probably the most undernourished in the hemisphere."[18]

In their arguments on behalf of the rural poor, the sisters appealed to Catholic social doctrine on equitable land distribution, reproducing the comments made by Pope John Paul II on his historic visit to Bolivia in 1988:

> The social doctrine of the Church has been constant in [maintaining] that the goods of creation have been destined by God for the service and utility of all God's children ... [and] in accordance with this doctrine the Church itself has always preached the equitable distribution of lands for cultivation ... in order to give to the campesino the possibility of a dignified life that permits the holistic education of his children and necessary progress in his health, method of work and marketing—at just prices—of his products.[19]

Unfortunately, the Bolivian government's NEP works against the "equitable distribution of lands," the "dignified life," and the "just prices" advocated by the pontiff. The devastating effect of Decree 21060 in rural areas was the subject of a survey of 172 campesino communities and a conference held in 1987 to analyze the ways in which the structural adjustment, designed by the IMF and the World Bank, "punishes the campesino agrarian sector" [*castiga al sector agrario campesino*].[20] The overwhelming complaint expressed was that Decree 21060 significantly increased Bolivia's dependency on food from abroad:

> In summary, Decree 21060 stimulated the transnationalization of the Bolivian food system, aggravating to an extreme our alimentary dependence since the free importation of agricultural products did not improve the efficiency of national agriculture. It did not guarantee that internal food prices would be regulated by international prices because the international markets are oligopolized. This means that commercial food importers have not sold in the internal market at the international price (in many cases substantially lower than the national one) but rather that they sell at speculative prices.[21]

As a consequence of the food dependency exacerbated by the NEP, indigenous cultures are threatened with erasure, because imported agricultural products flood the market and force out locally grown crops.[22] In *Resistencia campesina*, the authors of the study of the NEP's effects clearly recognize the relationship between Bolivia's lack of sovereignty, incarnated in the neoliberal provisions of the NEP, and the deterioration of the daily lives of Bolivia's campesino and indigenous groups. Guido Chumiray, national leader of the *Asamblea del Pueblo Guaraní* [Guaraní People's Assembly, APG], urged the government to intervene on behalf of the survival of the Guaraní people. Speaking in favor of the designation of a Guaraní territory, Chumiray stressed the Guaraní's need for vital services. Acknowledging that the government possessed scant resources, Chumiray suggested that, when government funds ran out, the state call on NGOs to fill the gaps, even though, when NGOs departed, the poor would be once again left stranded:

> Our idea is that all the plans for development of the indigenous communities should be carried forward by the state. If sometimes there aren't enough resources, there are institutions that help like the NGOs for example; but we believe that this should be something that the state supports, because at times plans of external cooperation end, and then we are left without that as well. I want to say that within our conception of our vision of integration, we believe that there should be more support from the state.[23]

In other words, campesino and Guaraní leaders were acutely aware of the relationship between the country's lack of real autonomy and their own increasing difficulties in feeding themselves and their families. Indigenous populations also realized that the result, if not the expressed intent, of the structural adjustments required by the NEP was to airbrush their cultures right out of the national picture.

Bolivia's historic dependency has been exacerbated by massive importation of foodstuffs. These imports have brought only hunger and degradation to the Guaraní farmers because they deprive them of their already meagre markets while pricing foodstuffs out of their reach. Economic decisions vital to the daily existence of the Guaraní are made thousands of miles away by a handful of individuals in global lending institutions who are accountable to no national group and certainly not to impoverished Indians.

Meanwhile, the Bolivian state accelerates its retreat from providing public services, which, except for the Revolution of 1952, has been one of its most constant features. Anthropologist Lesley Gill, in her study of the city of El Alto, observes that the Bolivian government has withdrawn to such an extent that state institutions, save for the military, scarcely touch people's daily lives at all any more.[24] Industries from transportation to communication, from tin mining to oil exploration, have been, or are becoming, privatized and squeeze the poor even tighter.

An increasingly unwieldy array of overlapping NGOs has sprung up in an attempt to fill the gap. Some of these perform vital functions typically carried

GUARANÍ WOMAN SHELLING PEAS, POTRERILLOS

out by national or local governments, such as securing potable water or building roads. It is difficult to imagine how most Bolivians and certainly the
Guaraní would survive at all today without the essential services offered by NGOs.
In the murky world of NGO sponsorship, one finds that the distinction between
governmental and nongovernmental is none too clear. For example, USAID, an
agency of the US government, is one of the largest and most important NGOs
active in Bolivia.[25] Funding sources of NGOs include liberal European and
North American groups that are holdovers from a more progressive period. They
sponsor community projects, education, and women's programs, although they
face an increasingly conservative climate for themselves in their home base as
well as for their organizations in Bolivia. Religious groups—Catholic,
Protestant, Mennonite, and other—are among the most longstanding of the
NGOs. They provide vital social, educational, and health services; a consistent
presence; and a defense of human rights. The Catholics and mainline Protestants
tend to offer a social model inspired by liberation theology, while other denominations project one more centered in individual morality and personal salvation. More recent neoliberal NGOs also sponsor much-needed community
projects and have been very effective, but they tend to require residents to
work or pay for services received.

Though NGOs unquestionably bring essential benefits, they are by no means uni-
versally acclaimed. For one thing, they are not accountable locally, for their sponsors are nearly all foreign; this is true even for the so-called "national" NGOs.
They often compete with one another and duplicate services, just as they do in Brazil,
and, however well-intentioned, they sometimes, as campesino leader Mario Gareca
says, promote their own vision at the expense of that of the community.[26]

The proliferation of NGOs is itself both a sign and a result of Bolivian development and dependency. It is also an indication of the difficulty of creating a broadly-based popular alternative to the poverty and social fragmentation that have been exacerbated by globalization. In her discussion of the relationship between the Bolivian state and development NGOs, Gill concludes that their increasing convergence "is less the result of the state's regulation of NGOs than the increasing control exercised over both by global financial institutions."[27]

Ironically, both economic plans crafted abroad and embraced by desperate governments and development projects sponsored by well-intentioned NGOs can conspire to erode indigenous cultures. In the case of the Guaraní, certain basic values, such as the preference for community and family over individual interests and their acknowledged connectedness to nature, are by no means rewarded by the global economy. Just as the Guaraní never espoused nineteenth-century liberalism or laissez-faire economics, so, too, have they rejected neoliberalism, for their worldview continues to be incompatible with individualistic capitalism. In order to understand fully this incompatibility, it is essential to appreciate the importance of the concept of relatedness to the Guaraní, their relatedness to nature and to each other in community.

The place to begin is with *maíz*, corn, for it is the fulcrum of Guaraní life. Corn constitutes the principal component in the Guaraní diet, the focus of their festivals, the fixed point of their calendar, and the basis of their economy. From corn one traditionally has attained social position, prestige, and political power. Respected ethnologist Bartomeu Meliá makes the important observation that without corn, a Guaraní is *desnaturalizado* [denaturalized], separated from nature, and from his identity.[28]

When the *choclo*, the first tender corn, is harvested, the pace of Guaraní social life picks up through *convites* [invitations] and fiestas. From then until the end of the harvest, women's tasks center around the preparation of *chicha*, the traditional corn drink, which may be alcoholic or non-alcoholic depending on the occasion and the length of fermentation. The women chew the corn, mixing it with their saliva, and then return it to the huge pot to continue cooking. Good chicha-making skills are a desirable trait in a bride because, for the Guaraní, chicha is all important. Fray Bernardino de Niño, writing in 1912, understood well the significance of *kangui*, or chicha, describing it as, for the Guarani, "his coffee, his soup, his wine, his dinner, his everything" [*su café, su caldo, su vino, su comida, su todo*].[29] This observation still holds true today.

The Guaraní practice a communal system of landholding. Traditionally each family was granted its parcel by community consensus, and conflicts were arbitrated by the chief. Division of labor among the Guaraní is according to gender. Men work clearing, weeding, burning the fields, and planting and harvesting corn. Planting beans and other food crops is women's work, as are cooking and chicha preparation. As with the rubber tappers, childcare is also women's work. However, the extent to which Guaraní fathers are involved in their children's supervision, education, and day-to-day lives is remarkable. They are gentle fathers; child abuse is rare, since the family unit is everything. Working in *motirō* [workgroups] is characteristic, not just for agricultural tasks but also for raising houses, clearing debris and stones from roads and paths, and building fences. The motirō is a deeply ingrained form of cooperation. The Guaraní prefer working in groups to working alone and invite others to work with them; this is true for both women and men.

The glue that holds the society of extended family units together is *reciprocidad* [reciprocity]. The basis of Guaraní social and economic relations, reciprocity involves the production and distribution of goods and a way of interacting with others. Reciprocity is not barter, as practiced by the rubber tappers, but rather a voluntary offering to someone else that does not require the receipt of something of an equivalent value in exchange. It is a gift; however, it does create a desire, not an obligation, for restitution. The best expression of reciprocity is the festive convite; the prestige of an individual, a household, or even a community is measured by its capacity to *convidar*. The expansive convite creates an obligation on the part of recipients who respond with diverse forms of generosity, such as moral support or participation in community jobs.[30] One can imagine the problems, complex and fundamental, that arise when one tries to determine how to integrate this indigenous economy into a market system.

The system of reciprocity depends on the convite, its most visible expression, and is sealed by the sharing of chicha. This custom has been vigorously defended by the Guaraní over the centuries in their contacts with outsiders, including Spanish authorities, missionaries, and NGOs. Padre Giannecchini, in his richly annotated *Diccionario*, understood the importance of the convite: "without these invitations and friendly get-togethers, each one would become independent and the tribe would dissolve" [*sin estas invitaciones y reuniones amistosas cada uno se independizaría y la tribu se disolvería*].[31] The diminution of convites and the abuse of alcohol, whether chicha or other forms, indicate hard times and increased dependence on economic sources from outside the community. Facundo Galeán, the captain of the village of Ñaurenda, addresses the serious problem of alcohol abuse in his candid interview, which follows.

Central to the chicha fiesta brought about by the convite is the *arete*, in which participants join hands and dance in a circle. The purpose of the dance is to celebrate the abundance of maíz and chicha and to forget times of scarcity. If the convite and the chicha are the cake, the arete is the icing. Affluence and generosity go hand in hand for the Guaraní. This is one reason that Guaraní culture has been so seriously damaged by grinding poverty, for, over the years, hunger, scarcity, and population decline have greatly reduced the number of convites and, therefore, the occasions one celebrates with the arete.

In his illuminating discussion of Guaraní culture, Meliá explains that, for the Guaraní, the worst shame is to be too poor to make chicha and, therefore, to be unable to carry out convites or obtain the cooperation needed for work in one's field or to build one's house. One who is poor has little corn and few relatives to supply obligatory solidarity, nor can he initiate the convite.[32] This is a very different view of poverty from that put forward by development organizations and international agribusiness, which deem people poor "because they do not participate overwhelmingly in the market economy, and do not consume commodities produced for and distributed though the market."[33]

The most authentic Guaraní political institution is the assembly, or community meeting. Bartomeu Meliá has described it as a type of generalized reciprocity in which what is exchanged is the free gift of the word, speech. The assembly determines the rules of the village and the rules of the convite; thus, when the economy of reciprocity becomes broken, the assembly no longer has meaning and disappears. Although the *mburuvicha*, or chief, presides over the assembly, ultimate authority is always retained by the group. Over the years, the karai have sought to promote the power of the captains at the expense of the community assembly. Meliá observes that the resulting *karaización* [becoming more like mestizos] "of the Guaraní world is in direct relation to the weakening of the assembly."[34] Within the community, the captain who imposes consensus is not regarded as strong; he is viewed as powerful only when he seeks and carries out the popular will. With such a strong community ethic, it is not surprising that the major Guaraní complaint about neoliberal policies is that they work to weaken this basic institution.

Some Guaraní, like members of other indigenous groups, are nominal Catholics, but much of their old religion remains. Though official figures show the Bolivian people are 95 per cent Roman Catholic, it would be more accurate to say that the majority of the population espouses a popular, indigenous, and/or syncretic form of Catholicism, while a rapidly increasing minority follows mainstream Protestant, Pentecostal, or other evangelical faiths. Most Guaraní believe in the *ija*—spirit-owners of the forests, fields, and river valleys—and in the *aña*—malefic versions of those same spirits. Observable in the daily life of the Guaraní is the figure of the *ipaje*, or *mbaekuaa*, or shaman. The prophetic shamans embody the Guaraní concept of the "divine" word as something given to chosen ones, who then become exceptional. The ipajes are beneficent shamans whose gifts are used for the welfare of the community, while the mbaekuaa usually represent malign forces. The ipajes are often advisors to chiefs, for they are empowered to interpret supernatural phenomena.[35] Moreover, they possess specialized gifts: one can bring rain, another can prophesy, while a third can cure ailments. The gift of healing is especially prized by the Guaraní, most of whom still consult *curanderos* [healers] today. The work of the traditional curandero/a, who is often also a *partera* [midwife], is described for us in two interviews with elderly practitioners.

For many Guaraní today, belief in good and evil spirits and in Christian practices, be they Catholic or Pentecostal, coexist. Though they intermingle syncretically to a considerable extent, they do not do so to the degree observed in the popular Catholicism of the rubber tappers. Rather, the two systems tend to co-exist in separate spheres. For example, in recent baptism ceremonies in several villages in O'Connor province, the Guaraní expressed interest in social benefits to be derived from baptism, like strengthening their acceptance among the non-Guaraní population, improving their status and self-image—those who are baptized are *gente de razón* [people of reason]—and attaining respectability through having a certificate of baptism, which serves as official identification for themselves and their children. Some also hoped that baptism would help them live better lives and become better people, while one elderly curandera thought baptism might help her arthritis. In her mind, baptism supplemented, but did not replace, her traditional medicine.

Thus, there are as many reasons for baptism as there are Guaraní who have chosen to participate in this basic Christian rite; however, in no instance is the appeal of the ipajes or *tumpas* [gods] diminished.[36] In fact, the native spirits remain untouched by baptism, for they reside in the sacred sphere of nature, while Christian rituals are more social and utilitarian. This is not to say that baptism is not a meaningful and deeply moving rite of passage for members of Guaraní communities today, for it is; or that it does not perform a profoundly spiritual function in validating a sense of personal, community, and even Christian identity, for it does. It is to say, however, that baptism and Christianity exist alongside, in parallel with traditional Guaraní beliefs.

The Guaraní of O'Connor province illustrate the struggle of traditional peoples to live with dignity, keeping intact their language, belief system, and basic values. Their 38 communities radiate north and east from the nearest large town of Entre Ríos, population 2,000. The Guaraní who have shared their personal histories for this study represent the communities of Ñaurenda, Saladito, Agua Buena, Potrerillos, and Yukimbia. In these and neighboring communities, residents shuttle back and forth, seeking work and visiting relatives, so that strict community lines are impossible to draw. A number of settlements were begun by Indians who withdrew to remote O'Connor in order to escape the patrones of the Cordillera, who were known for their cruelty.

The struggle of the Guaraní, like that of the rubber tappers, takes place within the broader context of a clash between two diametrically opposed attitudes toward the land: one advocating land use rights for the community and the other claiming private ownership for individuals. Hence, the clash of cultures and world views came to O'Connor province with the Agrarian Reform Act of 1953, concretized in the figure of the patrón. At that time, the Guaraní were very few in number and lived a reclusive, hermit-like existence in O'Connor. Their culture was degraded and in tatters; their numbers dangerously reduced after the devastation of the Chaco War and the subsequent haemorrhage of migration to Argentina. The diaspora and near genocide of the Guaraní produced severe demographic and psychological effects among the defeated remnants of their people.

A few Guaraní, however, had begun to create a peaceful and relatively prosperous life for themselves, only to have it shattered by the arrival of the karai—in this case, patrones. Respected elder Captain Sambo Gutiérrez, now in his late 80s, recalls learning how to hunt with bow and arrow as a boy and enjoying the many convites in his native village of Tentayape in a time before there were patrones and when Indians worked their own land.[37] Porfirio Novillo of Saladito, in his late 60s, relates how his father made soap, *cuajada* [soft cheese], and *quesillo* [melted cheese and rolled tortilla], which he sold on an itinerant basis. Porfirio sums up his placid existence before 1953, a time when he had corn and cattle, as *una vida feliz, no había cristianos por acá* [a happy life, there were no Christians (outsiders) around here].[38] However, when the "Christians" came, the Guaraní were no match for them; as the ranchers took over, the Guaraní were forced to acquiesce.

The principal patrones in the area were the powerful O'Connor and D'Arlach families, who for over a century controlled politics and real estate in the province. Those mestizos who worked for O'Connor as administrators or overseers of his vast holdings benefited directly from the Agrarian Reform Act of 1953. Doña Elvira Vaca de Vásquez, daughter of Antonio Vaca, former employee of O'Connor and later himself a harsh patrón of the local Guaraní, recalls that her father purchased land from the O'Connor family and obtained legal title through the 1953 reform. Doña Elvira remembers that O'Connor was *duro, duro* [extremely hard] on both peons and former employees like her father.[39] Dr. Guillermo Arancibia, currently Chief Justice of the Bolivian Supreme Court, was shocked when, as a young sociologist conducting field research, he observed the conditions under which the Guaraní peons lived and worked; they were, he says, treated "like slaves." [40]

For the most part, the mestizos who became patrones in O'Connor province after 1953 were not exceptionally wealthy men; they were not especially cruel; and they did not seek to eradicate the Guaraní. Some were recent arrivals; others had lived in the province for many generations. However, they all shared the deep-seated racism toward Indians that has plagued the nation since the conquest. The patrones bullied, threatened, cajoled, produced incomprehensible pieces of paper, and, when necessary, appeared with a show of force to take possession of their claims. For nearly 40 years, a few constables with antiquated shotguns were able to intimidate the Guaraní of O'Connor province, powerless remnants of a once indomitable nation, now indebted peons on their own lands.

Porfirio Novillo remembers how painful it was to go from being his own master to being a vassal. Above all, he recalls the sense of isolation that engulfed him: "In those days, we did not live in community. There was no unity, no spirit, everyone just set out to work individually, alone. You were isolated. There was no help of any kind, of any institution, nothing, nothing, nothing."[41] Nevertheless, like tender shoots of corn in rocky soil, as early as the 1970s extraordinary signs of change began to occur at the local level, change that would ultimately offer hope and restore dignity to the Guaraní.

First, the missionary Sisters of the Presentation opened an academy in the mestizo town of Entre Ríos in 1973. The *hermanas* [sisters] offered classes in typing and sewing to Spanish-speaking residents of the town, though not to the Guaraní who lived in outlying settlements, and they assisted the local priest in traditional duties. The sisters brought with them a social gospel that expressed clearly the preferential option for [the church's special commitment to] the poor in their every activity. For example, they began taking their classes, like sewing, to the outlying campesino communities where women could benefit their entire family by learning a valued skill. They opened a pharmacy in Entre Ríos and began offering classes in natural medicines. Area residents were too poor to buy standard medicines, nor did they know how to use medicinal plants native to the region. The sisters, along with local medical personnel, Spanish volunteers, and ACLO [*Acción Cultural Loyola*], a Jesuit-sponsored NGO, trained *promotores de salud* [health promoters] who lived in outlying communities and came to Entre Ríos for comprehensive workshops offered on several levels. Those who completed the advanced level were qualified to give injections and assist in childbirth.

Sectors of the Bolivian Catholic church had actively been promoting human rights and social justice for decades. The sisters worked with the diocese of Tarija in this area as they began catechism classes in the rural areas, in addition to the middle-class town of Entre Ríos. This rural pastorate [*pastoral rural*], which reached its apogee in the 1980s, not only prepared catechists [lay pastoral readers] for local communities, but it also became the training ground for future community leaders and directors of the local peasant's syndicate, much as we observed in the case of the Brazilian rubber tappers. Neither the rural pastorate nor the sewing and other classes sponsored by the *hermanas* reached the distant Guaraní communities; however, they were very important to the Guaraní nonetheless. For example, the campesino pastoral leaders, who were often also health promoters and respected members of their *pueblos* [villages], began to organize politically. As they did so, they themselves put the social gospel into practice by speaking out against the human rights abuses of the military dictatorships and, later, against the neoliberal NEP.

In 1982, in their regular newsletter to far-flung members of their order, the Sisters of the Presentation expressed solidarity with campesinos who were protesting spiraling inflation that made it almost impossible either to sell their goods or to purchase necessities. The sisters saw the peasants' protest, the work of Jesuit-supported Radio Tarija, and the rural catechist program that they themselves were wholeheartedly promoting as "making a difference."[42] Moreover, in various 1982 issues of *El Catequista* [The Catechist], a newsletter put out by the sisters on behalf of the diocese and intended for the campesino catechists, they denounced the government's abuse of human rights and urged catechists to take an active role in building a church that defends the poor and fights injustice. In various *El Catequista* bulletins, one sees citations from the Puebla meeting of Latin American bishops, which reaffirmed the church's option for the poor, interspersed with instructions on the medicinal uses of certain plants for a population too poor to buy medicine and directions for building latrines.[43]

Most rural pastoral agents became active members of the campesino movement [MCM], which sprang into action after the promulgation of the NEP in 1985. Campesino leader Gareca is a case in point. He recalls:

The church formed me; it gave me the first tools. It was the same for many of my companions. I'd say 80 per cent of the MCM comes from a Christian formation. Now if the church later condemned us a bit, well, we had a big problem with the special pastorates, and if at one time they called us communists, well, we have to remember that the church showed us the way. We should not reject that; I in no way regret it; I am proud of it. Sometimes I criticize the church, but it showed me the way.

He went on to say that the purpose of the MCM was to defend campesino lands from "assault by the oligarchy."[44] The defense featured rallies and protests against evictions of campesinos from their homes, repression by paramilitary organizations, and the silencing of Radio Tarija in 1986, the *antorcha* [beacon of hope] for the beleaguered campesino. The MCM depended on *reporteros populares* [popular reporters], like Feliciano Tárraga whose story follows, to keep close tabs on the local pulse. The reporters, most of whom, unlike Tárraga, were illiterate, would record instances of abuse, or simply items of interest to neighboring communities, and send the tapes to Tarija where they would be aired. In most communities, there were a few people who had radios, and in this way news was disseminated, communities came to know each other, and a sense of solidarity began to emerge. These were predominantly mestizo organizations and concerns; however, the MCM demonstrated solidarity with the Guaraní at crucial junctures, as we will see, and they repeatedly urged the Guaraní to organize in order to throw off the yoke of the patrón. Little by little, the work of the sisters, the health promoters, the catechists, and the MCM became known to the Guaraní. They began to believe that perhaps things could improve after all.

In the meantime, concomitant with these efforts, important changes were beginning to take place within the village of Ñaurenda. This small community of 227 inhabitants claims at least two natural leaders, Feliciano Tárraga and the late matriarch Nicasia, whose visionary leadership opened villagers' minds to the importance of education and to the basket-weaving project for women, now a crucial mainstay for Guaraní families. As was the case with the rubber tappers in Acre, the development of local leadership in O'Connor has been the critical precondition for fanning the embers of hope and overcoming fatalism and despair. Later, Jorge Gallardo (Machirope) of Saladito, whose story follows, became a forceful advocate of education and a respected Guaraní leader in the province.

Tárraga and Gallardo, for different reasons, were both deeply committed to building a school for the children of the community. When one considers the appalling literacy statistics for the Guaraní at the time and the discouraging figures for Bolivia as a whole, one can appreciate that it must have seemed a pipe dream, even to other villagers, to speak of a school of one's own in the early 1980s. But with the leadership and material assistance provided by Dr. Arancibia and CODETAR [*Corporación de Desarrollo de Tarija*] as well as the prestige of Nicasia, villagers became persuaded that a school was both essential and possible. Ñaurendans conspired secretly at night to plan their strategy. Finally, they summoned the courage to defy the patrón, who had angrily opposed their plan, but who reluctantly acquiesced when Dr. Arancibia convinced him that it would be in his interest not to oppose the school. The historic founding of the school in 1982 and its remarkable evolution into a *ciclo básico* offering grades 1-8 and the beginnings of a *ciclo medio* (grades 9-12) are detailed in interviews with Tárraga and Machirope. The school victory marks the first collective sign of Guaraní agency in O'Connor province during the time of the patrones. As such, it constituted the critical first step in their journey toward personal and cultural autonomy. Moreover, Ñaurenda's success served as a catalyst, with other communities following suit in rapid succession, as one observes in the interview with Valerio Muñoz, the captain of Agua Buena.

Meanwhile, the MCM was engaging in ever bolder acts and communicating more frequently with the Guaraní, while the rural pastoral agents and health promoters continued their effective work in the countryside. Outside the province, a very important event took place, one which has proved to be of major importance in organizing the Guaraní. In 1987, in the town of Camiri, in the Cordillera, the *Asamblea del Pueblo Guaraní* was born. The APG has as its goals:

1. stimulating production so that the Guaraní can feed themselves (as we have seen, a major undertaking in Bolivia);
2. creating infrastructure;
3. promoting health and education, especially bilingual education; and
4. securing land titles or a territory for the Guaraní.[45]

The APG aimed to promote unity among the dispersed Guaraní and to help restore a strong sense of cultural identity.

In 1987, the Guaraní of O'Connor province were still so isolated that they were not only unaware of the APG, but also ignorant of the existence of other Guaraní outside the province. Sr. Maura McCarthy comments that, in 1988 when she accompanied Guaraní women to their first festival outside O'Connor, it was as if two different worlds met. The Guaraní of the Cordillera spoke Spanish as well as Guaraní, were articulate, and possessed a sense of group identity, while the women of O'Connor spoke only Guaraní, were not used to expressing their opinions, and dressed in the traditional *tipoy* [dress of brightly colored material fastened at each shoulder with a pin] with their cheeks painted red. It was an eye-opener for both groups.[46] In 1989, the APG began sending representatives to O'Connor to explain their organization and to encourage the Guaraní to organize themselves locally, revive the assembly, and free themselves from the patrón.

That same year, at a historic meeting in Ñaurenda, the Guaraní re-established the ancient institution of the community assembly. They created the first *capitanía* [captaincy] of Itika Guasu—that is, of the Pilcomayo river area of O'Connor—with Saravia Novillo of Potrerillos as first capitán and Machirope as second. The *Acta* [minutes] of that meeting stated the reasons that the Guaraní had voted to organize themselves through the assembly: *para la comunidad, los hijos, y con fin que no seamos esclavisado [sic] como estamos hoy día* [for the community, the children, and so that we will no longer be enslaved as we are today].[47] This was, literally, the declaration of independence from the patrón system for the Guaraní of O'Connor province. The *Acta* bore as official witness the thumbprints of all those present at this watershed event.

After the first official assembly, the pace of events accelerated. Villagers in Ñaurenda carried out the first land seizure in 1989, with Tárraga and Machirope among the leaders, and with the crucial assistance of the MCM, other groups, and Guaraní from neighboring communities. Ñaurendans claimed a parcel of land belonging to the patrón and cleared it for use by the community, as was traditional Guaraní practice. This constituted the third act of defiance by the same community. The circumstances and significance of the takeover are recounted with emotion in the interviews that follow.

Earlier that same year, McCarthy and her Bolivian colleague, former rural teacher Renán Sánchez, began visiting Guaraní communities to acquaint themselves with their needs by means of an informal survey. These visits evolved into an enduring partnership with the Guaraní for the dual purpose of helping them survive economically while they struggled to free themselves and of supporting all efforts to rescue and reaffirm their culture. The following year, McCarthy, Sánchez, and a Swiss couple doing volunteer work in the region created the Support Team for the Guaraní People (*Equipo de Apoyo al Pueblo Guaraní*, EAPG), which provided a structure through which to carry out their assistance activities, a story described in depth in McCarthy's interview.

At the same time, the Guaraní women of various communities began to improve the quality of the tightly woven, colorful palm baskets, which they began producing shortly after the founding of the school, when Dr. Arancibia and Nicasia brought two Mataca women to teach them to weave fine baskets in addition to their crude *cedazos* [sifters]. Today, the income from the sale of baskets allows the Guaraní to feed their families. Times are very hard, the neoliberal NEP is still in effect, and men still hire themselves out to the patrón just to make ends meet. Now they are employed as day laborers rather than peons, though, in practice, this is sometimes a distinction without a difference.

Between 1990 and 1995, 38 Guaraní communities in O'Connor organized themselves. This means that they held community assemblies, discussed and reached consensus on community issues, recorded their proceedings in official registers, formed communal work groups, elected captains, and held regular festivals. Twenty work groups began functioning in 1991, reviving the traditional Guaraní institution of the motirõ. Also in 1991, the APG commenced operating as a regular presence in O'Connor with the collaboration of the Support Team. In 1994, because the community and its advocates insisted, education officials granted Ñaurenda the first bilingual teacher in the area; her interview describes bilingual education there. Authorities also approved instruction in Guaraní and Spanish for

CAPITÁN SARAVIA, FIRST CAPTAIN OF ÑAURENDA

the first three grades. This was the year that the first *postas sanitarias* [health posts] were created in some villages and that the Peace Corps began sending volunteers to O'Connor to assist in tasks such as irrigation, honey production, and marketing baskets. In 1994 CERDET, a Tarija development NGO, began helping the Guaraní with various projects to diversify production; in addition, they have urged the Guaraní to pressure the government on the issue of a Guaraní territory.

In 1999, the Support Team succeeded in funding a housing project requested by the Indian communities in which the Guaraní themselves built 33 adobe brick houses with tile roofs and cement floors to replace their packed dirt, open-sided, thatched homes. Villagers in other communities, including Susana de Chávez of Yukimbia whose story follows, eagerly await the opportunity to build their own new homes. That same year, CERDET, with funds from the British Embassy, helped villagers of Ñaurenda construct new classrooms, which allowed children to study at the secondary level in their own community for the first time. The Support Team continues working with the Guaraní to solve water problems, to promote family vegetable gardens that vary the Guaraní's limited diet, and to assist in advancing villagers' educational objectives.

Indeed, it is remarkable how education has become the top priority in many villages. For example, the Guaraní of O'Connor enthusiastically participated in the national Guaraní literacy campaign carried out in 1992, in which literacy volunteers known as *kereimba*, the Guaraní term for young warrior, blanketed communities in an all-out attack on illiteracy. Both the kereimba usage and the 1992 date—the one-hundredth anniversary of the devastating defeat at Kurukuy—were highly symbolic. They demonstrate a renewed cultural energy, this time focused on inclusion rather than resistance, but with the crucial caveats that their culture and language be respected, via bilingual education, and their history rescued from official distortion. As national Guaraní spokesman Chumiray put it, it is important "that the state not manipulate our history, that it be told to us the way it happened...."[48]

The supreme value the Guaraní place on education is unlike that of the rubber tappers, for whom education is of vital importance but still second to efforts at economic organization—the cooperative, the syndicate, and experiments in economic diversification. Like the rubber tappers, the Guaraní desire literacy so that they will not be cheated by the boss or when they go into town, but, unlike the tappers, they see education as the means for preserving and transmitting their ethnic history and language. Further, for the Guaraní, education is the way for their children to succeed and perhaps someday become *profesionales*. For example, Paulina Tárraga, a teenager from the village of Ñaurenda, hopes to complete secondary school, then go to Tarija for professional training, after which she intends to return to work in her home community. When asked how she will manage to pay for her education, Paulina replies that her father has told her that he will take on more jobs.[49] For the profoundly family-oriented Guaraní, no sacrifice is too great where the future of their children is concerned.

One wonders if assistance from NGOs, in education as in everything else, will eventually undermine or overwhelm local communities, resulting in new forms of clientelism and dependency. Thus far, such has not been the case, because the Guaraní themselves have set their own priorities and strategies for realizing them. Indeed, the Support Team is very clear that the Guaraní themselves must determine their own needs and projects. With each act, the assembly has been fortified, work groups solidified, and the community reaffirmed. The by-laws of

VILLAGE OF YUKIMBIA

the workgroups in O'Connor province embody the basic value of the communitarian message: "we are all responsible."[50] It is certainly true that the Guaraní cannot yet survive on their own. However, the assistance they receive, unlike that dumped on the country as a whole, is intended ultimately to promote independence rather than dependence.

A major challenge facing the Guaraní is posed by the extensive oil and gas exploration currently under way in the Chaco. Renán Sánchez, president of the Support Team, who works in the drilling areas, is concerned about the health, environmental, and cultural dislocations caused by the concessions the Bolivian government has granted to transnational companies for the next 40 years. He fears that the petrochemical industry may prove to be the most powerful threat that globalization poses to the Guaraní.[51] It is ironic that this threat comes at the time when the Guaraní are awaiting the final disposition of their territory, intended to secure their economic and cultural survival.

The Guaraní, like the rubber tappers, wish to survive with dignity, work the land, and retain their cultural identity while also contributing to the broader society. It is an extremely delicate balance, but if they can continue to make accommodations to modernity while exacting accommodations in return, if they can retain the communal, assembly-based root of their culture which makes possible the system of reciprocity, then there is hope. The outcome is uncertain, for their story, like that of the rubber tappers, is still unfolding.

In the meantime, with the centrality of corn production to their culture, the Guaraní reaffirm their place in the natural cycle, and, with their emerging political skills, they demonstrate their determination to preserve their basic values, antithetical to those of globalization. As they await implementation of a Guaraní Territory, they illustrate the fundamental importance of local control over local resources, something both they and the rubber tappers realize, but that the Bolivian government thus far has been unable to act upon. Bolivia continues to be a dependent, indebted nation with its sovereignty severely compromised by the dictates of global lenders. The interviews that follow consistently illustrate the importance of community to the Guaraní, a value constantly undermined by the neoliberal agents of globalization. They describe life under the patrón system and the struggle to be free from it. They also show the staying power of traditional religious beliefs and healing practices and their complex relationship with modernity. These Guaraní voices speak with eloquent simplicity of the struggle for land and survival and of the crucial role that religion plays in both.

NOTES

1. Bartomeu Meliá, *Ñande Reko: Nuestro modo de ser* (La Paz: Centro de investigación y promoción del campesinado [CIPCA], 1988) 3.

2. Francisco Pifarré, *Los guaraní-chiriguano: historia de un pueblo* (La Paz: CIPCA, 1989) 385.

3. Jürgen Riester, *Textos sagrados de los guaraníes en Bolivia* (La Paz and Cochabamba: Ediorial "Los amigos del libro," 1984) 19.

O'Connor province was named after the Irish soldier of fortune who was rewarded by South American liberators Bolívar and Sucre for his role in the wars of independence from Spain. O'Connor was granted the amount of land that a mule could travel in one day; that land became O'Connor province.

4. Sr. Maura McCarthy, PBVM, "Hacia la tierra sin mal: proyecto de promoción guaraní." 1989, n.p. Unpublished study available in the library of the Academy of the Sisters of the Presentation, Entre Ríos, Tarija.

5. Pifarré 209-11.

6. Sr. Maura McCarthy, PBVM, "God and the Lice," *Oak Leaves* 23,1 (June 1997): 2.

7. Pifarré 393, 395. The Spanish reads: "las injusticias y opresiones de los propietarios mestizos y blancos y la vergonzosa miseria que deviene como consecuencia."

8. Pifarré 396-99.

9. Herbert S. Klein, *Bolivia: the Evolution of a Multi-Ethnic Society*, 2nd ed. (New York and Oxford: Oxford University Press, 1992) 193-94.

10. Pifarré 410.

11. Barbara Schuchard, "La conquista de la tierra: relatos guaraníes de Bolivia acerca de experiencias guerreras y pacíficas recientes," *Chiriguano: pueblos indígenas de las tierras bajas de Bolivia*, ed. Jürgen Riester (Santa Cruz: Apoyo para el campesino indígena del oriente boliviano [APCOB], 1994) 469-71. The Spanish reads: "No sé por qué ha sido la guerra. Corría la sangre, los árboles se hacían pedazos. La ametralladora, esta arma. Están peleando. Hartos esqueletos. Los collas y los pilas, hartos muertos. Los árboles los picaron los collas que tenían su anillo de oro en la mano. Algunos no quieren morir, le cortaron su cabeza al pobre. Feo, feo. Los muchachos pobrecitos entraron en la guerra, les cortaron la cabeza. Feo, feo...."

12. Klein 235-36.

13. Pifarré 412-13.

14. Klein 238-41.

15. The COB document was published in July, 1980, and was reproduced in the regular publication of the Rural Pastoral Team of the Diocese of Tarija, *El Catequista*, available in the library of the Academia in Entre Ríos. The Spanish reads: "el pueblo ha quedado absolutamente huérfano de toda institución que vele por sus interses humanos y económicos."

16. Klein 271.

17. Marcia Stephenson, *Gender and Modernity in Andean Bolivia* (Austin: University of Texas Press, 1999) 188.

18. *El Catequista* 37 (1982); *El Catequista* 53 (1989); Klein 280.

19. *El Catequista* 50 (1988). The Spanish reads: "La doctrina social de la Iglesia ha sido constante en que los bienes de la creación han sido destinados por Dios para servicio y utilidad de todos sus hijos.... De acuerdo con esta doctrina la misma Iglesia ha predicado siempre la equitativa distribución de las tierras de cultivo,... para dar al campesino la posibilidad de una vida digna que permita la conveniente educación integral de sus hijos y el necesario progreso en su salud, en su método de trabajo y de comercialización—a precios justos—de sus productos."

20. *Resistencia campesina: efectos de la política económica neoliberal del Decreto Supreme 21060* (La Paz: Centro de Estudios para el Desarrollo Laboral y Agrario [CEDLA], 1989) 11.

21. *Resistencia* 27. The Spanish reads: "En resumen, el D.S. 21060 estimuló la transnacionalizacion del sistema alimentario boliviano, agravando a un extremo nuestra dependencia alimentaria ya que la libre importación de productos agrícolas no mejoró la eficiencia de

la agicultura nacional. No garantizó que los precios internos de los alimentos fueran regulados por los precios internacionales, puesto que los mercados internacionales de alimentos están oligopolizados. Esto quiere decir, que los comerciantes importadores de alimentos no han vendido en el mercado interno 'al precio internacional' (en muchos casos substancialmente menor que el nacional), sino que venden a precios especulativos."

22. Stephenson 194-95.

23. Kitula Libermann and Armando Godínez, eds., *Territorio y dignidad: pueblos indígenas y medio ambiente en Bolivia* (Caracas: Editorial Torino. Co-published in Bolivia with Instituto Latinoamericano de Investigaciones Sociales [ILDIS], Editorial Nueva Sociedad, 1992) 39. The Spanish reads: "La idea de nosotros es que todos esos planes para el desarrollo de las comunidades indígenas sean llevados adelante por el Estado. Si bien algunas veces no se cuenta con los recursos, hay instituciones que apoyan como las ONG por ejemplo; pero creemos que esto debe ser una parte que apoye al Estado, porque a veces terminan los planes de la cooperación exterior, y, si no es el Estado el que los lleva adelante, entonces nos quedamos sin eso también. Quiero decir que dentro de nuestra concepción de nuestra visión de integración, creemos que debe haber más apoyo por parte del Estado...."

24. Lesley Gill, *Teetering on the Rim: Global Restructuring, Daily Life, and the Armed Retreat of the Bolivian State* (New York: Columbia University Press, 2000). See Chapter 9, "El Alto, the State, and the Capitalist Imperium," 181-90.

25. Gill 152.

26. Mario Gareca, personal interview, Sella Cercado, 9 August 1998.

27. Gill 188.

28. Meliá 42.

29. Meliá 44.

30. Meliá 43-47.

31. Quoted in Melía 50.

32. Meliá 49.

33. The quote is from Vandana Shiva, cited in Stephenson 200-01.

34. Meliá 66, 68. For more on Guaraní customs see Xavier Albó, *La comunidad de hoy* (La Paz: CIPCA, 1990) 235-65. For information on Guaraní folklore and the local culture of Tentayape, see David Acebey, *Quereimba, apuntes sobre los ava-guaraní en Bolivia* (Bolivia: Ediciones Gráficas, 1992).

35. Meliá 59-62.

36. For more on baptism, see Denis L. Heyck, *Baptism Among the Guaraní of Bolivia*, n.p., 1998.

37. Captain Sambo Gutiérrez, personal interview, Potrerillos, 4 May 1997.

38. Porfirio Novillo, personal interview Saladito, 13 May 1997.

39. Elvira Vaca de Vásquez, personal interview, Entre Ríos, 11 December 2000.

40. Dr. Guillermo Arancibia, personal interview, Sucre, 17 December 2000.

41. Novillo interview.

42. Letter of 1 March 1982. Available in the library of the Academia of the Sisters of the Presentation, Entre Ríos.

43. *El Catequista* 14, 17, 37 (1982).

44. Mario Gareca, personal interview, Sella Cercado, Bolivia, 9 August 1998.

45. *Ñee Jeroata* 61 (enero/febrero 1997): 9.

46. McCarthy, "Hacia la tierra sin mal."

47. "Acta de Organización de Capitanía Guaraníes," *Libro de Acta*s, n.p., 3 March 1989. Available in Ñaurenda, Tarija.

48. Guido Chumiray, "La Asamblea del Pueblo Guaraní y sus 10 años," *Ñee Jeroata* 61 (enero/febrero 1997): 18.

49. Paulina Tárraga, personal interview, Ñaurenda, 12 May 1997.

50. "Estatutos, Zona Guaraní de Itika Guasu, Departamento de Tarija," appendix, McCarthy, "Hacia la tierra sin mal."

51. Renán Sánchez, personal interview, Entre Ríos, 11 December 2000. See also, Guísela López and Roberto Navia, "Boom: Tarija despierta y asume el liderazgo petrolero de Bolivia," *El Deber*, Santa Cruz de la Sierra (22 de abril de 2001): B12.

Interviews

Pascuala Arebayo, Rosario Mendoza, Gregoria Catuire, and Santos Arebayo

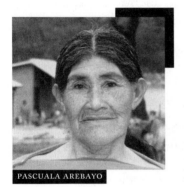

Pascuala, Rosario, and Gregoria are elderly curanderas *[healers]. Their interview reveals the remarkable strength of traditional healing practices today, despite the long process of erosion that Guaraní culture has suffered.*

Because they speak very little Spanish, Pascuala's son Santos, a healer himself, interpreted for the women when necessary. In this revealing interview, the curanderas *permit the uninitiated outsider an unusual glimpse into their secret world of cures, prayers, and spirits. Fascinating for the insights their comments offer on the traditional Guaraní world view and on the sometimes uneasy relationship between traditional healers and representatives of modern medicine, the observations of these wise women constitute a living history of Guaraní beliefs and practices. In addition, one cannot help being struck by the poverty of these women and their families, for, as Santos points out, food is scarce.*

PASCUALA AREBAYO

PASCUALA: I am about 75 years old; I am from right here in Ñaurenda. My *abuelita* [grandmother] taught me prayers, the *oración de puerta* [door prayer] to say when an illness first arises. Another is the *oración de pescadito* [little fish prayer], which, 15 minutes after you say it, the child is well. My abuelita knew how to cure headache, stomach ache, and *asustadura* [shock] for babies. Sometimes she would carry the baby to the ravine if it was *susto del agua* [water fright], and there she would purify him with the smoke from her cornhusk cigar [*se sahuma con tabaquito de chala*]. She would also spit on the baby. The combination of smoke, saliva, and prayers is what cures. You see the prayer comes from the mouth and the saliva, too; it is sanctified by the prayer.

Today there are still curanderas but most of them don't know anything about anything [*no saben nada, no saben nada*]. You can't just have anybody become a curandera. You have to be special; you have to be chosen and taught. I haven't taught my wisdom to anyone. I hate to see everything disappear. My son, Santos, knows the basic things, but I, like my grandmother, cure for many different things: asustadura, childbirth, and headache. There are many specialties because there are so many different kinds of spells [*malhechos*].

SANTOS: When Pascuala cures someone for asustadura, for example, she smokes to alleviate the person's distress. In order for the smoke to heal the patient, the cigar has to burn absolutely evenly, and the wrap has to be just perfect so that the smoke makes "little flowers" [*bien floreadito, florcitos, tiene que salir del humo de la chala para aliviar*]. If the *chala* [corn husk] burns badly, that is, unevenly, then the illness will not pass.

You make the cigar like you make a regular cigarette. You cut the tobacco up with a knife, and then you roll it in the husk, and then you light it. If it burns well, that is *parejo* [evenly], then the person gets well; if not, he doesn't.

You usually blow the smoke on the patient's head because that's a place the pain always attacks; also the hands and the feet of the *asustado* [one who has fright].

PASCUALA: [When it is removed] the spirit of the asustado may be in an animal, or somewhere else, but it no longer resides in the patient; that's why you have to go to where the person was *asustado* [frightened]. The curandera goes there and then calls the spirit to return to the person. The curandera's job is to try to get the body and the spirit back together. The spirit enters the person as it left, through the head, feet, and hands, also the heart. Often the asustado has fever too. The treatment takes three days. The patient brings all his clothes, and we have to purify them, too, if the asustado is seriously ill. And, of course, without prayers, the other treatment is nothing [*sin oración no es nada*].

The prayer is medicine; it is very valuable. That's why most prayers are secret. If a person is going to die and the treatment cures him, the person pays the curandera. You can't tell the patient how much to pay; that depends on that particular person, who decides of his own free will. Many women come to see me to cure illnesses or to consult during pregnancy. They come from here in Ñaurenda and from neighboring Saladito.

SANTOS: They are ashamed to go to the health post here [*tienen vergüenza*] because they have to pay, and sometimes Isabel can't cure them. Then they come and ask Pascuala for help. She helps them, but doesn't receive any pay for it [*no le llega su platita*]. The health post is not gratis. You have to pay for an aspirin or for them to cure a cut, and so on. Pascuala will take whatever people can give, a little flour or corn [*harinita o maicito*], sugar or rice.

PASCUALA: We are very poor because our patients are so poor; sometimes they cannot afford to pay us anything. It was the same way for my abuelita in the past. Paulina from Potrerillos is very poor too, for the same reason. The nurse observes us, but I haven't taught her specific things because she does not pay us for it. If she would give the curanderas a kilo of sugar, for example, she would show that she respects us [*nos respetan con la comida*]. She makes a salary, but she learns for free by observing us. That's not right, but she's not aware of the situation.

ROSARIO: I am 80 years old; I am from la Banda. I have had the same kinds of experiences as Pascuala regarding the *posta* and modern medicine. There were many curanderas in the past [*tenían hartas curanderas en el pasado*], but little by little, they are all dying out, especially the bad ones. There are those who cure and those who kill; the latter are *brujos* [witches]. It is good that so many of the brujos have died. They don't kill so many cattle any more, and the children are healthier. Before, many more children died. There are very few brujos now, that's why things are better.

When the *partera* [midwife] helps a woman give birth, in her prayers she tries to frighten away the brujos. Pascuala and I help out at the posta, only

ROSARIO MENDOZA

they don't pay us. I learned from my mamita who was an excellent curandera and who lived to be very old. She died here after she returned from Argentina where she had gone because there was no work here.

GREGORIA: Every time we have a meeting, we tell them about our problem. We include Paulina from Potrerillos too, because it's the same for all curanderas. Our experience and knowledge should be compensated, but they never do anything about it [*nada siempre*].

Life is better now than in the past because there are fewer brujos. Before, there were so many witches; they would kill people suddenly and eat them up, especially the children. Now more *hijitos* [children] are growing up. In the past, the witches would kill the children and carry them away. It's much better today.

It's also better with the *karai* [whites, mestizos], because before, the women were all afraid of the *cristianos* because they would come and drag us away with them to their bed. Now they don't do that.

SANTOS: I think what we need most is not to be so poor; there is so much need. The men have to leave the village to look for work. Some have to leave for a year or more until things get better because this year we have not been able to harvest much. We have nothing to live on; there is no work here now, and there is no help. We need assistance, credit. We have the *potrero*, the land, to work. What we lack is *plata* [money] and *garantía* [collateral]. We can't get a loan from the bank because we have no collateral. The big problems for us are food and work because this year there was no corn and now hunger is arriving at our homes.

The men are going elsewhere to try to find work, and the women are staying here with their baskets. From the sale of the baskets they buy rice and pasta. It is the only income for our families.

We would work for the oil exploration companies, say, for one, or at most, two months. But their contracts are for 90 days, and that is too long. We have to work our own individual plots here at home, and we can't leave them untended for three months. So, right now we are in a difficult economic situation.

Ñaurenda, 3 August 1998.

Paulina Muñoz

*Muñoz, like the curanderas of Ñaurenda, practices tradi-
tional healing in her town of Potrerillos, but, unlike them,
she welcomes the contributions of the "new" medicine. Also
like the curanderas of Ñaurenda, Muñoz is dirt poor.
Extreme poverty and ill health have aged her far beyond her
60-odd years. The Guaraní are too impoverished to pay
her, even with a little sugar, and Muñoz feels constrained
from asking them to give what they do not have. As a result,
women like Muñoz, who as curanderas and parteras [mid-
wives] perform essential and valued services, are often the
poorest members of the community. In her interview, Muñoz expresses her love of babies and
the pride she feels in helping new mothers. She also remarks on how much she has benefitted
from workshops on hygienic childbirth offered by Sr. Therese Marie and on family planning
offered by Project Esperanza, an NGO effective in promoting women's health. In the process,
Muñoz shares some old secrets and prayers which she mixes with modern medicine.*

I am a partera and curandera. I was born in Kawarina. From here in Potrerillos,
it's about, let's see, if you leave from here on foot mid-morning, you arrive sometime after dark. My parents are from there also; that's where I grew up. There
was a school where I attended until the second grade, but I have learned more
in my old age because of workshops and special classes given by health workers.
Now I do my own reports each month, about the babies, and about asustadura
and *lastimadura* [accidents]. I am not solely a partera, but also a curandera. With
this course that I recently completed, I learned a lot, what to do about colds, for
example. Sr. Therese Marie has given us excellent courses.

My mother was a partera and not a curandera; she practiced only childbirths
[*puros partos no má*s]. My *abuelita* [grandma] was a curandera in Kawarina. I grew
up over there in Kawarina with my abuelita; she taught me everything from the
time I was just a little girl [*por allicito iba aprendiendo desde jovencito*]. I learned
from her how to attend at childbirth, and I have continued learning and *capaci-
tando* [attending workshops] up until today.

As a midwife, the principal things that you have to learn are, well, I learned
from my abuelita, how to prepare coca water and the little prayer, little secret, that
accompanies it. If the baby is not doing well or is coming breech, she knew how
to deal with it. She also knew all about medicinal herbs. In 1992, I started taking
courses, and I have learned even more.

My abuelita also taught me prayers. One addresses the river, which brings us
a stick, referring to the baby in the womb. You say those words, then you have
to spit on the mother's stomach. Then the prayer says something like the river
carries things to where they should arrive, and this is what will happen with the
baby, because the *vientre* [womb] is like the river.

My abuelita taught me how to use some medicinal herbs. For example, there was a weed that was called *ororito*, or *calandrillo*, I forget the name exactly. You use it in the prayer for giving birth, along with five secret words. For the placenta, there was also a prayer, and also spitting; these were to ward off infection. *Tuopotá, tuopotá, puro de bombá* [roughly, "come out, come out," followed by words chosen for their sound]. That's what you say when one can't expel the placenta. The saliva of the curandera is like a tablet; it's considered to have curing power.

I started as a partera when I was 12, always with my abuelita. The difference between a partera and a curandera is that the curandera knows more because the partera knows only about childbirth. She does not know prayers, nor does she apply ointments or potions. One learns these things from mother to daughter if the daughter is interested. There are also men who are curanderos. They're both still common. There are also male parteros but they are usually cristianos and they make their little *santiguaditas* [signs of the cross].

The biggest problem I have is when the baby dies in the womb and it is difficult to remove it. One that I was able to revive is Señora Tomasa Velázquez who lives in Entre Ríos, I brought her out by her spine, doubled up, and I nearly gave her up for dead. I tried to get her to start breathing, but with no results. However, I kept on rubbing her until she finally revived. I will never forget the happiness, because usually, in a situation like that, they are gone.

In those days we didn't know about hospitals. I have 18 children, but all those who were born in the hospital died there too. I guess it is because I was malnourished; that's what they said. I have seven living children. Women mostly come to me only to give birth; a few also come for care during pregnancy.

After childbirth, there was better care in the past. I think our ancestors were more healthy and clean than we are today. Now, the time after birth is less healthy and we are more careless. Before, our ancestors would take great care with the new mother's nutrition. They would give a woman who had just given birth *maíz tostadito* [roasted corn]; they would grind and boil it. But now, they just give them rice and potatoes, which are not as nutritious. Corn was better; they recovered faster. Now they get up too fast and are not healthy. Before, it was 15 days; now it's one day, that's no recovery. The advice I give all new mamás is to look at their babies, that's very important so they know you love them, and to eat well.

The practices of the partera have changed much in the past decade or so. For example, we now have *parto limpio* ["clean" childbirth], which we didn't know about before. It used to be that there was no bed. You would just kneel down on the ground, and we would take the baby out with our hands, clean the baby with water, the mother too, and cut the cord. Now, we have a little packet for the parto limpio. The new practice is in bed; there is less pain in bed, and it is more hygienic. I think it is better. Also before, the *guagua* [baby] would hit the ground. The mamá gets some pain medicine in the packet. There's also a brush, soap, thread, scissors to cut the cord, and towels. Then we bathe the mother in water that has been boiled. Before, we used to bathe in just any water. This is better because it kills germs. As I mentioned, I started going to midwife workshops in 1992 when la hermana Teresa María first told me about them. They have been very important to me. I have attended here in Potrerillos and at other sites as well. They are optional, but I like to go because I love to learn new things. Others are not interested and stay home. I also go because we Guaraní have never before had the resources, the money, to go places like Tarija or even Entre Ríos.

That is certainly true for me because the partera is the poorest of the poor. I am ashamed to charge for my services because everyone is so poor, but people can pay with any little thing, perhaps a small amount of corn. Sometimes I am sick and can't plant my corn; then people I have helped give me a little *mate* [bitter tea drunk with sugar]. The partera is respected in the community, but terribly poor.

I cooperate with the personnel in the hospital here in Potrerillos. I bring the newborn to the hospital, leaving the new mother in her bed. I take the baby immediately to *control* [registration] so the doctor can give him his *carnet* [identification card] and a checkup. Whenever any children are sick, I take them too. I go get the *camilla* [stretcher] if necessary. Some are evasive and run away because they don't want to go. Often, their parents don't want to send them because they have no money. But I take in many, especially with diarrhoea. The hospital will help you even if you don't have any money. We helped build the hospital. There has been a good relationship from the beginning.

We will continue to need both parteras and nurses in the future because the Guaraní have so many serious health problems. I have two nieces who are interested. They are studying in *el segundo medio* [secondary school], but it's a struggle for their families to keep them there, and the nieces are working and studying all the time. It's a sacrifice for everyone, but they are dedicated to becoming health workers.

The Guaraní have so many grave health problems because most of us have nothing, we have no money. I don't know why we can't get money, but we don't have it, and so many are sick. The Guaraní know they should have good health; they don't want to have malaria, or malnutrition, or diarrhoea, but they don't have the wherewithal. Sometimes when I cure a cristiano, they give me ten pesos. But yesterday, I cured a woman's child of diarrhoea, and she had nothing. That is the most common. It makes you very, very sad. Rare are those who pay, because they have nothing. The Guaraní lack everything, even sugar. Sometimes when my kids are still hungry, I start crying. I want to go buy something, but I can't. The most basic thing is salt, but I have none, and I cry. One has to grow a few peanuts and potatoes in order to eat. All my kids go to school; I think that's the only way for us to do better.

Since 1992 I have been educating myself, involving myself in various organizations, meetings, and courses to improve in my profession, but the community has never supported me by paying my expenses to go to those courses in Entre Ríos, Tarija, Villa Montes, or wherever. They just can't do it. The courses are on the reproductive system and on psychology. We learn about the special problems of women. We encourage the mothers to go to meetings, like they have in the hospital, and with the support of Project Esperanza, the mother talks about her problems and shares them. For example, the mothers often talk about having so many kids and about not knowing how to keep them well and fed. I tell the women to try not to have too many children, to go to the hospital to the doctor who can solve that problem. I also talk with the couples, the husband and the wife together, about having fewer children. Many fathers help with child care, and everyone is interested in having healthier children.

People with Project Esperanza tell the women about birth control methods. So many women have headaches, attacks, depression, anemia, but they don't have the money to go to the hospital; others don't go because they are afraid. It's a serious problem for women and for the whole family. Women's health is a family issue as well as a personal one.

I believe that the future will be better because we will be more educated, and I think that education will definitely help Guaraní women. We will know more about health and diet, and we will be able to help ourselves more. We are a very capable people; we are able to improve and we want to improve.

I love being a partera because I love guaguas. It breaks my heart when they are sick. Many, many are born with illnesses. Sometimes I still use some of my grandmother's old prayers for asustadura for the babies and for insomnia for adults. We say something like this: *Lo está llamando que venga, que venga a jugar aquí; tengo flores* ["come, come and play here, I have flowers"]. You are calling the spirit to leave, to come and play here; you are offering flowers to attract the spirit. You cure by spitting and by smoking a cigar. You spit on the head of either the guagua or the adult. It is a kind of cigar that, when you smoke it, it produces a dizziness. Sometimes I use the cigar and sometimes I don't, but it is usually more effective with it. I wish I knew what causes asustadura. The symptoms are that they can't sleep, they hear a wind, they see an animal, they fall in water, sometimes they can't speak. If the cure doesn't work, then it may be that there is another person, say a nurse, who could cure the person, and I try to get that nurse. I learned from abuelita; she nursed me, and I lived with her. I never had much contact with my mother. Catalina was her name, and I called her Catalina, never *mamita*; that name was reserved for my abuelita. She taught me all that I know, and passed on to me her healing secrets and her love of babies. My nieces will learn even more because they will be educated and benefit from both the old and the new.

Potrerillos, 11 May 1997

Jorge Gallardo (Machirope)

Machirope lives in tiny Saladito, which borders Ñau-renda. A Guaraní, he is steeped in the folklore, religious beliefs, and history of his people. He is one with nature, communing daily with the spirits of the forest as his feet fly effortlessly up steep mountains or rest tranquilly in the damp river bed. One of the most respected Guaraní leaders active in the life of the province, Machirope has worked ceaselessly on behalf of the Guaraní of O'Connor and was, with Tárraga, a forceful advocate of the landmark school in Ñaurenda. The gregarious Machirope is a born storyteller who relishes any opportunity to recount tales of Guaraní heroism and resistance as well as of everyday life. Machirope, former first captain of Ñaurenda and second captain of the zone, is an articulate advocate of Guaraní culture, and a powerfully effective proponent of education, the institution of the assembly, and the Guaraní language. Despised by the patrones, the wily Machirope has delighted in defying their authority and deftly leading fellow villagers in their journey toward independence. Machirope believes one thing above all others: that the Guaraní will never be able to live with dignity and independence or preserve their past without the education that eluded him, but now must be the number one priority for Guaraní children.

I am from Ingre in the department of Chuquisaca, in la Banda. I came here in 1965 when I was about 20, fleeing from the patrones in la Banda. What happened was that my father, who was the capitán grande in the zone of Ingre, went to Argentina to work and didn't return, so there was no leader to protect us from the patrones, who came in and took the Guaraní to serve them. I had to escape, because, in those days, you couldn't choose not to work for the patrón. There was no *escritura* ["writing," law] for the Guaraní; that was for the *cristianos* [whites] only. That's still true today. So I had to escape under cover of night. If they caught me here, for example, I would have to carry a heavy stone all the way back on the return trip. That was the usual punishment. Of course, with the *chicote* [whip] too; that was standard. They would always tell people that they treated us well, but that was perhaps once a year.

I escaped alone. I didn't tell anyone before going. I came by way of Altamira here to Timboy and Ñaurenda, where I worked for a year. Then, in 1967 or so, I went to Argentina and stayed for five years. At that time I spoke very little Spanish and didn't know how to pronounce the words at all. Still, I liked Argentina, and I learned some castellano. I would work for six months in the vineyards and in the grape harvest, and then I would go to Mendoza and Buenos Aires.

In 1972, I entered military service in Villa Montes; it was obligatory. To this day I have not known the door of a school. I wish I could read and write; I was interested, but unfortunately I was never able to take any classes. I had hoped to learn in the army as they promised, but there was no opportunity. At that time Hugo Banzer was President. Service was for one year and eight months, almost two years of punishment. In the army we worked in the mines, *yeso* [gypsum] and *cal* [lime].

After I was discharged, I returned to my little pueblo here in the *monte*, but my brother came searching for me to ask me to go back and help move my elderly mother and all the family down here to help provide for them. That's what I did, and I have lived here ever since; that was about 1975.

It made me angry to see my former village fenced in by the patrones; they were closing our people in. At that time I began a campaign trying to get the Guaraní of Ingre to organize themselves. I went around for three months with a "brother" from the US, named Benítez. He works as a sociologist in Monteagudo, and I joined up with him. However, we could not organize the people because they were afraid of the patrones. To fight, for whatever issue, one needs a base, and there was absolutely no base. If there is unity, you can do it, but we had none. The patrones threatened everyone; you realize that those of la Banda were widely known to be the most violent.

I have been rebellious since youth. In large part, it's because of my mother's influence. When I was very young she would tell me stories about the history of our struggle and its heroes. I always paid close attention because I was interested in our history, and she was passing it down to me. She told me about when they killed my great grandfather, Andrés Pérez, because he was a leader; the patrones did not want there to be any Indian leaders at all. It was difficult in those days, no?

The patrones back in Ingre wanted to burn me, hang me, shoot me; they threatened to do all those things. Now, however, I can go and visit and see that many things have changed.

When I first arrived in Ñaurenda, it was very different from the way it is today. There was no school, medical post, or *sede* [assembly hall]. There were just a few houses, nothing else.

At that time I was working for the patrón, Antonio Vaca, here in neighboring Timboy. He never even gave me an old rag, but others were worse. He was very suspicious of all outsiders who were trying to help the Guaraní organize, including the sisters. He called all foreigners communists and tried to scare me away from associating with them. He would say to me:

> Don't trust those foreigners, *no te conviene* [it's not in your interest]; they come from the outside. One of these days they're going to deceive you, and it will end badly. They are poisoning you with their ideas. Look Jorge, you've done your military service. Why, you're almost a *cristiano*! Don't get involved in this, understand? Those foreigners, the sisters, are no good for you. Just tend your *potrero* [cornfield] and I will lend you what you need. Don't stay there in Ñaurenda and get involved in scandals; come and live here in Timboy. You have lived in the barracks; surely you have learned a lot, you are more like a karai now. These organizations are communist.

—I didn't understand what communist meant; all I knew was that Vaca wanted to have total control over us, for us to continue to be completely helpless. I would turn on the radio to hear the news broadcast, but he would turn it off, saying, "You don't want to listen to that. That Radio Tarija isn't worth shit [*no sirve para mierda*]. You're young, don't waste your life with these things." And then Benito Herrera, another powerful patrón in the area, would threaten me saying, "One of these days I'm going to throw you into the truck and dump you out in el Beni [the jungle in the north]." "Well," I would answer, "at least that way I'll get to see el Beni."

I didn't let them frighten me, and I kept going to meetings in our community and in neighboring ones. We also went to several meetings in Tarija with the MCM who helped us in everything. If you let them [the patrones] intimidate you, you are finished. At that time I was campaigning for the potable water project, and they would tell me to give it up. First, Vaca offered me a set of chairs and table if I would quit the organization. But the table and chairs never arrived! I had to leave my family and go tend the oxen for the harvest. I was working for the boss, gone for weeks, but when I got back, still no tables or chairs. He also told me to change my name, that Machirope *no sirve* [is no good]. Vaca was rabidly opposed to the organization, by which I mean the capitanía, which we developed ourselves, and he threatened us constantly. He would also belittle us, saying, "You are too poor, you will never be able to make it on your own."

But I would slip out at night and go to the meetings in Saladito where the organization began and where our first capitán, Saravia, lived. Always, the day after a meeting a "commission," that is, a group in the pay of the patrón, would arrive and ask us what we had discussed. They would push us around and threaten to send the police to beat us. But we kept on. First, we organized by ourselves; then we allied with the MCM and with the sisters and later with the APG.

—Relations are better now, and they have stopped persecuting us. The change is because we have our own voice now that the communities are organized and connected to each other. The biggest problems we have now in the community are education and health. Before, everything was against us. For example, it was very difficult to learn how to organize ourselves to work for the school. They kept telling us that we didn't need a school, that all we needed to know was how to sign our names. Then there were the threats to close the school if we didn't comply with all the rules exactly, or if we didn't coordinate things perfectly with the teachers.

With health it was the same thing. The patrones would say, "These Guaraní, what do they know about *botiquines* [medicine kits] and medical posts." A doctor from Santa Cruz sent the first *botiquín* to us; he was a good doctor, but the patrón didn't want us to have medicines or receive treatment. "It's not the custom, son" [*No es costumbre, hijo*], he said when I asked if I could go to the medical post. I had a bad throat infection and I couldn't eat, sleep, or drink. "No, it's nothing, *hijo*, you're okay." Things are better now. It's important that we have a reporter who covers health issues too, and a *promotora de salud* [health worker] in the community.

For bilingual education, it was the same story, but we fought for it with Sr. Maura by our side all the way, until we finally got Angela, our bilingual teacher, in 1994. At first, they were telling the community that Machirope was going to ruin everything for the villagers, and that it was foolish to learn Guaraní. "No business is conducted in Guaraní, just *castellano* [Spanish] for business," the patrón would say. They absolutely despised the idea of Guaraní instruction. I kept telling them it was bilingual, Guaraní and castellano, but all they heard was Guaraní.

Our move toward freedom all started with the school; that was before there was any organization whatsoever, and before we were allied with any other groups. The encouragement and materials for the school came from Dr. Guillermo Arancibia who worked with CODETAR [*Corporación de Desarrollo de Tarija*, Tarija Development Corporation] at that time. He and Nicasia worked to win the people of Ñaurenda over. But Feliciano and I already wanted our people to know how to manage notebook and pencil [*manejar cuaderno y lápiz*]. I believe that this has been my mission in life, that I was born to help get the school going for Ñaurenda.

But that was very early; their first visit was in 1977 or so, and I hadn't been living in Ñaurenda for very long, and, like I said, there was no organization. There was just the name, *capitanía* [captaincy], but no structure. I wanted very much to create an organization and establish the school so that we could recuperate our culture, our stories, our organizations as *mburuvicha*s [chiefs].

I had been wanting to work with our people so they would know what education is, and to convince them that even though it may change the culture some, it won't change our language, which is what concerned them most. That is what I kept telling our hermanos, but I had no authority at that time since there was no governing structure in our village, and, as I was a newcomer, I had no authority. Nicasia and Dr. Arancibia held a meeting with all of us, but still they did not go for the idea. They were all afraid that with education they would lose their culture. I would tell them no, that our culture will and must continue. Even if someday I wear a tie, I will still be a Guaraní; we can't forget. Our people were very suspicious of me, of outsiders, and of these new ideas. The elders and the grandmothers thought that our ideas would change everything and bring hard times to the village. The wife of the patrón encouraged these sentiments by telling everyone that I was an outsider and a troublemaker who should be sent back to Chuquisaca. I would just answer "We are all from the same Bolivia, it's as if we all had the same father."

Of course the patrones didn't want the school because they would say that once we had a school we would no longer want to sow or harvest for them. I would tell them that the important thing is for our children to become aware, to learn to identify wrongdoing. They did not like to hear that, but I didn't care. Education is the only way for our community to advance, to serve as a model to other communities, and so on, until all Guaraní are educated. I also kept telling our hermanos how important it is to remember those who came before us, that we can't forget our history. Of course, we don't want to return to those years, but we have to talk about them, to know about our ancestors; that is part of our identity. A few of us, like Feliciano, just kept on talking it up, and with the leadership of Dr.

Arancibia and Nicasia, finally the community agreed to start a first grade.

This was a very big step because Ñaurenda and neighboring villages had not yet begun to organize politically when we arrived. In fact, there was absolutely no political consciousness at all among the people. The capitanía existed in name only. I was very interested in organizing from the very beginning. I would always go to meet with the brother of the capitán grande of the Cordillera, from Santa Cruz, whenever they came to Villa Montes. I would tell him that my father had been a capitán, that I knew a little about organizing, and that I wanted to learn more. With the school issue, we took the first steps toward organizing, which we continued in earnest throughout the 1980s. Once the patrones found out what we were doing, we had to meet and travel at night. We would leave about 8:00 p.m. for example, to walk to other villages to talk to our compañeros there.

I have been capitán grande since 1991. That means I represent the three zones here in O'Connor province, and I have to go on foot to visit all the pueblos and try to organize them and introduce them to the idea of *asambleas*. They would also come visit Ñaurenda and observe our meetings and learn that way. But sometimes I would get discouraged because we were so dispersed.

One thing I helped to institute was the *grupo de trabajo* [work group], which exists in all the communities now, and works *chacras comunales* [communally worked fields]. We plant corn, peanuts, beans, for example, and everyone works the common field. We had to initiate them in all the communities because it's not possible for one person to be the leader of every group. The first grupo de trabajo in our zone was here in Ñaurenda. If there's a problem within the grupo de trabajo, it's the leader of the group who has to deal with it, not the capitán, though we try to coordinate our efforts.

All these efforts came after the school and as a result of that first success at organizing. That's what we tried to build on, that success, because before, no one thought there was anything that we could do to change our situation. It seems a small thing to start with one grade, but it was important for people to get used to the idea that we ourselves could change our lives.

I had always wanted to learn to read and write, but it didn't happen. After my father left for Argentina, this was in the 1950s, all I was considered good for was going to the fields. To the patrón, I was no different from the farm animals that he owned. It was absolutely ridiculous to think of a Guaraní in the classroom. That's why I think I was born for this initiative, because I always wanted to have an education. I can't write my name, but I can speak castellano, and I have a good memory.

Where I got my dedication to learning was from my mother; she was very wise, and she taught me many stories from her memory. Marayí was her name. She was the captain's wife, a leader in the community. She told me all about my great grandparents and what life was like in the olden days [*aquellos tiempos años*]. I would listen carefully, and then I would keep the stories in my head. So, when I was in the army, I thought that would be the opportunity to take classes, but I had bad luck [*me quema la suerte de mi persona*]; however, I reflected and planned a great deal. I offer a thousand thanks to my mother who gave me my education, who taught me how to behave and get along with my fellow Guaraní, stand up for what is right, organize, and appreciate how our ancestors lived. I learned all of this at her knee, listening to her stories.

For example, in the time of our grandparents they married late, at 25 or 28 years, not like at 14 or 15 years as they do now, and that made them more respectful of each other. They also had a much better diet and were stronger. They ate corn and drank *chichacauí*, and they lived from the fruits of the countryside, whose names we have now forgotten. There was the *algarrobo, mistol, chañal, pocochi, guayabilla*. One that is especially delicious is the *caranti*, which is a kind of potato that is sweet like honey, but most people don't know about it any more. They did not eat rice, noodles, or sugar, which are making us weak and hurting our teeth today. They didn't know alcohol, just chicha, there was no coca or tobacco either. They didn't have those vices, and they only got drunk during fiestas, not the day before and the day after like people do now. They were healthy and strong.

Our grandparents were intelligent too. For example, now we call the months January, February, and so on. Back then, they didn't know what January and February were. They knew the differences in the months because the birds that sing in August are different from those that sing in March. Our ancestors, although they didn't know how to read, knew many things.

And they were never lazy. Today, at 7:00 a.m. people will still be sleeping, and the sun is already high in the sky. They were up at the rooster's first crow doing their chores, grinding corn, hauling water, harvesting the crops. And on San Roque's Day, or San Juan's Day, they knew those dates by the birds and the stars, and they knew they did not have to go work for the patrón on those days. They had all they needed, not much in quantity, but sufficient to maintain themselves: goats, pigs, cows. When they needed clothing, they would go to Argentina to work for a time, finish the job in two or three months, and return with their purchases.

They worked in groups, this was very traditional. They grew corn in their individual plots, but they worked together in the larger one too, and on all community projects. For example, they would decide together when a party was to begin and when you could start and stop drinking chicha. They would notify people at 1:00 a.m., and guests would start to arrive at 8:00 a.m., drink and party and dance until about 2:00 or 3:00 p.m. Then they would stop, even if there was chicha left. If it was a two-day celebration, they would not drink again until the next day. People would sing Guaraní songs, dance the *atiku* [traditional Guaraní dance], play the *bombo* [drum] and the *terere* [flute]. It was all very sociable, and everyone came together. Those who did not come to the fiesta would have a spell cast on them by the *ipajé* [shaman] whose name was *Buricanambi* [Burro's Ears], and some would even die; that's how critical it was to participate socially. Of course, it was different in those days, but sociability is still important, and I keep my chichacauí in my house ready in case I have a visitor, or in case I decide to have a fiesta.

There were love songs and counterpoint songs, that is, songs that were like verse contests, where you would insult the other person with a clever rhyme and they would try to answer. At times they would fight with knives, with the poncho wrapped around their arm, as in Argentina, but if after a brief time they had not hurt each other, they would go off together to share a drink in friendship.

They had many prayers in those days. Prayers were very important, not like now when hardly anyone can remember them. For example, if I needed to "stretch my arm," that is, to be especially strong for some task, I would put rubber on that arm and say a prayer and the arm would stretch. Or, if I was going to a fiesta and I thought there might be trouble, I would say a prayer, spit on my knife, put it at the head of my bed overnight so the prayer would "mature," and then the next day the knife would be like fire, strong and sure. The so-called "fly prayer," I don't know why they called it that, also had to do with protection in a fight. If I said the prayer and was cut with a knife, in two hours the wound would be healed. The prayers helped our great grandparents; they didn't have police or jail, just themselves to keep order, and the prayers helped.

The curanderos were very powerful. Some of them, men and women, learned from their parents how to heal, cast evil spells, or make it rain. But there are also others who didn't have to learn from their parents or grandparents; either they were born knowing, or else they had an experience. For example, say someone goes out to work on the mountainside; spends the night there, has visions and becomes *asustado* [frightened]. We say *tapuh*, or *coquena* in castellano, that is, the spirit of the forest, would enter the person. It's like a spirit because you can't touch it, but it is very real. The coquena, the spirit owner of the forest, also known as the *dueño del palo*, would come because that person was open to learning. Then the spirit would make the person sleep, dream, become ill even. Sometimes that is because the dueño del palo would be angry because of the way people were treating the forest. The spirit would make the person sick as a way of teaching things for that individual's own good. Through that experience, the person would learn to become a curandero and practice for the good of the community what he or she had learned from the dueño del palo. It's that the owner of the mountain saw in that individual an aptitude and a capacity for understanding, so the spirit chose to improve and instruct that person.

The only prayer I can remember is the one for snakes. There are snakes around here that grow to 20 or 30 meters, and they are taken away by the wind if you say the prayer. If you say the words through your nose the snake disappears. There are only three words that I remember, which in Spanish are: *pasa, pasa por favor* [pass, pass, please]. I have tried these prayers, and they have worked. Once a large snake crossed my path and didn't harm me. It was ten meters long and had a head like a cow, large, with yellow eyes. But the coquena protected me because that day the snake didn't bother me.

Another thing I've learned is that if a newborn baby [*guaguita nacida*] urinates on your shirt and you climb the mountain and there are snakes, they are carried away by the wind, you are protected by the baby's urine. My mother told me all these things, and I have seen them myself.

Everyone used to believe in the *ipajés*, many of us still do, because it's just like there is an herb that cures and one that kills also; so too are there those who can do good and those who can cause harm with their spells. I believe in the ipajés because there are things that happen that you can't explain otherwise. For example, an asustadura cannot be healed with medicine because the bad spirit remains inside the person, and the person's spirit remains where the event or accident occurred. For example, a child who falls here and gets a "fright," his spirit stays right here. When it's a case of asustadura, it will never be cured with prescriptions or doctors or surgery. I had to explain this to a doctor before when he didn't understand why his medicine wasn't working. People say that *podemos asustar muchas veces porque no somos bautizados* [we suffer from fright many times because we are not baptized]. I don't know, perhaps so, but we still believe in the ipajés because there are strange things that happen.

I have a book of stories about the olden days, from 1894, it's called *Marabundi*, and it's in Guaraní. It's all about capitán Machirope and the Guaraní of Ingre, when they warred with the missionaries and had only bows and arrows; that's when the missionaries killed my grandfather. I took Machirope's name to honor him as a great leader from whom I am descended. My mother would tell me that I needed to learn the stories of Machirope's bravery so that when I became a *dirigente* [leader] I would behave like Machirope and not take advantage of others.

Everything is changing now. For example, in the old culture, the way they buried people, their marriage customs, the dances they knew, what they ate. I was born around 1947, and they still buried people in *cántaros*, large earthenware urns. Now we make coffins from wood, and we need a carpenter. In the old days, no, we just dug a hole two or three meters deep, and we wrapped the dead up very nicely and buried them seated and then put the top on the clay coffin. The dead would take with them chicken, *muiti* [a corn dish], and *kägui mascadito* [well-chewed corn]. The older people would always do the *yerure*, that is, prayers for the dead that wish them well and that express hope that the family members do not suffer from asustadura. They will send the dead off with this prayer, a *Váyase bien, ya va a ver el tumpa* [may it go well with you, you are going to see the *tumpa* (the great god)]. They say prayers for nine days.

Now, we take the dead to the cemetery. And with our new houses in Ñaurenda that have cement floors, how are we going to bury the dead under the house? People no longer lament for nine days; they see the dead, cross themselves, and leave. I guess it is more civilized now, but there was a lot of respect for the dead then.

I believe that we are going to preserve our culture, even if some things change. We just always have to be aware of what is happening, understand why, and think about what the consequences will be. The most important things are to maintain the language and the tradition of work. Another important thing that is in danger of being lost is the custom of hospitality [*convidar*]. People don't invite others to anything anymore.

But there are new practices that are very good for us and help us retain our culture. For example the assembly. Before the time of Machirope in 1894, they didn't have assemblies. But it is very important for our group identity to have common meetings where we discuss everything and everyone has a vote.

I want to tell you a little more about the food at the fiesta in the old days. First they had to have an *olla común* [common pot] that the woman of the house made. Every male old enough to drink chicha had to go to *el monte* to hunt; they hunted wild pigs, deer, and turkey; the first two they hunted with dogs. They would kill five or six, then they would make an *asado* [barbecue], and a soup for the guests when they arrived.

The young boys would go out to hunt doves. They would make traps with sticks and they would put a little food on top to attract the bird. They would set 40 to 60 *tilincas* [traps]. Then they would take the birds they had caught for the stew. That's how they used to do it here in the Chaco; they had plenty to eat back then. We still hunt, but it is just for one's family, not to invite others. We also still have the olla común and chicha. But that dove soup they used to make was delicious and it kept them strong.

There are other things that make one a Guaraní. If I am a true Guaraní I have to recognize my parents, that is, honor them and the past that they represent. I do this by the way I eat, dress, celebrate fiestas, with the arete, for example. I also honor them by maintaining our way of speaking. If I go to Tarija, I speak Guaraní with a different sound there, more like the sound of Spanish. But in my village, I speak Guaraní the traditional way. In both ways, when I do those things, I feel that I am Guaraní. The name Guaraní suggests all those things to me. The name is an important part of the identity, but it is not something you can see and say, ah, yes, that is what it means to be Guaraní. It's like the tumpas; you can't see them, but you know they are there. It's interesting that we identify ourselves with the name Guaraní, because it is one the Spanish gave us. We were from the Tupi Guaraní group originally in Brazil and Paraguay, and here, locally in the Chaco, we were called *mbúa*, or *ava*, not Guaraní.

What we want to do is keep our culture and not become just the same as the *entreriano*, the karai from the town Entre Ríos, for example. We can wear shoes, but our faces will still look Guaraní. I may be with a lawyer, or my educated friend, but if I run into my paisano, I have to speak to him in Guaraní. That way I am valuing my person, my culture, my customs, my local way of speaking, my parents, and my blood heritage. I am worth two men because I can speak Guaraní and castellano, I am two persons. I can't divide myself, but I feel that way. It's good to be two people; I just can't forget to honor my Guaraní parents.

There are parts of our culture that we are losing, old customs. For example, a young girl goes to the city and returns with a cassette player. Then she goes to a party and drinks chichacauí, sees people with watches and fancy decorations, and her eyes begin to shine. She wants to wear shoes, paint her fingernails, put on eye makeup, curl her eyelashes, and she no longer wants to go to school or dance the arete. I say, "Let's all dance the arete!" They say to each other, "Let's go over there," and they go off to the side to listen to their cassettes of modern music. I had first seen that when I was in the army, and when I began organizing our villages in the entire zone, I would tell the villagers and caution them, "We must organize so that this kind of thing doesn't happen."

It's okay to wear shoes and ties or makeup, but one must remain Guaraní. The muchachas who wear makeup and listen to the new music are also Guaraní, but they are not aware of it, that's the problem. I tell them, the paint [*la pintura*] is borrowed, it will always be borrowed, but your native culture is not. But some of them no longer want to speak Guaraní. They come back after two or three months in the city all *castellanizadas* [hispanicized], and soon they forget our language. For those who go to Argentina it's often the same thing; they return as gauchos. Whether you wear *ojotas* [Indian sandals] or *zapatos* [shoes] is not the important thing; it's whether you continue to recognize and value your Guaraní culture and language.

Because I am balding, many people mistake me for a karai; they say I am a cristiano. I always feel like I am valuing my culture when I make a little joke and tell them that this is how all us intelligent Guaraní look. I was in Argentina for many years, but I still returned as a Guaraní. Others go for two months and forget everything; they no longer want to go to school or grind corn. We need to leave the village, go out and see the world and learn many things, but we need to return speaking our same language. We are trying very hard to do both things.

We feel that we are valuing our great grandparents by our organization, our school, and our own persons. If I try to be a karai, if I drink alcohol instead of chichacauí, I am deriding my own person. But if I recognize what chichacauí is, what it is made from, how it is made, that is valuing my culture. We have to understand all this well and be clear about it so that we don't become *cristianos a la fuerza*, so we're not pushed into becoming cristianos; we have to resist that. I am Jorge, but I am first of all Machirope, which means monkey's eyelash, *machi* is monkey and *rope* is eyelash.

If our organization stays strong, with our regular assemblies and work groups, and if everyone participates in the school, fiestas, and community projects, then I believe that we can maintain our culture and at the same time advance. We are determined to do both. That is why education is so important; it is the key to everything. It is essential that we keep bilingual education, and not just learn castellano. My son can write in castellano and in Guaraní too, and that's the way it should be. That way he will come to learn our history too. Writing in Guaraní, they can search for our past, the story of our forbearers, how they lived, what type of housing, what type of food, what type of entertainment, work, and what type of social organizations kept their culture together. I know that education will change our culture, but without education we will never recover our past.

I go back to what I said at the beginning. Even though I cannot write my name, I believe that education has been my mission in life, because that is the door to the future for the Guaraní people.

Timboy, 4 May 1997; 2 August 1998

Feliciano Tárraga

Gentle, good-humored Feliciano Tárraga has occupied numerous positions of leadership within his village and province. As one of the few literate Guaraní of his generation, he is a much sought-after spokesman for the cause. He served as people's reporter with the MCM [Movimiento Campesinos en Marcha, Movement of Campesinos on the March] *during a time of widespread political unrest, participating at considerable personal risk in various MCM demonstrations on behalf of the rights of both mestizo campesinos and the Guaraní. Tárraga has served as secretary to the assembly in Ñaurenda, a highly regarded duty which requires him to be custodian of the word in the Actas [minutes]. Tárraga has also acted as secretary at zonal and regional assembly meetings, in addition to working as representative of the APG [Asamblea del Pueblo Guaraní,* Guaraní People's Assembly] *in Ñaurenda and member of the Support Team.*

Tárraga's dream is that one day the Guaraní communities will be able to survive on their own, free both of the patrón and of outside assistance. To this end, he has worked from the beginning to establish the school, the communal field, and the assembly in Ñaurenda, and he has assisted neighboring villages in doing likewise. He believes profoundly that education is the key to preserving Guaraní history and language, securing a future for Guaraní children, and empowering Guaraní communities to chart their own course.

I am from Camiri in Chuquisaca; I came here to Ñaurenda in 1971 from Altamira in La Banda. There were just two houses here at the time, that of Santos's father, Miguel Arebayo, the first capitán, and that of his cousin. As capitán, Arebayo was our intermediary with the patrón. Capitán Arebayo would tell us many stories about the struggles of our forbearers; he himself came here to Ñaurenda fleeing a cruel patrón. I first learned about organizing from the capitán; he was also the one that Dr. Arancibia, from Tarija, would come and talk with when he started visiting Ñaurenda about 1979, encouraging us to build our own school. I also learned about organizing from the compañeros in Tarija, but I'll get to that later.

I never knew my mother; she died soon after I was born. My father and my stepmother went to Argentina to work for a year, and I stayed at home with my four brothers and sisters. Then we moved to Ñaurenda. My grandparents and brothers and sisters came too.

I attended school in nearby Timboy until the fifth grade. It was very hard to find time to go to school because there was so much work to do to help the family, but school was required by law even though the *corregidores* [city officials] didn't want the Guaraní to attend. I liked school very much; I remember one teacher in particular, she was good, and I was a good student. But, for the slightest thing, she would punish you. She would pull your hair if you misbehaved. *¡Ay mi* *madre, dolía!* [Ouch! How it hurt!] I had two friends who would act up and she would hit them on the head with a blackboard. It was prohibited to speak Guaraní; everything was in *castellano*. *Patitos* was the punishment for speaking Guaraní, that is, they would strike you on the bottom with a large rod. I learned by force [*a la fuerza*]. I repeated the fifth grade twice. I would give anything to have been able to continue. I loved reading and writing, and, as you know, they have been essential in my work ever since.

The situation with the patrones back in Chuquisaca was that they treated us like property, not like human beings. For example, if the patrón saw a child, six to eight years or so, this was in Altamira, he would just steal him, pick him up and take him away as if he were his own property. I had a cousin who was stolen that way while he was playing in the ravine. The patrón came galloping toward him, lassoed him, put him on his horse, and rode away with him. We never saw him again. We knew that if we saw the patrón coming toward us on horseback that he was probably going to *zambear* [take one of the kids].

My grandmother was so afraid that he would come back and take the rest of the children away that we came here to escape the child-stealing. We left behind a family orchard there in Chuquisaca, orange and lime trees, plátano, sugar cane; we even had a few pigs. There, men, women, children all worked for the patrón. Mothers would have to leave the very young children locked up at home. They would come home at noon to nurse them, and then go out again to work in the fields, leaving the little ones crying. It was very sad. Of course no one went to school; that was for the *karai* [whites, mestizos]. I think that part of our children's education here in Ñaurenda should include the story of how things used to be; our kids should know about the things that happened to us.

I began working for the patrón here in Ñaurenda when I was in the fifth grade. As *no había económico*, that is, my grandmother couldn't afford the uniform and school fees, I had to hire myself out on credit to the patrón. I had to work off the loan for my school expenses, except, no matter how hard I worked, I could never cancel the loan. Every Saturday and Sunday, I worked for the patrón to pay back what he had advanced us. During vacations, I worked for him full time, as well as from the fifth grade on. We worked from before dawn until 8:00 or 9:00 p.m.; sometimes we only had a handful of ground corn with a little oil, nothing else, to eat. That's the way it was. There was no breakfast, or lunch, nothing until evening. It was difficult.

About 1980, we began to organize in Ñaurenda. There was just myself, Jorge Gallardo (Machirope), Sebastián Catuire (Arakaio), Saravia Novillo, and Porfirio Novillo; others wanted to organize but they were afraid. The majority of the people you see now in the village are not from here; they came to Ñaurenda from la Banda like we did, and with fresh memories of harsh treatment. They were afraid to take any risks. The patrones around here wanted me to leave: "You're not from here," they would say, "don't organize here; go back to La Banda. This is Tarija, not Chuquisaca." I would respond, "If I go to Tarija, I am still in my land because it's all Bolivia."

At the beginning, it was just us, and we wanted a school, but the boss was totally opposed to it. He didn't like it when Dr. Guillermo Arancibia came to help us with our plans. One day, an official asked me if this was my land. I said, "Yes, this is my plot." "Well, you have to have it in writing," he says. "We'll have to see what Antonio Vaca [the patrón] says about that." They knew I was very involved in the school project and were trying to intimidate me. Then one day a policeman shows up and says, "Is this your land? Why do you want a school if you've got one already in Timboy?" See, Timboy is a long way for our children to walk, especially the younger ones, and it is impassable during the winter floods, so that's why we wanted our own school. They arrested me for two days on some charge they made up and set my fine at 360 bolivianos! That was a large sum for me. Finally, I said I could come up with 280 and they said, "Okay, we'll take this but you need to find 360 more!" After a while, they let me go because they knew that I would protest. They still made me pay the fine, for doing absolutely nothing wrong. I finally worked it off. All this just because the boss didn't want a school in Ñaurenda.

Well, we had a meeting when the patrón was gone to Tarija for a week. Capitán Saravia asked, what did we want to do? We all decided then and there to take advantage of the patrón's absence and clear a spot for the school and soccer field. So we set to work and did it. When the patrón returned, oooooh, he was furious. He almost ate us up he was in such a rage. He called everyone together, and then he demanded that we put everything back exactly as it was when he left. Can you imagine? Put the trees back? His way of doing things was by force; he was dangerous and was always our worst enemy. But we didn't give an inch. Soon after *el desmonte* [the clearing], I went to Villa Montes for a few months. By the time I returned home, the school was all built. It was then that we really began organizing in earnest.

On my return the MCM named me *reportero popular* [people's reporter] since I could read and write. It was a very difficult time because the patrón was after me. But we persisted and got the organization going. As reportero popular, I informed the Guaraní about everything that was happening, whatever problems existed, abuses by the patrón, everything, and I would send my reports to Tarija. The patrón absolutely hated me; you can imagine how he wanted to kill me. I was very frightened during those years. Afterwards, when we had built the school, when it was all finished, years later when it was clearly a big success, he claimed that it was all his idea. Can you imagine? Anyway, that was the first big battle, the school. However, we were still peones; freedom from debt peonage came later.

I served as reportero popular roughly from 1982–84; the school was built just a little before that, about 1982. The MCM were much more advanced than we were, they were very organized. They, too, were exploited because they were poor like us. They would invite us to their meetings in Tarija. There were about five or six of us from here who would go, and I was always the one who liked to talk the most. The MCM wanted us to link up with them and also with the APG when it was created some years later; for a while, I served as representative both to the MCM and the APG. The campesino organization's members are not Guaraní, they are Spanish-speaking, and their meetings are in Spanish. But by then my Spanish was pretty good, and I learned a lot by listening too.

The same compañeros I mentioned before, we would go on foot from Ñaurenda to Entre Ríos, and then take a *flota* [bus] to Tarija. We did this about three or four times. The leaders of the MCM of Tarija were some companions from Valle del Medio: Emilio Guerrero, Lucinda Labra and her husband Gabriel Sánchez, also Mario Gareca. They named me reportero popular so there would be more communication; that was a big problem, just communicating among the villages. They would tell me not to be afraid, that they would publish everything on Radio Tarija, and that they would support me, which they did.

The patrones were furious: Antonio Vaca, Benito Herrera, Juvenal Sorucco, Amaro Sorucco, Walter Herrera, Rafael Zambrana. I took a training course for ten days in Tarija to learn how to write a report. After that, I went twice a month for training and meetings. I sent all my reports to Gabriel Sánchez in Tarija; he was the one who gave us our training. I kept copies of a number of my reports, but a flood came, and they were all swept away. I was very disappointed because I think they are very important for our history. I had this form to fill out for each report about what was going on in Ñaurenda, Mokomokal, Tomatirenda, all the nearby communities. I would send it to Tarija, and then two or three days later we would listen to the report on the one o'clock program on the village radio.

Sometimes after a broadcast I would see the patrón and he would say, "Stop doing this or I'll have you thrown in jail." But I had to keep on reporting because it was important to let other compañeros know what was happening in each community. Whenever we had a problem, the compañeros from Tarija would come to help us out. And every time they did, the patrones would say, "*Feliciano, te vamos a joder*" [we are going to screw you].

By the time I finished my assignment as reportero popular, we were more organized here in Ñaurenda. For example, we named a capitán, Saravia Novillo. Then we named a capitán grande; that was Machirope. That was still before we had created the assembly here. We were about 150 people here in Ñaurenda, but just about 10 or 20 of us were involved in organizing. I was named secretary of the capitanía. At that time, I had three positions, secretary, reportero popular, and nurse or health worker.

The whole community, men and women, are the ones who select the capitán. The captain's job is to begin more communities, not only Ñaurenda, but beyond; to resolve problems in the community; and to speak with the patrón on behalf of the compañeros.

The patrones did not like it one bit that we were electing captains. They would send people out to beat up our companions to frighten us away from organizing, and they were always threatening to send the police to throw us in jail. It was essential that we had the support of the MCM during that time and that they would come and help us whenever we needed them. Compañera Lucinda Labra was a courageous fighter and a wonderful person [*pucha bien*]. She's the one who trained us, helped us develop an awareness of our rights, and, most important, she taught us how to face the patrones.

Once, as we were finishing a course for reporteros populares, a young campesino arrived breathless from Santana Nueva, telling us that a karai had just thrown his grandparents out of their home. We thought it was terrible to treat *los ancianitos* [the elderly] that way, so we all went out there and found the *compañeros abuelitos* [grandma and grandpa] sitting under a Churqui tree, like they were no more than dogs, and the ancianito was crying. At that sight we lost our fear. We became angry because we were fed up.

By the time we got there, the patrón was seated inside the house of the ancianito, as if it was his, and he wouldn't come out. What's more, he had ordered large amounts of wood to be cut and stacked, at least two truckfuls. It wasn't for firewood, but to sell. This was a terrible thing! I was the spokesman for the group, and I became nervous because I had never before talked back to a karai. I said, "What are you going to do with all that wood?" "It's my land, and I can exploit my wood," he answered. Imagine, it was all stacked up, there was so much. I asked him for his receipt of purchase for the land. He wouldn't produce anything; he just kept saying, "It's my land." I told him, "You can't take away someone else's house" [*no puede quitar casa ajena*]. I was facing down the patrón and two of his sons, and I was shaking all over. Then I saw that they also had a big hose that could carry water about 500 meters. "We're going to take that hose for our school," I announced. "What? How can you do that?" "The same way you took their house," I responded. We took the hose and later gave it to another community. "We can use this wood to help build our school," I added, which we did. Several of us removed the patrón from the house and then locked it. Afterwards, all the campesinos were singing and dancing, but I was still trembling. We had a song that we sang about the struggle for justice, *todos estamos en la lucha para hacer la vida mejor* [we're all in the struggle to make life better]. It was a decisive moment. That was the first confrontation we ever had face to face with a karai. This was 1982.

It was about 10:00 p.m., and we all returned to Tarija where I went to the Human Rights office to file a report with Sra. Miriam Castillo. The patrón appeared before Human Rights also, and the case went on for about two months, but we actually won that battle, and the elderly couple got their house back. It was the first legal victory.

We kept on with meetings, courses, working with the MCM and with Radio Tarija. There was a great sense of solidarity. Radio Tarija was extremely important, because we could listen to reports and the news was reported so quickly. The karais would go and cut antennas. They couldn't stand Radio Tarija, because it informed everyone about everything that was happening in all the communities. It connected us. We would interview people; they gave us reporters cassettes and recorders, and then they would play the cassettes on the radio. Hardly anyone had a radio, but the news got around fast anyway.

There were other important cases, like ours here in Ñaurenda later on, about 1989 when we made our *potrero comunal* [common field]. We had asked the patrón, Antonio Vaca, to give us the land where we now have our communal plot. *No, no, nada*, he said. Twice more we went to ask because our families were hungry. But he refused to give us even one stick. You see, until 1989, no one had a plot, individual or collective; we had nothing. We had to live from whatever the patrones would give us; we were totally dependent on their whim. They were always telling us that we were lazy and didn't deserve what they gave us out of the goodness of their hearts. How could we possibly work our own plot when we were too lazy even to work theirs?

Finally, I went to Tarija with a compañero and we told our compañeros campesinos about the problem. They said that we have a right to our potrero and that they would mobilize the campesinos to come out and help us. Our *hermanos* [brothers and sisters] from the *Federación de Campesinos* and from *Derechos Humanos* [Human Rights] helped us plan our strategy. They came out in three truckloads and three or four pick-ups. We were more than 300. We were all organized, so we worked together and *desmontamos todo*, that is, we cleared the land with our axes, machetes, and the chain saws they had brought. Then they raised their brightly colored banners on the field, and we all sang; it was very emotional. Men and women worked together cutting the trees, pulling up stumps, so that we could plant for our families, and we all celebrated afterwards. The patrón was there in his house, fuming, but he didn't do anything. There were too many of us, and we were in solidarity. It was a hectare and a half that we cleared for the community. Compañeros came to help from Tarija, San Josecito, Pampa Grande, Bandejas; it was unforgettable.

Before, we had been alone and isolated, and had lived in fear. Now, we were part of a group that would support us. This was a long time after we had established the school; that was the first great act, in 1982, and that we did all alone except for the help of Dr. Arancibia. But this was even more risky, because by taking land for the community, we were saying that we wanted to feed ourselves, to be independent. Before, we had to go in debt just to be able to eat, and we could never pay it off. It was a matter of survival; we had to do what we did.

Well, in two weeks all the claims against us start coming in. The patrón filed a report against us with the Reforma Agraria in Tarija. We went there too and filed our report, and we also went to Human Rights; they were two different groups. I remember Alipio Valdéz was with Human Rights, and there was also a padre. Well, needless to say, Reforma Agraria voted against us because the patrón had paid them off, and Human Rights was for us, saying that we had the right to take the land. Even though Reforma Agraria supported the patrón's claim, he did not throw us off. I think it's because there would have been too much negative publicity.

Little by little, we stopped working as debt peons for the patrón because we were at last working our own communal plot. Not too long after that, we got individual plots as well, of between one half and one hectare each. We kept in communication with Human Rights. There still was no APG here in Ñaurenda; it didn't begin functioning here until 1991, although it had been formed in Santa Cruz in 1987. But we were organized locally among ourselves, and with the help of MCM, Radio Tarija, and Human Rights, we brought about the communal and individual plots.

Later, a group went to Tarija and gave a report to the Agrarian Reform office, explaining why we were justified in clearing that land to feed our families. The Agrarian Reform at that time was completely in the pocket of the patrón, so, of course, they rejected our case. After I arrived back here in Timboy, I met up with Gabino Barrera, a powerful patrón in our area. He says to me, "Tomorrow a commission of three soldiers is coming to investigate what you have done and the grievances you say you have against the patrón. You better prepare yourselves."

I came here to Timboy to use the short wave radio to communicate with Gabriel Sánchez to ask him what to do. He advised several of us to meet immediately with representatives of the Human Rights commission so that they could help us get ready for the delegation that was being sent by the patrón. In fear, several of us left that night, not knowing if there would be soldiers along the road to stop us. An hour earlier, two *camionetas* [trucks] filled with people had entered the area; they were the patrones' commission from Tarija. We waited nervously for our ride to pick us up so we could talk to the Human Rights representatives. Finally, about 4:00 a.m. they showed up and took us safely away.

At the beginning, when we decided to do the *desmonte* for our communal plot, we never dreamed that anyone would send a commission from the Reforma Agraria out to investigate us. You have to realize that the Agrarian Reform office sounds like a good thing, but the members were totally "owned" by the patrón. We knew that they would vote against us because we didn't have the patrón's permission for the desmonte. Machirope, Juan Acerri, Sebastián Catuire, and I had made the report in Tarija earlier. There we were told that we were *malcriados* [ill-bred] and that the land was not ours.

Of course, some of the patrones didn't have written titles either. Their "godfather" [*su papá de santo*], they would say, passed the land down to them. When we were in Tarija, where we had gone immediately after the desmonte to give our version of events, we began the discussion at 9:00 a.m., and we were still there talking at 2:00 p.m. We had a lawyer arguing for us; she told them that we had a right to agrarian reform. But, in the end, we got nothing, because Sebastián Vázquez, that's the son-in-law of Antonio Vaca, had two lawyers and lots of money. This was in 1990, on behalf of Saladito and Ñaurenda, which were a single community then. Sebastián Vásquez said to me on the way out, "Why are you doing this to me? I've always treated you like a son!"

Later, there was a trumped-up murder charge against one of our compañeros, Juan Acerri. He was in jail for about five years, but he did nothing wrong. As you can see, we have had a struggle, but we have continued, and we have not given up. Anyway, the report of the patrones to that Agrarian Reform commission in Tarija was completely negative against us. They had two lawyers, remember.

That's how they tried to intimidate us, with lawyers and commissions. For example, in the afternoon, when we would come home from the fields to eat, the patrón would come up to us and say, "Look, 'son,' you've almost got enough to pay your bill. Why don't you work afternoons?" He wanted us to work his fields afternoons too, and if we didn't want to, he would threaten us with another "commission." That was how they did it, not directly, but with threats of dishonest legal action, tricks by groups that always favored them. They did all their work through commissions. So we were always fearful, and we felt that we had to work to pay off our debts and interest to the patrón. If we didn't, we were afraid they would find any pretext at all to close the school. The APG still hadn't come on the scene here yet, so the patrones held all the cards. That's why the clearing of the land for our communal plot was like a declaration of independence; however, we had no idea whether it would work.

Then things started happening elsewhere. There was a problem in Pampa Redonda between the compañeros campesinos and the karai there. We had a meeting and helped them out like others had helped us out here in Ñaurenda. Then we went on and helped others in Yukimbia and Tentaguasu. The same people went to each place, organizing, explaining why we are doing this, what is the purpose. Some did not understand or were not interested, but others were, and little by little. they began to develop a consciousness and to understand the importance of organizing.

When we spoke to the various communities about *la organización*, what we meant at that time was the capitanía that we all formed part of. For example, they invited us to Pampa Redonda because they wanted to make a communal plot like we had done in Ñaurenda. Pampa Redonda is in our captaincy and they are our brothers, so we went. Human Rights and Radio Tarija always gave us transportation; 150 of us went to Pampa Redonda. We worked for two days building a stone fence around the communal plot for our companions. We made our fence, and the patrón made one too, but our compañeros took his down. Then the patrón filed a complaint and called out about 30 soldiers, fully armed, to throw us off the land. We walked up to them and four or five of us began talking to them, explaining what we were doing, even though we were all frightened and completely without arms. The patrón and his men retired, and it was a miracle that no one was killed. This was in 1990.

But this was what we meant by organization within the captaincy. I was the secretary of the captaincy; Machirope was the capitán of the capitanía grande, and the second captain was Sebastián Catuire. The idea of the capitanía came from our need to organize ourselves in order to survive. We still didn't have the assembly; that came even later. Things came bit by bit, because we were always having to convince our compañeros to participate in the organization. Because they would say, "Well, if I join the organization, who will feed me? What are we going to gain from all this? We won't gain anything. We will just lose." They didn't realize that you have to look beyond the present.

I am grateful for this opportunity to look back, because I see that we have accomplished a lot since the early 1980s. First, we were a very small group within the community, just a few of us really. Then, the next year we grew a little, and we kept on. Our first year there was no organization, this was before la hermana Maura McCarthy and the *Equipo de Apoyo* [Support Team] began assisting us. We gave *el arranque* [the start up] to the organization. Afterwards, it spread to other communities and then the next year to other zones.

We were totally allied with the campesinos during the 1980s. The ethnic, cultural question came to be important after we were already organized in the capitanía grande and the *Asamblea del Pueblo Guaraní* began to become more or less important here. The APG was open to our compañeros campesinos because our struggle is together, a common one, and many campesinos entered the APG; for example, the capitán of Ñaurenda, Facundo, is a campesino and a member of the APG. But others decided that it was more for the Guaraní. And some Guaraní didn't like non-Guaraní to be members of the APG because of past experiences. The APG is largest in the Cordillera, where it has its headquarters. We went to Camiri to participate in 1993, and in 1994 we began to collaborate. We were a little slow because of our isolation, because it wasn't until 1992 that we were even aware that there existed another Guaraní organization!

The function of the APG is to find more members and to raise consciousness, also to find funding. It has similar functions to the Support Team, it's just that the APG is a lot larger, of course. I was named to the Executive Committee in 1994 when we had an assembly here with the APG, so I'm also the secretary of the APG here in Ñaurenda, elected in 1994. The work of the Executive Committee is also to *concientizar* [raise consciousness] and get funding.

The MCM still exists, but it is no longer very important for us; we began going our separate ways once we had the APG. It was very lovely though, the close relationship we had for so long.

At the zonal level, I served as secretary. As the idea of organizing spread, it became difficult because I had to travel long distances for meetings. I was secretary of the capitanía for about three years and then secretary of the zone later. When the APG finally got an office, I left to come and help them. In 1994, I was also named an officer of the APG, as well as the *Equipo de Apoyo del Pueblo Guaraní* (EAPG). We've been working with other branches of the APG, like the Santa Cruz branch, and we have become stronger.

One of the hardest things about becoming organized are the long distances between pueblos, the lack of vehicles and roads. We walk very long distances whenever we have to perform our duties. For example, more than four times I had to walk from Ñaurenda to el Barrio del Medio for a meeting, leaving about 9:00 a.m. and arriving about 2:00 p.m. At times, I have had problems with my family; it makes me sad to leave them. After I finished my other assignments in 1997, I began to work with education, going around to the communities and conversing with parents to explain to them why it is so important. Some still don't understand; others think it is beautiful, but they can't buy the pencils and notebooks.

I tell them that education is so important because that's how we will advance. If we do not have education, we do not have power. Where there is education, there is power. If you don't give importance to education, you will never be anything, all your life you will be like a burro. We are still trying to convince some parents. Many adults, however, are studying in the afternoons. My daughter is continuing to study at the secondary level. She went to Entre Ríos last year because we did not have secondary school here, but she has returned to Ñaurenda because we have built our new addition, through the *tercer intermedio* [third year of secondary school, eighth grade].

Some people say that education will change our culture, that everything will be different. I don't think so; the APG is helping in that regard, and they are supporting education. Bilingual education helps too; we have a Guaraní teacher for our children, something that was unthinkable not too long ago. We began bilingual education here in 1994, and it continues for the first three grades. I believe that with the right kind of education, our children can become professionals and still be Guaraní. By being Guaraní, I mean being of Guaraní origin, being Guaraní by birth, by blood. I also mean by customs, traditions, and language. I want the young people to be proud of their heritage, and that's one reason I want the teachers to learn and pass on the history of those who came before us. They don't do it yet, except for some legends and stories, but the actual history of what happened and when and how, they are still learning. We have been thinking of making a book where we would at least contribute how Ñaurenda came to be.

What I wish for our people is, first of all, that our families stay together; and second, that we become educated so we can advance, no? What I want more than anything is for us, we Guaraní ourselves, to take charge of our own future [*que los mismos guaraní que hagamos cargo de nuestro futuro, nosotros mismos*], la hermana Maura and the groups that are helping us notwithstanding. If some day God were to give me the power to do a little more, I would like to be a leader of our young people, to show them what they can become if they are educated.

We still have very serious problems, such as lack of education, health services, roads, transportation, and of course, markets for our crops. Until recently, the patrones were our biggest problem. Now they have lost, and the problem is production. We can clear the field for planting, but we need seed, a community tractor, and fences to keep the patrón's cows from eating up our crops. A fence is very expensive, so we have to cut down trees to make a log fence because the cattle are unbelievably destructive. In the common field we have a log fence because the Support Team solved that problem. Now we need to fence the individual plots, but the problem is finding the funds. Of course, there are many other things that we also need, so we have to prioritize.

The thing that is holding us back the most is our low production. Sometimes, it is because of the weather, either drought or flood; sometimes, because of lack of organization of the work group and lack of training in how to work well together. There could be much better administration of the work groups. Usually there are personal differences that weaken everything; that's very common.

Another serious problem is alcoholism. For example, today two compañeros are friends; then they get drunk and fight and become enemies. Sometimes someone gets beaten up, and then, out of shame, he doesn't participate in the work group. Then it becomes a productivity issue as well as a personal and family problem. I think that only self-control and self-knowledge will solve the alcohol problem. We've tried to get the shopkeepers to stop selling alcohol, but they just keep on.

It's clear that we have many problems to work on, but we also have come a great distance from the time when we were alone, hopeless, and afraid to look the patrón in the eye.

Timboy, 4 May 1997; 3 August 1998

Facundo Galeán

Bible-quoting, teetotaling Facundo Galeán is one of the few evangelicals and mestizos in the village of Ñaurenda. He is a passionate admirer and defender of the Guaraní, with whom he came to live many years ago, a choice for which he continues to be criticized by other mestizos. Galeán admires the "Christian" virtues of the Guaraní, especially their generosity in sharing their meagre resources, and he maintains that they have much to teach so-called Christians. As a recovering alcoholic, Galeán is concerned about the problem of alcohol abuse among the Guaraní, but he believes that with Bible reading and reflection things will improve. The residents of Ñaurenda demonstrated their affection and admiration for Galeán by electing him first captain to succeed Machirope. It is less important to them that Galeán is mestizo and speaks little Guaraní than that he is deeply committed to the welfare of the community.

The Assembly has named me capitán. Unfortunately, I cannot speak much Guaraní, but I feel a great sense of pride, and I give thanks to God that my Guaraní compañeros understand Spanish perfectly. That is a beautiful thing, so I say that although I know how to read and all, in every moment of every day, I respect the Guaraní to the highest degree possible because they know two languages, even though they do not know how to read and write. I know how to read and write, but only in one. In this sense, I feel inferior to them. I would prefer that they be the authority that tells me what to do, but they have chosen me.

However, I'm not the only authority because we always work in groups to consult and solve problems together. We include the former capitanes and others who are good at making recommendations and who can serve as *testigos del arreglo* [witnesses to an agreement] and can assist in deciding disputes. When settling grievances, we all help encourage the person who is at fault to stop doing what he was doing; we keep after him trying to convince him to behave.

For example, at a recent fiesta we had, the Feast of the Cross, everything started out really nice. But the problem is that there is a lot of alcohol consumption, and that makes people remember earlier grievances, grudges; it revives rancor against a compañero. Words are exchanged, then blows, then the knife comes out. Before, the *castellanos* [Spanish speakers] in this area would settle disputes between the *demandante* [plaintiff] and the *demandado* [defendant] by themselves. I know, I used to be *corregidor* [town official].

We, however, try to settle disputes in the organization with at least five, six, or seven people participating in the settlement. We want to resolve these things here ourselves; we don't want them to drag us off to Entre Ríos or Tarija. Because we, as poor people, are aware that, as God commands, it is important to pardon offences, but the castellanos around here, they don't pardon. And we don't want our Guaraní compañeros to fall into the hands of a higher authority. That's why we try to resolve everything in community.

For example, in the case I was describing, we asked the aggressor why he beat up the other compañero. "I don't remember," he said, "I was drunk and I don't remember anything." "*¿Por qué tomas si vos sos un mal borracho?*" [Why do you drink if you're a mean drunk?] "I don't know," comes the answer. We decided on the sanction, which was to pay the nurse for tending the person he hurt, but, of course, he doesn't have any money. So he has to pay in work, community work, for the school, or the road; the number of days varies according to the seriousness of the crime. He finishes the work, then he signs the *Libro de Actas*, that's our official village record book, saying that he promises to respect others and never to repeat those offences. In the event of noncompliance, let's say he goes back and commits the same offence again, then the sanction will be 500 bolivianos. Then we all sign the Libro to that effect. The second time we are much stricter, even if it pains the compañero. Alcohol is the central problem in all our serious disputes. It makes the best man unreliable; it ruins the person completely. He loses his creativity, begins to fight, sometimes he beats his wife or his mother, rarely his children.

I used to be a *tomador* [drinker] and a *peleador* [fighter]; the police would come and I would land in jail. Then I would have to pay 150 bolivianos, and a poor person doesn't have any money; it was a terrible way to live. I needed the Bible to set me on the right path. Now I am *recto* [a straight arrow], and I want to be an example. I don't want any of our hermanos to go to jail because it is so expensive. The Bible says that drunkenness is wrong. One reads the Bible and focuses on obeying the Ten Commandments, which tell us how to live our lives. As *mburuvicha comunal* [community chief], I have to be more recto, more of an example, and not drink. Well, perhaps a *copita* [a little glass] just to be polite, a little *chichita de maíz*, but not alcohol. I tell them, if I drink, then I am not worthy to be your authority.

I think it's important to have a strong morality; my morality comes from reading the Bible. The Ten Commandments are the most important, not to steal, to love your fellow man. If we learn, little by little to obey the commandments, then we will improve the way we run our community. We will learn to manage our funds more honestly too, because we will not dare put our hand in the till that belongs to everyone without the full consent of the assembly. Sometimes, some of our *dirigentes* [leaders] have fallen a bit in this area, and others are a little cowardly, and don't say to the dirigente, "You shouldn't do that." But I am not afraid, and I tell them with affection, "*Es plata de todos* [it's everyone's money]. Let's begin work anew; if we have fallen, let's get up." If there's a problem within the organization, my feeling is that we shouldn't run from it, or pretend it doesn't exist, but try to get involved in solving it and try to *recapacitar* [re-educate].

The Bible is my guide, but it's not that of the Guaraní. All their attitudes and practices are Christian; they lack just a few small things to become Christians. Actually, they are better Christians than the so-called cristianos. That's because they are loving; they are not reproachful. They welcome everyone, they are very hospitable, and they invite everyone to everything. When they kill a cow or a pig or a goat, they give some to everyone; they are very generous. That is lovely. That is Christian.

I became interested in the Bible because I was a disaster. I had fallen into a series of bad problems, all because of alcohol. My wife would scold me and say "How are we going to get the 150 bolivianos to pay the sanction? We are so poor, we don't even have a cow, a burro, or anything at all. We can't even buy our kids *chinelas* [plastic sandals] or food." That was my shameful lesson. A friend gave me a New Testament, and I began to turn my life around.

We could have much better fiestas. You know, the Guaraní have the custom of participating in fiestas even on Sundays, and the kids see *las malas actitudes* [bad attitudes, behavior]. If we look for an alternative to brake a bit our alcoholism, we can share our fiestas better with our children. I haven't brought this up yet with the compañeros; I'm still studying it, because I want to do it right. But everyone agrees that alcohol makes us *desconocer* [disavow] each other; it makes us fight, and it makes us demoralized. The castellanos ask me, "What do you think you're doing, living with those Guaraní?" But I read my Bible, and I am calm; they don't bother me. If I don't know my Bible well, I will fall. And I want to know more; I need to become more involved with the oppressed, the poor, where they need moral support. I live here with the Guaraní, but at the same time I want to help them to *superarse* [overcome their situation]. The castellanos say they are slow, that they don't know how to think or offer an opinion, but it's just that they don't articulate things in the same way as the castellanos. They have spent so much time obeying the patrón, that now they're just beginning to learn to do things, including thinking, for themselves. Every morning the patrón would come and tell them to go take care of the pigs, the cows, do this, do that, and so they haven't been brought up knowing how to use their own head.

I was employed by the patrón when I was younger as a truck driver. I'd say the power of the patrón in this area goes back 30 years or more. The patrón lived in Tomatirenda. I would drive from Tarija to Tomatirenda to Ñaurenda, just doing errands for him. I see how the Guaraní got used to sitting around waiting for the castellanos to tell them what to do and not thinking for themselves. Not now, though; those days are over.

I am from Tomatirenda. I came here because I had been a teacher. I am 33 years old. We wanted to have a school in Tomatirenda because there were lots of children, but they had to come here to Timboy, which is very far. So the comunidad named me professor because I can teach first and second grade. Trying to hurry the school project along, I would get all the kids together and start teaching them so their parents would see how they were learning and would hurry up with the construction. I did that for two years until they got the school built.

There was a social problem though. The rich were angry about what I was doing. I was always with the children, and the patrones needed them to go fetch water, feed the chickens and pigs; however, as the children were in school, they were no longer available to do these tasks. The patrones threatened me repeatedly, and that's why I finally left.

I came to Ñaurenda because there was already an organization, and because my sister lives here. So I came to live in Ñaurenda too, and I've been here for six years now. I had to leave Tomatirenda because of the patrones, but they have a teacher there now. The organization here in Ñaurenda has been good and it has been bad, but it keeps on going. When I arrived, they already had their school, they had their asamblea, and they had their capitán, at that time it was capitán Saravia.

Then I would go back to my community and I would tell them organize, organize, organize! Tomatirenda is 50 per cent Guaraní and 50 per cent castellano. I went back to encourage them because everyone was working for the patrón. If you didn't want to work for the patrón, he would come and throw you out, make you leave for good. The patrón was Benito Herrera. But I would go back to talk with my compañeros there, to tell them about the organization in Ñaurenda. The patrón was still threatening me, but I was no longer afraid. I kept telling them that if they would organize, then they would no longer be peones. From so much coming and going and talking to the compañeros, we organized there. We formed a group and planted our own potreros; this was about three years ago. So, the organization arrived at Tomatirenda and now they have their own capitán, leadership, and the castellanos and the Guaraní get along very well there.

Here, people get along with each other very well, except for the alcohol and fiestas, and then no one wants to work, and they are hung over. If it weren't for alcoholism, there would be no problems here. What I am doing now is talking individually with members of the community, saying, "Look, brother, let's don't drink because it is the road to ruin. Perhaps now we are handy, good workers. But if we keep drinking, we'll end up stretched out on the ground. Then comes illness." Some listen for a little while, but then they go back to drinking.

The other problem is that our community is very poor. Last year, we couldn't afford to sow the common field, and we didn't have enough food to make the *olla común* [common pot] or to contribute to the *canasta familiar* [family basket]. Sometimes we went hungry. Sometimes we get credit from *la hermana* [the sister] until we can pay her back. Now we're trying to make the common field go forward. We all think it's a good idea because income from its produce will go to health, education, notebooks, medicines for the village. Right now, we don't know exactly how we are going to be able both to use the *comunal* and set aside more money for the community, but we're trying to figure it out. We don't have the custom of having money, so it is hard to figure out how to manage it and to plan for when we might have money.

I've been capitán for about a month. I'm not the first capitán castellano, but the previous capitán castellano knew Guaraní. As for my Guaraní, I guess I speak about 20 per cent; that is, for every 100 words, I know about 20. It's great that the children are learning both languages.

Our main problem is our economic situation. We have to find a way to improve, because whenever we get any money, we spend it right away. We need some kind of *administrador de sus bienes* [financial administrator].

Coqueo [I chew coca leaves] a little; at first, I didn't like it, but I find that it does help me work. But you can't spend too much on it for the good of your family. But coca is not the big problem, not like alcohol.

I understand that, in the past, before the men would go out to work they would *coquear* [chew coca] and *orar* [pray] that their work go well and that God, or the tumpa, would protect them. I would like to revive that tradition, to ask God's blessing on our work. I would also like to ask that we all stand and start our assemblies with a prayer, asking God to put good words in our mouths, to help us come up with good ideas, to help us be good workers, to be strong and courageous, and always to maintain our unity so we can accomplish our work and do it well. That way we would always be reminded that our work is under God; first God, then work. God wills that we work united, shoulder to shoulder to maintain our families, and that is, in fact, what the Guaraní do.

Currently in the village, some social organization is giving a course on violence against women. I think that is very important, and I hope to continue those kinds of workshops and to use their methods in order to help educate all our compañeros. It is also a good way to talk about the violence that results from alcoholism; that's the cause of almost all our violence, including domestic violence. I plan to read to the compañeros the level of punishment given for each kind of violence, including the kinds for which they send you to Tarija. Then I could explain to the people, in a course, and we could little by little improve our living conditions. This is a strategy that I was discussing with Feliciano, and he agrees. First, we're going to start in informal conversations with people, talking up the idea, with Don Jorge (Machirope) and others, gathering support little by little.

They don't know what the law says; they don't know what level of violence will get them taken away. They don't think about those things when they are drinking, and then violence erupts, and then they get sent to jail. Meanwhile, the potreros go to ruin and our children too. We want to explain all this to them. We would like to do it the same way they did it for the violence against women class. That was very effective. They read the law to the compañeras and explained it. I want to follow up on their lead and talk to the women about the relationship between domestic violence and drunkenness, so that they, too, will push against alcohol.

You know, the Guaraní and the castellano way of life are very different. As I mentioned earlier, the Guaraní are much more Christian than the castellanos in the way they live their lives, in the way they live in community; united, it's almost like they form one large family. I think that's the way God wants us to live, in harmony and respecting each other. But the castellanos do not live in any kind of unity or brotherhood. They are always fighting among themselves and trying to be the most important or powerful. In God's eyes we are all equal; the Guaraní are not less. I am not ashamed to have chosen to live with the Guaraní because

I love and admire them. The castellanos criticize me for my choice; it makes them angry that I respect the Guaraní.

Some people say that Christianity will totally change Guaraní culture. I don't see that. What I see is almost a perfect harmony between Christianity and the Guaraní culture. And they can continue with their fiestas, but healthy fiestas because our children participate in them. We can make chicha de maíz, have plenty of food to eat, they will be happy fiestas, but the happiness will be in thanksgiving for the blessings of this life. We could start the fiesta with a prayer also, giving thanks for the corn, the chicha, the *mote* [corn dish]. We should celebrate on the day of the fiesta, and then the next day get up and go to work, tranquilly, instead of losing another day's work, which we can't afford.

The evangelicals want to make a church in Ñaurenda. The community is opposed to it because the católico and the evangélico don't go together. I think that in the eyes of God we are both equal. The most important thing is the practice, what one does. Catholics drink too. The problem is that the compañeros think that if the Bible is introduced here, there will be no more fiestas [*si se introduce la biblia no va a haber fiesta*]. But you can have a great fiesta with lots of good things in the olla común and not allow them to add alcohol.

With regard to the Guaraní religious practices, there remain only a few of the old customs. For example, mourning. When a family member dies, they mourn for a period of months or even a year. They drink chicha, and they use leather straps to beat each other on the shoulders and back, in a kind of *martirio* [flagellation]. I haven't seen it but my brother has. They play the *bombo* [drum] for about 20 minutes at a time. Another custom is when they are waking a family member, they prepare all kinds of food for the departed to take on their journey. There is still witchcraft too. It's dying out, but there are some who practice good and some who practice bad witchcraft. Some know how to cure you of snakebite and *recalcaduras* [pressures, swellings]. They cure with secret prayers, talking and spitting, and they can also cure you of spider bites. There are some people in the pueblo who still can do this; for example, Valerio Arce can cure snake bites. He learned from his father. Some of them learn in dreams, that's what they say. They keep their custom of curanderos, and they produce results.

They also have an environmental consciousness. They respect nature [*respetan el monte*]. The castellanos are the ones who do the most harm to nature; the Guaraní never. The castellanos deforest in great quantity, but the Guaraní never deforest. The castellanos believe they are Christians, but they don't have the slightest idea what that means because they destroy the forest to exploit the wood. If the Guaraní cuts down a tree, it is for everyone, not just for oneself or for a profit.

We need irrigation in the village because malnutrition is a serious problem. We need vegetables. A group of mothers produces a little, but it is not enough. So we're thinking about starting family gardens for individual families, very small. We need a little help, a small roll of wire to fence off the *huertos* [gardens]. I would like to use a little bit of my land to try out new things. For example, I'm now cultivating soy with the assistance of CERDET, an agricultural organization that helps poor people. I would like to have a little hand mill for grinding corn and mixing it with soy, and, if the compañeros like it, that could improve our nutrition.

I would also like to have some chickens, for eating and for laying eggs, about ten of each. That way, each family could have eggs. I'm going to Tarija next month to get some chickens. I will try to get them myself, CERDET helped only with the soy. We need chickens because we don't have any. We need them for when visitors come, like when education officials come to visit our school, or when compañeros from other villages come for meetings. When the educators came the other day, we had to get up way before dawn and go to Tomatirenda to get a chicken because we didn't have any in Ñaurenda. We need to have chickens for Mother's Day too. Corn sells for such a low price that we get very little money, but chickens are not very expensive, and this way we would have both eggs and chickens.

I also would like to set up a little store, my wife and I would run it. Then I could really dedicate myself to *incentivando* [encouraging] my compañeros. If I could do these things, I could dedicate myself exclusively to being capitán. I could attend more meetings outside the community; if you don't, then you don't know what is going on. The family garden could be the market of each family. Yucca, sweet potato, peanuts, soy. They could save whatever small amount they receive for an illness or emergency, and they wouldn't have to spend so much for food. I want to encourage them to do that themselves.

Maybe I could get a little credit with interest to get my little shop started. It's okay if I lose my *jornal* [wage for daily labor in the field]. At least if I had a store I could help my compañeros more, saying let's do this, and helping everyone equally. But first, I want to start with small family gardens. I want to help *levantar el otro* [lift the other person]. I have an evangelical friend who tells me, "If someone asks for a fish, teach him to fish." That's what I'm trying to do, so that all our companions will have something.

Timboy, 13 May 1997

Valerio Muñoz

Like many other Guaraní, Muñoz fled to O'Connor to escape bondage to a patrón in another department. As mburivicha, or chief, of the community of Agua Buena, which is even more isolated than Ñaurenda, Muñoz has worked hard to reduce the nearly insurmountable natural barriers to communication between the Guaraní of Agua Buena and those elsewhere. Like other Guaraní, he is a staunch advocate of education as the only way to overcome fear, stand up to the patrón, and take charge of one's life. Muñoz also expresses an environmental consciousness as he condemns the illicit cutting of trees in nearby forested areas. Muñoz, who also serves as a health promoter, is an extremely able captain, and one who gives his personal account of how the Guaraní of Agua Buena came to organize politically.

I am the mburivicha of the Agua Buena community. I am a Guaraní, and like so many others, I came here fleeing from a patrón. We formed a community in Agua Buena, which is some distance away and difficult to get to, but I settled there, and they named me chief. We organized ourselves in 1993.

There are 40 families in Agua Buena, counting all the karai and the Guaraní; there are more Guaraní. We began to go to meetings to get to know our hermanos better, and that's how we got started. It was very difficult at first, since no one wanted to break with the patrón because it was costly. We had to lose our fear above all. That was the most important, not to be afraid of the patrones and to defend our brothers who were suffering at their hands.

I think that the only way you can overcome fear is by having a grassroots base of support. When one has a base, one gains confidence in oneself and trust that with the others you can face the problem before you. We had to band together to face some of the abuses of the patrón. For example, deceit, charging us twice or three or even more times what something costs because we were ignorant. And not allowing mamás and papás to accompany their very young children to school. It's that they didn't want the children going to school at all because if they study, learn, if they are educated, then they can stand up for themselves. When they get a little older, they can think about situations and realize that, no, this should not be this way. However, if one does not go out and study, one knows nothing. One is just an *animalito* [a little animal], nothing more, who, if you give them something to eat, they eat, and if you don't, they don't. Maybe you will be able to work for your food, but you will never know if you will be able to make enough to feed yourself, and people can get away with taking your work away from you, just because you didn't go to school. It's impossible to know the words to use to talk to the patrón if you haven't gone to school, and that's part of the fear. Then you're set up for a brutal deception, because they twist words around and sweet talk you [*con boca dulce te hablan*]. They confuse you, and you go away thinking that you are just fine and that they treat you well. Of course, the patrón cheats the workers at every turn because of that. Without education, without knowledge, without awareness, you will always be tricked and taken advantage of by those who have power, not just the patrón, but any powerful person. There are others who are not patrones, who always try to deceive. They promise you something, take your money, and leave, or they ask you to do some work for them, and you do it, and then they don't pay you. These people are usually karais.

For all these reasons, we had to organize ourselves. People came from Ñaurenda to help us, like Machirope; they also sent a paper inviting us to one of their meetings. We went, even though it's an extremely long walk through difficult terrain. It's a sacrifice just to get there, because we are isolated in Agua Buena. We have always looked for a way to have a better road than the one we have, which you can hardly call a road, and also to try to reach the villages that are even more remote than we are to help them organize too. We are far, but there are several that are even farther away, and they still have patrones.

In Agua Buena we have our *terreno comunal* [common field] and our individual plots as in Ñaurenda, but we still don't know who the lands belong to. We're still dealing with the question of ownership, titles. We think that with this law we can now have our own territory, have title, so we can say this is ours and work it for ourselves. The patrones really aren't claiming ownership anymore since we have become united and have figured out our ideal, which is to be one, that is, to act as one and speak with one voice. We clarify all that through conversation, meetings, planning sessions, and by all of us looking out for the *medio ambiente* [environment].

Our forests are important and should not be exploited. We have to protect them; it's a big problem because people enter and cut. They come in and say they have permits, and then they take out huge loads of wood. We can't figure out how they get the permits or if they're lying, because it should not be authorized; it is against the law. We had a meeting, all the mburivichas of communities, to condemn the cutting. If we don't, then, sadly, they will be taking the food from our mouths [*lastimosamente, la comida de nuestra boca se nos van a llevar*].

The community is participating actively in the political process and is concerned about the medio ambiente, because they are taking out a great deal of wood. We have enough palm, but wood for our own construction we have very little, but for firewood there is plenty. We use different wood for firewood and for construction.

We chiefs are working on this in each of our communities, trying to defend the future of our communities and to orient our hermanos about the importance of the forests, to give them training so that they can help us help the community. Training has been very helpful for us; it has really educated us to the importance of the forest. Thanks to it we have increased our understanding, but many of the mburivichas can't read or write, and that's a limitation. In the workshops there are some who can read and take notes, but most of us cannot. That's also one reason we want bilingual schools, so that at least we can understand what's being said, whether it's in Guaraní or castellano.

I learned castellano as a first language, and Guaraní as a second. From the time I was a very young child I worked for the patrones who didn't allow me to speak Guaraní, and, because of that, my Guaraní isn't as good as my castellano. Since stopping work for the patrón, I have improved my Guaraní quite a bit. Sadly, to work for the patrón is to lose everything. Soon, you have a houseful of kids to try to support and you can see no alternative for your life. Everything is for the patrón, for the patrón. When you are old and can no longer work, you look back and see that all your strength went to the patrón, and you say, "This is what I lived for?"

Our school is pretty, our maestro Ramiro is very good. We have four grades and 50 children already. I fought hard to get a fence for the school; I even went to the county to get help to purchase it. We were free by then and working in community. We have been fortunate to count on the Support Team, la hermana, CERDET, and others, to help us keep going because our community has no money. We have learned to work with each group and to benefit from what they have to offer us. It has been a wonderful partnership.

A big problem for us is the so-called road and how to keep it clear, because the poor are very isolated. In Entre Ríos and Timboy we got help from CERDET to help us clean the road, that is to clear the boulders, branches, and debris. If we hadn't cleared the rocks away, we wouldn't have been able to get there to pick up the people to come to the workshop here. We need to have our road clear so that a *movilidad* [vehicle] can have access, but we also need to be able to walk it on foot.

I think what our community needs most is communication. We need a short wave radio, a Dieter, for example. We also are greatly in need of medicines and potable water. The rains have washed away all our construction for a water pipe. This is a big problem, because we had just about finished. The man who was responsible for the project never showed up to complete it. He was supposed to bring different pipes, because what he brought out at first wasn't any good. With the water pressure it broke, so he was going to come out and install a new system. We have everything prepared for him; the only thing missing is the *cañería* [piping] and the man who was to come from Tarija to put it in. We have sent him a letter saying that, if he doesn't do it soon, we will have to file suit [*seguir un proceso*]. There is a lawyer, Dr. Guillermo Castro, also in Tarija, who is helping us. We can communicate by radio with him, but not in Agua Buena. We have to go to another community where they have a short wave radio.

I have seen a number of important changes just in the years since we have become a community. First, the patrones have to respect us. Now, we have the freedom to go out when we want and participate in meetings, to do public work here in the community, and to send our kids to school. There was none of that before. First of all, there was no school, and there was no participation in anything; everything was through and for the patrones. They would never let us work together to build a school, or to do any other work as a community. Our little palm school began in 1986, and the current school is just three years old. It's made of adobe, cement, and plaster.

Being a capitán is a full time job [*trabajo todísimo*]. It depends on the people how long I will be capitán; I asked them if they wouldn't like for someone else to take over, but they want me to stay on. As capitán, I don't have the time to cultivate my own plot. This year I've just planted a tiny bit. I had to bring this up at a community meeting and to tell the hermanos that they couldn't name me *dirigente* and leave it at that. I needed for them to help me with my field. Lately, however, they have understood and have been helping me in my *individual*, because, otherwise, I can't feed my family. Community service is a big honor, but it is a big sacrifice too.

We didn't plant much in our terreno comunal this year, just about a hectare because of the heavy rains and flooding. We want to sow improved seed like we did in the individuales. The terreno comunal is worked in *grupos de trabajo* and each person is paid according to the work that he has contributed. The president of the work group keeps records of all this.

The most difficult thing for me is that I have two jobs: health promoter and capitán, and that means that I travel everywhere. That is actually quite difficult because of the distances, the terrain, and because so much of it is on foot. I went to Entre Ríos some time ago, in 1992, and finished the four levels of training required to become a *promotor de salud* [health promoter]. In the fourth level we give injections, take care of pregnancies, assist in childbirth, and more or less detect illnesses. We instruct villagers in how to boil water, but they don't do it. They say it doesn't taste as good. Nor do they build latrines. When we had the cholera epidemic the first year, they did, but now, they're forgotten.

I see a much better future for my son than I had for myself. We get along pretty well in the community; we have some problems, and some of the hermanos are still tempted to go back to the patrón because it is so hard to make it on your own, but that is just a few.

Ñaurenda, 7 May 1997

Angela Tagüe

Angela Tagüe, who comes from a town near Camiri in the Cordillera, is Ñaurenda's bilingual teacher. She arrived several years ago after having completed her required training and practicum and after working briefly as a translator of bilingual tapes to be sent from Camiri to places like Ñaurenda. Tagüe describes the bilingual curriculum and her life in the community in this brief, but informative, interview.

I come from the Guaraní community of Urudaiti, about 15 kilometres from Camiri in the Cordillera. There was a school in my village up to the *quinto básico*, that is, the first five years, and then I was an internal student in Camiri after the fifth grade until I graduated when I was 20 years old. I am 27 years old now. My education was in Spanish only; that's how I first learned the language.

Later, I studied bilingual education in Camiri. It was a great educational and cultural experience for me, because, although I spoke Guaraní, I could not read or write it. First, they taught me the Guaraní ABCs, and then I took bilingual practicums in other schools, 15 each in two different schools. I also went to numerous *charla*s [talks] on bilingual education. I did my practicum, worked as an assistant in a bilingual classroom, observing, practicing, teaching some. I think I have a knack for bilingual education; I really loved all my education and the bilingual training especially.

The *Teko Guaraní* [*Talleres de Educación y Comunicación*, Education and Communication Workshops] office is in Camiri; that's where they translate into Guaraní the cassettes that they send to this region. That's what I was doing too, translating tapes. Then they told me that I could be a bilingual teacher if I wanted to. I would have to study for two additional years after high school. I thought it over and decided I really wanted to do it, so I did.

They assigned me to this pueblo. I came here in 1995 and have been here two years now. At first, I really didn't want to come, because it is so far from my home. But I have a cousin who lives fairly close by, and he told me that this was a nice pueblo, that they would treat me well, and that I would like it here. I had really wanted to go to Ingre because it's closer to home, to my mama, and there was a movilidad that regularly entered there, so getting around was not so difficult. In the end, I decided to come here, and I'm glad I did.

I didn't know a soul when I arrived in the village; that's why it was so important that the people here are very good. I arrived at night in a pickup, and they put me up in Don Feliciano's house. The medical post was vacant because we didn't have a nurse then, so I stayed there for two weeks. When we got a nurse, I had to move again, this time to the *sede* [assembly hall] where I stayed for a while.

Then I began classes, the *primer básico*, grades one through four, and I did everything. I began with a guide called *Ararundai*, which means "clouds" in Guaraní. I am the only bilingual teacher. They had a school in Ñaurenda when I came and a teacher; they just didn't have a bilingual teacher. *La hermana* Maura had requested a bilingual teacher, and she sent money for my transportation. I came to Entre Ríos where we met and talked about bilingual education. Then we came here, and the parents received me warmly.

In class, we spend half the time in Guaraní and half in castellano. It's not just speaking Guaraní, it's also teaching castellano; that's my job, teaching both of the languages. I teach Guaraní so that they will not forget their mother tongue. They all know how to speak Guaraní and castellano when they enter first grade. We translate back and forth. We continue to learn both with and without a text, through conversation and activities in both languages. We use a first grade text that's in Guaraní only to teach them words, more vocabulary. It uses drawings and pictures to teach the names of things. For example, they learn to recognize the letters for "chicken" in Guaraní, which is *uru*, for "fox," which is *aguara*, and "pot," which is *yapepo*. They learn a great deal of vocabulary that way and also how to make the letters and form words. In second grade they have a text in Guaraní and Spanish, a parallel text, and they also learn how to write in Guaraní and Spanish.

Bilingual education is important because some children no longer want to learn Guaraní; they want to forget their own language. Bilingual classes are important so that they continue their language, customs, and culture. Their culture is their way of being that is peculiar to them [*su forma de ser que tienen ellos*], their language, their fiestas. Here, we have bilingual education just for the first three years, but where I'm from we have it for the whole quinto básico, the first five years. It's not possible here yet, because it's a question of having enough students. We have only two castellano families here who don't want their kids learning Guaraní. It's optional; no one is forced to be in a bilingual program. The other parents are all for it; they asked for it repeatedly, and Sr. Maura carried it forward. If not, I wouldn't be here now.

They requested a teacher from the Cordillera, because that's where the Guaraní organization is strongest and where there is more bilingual education. Nearly all of us bilingual teachers in this area are from the Cordillera. Bilingual programs began recently, in 1992, the same year as the March to La Paz.

I've always wanted to be a teacher. My cousin studied to be a bilingual teacher, and I have another cousin who studied in Santa Cruz to be an English teacher. He wanted me to study and teach English too, but I preferred bilingual education. I was very sad to leave my mamita at home alone to come here. That was the hardest part. The salary is not enough to live on; it's not enough for anything. They take some out of my salary for my house, and some for the teacher's federation. My check is 513 bolivianos per month; of that I get about 450. You can't live on that. My husband works as an assistant to the nurse, Isabel, who is also

Guaraní, and who is, I believe, the first Guaraní nurse in the area, and perhaps in all of Bolivia. My husband is from Ñaurenda; we met here in the village.

Supervisors from the Department of Education come to visit classes, to evaluate my teaching, our compliance with certain rules, and to give workshops, such as on the *Reforma Educativa* [Educational Reform]. For example, they came from Potrerillos to give a few suggestions about how to put the Reforma into practice. The Reforma is new; it's separate from and came after bilingual education. It's more about methodology than anything else. We have to teach students in small groups for example, and not just dictate information to them. It's more interactive, like that workshop on domestic violence that we observed this afternoon. They teach us how to teach our classes better. I think it's an improvement.

A few of the parents can read and write a little. I don't know if the students will teach their parents or not; I hope so. I give them homework every night, things to copy at home. The books include Guaraní myths and legends in both Spanish and Guaraní, such as one about the fox and the *tigre* [jaguar], which the children enjoy and they share these with their parents.

Ñaurenda, 6 May 1997

Susana de Chávez

Susana de Chávez's contagious sense of humor has served her well, enabling her to endure years of harsh mistreatment at the hands of her former patrón and patrona [patron's wife] in the Cordillera for whom she worked as cook and babysitter, though she was but a child herself at the time. De Chávez is perhaps in her 60s now, though she, like most Guaraní, does not know her age. In her recollections, her descriptions of traditional foods, festivities, and songs, as well as the situation of oppression, paint an accurate picture of daily life under the patrones. De Chávez, who now lives in the tiny, remote village of Yukimbia in an extremely arid strip of the Chaco, also recounts her first trip to the city of Tarija and shares some interesting insights on the differences between past and present for the Guaraní.

Before, things were bad. The patrones made us work very hard all the time, starting before dawn. At 3:00 a.m. I had to have the flour all ground to make the food for the peones. No matter how cold it was, I was up cooking, so that by 7:00 a.m. everything was all cooked. I had to dish out large amounts into a heavy iron pot that I would carry on my head long distances to serve the men, and it was scalding hot. Sometimes I would slip and fall. We suffered a lot in those days.

And now, here we are. I came to see what things were like over here, and I'm, well, I'm not grinding corn for anybody's meal but my own! In la Banda it's not like here; they still have patrones there, and things are still really bad. We came here to Yukimbia with all our children five years ago.

I can read and write a little. My papá put me in school there for two years. The patrona made me a babysitter, really more like a playmate and babysitter, because I was just a child myself. They told my father to send me to school so that I would be a better companion for the daughter of the patrona. The patrona decided that two years was enough for a babysitter. After all, as she said, "I'm not going to send you into town."

The patrona's daughter and I were the same age, and we played together; she would take me to school with her. She would give me pencil and notebook as well. There were only three Guaraní in the whole school. The teacher was cristiano; he was very good too. He himself was a student who was filling in until they got a regular teacher. They gave me a dress to wear to school; they didn't want me to wear a *tipoy* [Guaraní women's traditional dress]

After that, I continued working as a babysitter, but this time, for the teacher's wife, not for the patrona. I cared for their two little *chiques*, [kids] bathing them, dressing them, combing their hair. I lived in their house and they treated me well; the chiques were very good. I was a babysitter for some years until, at age 12, I began cooking for the peones.

I didn't marry until late; I was about 28. The custom was that the man would ask the patrona's permission to marry you. The patrona was the one who made me marry my husband, but I didn't want to because he had been married to my sister. He was my brother-in-law! I didn't want to get married at all, and I certainly didn't want to marry him when I saw how he beat my sister. My patrona asked me where I thought I was going to go to find a better husband. I said, "I'm old now, and I don't want to marry. Besides, a husband wants a young woman." Unfortunately for me, my husband wanted an older woman!

The patrona wanted me to marry him because she did not want me to leave. She said she didn't want some outsider to come and take me away. She wanted us to marry only her peones. I told her not to make me marry him, that he would beat me. But she didn't care. I couldn't complain because that would make him angry, and he would beat me more. He would beat me when he was drunk; he is violent when he is drunk. But now he has stopped beating me because he knows I know where the road is. I can leave whenever I want, and I know where I can go. I can go to Tarija to stay with my daughter! He doesn't want me to leave, so he treats me well.

I didn't come first to Yukimbia, but to Napichán where they have a dentist. I went there to have all my teeth pulled out. I asked the patrona for money to pay for the dental work, but she just said, "Go ahead and have it done; I'll take care of it." Of course, she never gave me the money, so I couldn't go back and have new teeth put in. The patrona also said that she would give me a tipoy for Carnival, but she deceived me there too. I was working and slaving for them, but they gave me nothing in return. Well, I say leave punishment to God; God knows all. I left there crying like a lost child.

I went to work for Dr. Walter [Raña] for a while before coming here. First, I went to make chicha for Dr. Walter for a week. Then, he said, "Let's go to Entre Ríos." He took me to Entre Ríos, where I stayed for about three months working for him, cooking his meals, and those of his workers. After that, he put my teeth in, and I came here.

There were already people in Yukimbia when I arrived, but I didn't know a soul. I came with my husband and five children. My children have now left for Tarija to work. They left because of the water. We had a cholera epidemic last year and that's why they left. My husband nearly died from it. Several of our family members were very ill, as was much of the village. My daughter works in a bakery in Tarija; her husband is a curandero there. It's so far away [lejos es]; I miss very much chatting with her every day like I used to do. She has five kids; three are in school. They are very happy in Tarija. I like it there too, except the first time I was too frightened to go outside. I stayed seated indoors. It was my first time in a city and I was afraid of making a mistake and getting lost. Ha, ha! Isn't that foolish?

I went to Tarija for a meeting on how to plant better potatoes and corn. We all brought work that we had done to show it to other people. Some brought their potatoes to exhibit, while others brought their baskets. We all participated and gave demonstrations; it was lovely. At that same meeting I met Doña Domitila Chungara [Bolivian women's and tin miners' advocate]. She came to speak to us; she told us about her life with her abusive husband and how they're divorced now. It was a meeting just for women, and we all danced the *atiku* [traditional Guaraní dance], the *chacarera* [farmer's dance, Chilean folk dance], and the *cueca* [Chilean folk dance]. Everyone spoke in their language and it was translated so we could all understand. Each group presented something from their region, something of their music, or art or crafts. It was wonderful!

According to our tradition, only men are musicians; they are the only ones who can play the *bombo* [drum] or the *flauta* [flute]. They usually learn by listening and observing. Singing was important for our ancestors. There used to be more singing in the past, and there was a great deal more singing for the children than there is today. My mamá's abuelito, when he was already very old, began to sing, but I was too young to remember his songs. My sister learned them, but I don't know any of his songs. He would sing and others would play the bombo and the flauta. We would join hands and dance a few steps forward and a few steps back, like this, all in a circle. You always carried a gourd of chicha in your hand. Men and women would also dance as couples. For the festivals of Carnival, Easter, and San Juan we would dance and sing, everyone, young and old. Singing and dancing were reserved for celebrations. Singers enjoyed a great deal of respect because they were usually captains, and they painted themselves with *urucu* [red plant extract] for all fiestas.

I do remember one Easter song. I'll try to sing it for you. It goes like this:

> *Jekoveyema, jekoveyema, ñande Iya,*
> *Santo Cristo ñande Iya*
> *Santo Cristo ñande Iya*
> *Aleluya, y jareluya*
> *Jareluya y aleluya*

Ha, ha, I don't sing very well do I, but you get the idea. *Jekoveyema* means "resuscitated." We are singing that our Lord, Jesus Christ, has been raised from the dead. We also sing and play the violin to accompany us during the Easter feast. Singing goes way back in our culture. I am baptized and chrismed too. In Rosario del Indio some padres came to baptize the poor. I was already old, but I wanted to be baptized because that means you are somebody. Here in Yukimbia, no one else is baptized because no padre has yet come out into this remote region of the Chaco. We need to have a little course [*cursillo*] to prepare us first.

There have been important changes during my lifetime. Now they are speaking more castellano, people are becoming baptized, they are studying, and learning how to read. We still continue to grind corn as always. Probably that will never change.

I think our health is better. Before, for example, there were no medicines at the posta. We would cure ourselves only with weeds [*corita*] and wild plants like the *picantilla*. For example, we would moisten it and put it on a headache. Sometimes it would cure and sometimes not. Everything we had before was natural.

We would wash with the picantilla when we had *carachi* [blisters, rashes]. Do you know that the patrona would not even prepare these things for us! She never fixed anything for us! And our children would just get worse and worse. We would also use the starch from the yucca for our children when they had diarrhoea. I get angry remembering that our children were always sick and the patrona did absolutely nothing for us to help them. However, when I took care of Dr. Walter's kids, and I did their laundry, he would give me medicines.

For pregnancy it's better now too. Before, we poor people were like animals. It is so sad, but we would go to the trash heap to give birth. That's what we had to do when we were under the control of the patrón. We would give birth in the trash heap and present the newborn baby to the patrona. She would not give us even one rag for our baby . We would tie off the umbilical cord and bring the baby with us in a little bed while we worked. When the guagua was two days old, we would bathe him thoroughly so that he would be nice and clean. Now, childbirth is at the post, very clean. Before, many babies would be born already sick.

Food has changed as well. Before, I didn't have any idea what rice and sugar were. I ate mostly corn, *anco* [*zapallo*, squash] and wild honey that my father would bring me from the fields. There was also *yerba mate* [bitter tea] when I was young. They would ferment it in a big tub and drink it like chicha. They would also eat *cuchimonte* [wild boar] and *urina* [deer]. These my father would bring back from the *monte* [hills]. We also had eggs because we had a chicken. And *cañazo* [cane alcohol]. We ate *mote* [corn dish] with honey.

As soon as I tasted rice I loved it. I tried it at a market stall where they have a tent and prepare lunch to sell. *Ven y comer* [come and eat] they invited, but I was afraid to sample it at first. They also had meat, but I thought it was probably dog meat and didn't want to taste any. They kept trying to convince me that it was all delicious, so I asked for corn, just to be sure, *api*, which is a corn drink, cuchimonte, rice, and potatoes. I could hardly believe how delicious the rice and potatoes were! I was already grown and had kids of my own when I first tried these foods.

I was also already a woman when I first tried yerba and coffee; I was still in la Banda. Before we knew about coffee, we would make burned corn for our "coffee," for our husbands. You burn the corn, put it in a big pot and boil it with water; it has a wonderful flavor. I no longer fix it because they told us that the smoke from the burning corn goes up to heaven and that God has complained that we are burning him. I don't want any complaints from God! The patrona told us this years ago. When we used to prepare it, it was delicious, but it did make a lot of smoke.

Life is better than it was before. I think it will be better in the future too. Some people already eat bread in the morning, and some have porridge. The diet is better, and that means that our life will be better. Other things are improvements too, such as the road, the post, having a house, and, one day perhaps, having a house of adobe.

It would be better to have adobe instead of our open houses because some-times a strong wind comes up and you get sick. Sometimes women are ill in child-birth, and the wind makes them worse. We have some strong winds in the Chaco and cold ones too. At times it's very cold, and we get sick because our houses have no walls. If you have a closed house, vermin [*bichos*] can't come inside. We would love to build a house.

We would be protected from snakes like that one over there that we killed yes-terday. If that kind of snake bites you, you die because there is no remedy for it. A 13-year-old girl died just last week from a rattlesnake bite. She was gone before they could search for a remedy. They didn't even have time to go to the post or to the curandero, nothing, it was so quick. The curandero said later that he would not have been able to save her because there's nothing you can do for that kind of snakebite. We would be more protected and healthy if we had adobe houses. Maybe one day that will come, too, along with the other changes.

Yukimbia, 7 August 1998

Maura McCarthy, PBVM

McCarthy is devoted to the Guaraní people, to enabling them to make it on their own, and to helping them preserve their culture and language. Her ardent wish is that some day she, and the Support Team, will work themselves out of a job. In the meantime, she is a fearless defender of the rights of the Guaraní and has stood up to religious and political authorities who have tried to silence her; she has carried on despite threats from area patrones. Her first ten years in Entre Ríos, McCarthy taught catechism in the town and typing classes at the Academia and prepared cat-echists in mestizo towns in the countryside. During the years of political repression, beginning in the 1970s, she was accused of communist activities and asked by the Bishop of Tarija to leave the country. McCarthy spent seven years in the US teaching and recovering from the injustice of her forced departure. When she returned to Bolivia in 1987, she dedicated herself to working with the scattered Guaraní communities so near to middle-class Entre Ríos, yet so far away in terms of culture and status. McCarthy's story reveals an abiding commitment to accompany the Guaraní come what may. The Guaraní regard McCarthy as one of their own, as well they should.

We Presentation Sisters, Eileen Sweeney and I, arrived in Bolivia in 1970 to begin our language school studies and to locate our new mission in the country. We decided to come to Entre Ríos in 1972, and because of ill health, Eileen Sweeney returned to the States and was replaced by Therese Corkery in 1972. We founded the *Academia de la Presentación* in 1973, offering sewing and typing, and we began a library for the town, all in response to requests from the local residents. The *promotores de salud* [health promoters] program was begun a couple of years after the catechists' program. This was a joint effort of the Presentation Sisters, the local doctors and nurses, some medical volunteers from Spain, and an NGO from Tarija known as *Acción Cultural Loyola*, founded by the Jesuits. After several years of work, in coordination with the local doctors and nurses, especially on the part of Sr. Julianne Brockamp, Sr. Therese Marie Hawes, and later Sr. Marge Healy, the promoters began making plant-based salves and other natural medicines. This program, one of the first of its kind in Bolivia, became firmly established and highly respected.

In 1975, Julianne Brockamp and I, with the Spanish volunteers, Acción Cultural Tarija, and the other sisters began the catechism program, but it was slow getting off the ground. We would travel with the priest, Rafael Romac, a Croatian Franciscan, to attend the fiestas in the *campo* [countryside], getting to know the people, and trying to encourage them to build up Christian communities and to have a catechist. The Guaraní communities, however, were not on the fiesta circuit at all; these were all campesino communities of mestizos that we visited. The catechist program during the 1970s was one way to facilitate community organizing. At that time we were living under the dictatorship, and sindicatos were *prohibidos* [prohibited]; this was General Banzer's first term. We did a lot of work promoting an integral type of community organization; it wasn't exclusively religious, but rather stressed the importance of becoming organized so that the communities could defend the human rights of their members.

Later, the catechists frequently became community organizers with NGOs; they became true community leaders. These were the seeds of base communities, but we never had the kind of success that you see in Brazil. Tarijenians live pretty isolated lives and want to become involved only if it is really important for their own welfare. Otherwise, they like to live an independent existence. That is so different from our experience with the Guaraní, but it is very true of the campesino communities. There are some that have had successful base communities, Potrerillos is one of them, but in general I'd have to say that our results were disappointing. We even found it difficult to persuade people to hold Sunday prayer services that might develop into a community meeting and, ultimately, an organization. We never had the success we would have liked.

But, as I said, there were individuals who later became very effective and courageous leaders of their communities. Also, the *Movimiento Comunidades en Marcha* (MCM), were practically all, in their entirety, catechists who became politically conscious. Between the time of my departure from Bolivia in 1980 and my return in 1987, the MCM had become completely transformed.

The whole idea of the MCM was for campesinos to organize in order to advance and protect their interests. The basic strategy called for catechists from different communities to come together and share their experiences and suggestions. In other words, for a long time it was more a support group for catechists so they would not be so isolated in their communities, and the idea was to meet together regularly. It is a marvellous structure, and the Guaraní use it today, with the *capitanes* from different communities holding zonal and regional meetings.

Why did I leave in 1980? It was a combination of things, but the most important was that our old pastor was seeing communists everywhere; he was reliving his years in Yugoslavia. Fr. Romac was very old, very nervous, and was becoming senile. He saw me as a communist ringleader who was influencing the sisters and everyone else and beginning communist cells in the community. Whether this was all his own invention or others manipulated him, playing on his fears and poor health, I don't know, but it got to the point where it was impossible for me to stay.

At times, he would accuse all the sisters of being communists, but in the end, he decided that it was mostly me. The sisters began to feel that it would be better for one of us to leave than for the situation to continue. The tension in our household finally became unbearable. I have to say that it was especially difficult for me and I didn't feel supported enough to stay. The attitude of the sisters in Entre Ríos was, "We can't take this tension," so it seemed better to leave. But I knew that I was not responsible for supporting communism in any way. *That* was the accusation after all.

I think that the priest focused on me because I was the one who was most fluent in Spanish then and at the time served as community spokesperson. I had been there the longest.

He wrote back and forth to our superior in Dubuque for a couple of years trying to convince her to remove me. However, our superior, Sister Martin McCormick, kept resisting because she felt that the Bishop of Tarija should resolve the problem. She even travelled to Bolivia to try to resolve the situation. The Bishop, Abel Costas, stalled as long as he could. Finally, he sided with Fr. Romac and asked me to leave the country. I know he felt badly about it afterwards, because when I returned, he was very, very supportive. That was an extremely difficult period, and there were times when I would "lose it," in that I would become very disillusioned and upset.

A precipitating event was the assassination of Fr. Ray Herman in 1975 or 1976 outside of Cochabamba. His was a politically motivated murder. Fr. Herman was never, ever, a political priest, but he spoke Quechua and had influence with the Indians, and for some people, that was indictment enough. We had invited him to help us out with a catechists' cursillo in Entre Ríos, but he was assassinated before he arrived.

Back in the States, I spent one year teaching at a grade school near Dubuque. By the time the year ended, I was already looking for a Hispanic ministry, which I found in Chicago. There, I lived at St. Dorothy's parish, an all-black parish with an all-black school, and I commuted by bus to teach at Our Lady of Guadalupe, an all-Hispanic school. I always felt that, in the providence of God, the Chicago experience was profoundly beneficial to me. The inner city life, the black neighborhoods, the Hispanic school expanded my world tremendously. It was totally different from what I had just come from in Bolivia, and it was good for me to see the world through new eyes.

In Chicago, I had six years to think about my life; that's a long time. It was a very difficult period because I had been broken by my forced return to the States. You see, my confidence had been shattered. It took me a long time to rebuild my self-esteem enough to volunteer for Bolivia again, although I desperately wanted to go back from the beginning.

In 1987, on my return to Bolivia, I began studying the Guaraní language. In 1988, I was still teaching religion, doing baptismal and confirmation preparation in Entre Ríos, and once a month, trying to get away to visit the Indian communities. In 1989, I began visiting the communities with Renán Sánchez. He was a rural schoolteacher who had worked with the Sisters, particularly Therese Marie, on many literacy projects and on base community projects with Nilda, his wife. Renán and I went around to the villages asking the Guaraní what they needed and how we could help.

It was clear from the outset that one of the things they most wanted was a common field, plus the tools and wire to secure it. So, we wrote our very first funding proposal to the Hilton Fund for Sisters for wire and tools. However, the people neglected to tell us that they needed groceries, and we didn't think to ask, although that was one of the biggest expenses, so we had to revise our proposal. Since then, I've always remembered to add groceries.

The Guaraní also requested an *item* [teacher] for their school. Tentapiau residents wanted a school, too, about then, and the village of Ivopeti soon followed. Tentaguasu already had a school, but it was falling apart, and they wanted help repairing it. From our visits, we saw that there was a generalized interest in having both schools and communal fields. Renán and I had no preconceived notions about what they would request, and no ideas that we wanted to push; the surveys were more like informal conversations as we visited from place to place. Actually, since we were both studying the language at the time, it was as much to practice the language and get to know the people as anything else, to learn what their life was like, their tribal values, and to develop a rapport. Every time we returned to a village we enjoyed greater rapport, and, in time, we were able to help them with the communal fields. Many times, we found out around a campfire at night what was most important for a particular community.

Ñaurenda was the first to acquire a common field, with Saladito a close second. We were involved in helping them plan the *desmonte* [clearing], which, as you know, was an act of defiance against the patrón. Because of our visits to the Guaraní communities, we already felt very threatened by the patrones. We felt even more threatened because the *Comunidades en Marcha* and other groups came en masse and held these big rallies, whereas our plan was to go in quietly from community to community and, in some cases, even to consult with the patrones about where the common field could be located. But the *Comunidades en Marcha* were much more confrontational, loudly proclaiming the rights of the Guaraní from the beginning. We, however, were the ones who were blamed for their presence because it was presumed that we had invited them. We always thought we could accomplish our objectives by being non-confrontational, but whether we could have or not is another matter. At that time we were receiving some back-handed death threats and threats to expel the non-Bolivians from the country. The patrones made numerous threats against the sisters and Renán. That's one of the reasons why the doctor who had been working with us left our group; he felt like he had an important profession to practice, and he didn't want to risk his life in this situation.

We always felt that it was unfair that the MCM, the farmers' syndicate, and NGOs from Tarija came in, held their rallies, and then got in their trucks and returned to Tarija, while we were left to suffer the consequences. But the Guaraní didn't seem to mind the confrontational meetings; maybe it gave them energy, and maybe we were the only ones who felt it was counterproductive. To the Guaraní it meant something entirely different from what it meant to us.

I think the patrones underestimated how badly the Guaraní wanted the communal fields, and that they would actually follow through on it. The patrones' experience was that the Guaraní would work for them all week and then drink all weekend, so they laughed at their desire for a communal field to work. As far as the land itself was concerned, it wasn't that important to the patrones; moreover, it was land that the Guaraní always felt was theirs, that they had a right to. I don't know why the patrones didn't resort to violence. Perhaps one reason is that they weren't united. They had no strong organization among themselves; rather, they were rivals one of another. Nor were they particularly wealthy. Some went into very serious debt around that time and didn't have land titles in their hands anymore because they had left them in the Agricultural Bank, which folded. It was almost always threats of violence rather than violence, but I can tell you that there was a time when we locked our doors well in Timboy, very well, very well.

The Ñaurenda desmonte for the common field was of great symbolic importance. It was carried out by the MCM, the sindicato, other NGOs, and the people of Ñaurenda in 1989, but the area wasn't fenced in, so it really didn't amount to anything in practical terms for a while. It wasn't until we were able to get some fencing, groceries, and tools that the desmonte became the common field. We had to buy groceries, because the Guaraní weren't working for the patrones while they were involved in the desmonte, and they had absolutely nothing to eat. They had to have tools as well, because, when they were carrying out the desmonte, some of the Guaraní were just standing there watching because they had not even a machete or an axe with which to work. The MCM brought chainsaws to lend. So they had nothing to eat, no tools, and their own fields were poorly fenced. The individual fields are mostly miserable hilly areas even today. As I look to the future, I see that they've got to have fields of at least two or three hectares of decent land or they can't make it. The *individuales* they were given by the patrones are all they have, and most of them are of such poor quality that they cannot provide a living.

We've also become aware that the common field can't provide a living for the families either. It's a help for them, but seriously inadequate. They need family plots also. They plant corn in the common field, but we're trying to diversify with some *maní* [peanuts], yucca, and especially beans. Traditionally they plant beans *asociados*, which means they plant beans and corn at the same time, and the nitrogen that is taken out of the soil by the corn is replaced by the beans. Ecologically, it's an excellent *socio* [partnership]. The beans are for their own consumption, while the corn is mostly for sale. However, I must say, you know, in these last two years of famine, they have had to eat from the common field, too; it's been a constant struggle for them just to survive.

I'd say for this reason that the recent housing project was very timely, especially in Mokomokal and Saladito, because it provided groceries for those months. This was the only way to enable workers to build their houses and feed their families. One of the reasons we couldn't do the *obra fina* [finishing] was that we had to invest so much in the groceries. It was absolutely necessary; there was no other way to do it.

The Guaraní must diversify in order to make it. They've got to have more beans, yucca, *camote* [sweet potatoes]. It's absolutely essential, but starting new things is a very slow process. We're really trying to get family gardens going, not just a common garden. It doesn't have to be big, but a plot the size of your back yard and fence that in. And, you know, beans and rice taste so much better if you have some vegetables to go with them, and a few vegetables make your soup taste so much better. Otherwise, it's so thin and watery day after day. Normally, your soup just contains a little rice or macaroni with water. If we could also use turnips, tomatoes, and onions, that would be wonderful. The Team is working with CERDET to get the family gardens under way. That's a priority for me, the fencing and seeds for family gardens.

After the first desmonte, in Ñaurenda in 1989, Saladito followed, as did Yukimbia. Then came others, one after another, so that the patrón system was broken in our area. Now, that doesn't mean that they don't work for the patrones any more, because they do. The break has been more successful in some communities than in others. It's very difficult because we're still having to provide money for groceries, and you know, if you don't have an individual field, how are you going to make it? It's a circle of poverty.

Even today, villagers in Potrerillos and Mokomokal spend a lot of time working either for patrones or for the non-Guaraní as day-wage laborers. I'd say in Mokomokal they work at least half time for the patrón. During the housing project they didn't work at all for the patrón; they worked steadily day after day and often into the night on their own houses. In Potrerillos, however, even during the housing project, some were working for patrones once in a while, and of course, they were working on CERDET's *microriego* [micro irrigation] project. For the 12 houses we built there, we had only about eight or nine people working full time; that's why it cost more. We're talking about at least $2,400-$3,000 more that the project cost in Potrerillos than in the other communities, mostly because people were working on the microriego project for CERDET.

We became the *Equipo de Apoyo* [Support Team] after the Swiss couple, Renzo and Francesca, came to work with us. The beautiful thing was that they didn't want to go off by themselves, but, rather, wanted to work together with us as a team, God love 'em. About 1991, we formally decided to become a Team. It turned out to be a tremendous blessing, because when they went back to Switzerland, Renzo and Francesca established a solidarity group there which now provides essential funding for us.

We didn't divide up our tasks into different zones for a long time; everyone went most places together. When we'd attend meetings in Yukimbia or Saladito or Ñaurenda, or if we started a new community, we'd go together, Renán, Renzo, Francesca, and I. Exceptions were that Renzo worked pretty much by himself on the *posta sanitaria* [health post] in Yukimbia, and Francesca, a nurse, took care of stocking it. Picking up baskets woven by the women at first was pretty easy because we had only one community to start with, and then two, and then it multiplied. We'd collect baskets together when we could, especially Francesca and I, but as the years went on, we came to the point that we had to get someone to help market them; that's when we began to work with the Peace Corps volunteers.

The basket project was nurtured by Therese Marie, Renán, and myself, but Renán soon became involved in other things. It is more the Sisters of the Presentation who have been the constant presence. The women learned to weave the baskets all by themselves. You know, they always visit their relatives anyway, and while they were sitting there visiting, they would watch how other women made baskets. Soon, we started picking up baskets in Ñaurenda and saying, "Well, if we can sell these, we'll pay you for them." As the project grew larger, the bookkeeping nearly overwhelmed us; we had to pay the women right away for their baskets and then try to sell them.

The women were dyeing the straw different colors from the beginning, but they didn't learn how to blend colors, light and dark, or combine different colors until after I returned from a trip to Guatemala. They saw a beautiful wall hanging I had brought back and became inspired. It was a nice refinement on what they were already doing. The women are justly proud of their contribution and the men do not feel threatened by it, perhaps in part because it enables the family to eat.

Another project the Equipo is working on is establishing cattle in the driest areas where agriculture is not appropriate. We're doing it cooperatively, with a cattle project in three or four communities together, with funding from Switzerland. The Guaraní are planting dryland pasture where you don't have to cut down the trees. There are special grasses that grow under trees in the shade and don't require much water. The cattle project is ultimately supposed to pay for itself. Currently, most of the cattle are bought from the patrón, but plans are being made to have more cattle projects, and soon we hope the cattle will come right from the stock that we now have.

Our honey project is expanding nicely. I can't believe how well the honey has sold in Tarija! These are wild bees, *de la selva*. The Guaraní capture them and put them into beehives. The honey is delicious and sells incredibly well. We take it with us when we go to the *ferias* to sell baskets. Eventually, we should be able to sell it in quantity. Fairs are a good thing because they are a way for people to become acquainted with your products. Sometimes the people who buy in quantity discover you through the fairs. Soon, people start coming to the fairs hoping to find your booth.

I've already mentioned the housing project. We have completed 55 houses so far, but we've got a long way to go, little by little. The Guaraní feel a strong sense of pride in their homes; they show them off when people from Santa Cruz or the Cordillera come to visit, and they say, "We did it all ourselves." We're hoping that in a ten-year period the recipients will be able to pay for their houses. We can't tell them to pay up or move out, so we will rely on their sense of honor. If they can do it, they will, and they will thereby help other people, because the money will go into a building fund. If they pay for their homes, it will be announced that they are helping make possible more houses.

NGOs need to respond to the community's stated needs. Sometimes they have things they want to fund, which may not be exactly what the community wants.

That's what happened in that micro irrigation project in Potrerillos; CERDET had to get it done and done now, so they had no wish to coordinate with our housing project because, in a sense, they couldn't. CERDET works in the same kinds of things as our *Equipo de Apoyo*, and, as you can see, our coordination hasn't been the best. We have duplicated efforts and we have not communicated adequately with each other. We have had lots of talks about our conflict over the micro irrigation project, for example, and they apologized, but financially, an apology doesn't help a whole lot. I have to say we try, and we're both doing better.

The *Equipo de Apoyo* consists of Renán Sánchez, the Director; Noé César, the agronomist who has been with us for a long time; Eulalio Torres, also an agronomist; two Peace Corps volunteers; and a forestry engineer, Víctor Hugo Sánchez, Renán's son. Víctor Hugo would like to help establish forestry reserves, but that effort has been frustrated because the land is "immobilized" while the INRA does its survey. Immobilized means that land cannot be bought, sold, or negotiated in any way in the designated area. Neither are new desmontes permitted, nor can *ganaderos* [cattlemen] move onto the land.

The forestry reserves that Víctor Hugo would have liked to see would be something different. The idea there would be to practice managed extraction with a *plan de manejo* [management plan]. You would use some wood from one area, then you'd move on to another part of the territory, and so on. But Víctor Hugo wasn't able to get that accomplished, so instead, what we are working on now are *reservas de palma* [palm reserves]. We will set off a *manga*, an area of one or two hectares close to each community and plant new palms, *karandai* they're called. Palm from these reserves will be used exclusively for *artesania* [handcrafts]. The tender heart of the palm makes the best baskets, so the palm you would use for artesanía would only grow to a certain height. The tall palms that you use for roofs also come from the karandai; we would allow those to grow taller. I am concerned about the future of the karandai, because it is disappearing from many communities. Yukimbia and Potrerillos no longer have any at all. For some of the roofs we had to haul in palm from a considerable distance, which is very worrisome.

Land and education continue to be the top priorities for the communities. It varies: for example, Ñaurenda has really prioritized education, and clearly in Tentaguasu, infrastructure for the school is the number one need. If the Guaraní are granted a territory, I think that in Zone One production will have to be a top priority because both the communal and individual fields desperately need to be expanded; they are too small to support a family, and the population is growing.

In Zones Two and Three, agriculture is not as appropriate as cattle raising, so, as far as production is concerned, cattle projects would be a major priority there because it is so very, very dry. They have small *microriego* [micro irrigation] projects for gardens and for citrus in Yukimbia, but it takes several years before the trees produce, so cattle are certainly desirable in those zones.

Zone One is both a cattle and an agricultural area. Cattle would provide milk, cheese, and income generation. We are planting dryland pasture for one year previous to any cattle being moved in. That's a Team requirement because the cattle will be much healthier if they have dryland pasture instead of just the fruits of the trees, and they'll give more milk.

Production is the main priority overall I suppose, although we never forget that we work in five areas: production, infrastructure, health, education, and territory. Territory means what the INRA (*Instituto Nacional de Reforma Agraria*, National Agrarian Reform Institute) is about right now, setting aside an area as indigenous territory. The Quechua and Aymara who were working in the valleys and the *altiplano* [mountainous region], in 1952 were already organized into sindicatos and thus received titles to land that formerly had belonged to the patrones.

Not so for the Guaraní. I remember capitán Araisi from Tentapiau saying that Victor Paz *uyapo una macana* [played a trick], because the agrarian reform was negative for the Guarani as well as for some indigenous peoples in Santa Cruz, the Beni and Pando. It was negative because the karais moved in and obtained title to the lands. Also, under the dictators, huge land concessions were made to their supporters, especially those of Banzer and García Meza. These were unjust concessions; land was simply taken right from under the feet of the indigenous people.

INRA is attempting now to redress that specific grievance of those groups. INRA will be looking at just how much land a hacendado actually needs. How much is he actually using? How many cattle does he have? They figure five hectares per head of cattle. So if you have 300 head, then you have a right to 1,500 hectares. In addition to that, how much of that land is being used for farming? Is it actually being used for farming? If not, then it should be available to the Indians. So, it's not intended to take away land that is socially justified. But if it's not justified, if there is land that is not being used, then it should be turned over to the government and eventually conceded to the indigenous.

The Guaraní, for their part, have to justify their land use and their requests for more land for individual and common fields and for cattle. It has to be taken into account that they do not have enough land now even to feed their families, which is why so many are still peones of the landholders. Title to the territory will be held by the Guaraní people, and the land will be managed by the Guaraní themselves. In the meantime, they can't expand without capital. In a sense, it's like starting all over again. They're going to need more fences, tools, groceries while they work. My question is how we as an Equipo are going to respond to those needs.

The patrones will continue living in the territory and will have whatever title is deemed just by the study. They call it a "mosaico" [mosaic], because within the territory there will be many titles held by non-indigenous people. The Guaraní are so happy about the territory, because, to them, it means regaining their homeland. It confers a sense of power and strengthens their identity.

The survey will take a long time. It's very hard work; they have to climb mountains, traverse very rugged terrain, and sleep in tents. The young professionals, with the Guaraní counterparts, are doing a good job, but I think it's harder than they imagined. Everything needs to be counted. The patrones are required to gather their cattle together to be counted; they must comply. Some Guaraní are starting to call those who still work for the patrones *terceros* [third ones], those who are not part of the demand for territory. They are challenging the peones, saying to them, "Are you a Guaraní or not?"

There is a noticeable political consciousness developing among the Guaraní. I have to say that CERDET has done a lot in that area, raising awareness for territory, that's a very positive contribution they have made. This thrust comes from the APG too, but they've received good counsel from groups like CERDET.

A recent situation that we are adjusting to is oil exploration in the Chaco. It affects the Guaraní in a number of ways. For example, in those areas where the companies are operating, the Guaraní ask them to give back something to the community. They have in mind cattle or fencing, but the oil companies don't want to comply in that way, preferring instead to put up a school. Well, the one they put up in Ivotepe is very poorly constructed; it was put up in a hurry, without any care at all. The community is quite disgusted, especially because they were already programmed with FIS [*Fondo de Inversión Social*, Social Investment Fund] to have a school built, which would have been much better constructed.

The baskets offer a curious example of the impact of the oil companies. Oil personnel tend to pay highly inflated prices for baskets that are poorly made. This practice discourages the production of high quality baskets, and it could have the effect of increasing sales to the drilling camps at the expense of our other markets. The oil companies won't be there forever; but while they're there, it's hard to deny that the women are better off receiving the inflated prices.

They are finding oil in the Chaco, but not without serious environmental risks, specifically the increasing contamination of the Pilcomayo River which provides a livelihood for most of the riverine communities.

Other problems are social and cultural rather than economic or environmental. For example, many Guaraní now work for the oil companies, which sounds good, but it brings social costs because those workers become less community-minded and less committed to the organization. Things such as cattle projects in the zone are less important to them when they're working for the oil company. They are hired to do manual labor, cutting down trees and making clearings in many cases, building roads in others. Some are day laborers, but others are gone weeks or even months, which often means that they drink all weekend. Some of the oil companies are famous for their workers being great drinkers; this is in no way a positive development for the Guaraní. On the other hand, the road into Puerto Margarita is now the best road in the province. They also have a big flatboat ferry that takes vehicles across to the other side, where they have also built a new road. They are not paved, but they are good gravel roads.

One of the recent developments in Zone One is that alcoholism is no longer a taboo topic of discussion. This is quite a step forward, because it is a longstanding problem, going way back, long before the arrival of the oil companies. Alcohol abuse was discussed in the reorganization meetings we had in Mokomokal and

Saladito, and it came up at the school meeting in Ñaurenda. It wasn't addressed by me, but by the Guaraní themselves. They said things like drinking shows a lack of responsibility to one's family and sets a bad example for the children. They also said that, here we are asking for land, and we talk about ourselves as responsible people, yet the karai see us drunk and say, "Look at them, drunk and lazy, they don't deserve more." The Guaraní talk about the image they wish to project as a people with a strong organization and close families and they conclude, "We can't do this and be drunkards." One who speaks this way is Capitán Ramón in Mokomokal, who feels very strongly about it, and he himself doesn't drink. Also leaders like Feliciano, Facundo Galeán, and the women.

The women speak up in assembly on this topic. They say that the money needed for the family is wasted on alcohol. What they drink is a cheap by-product of the sugar cane produced in Bermejo and Santa Cruz. The Guaraní often bring their own bottle and just fill it up. The women also speak up about domestic abuse. It's almost axiomatic that where there's a fiesta, there's drunkenness and domestic abuse. There's more and more consciousness among the men that this is a serious problem. What I'm pleased about is that it's no longer a forbidden topic. It used to be that all you'd see was grins, and nobody would say anything, but now it can be talked about openly.

The other thing they now talk about is the need for transparency and financial planning. For example, one item for consideration in a recent reorganization meeting in one of the communities was how to manage the sale of corn so that the whole procedure will be transparent, not *nublado* [cloudy] as it has been. It was decided that when the corn is harvested, it will be taken to the *centro de acopio* [storage center] in Timboy, weighed and stored in silos until it is sold. Let's say it sells for 25 bolivianos per quintal and they sell 100 quintales. That's 2,500 bolivianos. Of that total, 1,000 goes to a fund for cultivating next year; then so much goes to pay for transportation; some more to pay for the coca and groceries used during the harvest. Then we look at our *jornales* [daily wages]. So-and-So put in 10 jornales, another put in 15. We total the jornales and pay the workers. Say a jornal is worth eight bolivianos. If you worked 10 jornales, you get 80 bolivianos.

When we figure the jornales, we're including the women who cook. It was agreed that they would receive the same amount as the men who worked in the field. This was a step forward because, at one time, they received about half. Equal pay gives the women and everyone else a sense that their cooking is very important; it also encourages them to do a good job of it.

This kind of planning is very important, as is inscribing the financial arrangements in the Libro de Actas, the official record book of each community. That way, when the money comes in, the process will already be established.

Who knows what changes the future will bring? I am hopeful that many Guaraní will choose to remain in the communities. If there were a *subalcaldía* [sub-mayoralty] created that would provide jobs, either in Tentaguasu or Ñaurenda, I believe that many would remain here. I hope that there will be more bilingual teachers who will return to the Guaraní communities and that, in the future, education will be completely bilingual. That's a strong personal goal of mine, and one that the communities share because they feel that their language is the heart of their culture.

Will there be plumbing, electricity, TV, telephones, cell phones in these communities? I suppose so. There is already a proposal to bring electricity to the Timboy area. Cell phones do not function even in Entre Ríos yet, but they're putting in fiberoptic lines all the way to Yacuiba; who knows what all this will mean for us.

These are not things the Guaraní are very familiar with. For example, they don't go to the movies when they go to the city of Tarija. What you do see is people watching television when they go to Entre Ríos. They usually stand outside the window of the restaurant and look in at the TV. Sometimes, when some group sponsors them for a meeting in Entre Ríos, they go inside the restaurant to eat and watch TV, but even that is relatively new.

They tell me, just while I was in Tarija for the basket fair, that now there's a *micro* [minivan], part of the bus system, going into Ñaurenda every day. It's experimental, but that's a big change. There are micros in Tentaguasu and Yukimbia already twice a week, and now Tentapiau. The micros all come from Entre Ríos. The micro owners get together and decide which day who is going to go where, but the tickets are sold in common, and they are fairly affordable, 15 bolivianos from Timboy to Entre Ríos. Improved transportation will bring more changes.

I wish I could describe how privileged I am to be working with the Guaraní, and to be contemplating the future with them. My experience continually reinforces my great sense that God is good. Somehow all the difficulties that brought about my departure in 1980, who knows, if I had stayed in Bolivia, maybe I would never have been forced to reflect, re-evaluate, and commit myself to working with the Guaraní. It might never have happened. That was the lowest point in my life, but as I look back and put things together—usually I am so busy with the day-to-day concerns that I never step back to look at the whole picture—but as I do that now, I see how valuable those years of "exile" were for me. I also feel deeply honored to be asked to share the story of these beautiful people whose hopes, trials, and daily lives are also mine.

Evanston, IL, 5, 6 June 2000

Conclusion

The basic problem for the Guaraní of the Chaco has been to break free of dom-
ination by the patrones, thus regaining control over land, recovering their community self-control, and preserving their traditional culture. The concerns of the
Guaraní of O'Connor province and their daily struggle for existence and for independence from the patrones may seem entirely localized. Yet, their voices, like those
of the rubber tappers, speak to us of the profound ways in which they have been
affected by forces that have their origins in national and international developments.
While the impact of globalization and development on the rubber tappers has taken
the form of a direct, violent conflict, that on the Guaraní has involved since the
1950s a more indirect, low-intensity erosion of their culture. At the same time, the
Guaraní serve as a positive example of how a defeated, poverty-stricken people can
fight back, how they can rekindle hope, revive agency, restore traditional institutions, create a sense of solidarity, and work with, but not surrender to, outside forces.

For both the rubber tappers and the Guaraní, the struggle is about land, dignity, and power. Marcia Stephenson, in *Gender and Modernity in Andean Bolivia*,
speaks of the need to develop "AlterNative Institutions," which incorporate the
vision and values of the marginalized majorities.[1] Dignity has meant pride in
being Guaraní as well as refusal to serve as a wage slave to the patrones. Guaraní
leader Chumiray, for example, has consistently stressed this theme in numerous
speeches on *territorio y dignidad* [territory and dignity].[2]

The struggles of traditional groups are also about opposing views of land use.
For the tappers and the Guaraní alike, the important goal is to remain where they
are and work the land, not to own it or to get rich from it. Their respect for nature
and their sense of connectedness to it dictate a different land use ethic than that
of the patrones, who are the local face of capitalist entrepreneurship.

Certainly, the tappers and the Guaraní are each locked in a protracted struggle for economic survival. The tappers have adapted very quickly to new economic
arrangements, such as diversifying production and forming cooperatives, and
they have benefitted from the assistance of national and international environmental and agricultural NGOs. Further, under the leadership of Wilson Pinheiro
and Chico Mendes, they have created a strong union that has defended their human

rights and economic interests at every level. The Guaraní have been slower to diversify both because of the vital importance ascribed to corn cultivation in their culture and because of the environmental obstacles presented by the arid Chaco. NGO assistance is also a more recent phenomenon for them than for the rubber tappers. By any measure, however, both groups live on the edge of physical survival.

For the Guaraní, like the tappers, the struggle is not only about the obvious need for economic survival, but also the equally important requirement of cultural survival. Cultural survival for the Guaraní means, above all, education for their children, particularly bilingual education, so that their language and "true" history will be known and perpetuated. Education is seen as the way to preserve identity and honor their ancestors, while simultaneously preparing children for the future and integrating their culture into the broader national picture. As Chumiray put it, "We want to be Guaraní Bolivians."[3] Unlike the rubber tappers who are a product of Brazil's long tradition of miscegenation and who have not been persecuted as a racial, ethnic, or language group—though they have suffered severe abuses on other grounds—the indigenous Guaraní have been targeted for extermination by historically racist governments. Thus, the desire to preserve their culture takes on a sense of urgency not found among the rubber tappers.

The determination not to allow their culture to expire has awakened a political consciousness among the Guaraní nationally, galvanized recently by the proposed Guaraní Territory. In O'Connor province, the Guaraní do not yet possess a strong political sense, but one can observe the beginnings of its development. The recent recovery of the all-important tradition of the village assembly has done a great deal to strengthen a sense of community, a basic value among the Guaraní, and to promote a solidarity that is beginning to find expression in political action. This is different from the rubber tappers, who began building a sophisticated political awareness early on through their intense involvement in Christian base communities, the syndicate, and the Workers' Party.

It is difficult to imagine that the Guaraní of O'Connor would have progressed much in the economic, cultural, and political spheres without the "accompaniment" of the Sisters of the Presentation. The sisters are, of course, agents of modernization of a kind, as well as representatives of a global institution. They bring their own values and priorities, of course, but they have been very careful to listen to the Guaraní and to learn from them what the communities want and need. Thus, they have been very reluctant to impose the catechism. They quietly and effectively prepared the terrain for the emergence of a native leadership through the work of the Academia, the health promoters, and the catechist program.

What unites these two traditional populations is more important than what distinguishes them. In both Xapuri in the Brazilian rainforest and Ñaurenda in the arid Chaco, what may make economic and cultural survival possible are, above all, the creative initiatives at the local level generated by the people themselves and the courage, resilience, and determination not to be intimidated or broken by superior force. The endlessly inventive responses of both populations to the increasingly harsh and complex demands of daily life remind one that there are alternatives. As we will soon see, Nicaraguan *campesinas*, too, are putting forward fresh alternatives born of necessity as they do battle with sexism, a reactionary Catholic church, and a backlash against the Sandinista Revolution of 1979 in their determination to hold on to their lands and their cooperatives.

NOTES

1. Stephenson 204.
2. See, for example, Libermann Godínez. See also, *Ñee Jeroata* 61 (enero/febrero 1997).
3. Chumiray 18. The original Spanish reads: "Afirmar la identidad Guaraní siendo bolivianos."

PART THREE

Nicaragua

Introduction

The Nicaraguan women cooperativists whose stories follow, like the Brazilians and Bolivians we have studied, are part of the broader struggle for autonomy by a very poor segment of the population, in this case in a nation long dominated by the US. Like the Brazilian forest peoples and the indigenous Guaraní, the *nicas* have been caught in a bitter and protracted dispute over land ownership and usage of a kind that pits traditional against modern concepts and often results in increased impoverishment.

Unlike the seringueiros and Guaraní, however, the nicas do not constitute a separate cultural or ethnic group, nor are they members of a single, isolated traditional community. They differ also in that they have not benefitted from the protection of the official Catholic church; on the contrary, because of their close association with Sandinista social and economic policy—even though they themselves may not be pro-Sandinista—they are regarded with scepticism by the Church's conservative hierarchy. Further, during President Arnoldo Alemán's administration (1996-2002), cooperatives in general have suffered from increased government restrictions on NGOs, which are their lifeblood. In Nicaragua's current neoliberal political and ecclesiastical order, cooperatives and NGOs are unwelcome reminders of the Sandinista past. Thus, although the nicas have not fallen victim to armed bands of ranchers and loggers as did the seringueiros and although they have not experienced the racist attempts at extermination that have often marked the Guaraní's relations with government authorities, they have experienced the opprobrium of the country's two most powerful and patriarchal institutions, the Catholic church and the government.

These women cooperativists, like the rubber tappers and the Guaraní, make up a tiny minority of their country's population, but their experiences, too, are extremely instructive for what they teach us about economic survival in a time of globalization. What are the cooperativists' strategies? Their bedrock values? Their successes and failures? What can we learn from their example? To consider these questions, we must look at Nicaraguan history as it has been lived by the *campesino* [country person].

NORTHERN NICARAGUA NEAR SOMOTO

A breathtaking mixture of enchanted lagoons, rugged volcanoes, dense jungles, high sierras, and steamy coasts, Nicaragua, "the land of abundant waters" to its indigenous inhabitants, borders Honduras to the north and Costa Rica to the south. About the size of North Carolina, it is the largest and most sparsely populated (4.25 million) of the Central American republics. Though it may appear to be a tropical paradise, Nicaragua has been ravaged by the unrestrained use of pesticides and rampant deforestation of its precious hardwoods; this has had immediate deleterious repercussions on the health and economy of the campesino. In addition to man-made calamities, Nicaraguans have borne the natural disasters of earthquakes, volcanic eruptions, droughts, floods, and, in 1988 and 1998, hurricanes.

Nicaraguan campesinos have always produced raw materials for export to Europe and the US. Coffee, cotton, and sugar cane comprise the major products of the fertile west and north, or Pacific coast, while coffee and cattle are found in the central region and gold mining, shell fishing, and wood extraction make up the basic industries of the Atlantic seaboard. Banana, tobacco, sorghum, and sesame production also contribute significantly to Nicaragua's agro-export economy.

Nicaragua's population is predominantly mestizo (69 per cent), of Spanish and Indian mix, while smaller percentages are pure Caucasian (17 per cent) or of African (9 per cent) or Indian (5 per cent) origin. The last two populations are sprinkled along the Atlantic coast. Nicaragua is demographically skewed, with 90 per cent of its inhabitants living on the Pacific coast, while only 10 per cent call the Atlantic coast home.[1]

Nicaragua's population now is predominantly urban, as Managua and other cities are experiencing what E.F. Schumacher, in his classic critique of capitalism and growth *Small is Beautiful*, has termed the "revenge of the countryside":

the massive influx into urban centers of rural dwellers no longer able to make a living in the countryside, a phenomenon we also observed in Acre with the continuing migration of forest peoples to Rio Branco. Despite its burgeoning urban population, Nicaragua remains culturally a rural, campesino society. This means that basic values are traditional, family-centered, personalistic, and religious, and that an informal, often complex network of mutual assistance binds families and communities through a system of favors and the provision of basic needs and services. These values were strengthened by the common revolutionary experience and by the Sandinistas' social experiments to improve the lot of Nicaragua's poor, including their successful efforts at mass mobilizations of the populace. The experiences shared, the organizational skills imparted, and the traditional beliefs reinforced by certain Sandinista programs supplied the principal supports that helped campesinos withstand, if only barely, the neoliberal "structural adjustment" programs during the 1990s.

The vast majority of Nicaraguans, perhaps 90 per cent, are nominally Catholic, although statistics are very unreliable because of the highly individual and shifting nature of self-definitions. Evangelical denominations, especially the more enthusiastic varieties, are proliferating in Nicaragua as in the rest of Latin America. What is not in doubt is the integral role that religious faith plays in the daily life and language of most Nicaraguans, certainly of the campesinos, a quality more immediately observable among the nicas than among either the seringueiros or the Guaraní. Strong religious beliefs have contributed to the stoic resistance and faith in the future that have characterized the Nicaraguan people, especially the women here presented, in their long history of struggle. It is clear from the interviews that a local, popular ecumenism plays an important role in social cohesion and, therefore, in the survival of the families and local community. We did not find such ecumenism at the daily, practical level of lived experience among the seringueiros or the Guaraní. For the nicas of our study, religious support has come from their own personal faith. Unlike the seringueiros, who have been protected and encouraged in leadership development by the official Catholic church, or the Guaraní who have been accompanied and supported in community development by Catholic missionaries, the nicas have not been protected, accompanied, or encouraged by the official Nicaraguan Catholic church, which has sponsored few initiatives to improve the lot of the poor.

The capital city of Managua and the historic rivals, León and Granada, both founded by the Spaniards in 1524, are the centers of political and cultural leadership in Nicaragua. One of every four Nicaraguans lives in Managua, a surreal city in which axle-breaking potholes, pirated power lines, gutted ghosts of buildings destroyed in the 1972 earthquake, and piles of rubble exist alongside fashionable shopping malls, brightly illuminated Shell and Texaco stations with youthful guards toting AK47s, and ubiquitous SUV dealerships for the well-to-do, many of whom are former exiles who began returning from Miami and elsewhere after the Sandinistas were defeated in the 1990 elections.

Nicaragua is, after Haiti, the poorest country in Latin America. Except for the ten-year period of Sandinista rule, the country has been governed by oligarchs or US-approved dictators and presidents. Nicaragua's political and economic history bears some similarity to that of Bolivia both for its extreme dependence on foreign governments and foreign markets for a few vulnerable products and for the centrality of a limitless supply of cheap native labor. However, it is very unlike either Bolivia or Brazil in the preponderant influence exercised by the US, which has been a dominant factor in Nicaragua's internal affairs since the early nineteenth century.

From the founding of León and Granada, Nicaragua's history has been one of exploitation of people and natural resources by imperial powers such as Spain, England, and the US, and by local elites. As a member of the Central American Federation, Nicaragua gained independence from Spain in 1821, but it has still to achieve economic autonomy. Beginning in 1823 with the Monroe Doctrine, by which the US granted itself the right to intervene to protect its interests in Latin America, the US challenged British control in the region and by 1900 dominated Nicaragua's economic and political life. In 1855 American filibusterer William Walker, invited to defend the liberals of León against the conservatives of Granada, declared himself president of Nicaragua, introduced slavery, proclaimed English as the national language, and lasted two years before being deposed. The US was at one time interested in Nicaragua as a site for its transoceanic canal, but even after selecting Panama instead, it invoked the Monroe Doctrine to prevent incursions by other countries who also saw the economic potential of this strategically located country.

The other side of this history is the longstanding struggle to establish local autonomy. Nicaraguan nationalism frequently clashed with US manifest destiny, and resistance by nationalist leaders like José Santos Zelaya in the late nineteenth century and Benjamín Zeledón at the turn of the twentieth century had to be put down by US marines, who first occupied the small country in 1909. In 1927, the US became involved in the first guerrilla war in Latin America as marines tried in vain to capture the elusive nationalist guerrilla leader Augusto César Sandino, who became a hero to the Nicaraguan and Latin American people for confounding all of Uncle Sam's efforts to capture him. In 1933, when the last marine had left, Sandino laid down his arms as he had promised. Shortly thereafter, however, he was murdered in a double-cross by henchmen of Anastasio "Tacho" Somoza, the US choice to head the newly formed National Guard.[2]

Thus began the Somoza Dynasty (1936-79), the longest and most corrupt tyranny in Latin American history. Anastasio "Tacho" Somoza García ruled from 1936 to 1956, when he was assassinated by the poet Rigoberto Pérez López. Tacho was succeeded by his clever older son Luis, president from 1956 to 1967, when he died of a heart attack. Luis was replaced by the brutal "Mafioso" godfather Anastasio "Tachito" Somoza Debayle, who ruled with an iron fist from 1967 to 1979, when he fled Managua shortly before the Sandinistas' triumphal entry.

What was life like for the campesino, that is, the majority of the population, during the Somoza years? The answer almost exceeds the bounds of credibility.

First, a startling gap between rich and poor shaped life for the campesino major-ity: 1 per cent of the population controlled over 50 per cent of the land, and the Somoza family alone owned an estimated 30 per cent of all arable land—*Nicaragua es mi finca* [Nicaragua is my farm], Tacho was fond of saying. Rural illiteracy stood at more than 90 per cent, more than 50 per cent of all children were mal-nourished, and Nicaragua had the lowest life expectancy of any Central American nation.[3] Beginning in the 1950s and continuing through the 1970s, the landown-ing elite promoted the mechanization of agriculture as part of a drive to modernize the economy. As a result, the agricultural population declined rapidly, and coffee and cotton estates became more concentrated in the hands of a few oligarchs; this process, as we saw in Bolivia and Brazil, precipitated the campesinos' migration to the cities in search of work. Nicaragua received generous grants, $50 million each from the Alliance for Progress and the Inter-American Development Bank, in order to diversify agriculture; inevitably, these funds found their way to the agricultural enterprises of the oligarchy. Agricultural entrepreneurs evicted small farmers from their fields and purchased mechanical cotton-pickers in an effort to increase pro-duction for export. Unfortunately, not only did this practice evict campesinos, but it also made the economy less diversified and more dependent on volatile world market prices, which declined in the 1960s and 1970s.

For campesinos in León's cotton growing area, the modernization of agriculture also meant exposure to massive amounts of pesticides, including 12 million pounds of methyl parathion in 1951 alone. Despite widespread illness and death, the indiscriminate use of toxic substances continued for over two decades. As these entered the water table and the food chain, they caused more illness and death. By the 1970s Nicaragua was a world leader in the use of DDT, a substance banned in the US and many other countries. One study carried out in León in 1977 showed that the breast milk of mothers there contained 45 times the danger levels for DDT as determined by the World Health Organization.[4]

The Somozas also promoted cattle-raising and wood extraction in the rainforests in central and eastern Nicaragua; they did so to such an extent that by the 1970s Nicaragua had lost 30 per cent of this fragile ecosystem. These policies, too, affected the campesinos, pushing them off their land and deeper into the rainforests. There, they would farm for a few years until the land was exhausted and then pull up stakes and move on, in a cycle of environmentally and economically unsustainable prac-tices. This situation is very similar to that of the farmers from southern Brazil who, beginning in the early 1970s, were displaced by the expansion of cattle and agro-export industries and who relocated to the Amazon in hopes of making a living there.

One can scarcely imagine a more stark contrast than that between the daily strug-gle for subsistence of Nicaragua's campesino majority and the profligate lifestyle of the minuscule elite, who dined on imported wines in their exclusive clubs and whose conspicuous consumption rivalled that of the earlier Amazon rubber barons. The levels of personal corruption of the Somoza family are especially startling. When the first Somoza took power in 1936, he owned one broken-down coffee plantation, but, by 1978, through the calculated elimination of competition and the use of government funds and foreign loans, the family's wealth reached an estimated $500 million, not counting holdings in foreign countries. Tachito personally exploited Managua's devastating earthquake in 1972 to expand his financial empire, benefitting through his own construction companies from the $78 million in relief from the Agency for International Development (AID) and the $54 million from the Inter-American Development Bank (IDB) that were targeted for reconstruction. Meanwhile, his National Guard looted freely and sold desperately needed relief supplies and medicines from the Red Cross on the black market.[5]

In the wake of public outrage and unrest following the earthquake, the government cracked down on dissent, which by then came from all quarters—unemployed laborers; landless farmers reduced to squatter status; student groups; Christian base communities, which, as in Brazil, had been gathering strength during the 1960s; elements of the small middle class; and Pedro Joaquin Chamorro's opposition newspaper *La Prensa*. As repression increased, these groups became further radicalized, more organized, and more amenable to the objectives of the growing band of Sandinistas, who in 1974 demanded and obtained the freedom of previously jailed Sandinistas, including Daniel Ortega, who had been incarcerated since 1967. Protests, riots, work stoppages, and general strikes became widespread, and, by the late 1970s, they were supported by all sectors of society, including Nicaragua's most prominent businessmen. The spark that ignited the fire of revolution was the murder of the widely respected Chamorro on orders of Anastasio Somoza Portocarrero, Tachito's son. Chamorro's assassination provoked the largest mass protest in Nicaraguan history as 120,000 people spilled on to the streets of Managua during his funeral procession, which was followed by a crippling *paro cívico* [work stoppage]. The Catholic church, represented by then Bishop Miguel Obando y Bravo, finally broke with the regime, protested the slaughter of over 6,000 innocent campesinos, and vigorously denounced Somoza's bloody tactics of calling in air strikes on civilian populations and taking no prisoners. Thus, campesinos, urban workers, neighborhood defense committees, students, the official church as well as the base communities, and the bourgeoisie arrayed themselves against Somoza, reducing him to total dependence on his reviled National Guard. Seeing that the end was at hand, Somoza left for exile in Paraguay, where he and his armor-plated Mercedes were blown to bits in 1980.[6]

The Sandinista National Liberation Front had been founded in 1961 by Carlos Fonseca, Silvio Mayorga, and Tomás Borge as an anti-imperialist pro-nationalist guerrilla group. Inspired by Sandino and the example of Cuba, especially that country's charismatic Che Guevara, the FSLN was dedicated to attaining national self-determination. It was a radical, revolutionary mixture of nationalism, Marxism, and liberation theology and was committed to the twin goals of economic and social justice. Once the FSLN was in power, they moved quickly to make good on their promises.

Immediately after assuming office, the Sandinistas put into motion the Literacy Crusade (1980), plans for which had been laid earlier by Sandinista leaders in exile. Teams of educators, including Fr. Fernando Cardenal, later Minister of Education, and Dr. Carlos Tünnermann Bernheim, later Ambassador to the US, studied the literacy programs of other countries and invited the renown Brazilian educator Paulo Freire to visit Nicaragua. As late as 1979 the illiteracy rate for the population as a whole was 60 per cent, but for rural women, such as Juanita Medina de Matus and Zoila Rojas Calero whose interviews follow, it was closer to 100 per cent. The goal of the literacy program was to bring functional literacy at about third grade reading level to 50 per cent of the population, both rural and urban. For the urban population, this meant that homemakers, government workers, and factory laborers received instruction from volunteer teachers at city neighborhood sites during the evening hours. To reach the campesino population, young *brigadistas* [volunteer teachers] set out to spend March through August in the countryside, armed with hammocks, chalkboards, and lanterns. After working in the fields during the day, campesinos and teachers would gather for classes of maybe five or six students for two hours in the evening. Literacy workers reached out to some 500,000 people, including Edmundo (Mundo) González Matute, whose interview follows and for whom the literacy campaign was a life-changing experience. Government figures claim that the illiteracy rate was reduced to 13 per cent; however exaggerated the official figures may have been, there is no question that the achievement was impressive.[7]

The health campaign (1981) followed on the heels of the literacy drive, with large segments of the general population mobilized as volunteer health workers. These volunteers immunized citizens in the city and the countryside against malaria and polio and offered instruction in basic hygiene and sanitation. The eradication of polio was a major accomplishment of the campaign.

The promotion of women was a vital feature of the revolution, but one often neglected by foreign observers. It was a clearly stated goal of the Sandinista program, and the active participation of women was recognized as essential to the triumph of the revolution. The party leadership acknowledged women's contributions to the effort and supported the principle of gender equality. Women constituted 20 per cent of the guerrilla columns in the revolution, and several women headed combat battalions. During the 1980s, women made up 22 per cent of FSLN membership and held about 37 per cent of the party's leadership offices. In the CDS's [Sandinista Defense Committees] and the local militias, roughly 50 per cent of the members were women. Also during the 1980s, the Nicaraguan Women's Association (AMNLAE), an official organization of the Frente Sandinista [Sandinista Front, the Sandinista political party], claimed a membership of about 85,000.[8]

After the FSLN's defeat, AMNLAE's membership declined precipitously, but women's organizations in general proliferated during the 1990s. Most are more independent than AMNLAE and are dedicated to such issues as women's and children's rights, health, and nutrition. Beginning with the revolution, women have literally fought their way to a new status, challenging old notions of male pre-eminence including within the Frente itself; however, as Olfania Medina, Gloria Siesar, and Rosario Flores point out in their interviews, the battle against machismo is far from over. Today, whether the younger generation of women realize it or not, whether they regard themselves as Arnoldistas (supporters of Alemán) or Sandinistas, or express an aversion to politics altogether, many of the life choices available to them and the very terms of their discourse are important features of the revolutionary legacy.

The Sandinistas were the first Nicaraguan government ever to represent the interests of the campesinos. For them, the Agrarian Reform Law of 1981 enshrined the Sandinista promise of economic justice. The law protected the private property rights of all those who farmed efficiently, but those who did not were likely to have their abandoned or neglected fields expropriated and turned over to Sandinista Agricultural Cooperatives (CAS) or to small private farmers. The first to go were the vast landed holdings of the Somozas and their associates (most of whom had fled), which were turned into state farms that, for a time, accounted for about one-fifth of the nation's agricultural land.[9] Eventually, the agrarian reform provided the majority of campesinos either with new land or with titles to land they had already been working. This is the case for Nubia Boniche and the family of Gloria Siesar in the department of Masaya.

It is fortunate that the Sandinistas moved so swiftly to implement their program, for their efforts were almost immediately hamstrung by a series of difficulties: growing disagreements among the various Sandinista factions, increasing verticalism in decision-making, mistakes in Sandinista policies, the US-sponsored contra war begun in 1981, the US embargo on trade with Nicaragua from 1985 to 1990, the departure of some 20,000 middle-class professionals, and the exodus to neighboring countries of campesino families and young men fleeing the draft and the war. The contra war in particular was a nightmare for the Sandinistas and the Nicaraguan people, a low-intensity conflict with high-intensity suffering that ultimately undid the Sandinistas. As the war ground on, the Sandinista government, headed by Daniel Ortega, was forced to move into a wartime mode, forcing drastic cuts in allocations for social programs, while military expenditures ate up 50 per cent of the budget. The administration also became more top-down in its decision-making and less open to criticism from the outside. As the suffering of the populace intensified, the FSLN leadership became more remote from its constituency, seriously weakening its close ties with the ordinary citizen and campesino, the base of Sandinista support. By the time of the 1990 elections, many campesinos had come to feel abandoned by the party, families had lost too many sons to the war, and all Nicaraguans desired an end to the draft. Further, most everyone expected that the election of Violeta Chamorro would bring in US dollars to rebuild the shattered economy. Ortega was voted out, and Chamorro was voted in. Her inauguration marked the first democratic transfer of power between parties in Nicaragua's history.

When one considers the devastating effect of the contra war on Nicaraguan families, the high-handedness and/or inexperience of many Sandinista officials, and the extremely conservative (i.e., neoliberal) nature of the succeeding Chamorro and Alemán administrations, it is surprising, indeed, that any revolutionary heritage at all still remains. Elements do remain, but for how long is an open question. The revolutionary heritage is found not only in the continuing push for women's rights, but also in a widespread sense of self-awareness and self-confidence exhibited by campesinos generally. It is a legacy of legal rights, but it is also one of self-worth and dignity. In part, that legacy came about through means that are outside the scope of our study, such as intense political organizing and promotion of labor unions prior to and during the revolution and the highly effective work of Christian base communities (CEBs), feminist organizations, and NGOs. To some extent, the fruits of all these efforts are represented in Nicaragua's cooperatives, which offer concrete examples of the sometimes surprising ways in which the revolution has left its mark. This heritage is what most sets the women cooperativists apart from the rubber tappers and the Guaraní.

From the peasants' perspective, the Sandinista years brought the hope, at least, for an end to hunger and injustice. The "new" Nicaragua was to achieve food self-sufficiency through a restructuring of the system of agricultural production and the creation of a mixed economy in which the state played the major role. This was a tall order for a new government recently emerged from insurgency and heir to a bankrupt treasury, but the Sandinistas at once set about redirecting the economy along more socialist lines. The government immediately confiscated the 20 per cent of agricultural land that had belonged to the Somozas and their allies, roughly 2 million acres, which they termed the "Area of the People's Property." These estates were converted to state farms, large state-run businesses producing for export, much as the capitalists before them had done, so great was the need for dollars.[10] In part, the state farms were created because the Sandinistas feared that campesinos would invade the former Somoza and other estates and break them up into small, inefficient tracts, which, indeed, they had begun to do.

The government wanted to discourage takeovers while also demonstrating concern for the plight of the campesino. Ortega expressed his sympathy in 1980 by declaring that it was "not acceptable that while there are peasants who have to scratch among the rocks to sow their crop, there should be landlords with fertile land unused except for contemplation by its owners...." The Sandinistas, however, definitely did not want takeovers because they needed the campesinos to provide labor for the export crops that brought in 80 per cent of the nation's foreign exchange. In the early years, the Sandinistas suffered from what Dennis Gilbert terms "technofascination"—the dazzling possibilities of modern technology— and by a desire to proletarianize the campesinos, converting them into wage-earners.[11] A series of factors led to the failure of this doctrinaire, top-down approach to a reality resistant to Marxist theory, but for the first five years this direction prevailed. Although the campesinos' goal was food self-sufficiency and an end to hunger, the Sandinistas' was increased export production and only modest land reform.

Thus, the Agrarian Reform Act of 1981 was a conservative, compromise document, which guaranteed the right to private property to those who worked it efficiently and productively [*garantiza la propiedad de la tierra a todos aquellos que la trabajan productiva y eficientemente*]. It is still on the books, though a number of amendments have been enacted. The law recognizes the huge debt the Sandinista government of national reconstruction owed the "best sons and daughters of the country" [*mejores hijos de la patria*] who died for the revolution as well as the goal of social justice, or social redemption [*redención social*], championed by Sandino. Moreover, the law guarantees the right of the campesino population to live with dignity from working the land [*el derecho del campesinado a vivir dignamente del trabajo de la tierra*].[12] It places no limit on land ownership, unlike other agrarian reform programs in Latin America; moreover, it sets out reasonable criteria for deciding if land is being used efficiently, and it applies only to very large estates of over 850 acres. Unlike other Latin American cases, the Nicaraguan law provided specifically for the inclusion of women and mandated compensation for underused or idle lands taken over, while prohibiting land seizures.[13] Peasants and rural workers were to receive land free of charge; titles were not to be sold. Agricultural reform land could not be divided, sold, or rented, and title was given in perpetuity to beneficiaries and their descendants.

From 1980 until the end of 1983, 80 per cent of reform lands went to production cooperatives, with preference given to heroes and martyrs of the revolution.[14] The Agrarian Reform was central to the Sandinistas' desired transition to socialism, because it would begin the shift from individual to collective farming, bringing greater social justice; a more rational, or efficient, use of the land; a transformation of the social relations of production; and, of course, a strengthening of the relationship between the campesinos and the FSLN. These were all objectives pursued by Jaime Wheelock, the Minister of Agriculture and Agrarian Reform, but the original inspiration for cooperatives comes from the peasant cooperatives organized by Sandino in 1932. The Sandinista's evocation of Sandino's revolutionary mystique identified their cooperative program with the nationalist tradition in Nicaraguan history. The government also promoted cooperatives because they offered a system for distributing credit and technical aid, and they justified the purchase of agricultural machinery to be shared among cooperatives.[15]

There are several different kinds of cooperatives in Nicaragua. By far the most numerous, the Credit and Services Cooperatives (CCS), resemble farmers' associations in the US or the seringueiros' cooperative in Acre. In these cooperatives, small farmers retain their own property, but unite to obtain seed and fertilizer more cheaply and to apply for loans via their elected president. Members receive credit for their own production expenses and are responsible for paying their own loans. In the first year of the reform, 1,200 credit associations were registered, though many failed the following year because of the difficulties involved in adjusting to and administering the new arrangement. The CCS were the cooperatives least favored by the Sandinistas, who initially regarded them as primarily a first step in promoting collective work situations and as a means for channelling credit to increase output.[16] Four of the cooperatives to which the women interviewed belong are of the CCS type: AMOC (The Association of Rural Women Workers) in Chinandega; the San Francisco de Asis Cooperative in Malpaisillo, León, with overlapping membership in the Cooperative of Widows and the Retired; and the Multiple Services Cooperative in Masaya.

The government favored a different type: the Sandinista Agricultural Cooperatives (CAS), in which small farmers pool their land, tools, and livestock. In these, profits are allocated according to the amount of work each individual performs; to community projects, such as schools or roads, collectively determined; and to capital improvements such as tools, plows, and wire. This type is very similar both to the Guaraní work groups and to the Guaraní *comunal,* or common land arrangement, except that each Guaraní farmer has his own small plot in addition to the comunal. After three years, there were only two dozen CAS established by former small landowners, for peasants were chary about letting go of their own land. They were, however, agreeable to joining "dead furrow" [*surco muerto*] cooperatives, in which land is divided into individual plots separated by untilled furrows, with campesinos sharing equipment and work activities.[17]

By the end of the second year of the reform, there were officially 3,820 CSS and CAS cooperatives in operation, with a combined membership of 62,359, totaling 53 per cent of all small farmers. By 1984, 2.4 million acres had been granted to 45,000 family farmers or cooperatives, controlling about 20 per cent of Nicaragua's farmland, more than ten times the amount owned by peasants before 1979.[18]

The Sandinistas' transformation of the structure and relations of farm production occurred at precisely the time of the greatest violence and destruction of the contra war, which heated up considerably in 1984 and reached its peak in 1986. The primary contra objective in the countryside was to disable production; thus, they made agricultural cooperatives their prime targets. Partly because of the dislocations and suffering caused by the war and partly because of the increasing clamor of the campesinos for their own land, the government began awarding more titles to individual campesino families; they were, after all, bearing the brunt of the war.[19]

The Masaya Plan offers the best example of the move away from collectives and toward accepting a variety of arrangements to increase production. In Masaya, the most densely populated rural area in Nicaragua, the concentration of land ownership originally brought about by cotton farming had been especially acute, to the extent that during the revolution many landless campesinos had taken over estates and immediately planted food crops. The *minifundio* [extremely small farm] problem in Masaya was the most acute in the nation, and the campesinos' land hunger needed to be addressed. As campesinos' frustration with their situation increased, their support for the government began to flag. They reduced their participation in UNAG (National Union of Farmers and Ranchers), began evading the draft in larger numbers, and emigrated to neighboring Costa Rica and elsewhere. The Sandinistas were in danger of losing their rural base of support. Combined membership of the ATC (Association of Rural Workers) and UNAG fell to less than

150,000.[20] To shore up UNAG, the able Daniel Núñez assumed leadership in 1984; he worked hard to increase UNAG's membership rolls and influence by making it more inclusive and more independent of the FSLN. Acknowledging that the Sandinista government had miscalculated key aspects of its agrarian policy, agricultural minister Wheelock told peasants that they themselves would have to decide how to organize the expropriated lands, confessing, "Obviously, we don't know how to do these things, so it's up to you."[21] Campesinos mainly wanted their own land, not collectives, but the government was reluctant to confiscate large estates because they needed their contribution to the foreign exchange earnings, and they wanted to de-emphasize their radicalism in view of the hostility of the US. Using a special provision of the law allowed for Agrarian Reform Zones, something akin to eminent domain in the US, the government expropriated a number of large producers' estates for campesino use and offered owners cash or land of equal quality elsewhere. All producers agreed save one, Enrique Bolaños, the head of the Superior Council of Private Enterprise (COSEP) and later vice-president under Arnoldo Alemán, even though he was offered twice as much high quality cotton land in León as he possessed in Masaya.[22] [Bolaños was elected president of Nicaragua in November 2001.] A total of 4,509 manzanas [1 mz.=.7 acre] of prime land was awarded to 1,011 campesino families in Masaya and Diriomo, who chose chiefly the credit and services type of organization.[23] Nubia Boniche, an organic farmer whose interview follows, is one of the campesinas to benefit from the expropriation of Bolaños' property, although she still worries that his lawyers could evict her and her family. Plan Masaya was a successful government effort to address the land needs of poor campesinos, increase and mechanize basic grain production, improve the standard of living of the beneficiaries, and retain the loyalty of the campesinos. New agrarian reform titles for 1985 totaled 1 million acres. By early 1986, 60 per cent of Nicaragua's campesinos had received land titles to 4.5 million acres, one-third of the nation's agricultural land.[24]

Economic pressures on the Sandinistas intensified, culminating in the Agrarian Reform Law of 1986, which revised the 1981 law in two important areas: it no longer exempted unproductive farms under 850 acres, and it allowed peasants to sell their land.[25] The second provision unintentionally paved the way for a flood of distress sales among campesinos themselves as credit became more and more difficult to acquire. In the meantime, the Sandinistas' distribution program reached its height in 1986 with a record 35 per cent of the 315,032 manzanas turned over to individual ownership. The government no longer regarded the campesino as in need of proletarianization, but rather as a productive source to be encouraged and as a group whose hunger for land needed to be satisfied.[26] For all their failings, the Sandinistas were attempting to create a more equitable distribution of resources under extremely adverse conditions.

With the inauguration of the Chamorro administration, the orientation toward campesino producers shifted precipitously back to large, highly capitalized enterprises. Like the Sandinistas before her, doña Violeta inherited a war-torn, impoverished country, but her repair kit included very different tools from those of the Sandinistas. Before receiving the foreign aid desperately needed for reconstruction, Chamorro's government was required by international lenders to stabilize the economy through draconian cuts in public spending and severe reduction of the money supply.[27] The structural adjustment package mandated by the IMF emphasized deregulation, which eliminated state-run businesses and nearly all price controls; banking reform, which favored private over state banks; integration into the global market, which removed import quotas and lowered tariffs; sharp reduction of the state's economic role through privatization; and drastic cuts in social spending.[28] Thus, there is a struggle for land in Nicaragua between large landowners and campesinos, with the large landowners working in concert with global economic forces.

Neoliberal policies, fostered by the IMF, have tended to bring about the desired economic stabilization and reduce inflation, but they have hit the poor population in Nicaragua like a sledgehammer, resulting in soaring unemployment, the drying up of credit sources, and devastating reductions in education and health care. Moreover, their "one-size-fits-all" prescription runs roughshod over local differences. Nicaragua scholar Richard Stahler-Sholk describes the IMF as a "kind of global capitalist planner," but one whose agenda in the short term immediately lowers the living standards of the poor and strengthens the hand of undemocratic governments.[29]

The Chamorro administration's implementation of IMF conditions, as well as those imposed by other international financial institutions such as the World Bank, the Inter American Development Bank, and the US Agency for International Development (USAID), clashed with the high levels of mobilization the populace attained during the Sandinista era, such that initially there was strong resistance from labor unions and farmers. Their resistance, however, waned with the grinding effects of neoliberal measures, exacerbated by deep divisions within the FSLN, evidenced by the party's split in 1994 into the Sandinista Renovation Movement (MRS), led by former Sandinista vice-president Sergio Ramírez, and the orthodox FSLN, led by Daniel Ortega.

Credit restrictions hit the campesinos hard. During the Sandinista period, families attended by BANADES, the Nicaraguan National Development Bank, grew from 16,000 in 1978 to 102,200 in 1988. This number was reduced to 31,700 families in 1991 and further to 12,000 families by 1995. The policy shift was intensified by the government's partial privatization of the banking system. Seven new private banks were in operation by 1992, while the staff of BANADES was slashed by 61 per cent and its branches by 46 per cent. The rural poor were hurting; even though the small and medium producers furnished 60 per cent of agricultural production in 1990, their share of credit fell from 56 per cent in that year to 23 per cent in 1993. USAID, a supporter of neoliberalism, chided the administration for foot-dragging in extending titles and credit to small farmers, without which they were ineligible for credit. The credit vise was a major cause of economic hard times generally, but for cooperatives it was devastating. Stahler-Sholk claims that it was the principal reason for the decrease in the number of agricultural cooperatives from 3,000 to 1,400 in 1995 alone.[30]

In 1990, 60 per cent of the population lived in poverty; by 1994, that number had increased to 70 per cent. Much of the increase resulted from the 63 per cent reduction in public employees, many of whom were unsuccessful in locating positions in the depressed private sector.[31] Further, many middle-sized and large capitalists who wished to increase production, including returnees from Miami, found it impossible to compete because of Nicaragua's archaic infrastructure and the extreme shortage of credit, even for entrepreneurs. The Superior Council of Private Enterprise (COSEP) itself complained about the SAP (Structural Adjustment Program), because the closed decision-making process and chokehold on credit excluded them from playing the role they desired in their country's recovery.[32]

Policy decisions were made by negotiations between Managua and Washington in what constitutes perhaps the greatest of all repudiations of the Sandinistas' nationalist legacy. The Nicaraguan government, like the Bolivian government, willingly removed itself from economic intervention to the extent that it would have a difficult time reinserting itself significantly even if it so desired, so limited is Nicaragua's economic autonomy. Meanwhile, the country's traditional economic role has been reinforced—as a dependent exporter of cotton, coffee, bananas, sesame, sugar, tobacco, and other agricultural commodities, and a dependent market for manufactured products and investments from developed countries and transnational corporations as part of a globalized economy.[33]

By 1994, Nicaragua's foreign debt of $11.5 billion was the highest per capita in the world. Economic structural adjustment reduced inflation, but it did not increase production or income, only unemployment, and it further skewed the class structure. The United Nations Development Program (UNDP) report of 1994 figures show that the wealthiest 20 per cent received 65 per cent of the national income, with the poorest 20 per cent, including those of our study, living on only 3 per cent. Nicaragua's income distribution was among the most unequal in the world. The slogan popular in the 1990s, *La priva nos priva* [Privatization deprives us], sums up the effect, if not the intent, of the SAPs.[34]

When considering the local impact of global neoliberal policies on developing countries such as Nicaragua, Brazil, and Bolivia, it is important to bear in mind that it is gendered—that is, neoliberal policies in actuality affect women and men differently. In addition to the increased impoverishment of the general population, structural adjustment policies have augmented women's share of "invisible" labor, their unpaid work, as well as their "double day," their paid work plus their domestic responsibilities. Gender inequality in terms of economic wealth is a worldwide phenomenon. UN statistics reveal that women constitute one-half of the world's population, carry out two-thirds of the work, but receive only one-tenth of the world's income and own less than 1/100 of the world's property. This gulf between the portion of work carried out by women and their income illustrates the "invisible" nature of women's economic contributions. More and more, women have to engage in some sort of wage-earning activity, such as participation in seasonal harvests, as well as maintain the household. Their traditional workload at home remains unchanged, resulting in the "double burden," which becomes heavier in times of acute need. Not only have policy-makers been unaware of the burden, they have come to count on women to increase their load, paid and unpaid, but still invisible by most official measures. A UNICEF report in 1989 determined that "poor women working harder" had permitted the lowest one-third of the Latin American and Caribbean population to survive the crisis of that decade.[35]

Women in Nicaragua face the same challenges as poor women elsewhere, and their domestic labor contributions have only recently begun to be studied. For example, a comprehensive statistical study on rural Nicaraguan women published in 1997 by the International Foundation for the Global Economic Challenge (FIDEG), made visible through quantification the productive work that rural women do, such as 97.8 per cent of food preparation, 98.3 per cent of childcare, and 94.3 per cent of housecleaning. It concluded that women contribute 85 per cent of all nonremunerative tasks, while increasing numbers also engage in temporary wage labor and prepare food and other items for sale.[36] Although the study shows in black and white the extent of women's economic contributions, these are still taken for granted, for the underlying assumption is that women can always take on more in times of crisis. In 1987, a UNICEF document termed the notion of infinitely elastic home work hours the "invisible adjustment."[37] The UNICEF report reveals the gender bias inherent in SAPs, not just in Nicaragua, but for women and children on a global scale.

Life has always been hard for rural Nicaraguan women, but hopes had been high that cooperative associations would ameliorate their hardships. To some extent,

CAMPESINO'S HOME, MALPAISILLO

and in some unexpected ways, this proved to be the case. A study carried out in the 1980s by the Rural Women's Research Team of the Center for the Study of Agrarian Reform (CIERA) reveals that in agricultural Nicaragua in 1978, only 22 cooperatives were in existence; by the end of 1979, the year of the Sandinista triumph, there were 1,976. By 1982, 2,849 cooperatives listed a total of 68,434 members. National Cooperative Census figures show that by 1982, 44 per cent of cooperatives, mostly of the CCS type, had incorporated women, even though only 6 per cent of all cooperative members were women. The average cooperative according to this census, consisted of 22 men and three women. In most of the production and the CCS cooperatives, the majority of women members were the sole or principal support of their families. In 1982 there were four all-women production cooperatives in Nicaragua, and 16 in which women constituted over 50 per cent of the membership.[38]

Women were slow to join cooperatives in part because, despite the revolution, they were still very much relegated to the private sphere and subject to their husband's will; in part because of traditional views of what constitutes women's work and place; and in part because the invisible work of childcare and household maintenance claim so much of their day. Even where women are admitted to membership they have had to struggle for real equality with men, and they have to raise consciousness of both women and men regarding women's changing roles and their abilities as workers. The CIERA study points to women's participation in both the revolutionary effort and the struggle for the land as having favored their incorporation into cooperatives, but women have had "a tough row to hoe" in agricultural cooperatives. As late as 1999 women received only 11 per cent of all agricultural credit given.[39]

The cooperatives in our study are run by women. They accept male members, but they are founded, organized, and headed by women. The San Francisco de Asis Cooperative in the village of Malpaisillo in the department of León is one of the oldest in the country, founded in 1975 as a credit and savings association. The other four cooperatives were all formed in the mid-1990s in response to the economic crisis. Three of these are of the CCS type: the Cooperative of Widows and the Retired, also in Malpaisillo; the Association of Rural Women Workers (AMOC) in Chinandega; and the Multiple Services Cooperative (Cooperativa de Servicios Múltiples) in Masaya. The last cooperative of our study is that of the Women Producers of Guanacastillo; it is *agropecuaria*—that is, it produces both crops and animals. These cooperatives were cobbled together out of desperation and in the belief that, as cooperativist legislation proclaims, "there is strength in numbers" [*la unión hace la fuerza*].[40]

In the countryside, the government's neoliberal budget cuts have been a painful reality, not just a column of statistics, and they have made a difficult existence even more precarious. The desperation of the women's situation comes through clearly in the founding statutes of their organizations. For example, among the basic objectives of AMOC is to "promote accessible alternatives for the

PREPARING TORTILLAS, MERCADO ORIENTAL, MANAGUA

survival ... of the poorest sectors of the Nicaraguan population." Specific goals include promoting *micro-empresa* [microenterprise], resolving problems in health and education, raising consciousness regarding the "ecological disaster we are living," and stimulating the "effective integration of women in all spheres of society."[41] The Women Producers of Guanacastillo, in their statutes, state their objectives succinctly: "to search for a better family income that would represent a dignified and just life, and to develop relationships of brotherhood, cooperation and solidarity among our members and those of other cooperatives."[42]

In organizing themselves, the women were responding to their own concrete experiences. For example, the lack of credit forced them to take up additional wage-earning activities, such as selling used clothes, or cheese, or sending their school-aged daughters to do so. In the San Francisco and Multiple Services cooperatives, lack of credit so reduced women's capacity to support their families, that a number of members in desperation left the countryside for the city, seeking work in Managua as domestics and leaving the remaining associates to assume a greater burden. Lack of credit translates into lack of food for one's family. To compensate for food shortages, the women commonly eat less so that their children may have a meal.

Hunger is a serious problem in Nicaragua; recent figures reveal that 35 per cent of the deaths of children from one to four years of age result from malnutrition.[43] Cardinal Obando y Bravo, on responding to a critique of neoliberal policies made by the broader Catholic church, agreed with the critique and drew a parallel between neoliberal policies and hunger in his country: "If it is a market economy not well controlled by the government, I consider it problematical. There is an enormous gap [between rich and poor] and many have nothing to eat.... I think one has to regulate a market economy. If it is not controlled [the market], it creates even greater inequality."[44] Pope John Paul II himself in 1997 spoke of hunger as the great challenge and accusation of our time.[45] Joseph Collins, author of the widely read *What Difference Could a Revolution Make?*, is even more direct. He states that in virtually no country is chronic hunger the result of scarcity of resources; rather, the problem is that the hungry "have been dispossessed—deprived of control over the resources rightfully theirs, which they need to free themselves from hunger."[46]

The World Food Program (PMA) has been a lifesaver for the San Francisco, AMOC, and Women Producers of Guanacastillo cooperatives. PMA assistance was especially critical in the sectors of Chinandega and León where, in October 1998, Hurricane Mitch swept away all the crops and the six cows belonging to San Francisco cooperativists and left communities "submerged in despair."[47] Donations of corn seed, beans, oatmeal, and used clothing from Casa Ave Maria, a Nicaraguan and international NGO, enabled the community to survive.

The women neglect not only their own nutrition for the sake of their families, but also their general health needs now that health care is privatized. For example, a woman will forgo medical attention for herself in order to obtain medication for her children, though she can usually purchase only a few pills of the prescription. A Witness for Peace publication in 1995 records that one in every 66 women who die in childbearing years dies of pregnancy or child-bearing causes, an exceptionally high figure compared to the 1 per 10,000 women in developed countries.[48] Women also lose valuable work time and pay costly transportation fees to take their children to clinics where lines are long and medical staff are overburdened because funding cuts have forced so many centers to close. The Cooperative of Widows and the Retired in Malpaisillo was formed in 1997 in response to this situation. It provides a tiny subvention to help cover basic medications for members' children, emergency transportation to León, and funeral expenses. Stress from the constant search for work and food presents an additional health problem; the headaches that Olfania Medina suffers are a consequence of that daily tension. There is also the problem of increased alcoholism among male partners who, as Gloria Siesar observes in her interview, frequently turn to alcohol to escape what they perceive as a hopeless situation. Alcoholism creates additional problems for the entire family, including domestic abuse, and it is hard on the budget. The lack of potable water and near absence of plumbing present health problems as well. Now that spending restrictions make maintenance, let alone improvements, prohibitive, women and their children are traveling greater distances to fetch water suitable for drinking and cooking.

The biggest struggle, aside from putting food on the table, is educating one's children. The women sacrifice continually in order to cover school fees, bus fare, books, and uniforms for their children's "public" education. It is rare indeed to be able to send one's child through university, though Nubia Boniche of Nindirí has somehow managed to do so. Rosario Flores observes of AMOC members in Chinandega that many are unable to pay school fees, in addition to which they need

"CAPACITACIÓN," COOPERATIVA DE SERVICIOS MÚLTIPLES, MASAYA

their children's labor; therefore, it is difficult to convince desperate parents to keep their children in school. Recent estimates place at 24 per cent the primary school age population that is not enrolled in schools.[49] Privatization of public schools has made them increasingly inaccessible to rural children. The long-term consequences of lack of schooling are sobering. UN population figures show that, in 1998, two of every five Nicaraguans were younger than 15 years of age. If these children are not schooled, it will compound a situation in which 68 per cent of the economically active population under 25 years of age lacks formal education or has logged only a few years of elementary schooling.[50] Childcare facilities, too, have fallen victim to the budgetary axe. Women have to leave their children untended in order to carry out field work, sell, or assist as temporary hands at harvest time. Sometimes they leave their oldest daughter in charge; but she may be only six or seven years old, and while she is tending her younger siblings, she is not attending school.

One of the biggest educational blows to women is that funding cuts have affected *capacitación* efforts, that is, training sessions, seminars, and workshops. It is difficult to overestimate the positive impact such programs have had over the past two decades or so on the development of cooperatives and the enlargement of women's understanding of their work and their world. It is no exaggeration to say that they have functioned as an alternative educational system for campesinos, women and men alike. The technical workshops have benefitted both populations, imparting invaluable knowledge and raising environmental consciousness.

The non-technical *talleres* [workshops] have been of special benefit to women. Rosario Flores, president of AMOC, refers to the human development manual provided to her by the Ministry of Social Action (MAS) and funded by the United Nations Development Program (UNDP) as her bible. It offers her a general philosophy in which to contextualize her work with AMOC, that of *la hermandad de los seres humanos* [the brotherhood of humankind], while it also suggests motivational activities; ideas for group process, raising self-esteem, and setting goals for personal growth; and topics for workshops, speakers, and small group work, complete with a model plan for an agenda and workshop evaluation sheets.[51]

In addition to the regular technical workshops, Rosario has sponsored classes on self-esteem, women's health, and identity. The identity workshop was extremely well-received as it allowed women the opportunity to discuss the topic from three different perspectives: Who am I? Who do people say that I am? Who do I want to be? Other workshop materials come from instructional booklets published in neighboring Costa Rica. One such booklet focuses on the personal difficulties of working collaboratively, with role-playing suggestions of several difficult types, including Miss Unreliable [*Doña Incumplida*], Miss Egotist, [*Doña Egoísta*], Miss Resentful, [*Doña Resentida*], and Miss Know-it-All, [*Doña Toda*].[52] Such activities and publications offer members the opportunity to develop their human potential, socialize, share questions, exchange experiences, and strengthen common bonds. In the agricultural cooperative, the Women Producers of Guanacastillo, regular workshops on bookkeeping, animal husbandry, pesticides, and organic fertilizer have proved essential in enabling the women to increase production enough to feed their families.

Unfortunately, funding for such vital functions has been slowed as the Alemán government tightened up regulation of NGO activities. Women in the San Francisco cooperative of Malpaisillo for example, have been unable to hold workshops since 1998 because of lack of funds to pay even modest fees to technicians and other specialists who may be willing, but who cannot afford to provide their services gratis. The San Francisco women hold frequent raffles of shoes, towels, clocks, and, once, a night table with cosmetics inside, as a way to *levantar la cooperativa* [lift the cooperative].[53] It is unfortunate that, according to FIDEG figures, only 1 per cent of the 15.5 per cent of women in agriculture receive any kind of workshop training at all. It is interesting to note that 72 per cent of all workshops, rural and urban, for all populations, are offered by NGOs while only 8.5 per cent are sponsored by the state or its institutions. Workshops and educational tools are desperately needed in the countryside, for 95 per cent of the rural population lives in poverty.[54]

Clearly, the women of our study continue to experience severe hardships in their daily lives. They have learned that cooperativism carries with it the continual difficulties inherent in sharing—work, responsibilities, resources, and decision-making—with others. However, as hard as it is to cooperate, it is nearly impossible to go it alone.

The women whose interviews follow have also come to know the distinct rewards of cooperative membership, which, along with the crucial assistance provided by NGOs and their own deep sense of religious faith, constitute the main strategies they draw on to help them survive neoliberalism.

NOTES

1. Philippe Bourgois, "Nicaragua's Ethnic Minorities in the Revolution," *Nicaragua: Unfinished Revolution*, ed. Peter Rosset and John Vandemeer (New York: Grove Press, 1986) 459-72.

2. For more on US/Nicaraguan relations, see Walter LaFeber, *Inevitable Revolutions* (New York: W.W. Norton, 1984).

3. Joshua Karliner, Daniel Faber, and Robert Rice, "An Environmental Perspective," Rosset and Vandemeer 396.

4. Karliner et al. 403.

5. Denis L. Heyck, *Life Stories of the Nicaraguan Revolution* (New York: Routledge, 1990) 7, 10. *NACLA [North American Congress on Latin America] Report on the Americas* 12 (November-December 1978): 6-7.

6. For an account of political developments during the 1970s, see *NACLA Report* 6-7.

7. See Sheryl L. Hirshon and Judy Butler, *And Also Teach Them to Read* (Westport, CT: Lawrence Hill and Co., 1983).

8. See Maxime Molyneux, "Women: Activism without Liberation?," Rosset and Vandermeer 478-81.

9. See David Kaimowitz, "Nicaragua's Agrarian Reform: Six Years Later," Rosset and Vandermeer 390-93.

10. Joseph Collins, with Frances Moore Lappé, Nick Allen, and Paul Rice, *Nicaragua: What Difference Could a Revolution Make?* (New York: Grove Press, A Food First Book, 1986) 3.

11. Dennis Gilbert, *Sandinistas: The Party and the Revolution* (New York: Basil Blackwell, 1988) 90, 93.

12. *La Gaceta* (Managua) 188, 21 (agosto 1981): 1738, 1737.

13. Gilbert 92; Collins 90.

14. Gilbert 92.

15. Collins 97-98.

16. Collins 99, 101.

17. Collins 102; Gilbert 102.

18. Collins 105, 151.

19. Collins 155-59.

20. Gilbert 98.

21. Gilbert 101.

22. Collins 246.

23. Laura J. Enríquez, *Agrarian Reform and Class Consciousness in Nicaragua* (Gainesville, FL: University Press of Florida, 1997) 105. For more on agrarian reform, see also Laura J. Enríquez, *Harvesting Change: Labor and Agrarian Reform in Nicaragua, 1979-1990* (Chapel Hill, NC: University of North Carolina Press, 1991).

24. Enríquez, *Agrarian Reform* 123; Collins 247.

25. *La Gaceta* 8,13 (enero 1986): 58.

26. Enríquez, 110, 113. See also, David Núñez, "Talar los grandes árboles," *Pensamiento Propio* (Managua: CIERA, 1986) 31-36. For more on the Sandinistas' conceptions of democracy, see Katherine Hoyt, *The Many Faces of Sandinista Democracy* (Athens, OH: Center for International Studies, Ohio University, 1997).

27. Gary Prevost, "The Status of the Sandinista Revolutionary Project," *The Undermining of the Sandinista Revolution*, ed. Gary Prevost and Harry E. Vanden (New York: St. Martin's Press, 1999) 15.

28. Sharon Hostetler, JoAnn Lynen, and Leia Raphaelidis, *A High Price to Pay: Structural Adjustment and Women in Nicaragua* (Washington, DC: Witness for Peace, 1995) 9.

29. Richard Stahler-Sholk, "Structural Adjustment and Resistance: The Political Economy of Nicaragua under Chamorro," Prevost and Vanden 76. See also David Close, *Nicaragua: the Chamorro Years* (Boulder, CO: Lynne Rienner Publishers, 1999).

30. Stahler-Sholk, 90-91, 103.

31. Hostetler et al. 9.

32. Stahler-Sholk 93. See also Rose Spalding, *Capitalists and Revolution in Nicaragua: Oposition and Accommodation, 1979-1993* (Chapel Hill, NC: University of North Carolina Press, 1994).

33. Gary Prevost and Harry E. Vanden, "Introduction," Prevost and Vanden 4.

34. Stahler-Sholk 94, 95, 74.

35. Cited in Hostetler et al. 3.

36. María Rosa Renzi and Sonia Agueto, *La mujer y los hogares rurales nicaragüenses: indicadores económicos y sociales* (Managua: Fundación Internacional para el Desafío Económico Global [FIDEG], 1997) 173; Ligia Blanco, "Mujer, trabajo y pobreza," *Barricada* (24 septiembre 1997): sec. 6A,54.

37. Hostetler et al. 4.

38. Lucia Aguirre, and Martha Luz Padilla, with the collaboration of Carmen Diana Moore, *Tough Row to Hoe: Women in Nicaragua's Agricultural Cooperatives*, tr. Paola Pérez Alemán and Phil Martínez (Managua: Rural Women's Research Team [CIERA] and San Francisco: Food First, 1985) 9, 11, 16, 25.

39. Aguirre et al. 26, 22; Mariana Young, "Las mujeres son mejores pagadoras que los hombres?," *El cooperativista* (Managua) 3, 17 (1999): 11.

40. René Miranda Meléndez and Leonardo Chavarría Balmaceda, *Legislación cooperativa* (Managua: Fundación para el Desarrollo [FUNDER], 1995) 9.

41. *Estatutos de la Asociación de Mujeres Obreras y Campesinas, 1997*: 1-2. The Spanish reads: "promover alternativas accesibles para la sobrevivencia, el desarrollo económico, social, ecológico y cultural de los sectores más pobres de la población nicaragüense. ... promover la micro empresa productiva, promover participación activa de la población en resolver problemas de salud y educación, contribuir a la toma de conciencia sobre el desastre ecológico que vivimos; y estimular la efectiva integración de la mujer en todas las esferas de la sociedad."

42. *Estatutos de la Cooperativa Agropecuaria de Producción, Productoras de Guanacastillo, 1997*: 2. The Spanish reads: "procurar un mejor ingreso familiar que represente una vida digna y justa y desarrollar relaciones de hermandad, cooperación y solidaridad entre sus afiliados y entre éstos y otras cooperativas."

43. Hostetler et al. 13.

44. Quoted in Andrew J. Stein, "The Church," *Nicaragua Without Illusions*, ed. Thomas W. Walker (Wilmington, DE.: Scholarly Resources, 1997) 243.

45. "Editorial," *Carta alimentaria nicaragüense* (Managua: Publicación del Grupo Propositivo de Cabildeo e Incidencia) 1,5 (setiembre/octubre 1997) 1.

46. Collins 261.

47. *Acta* 360 (18 November 18 1998).

48. Hostetler et al. 13-14.

49. Hostetler et al. 14.

50. "Estado de la población nacional, 1998, Las nuevas generaciones: Nicaragua" (Managua: Fondo de Población de las Naciones Unidas [FNUAP], 1998).

51. *Compendio para la preparación de multiplicadores de desarrollo humano*, (Managua: Ministerio de Acción Social [MAS], con el apoyo del Programa de las Naciones Unidas para el Desarrollo [PNUD], 1995) 2.

52. *Para que el grupo permanezca unido* (San José: Centro Nacional para el Desarrollo de la Mujer y la Familia, Ministerio de Cultura, Juventud, y Deportes, 1989).

53. *Acta* 320 (10 junio 1995).

54. Blanco.

Interviews

María del Rosario Flores Neira

Founder and president of the credit and savings cooperative, the Association of Rural Women Workers (AMOC), former soldier in the Sandinista Army (1978-90), and feisty reformer, the spirited, straight-talking Rosario Flores helps women earn their daily bread and pushes them to stand up for themselves. Flores describes for us the workings of AMOC, the circumstances that led to its creation, and the army experiences which spurred her to develop her home-grown brand of feminism. As she discusses AMOC's many projects, she points out ways in which gender relations and women's health issues have been addressed through cooperative-related activities, and she highlights the crucial role that individual responsibility plays in making or breaking a cooperative. Flores details the complex challenge of changing traditional attitudes regarding saving money, paying back loans, and planning ahead, pointing out along the way the error of machista and asistencialista attitudes [promoting dependency] that have kept campesinas passive and subservient. Flores's observations reveal her practical nature and sense of humor, as well as her deeply-held belief that rural women must organize in order to survive.

I've been working with country women since March 25, 1995, when AMOC [*Asociación de Mujeres Campesinas Obreras*, Association of Rural Women Workers] was created to help women survive economically and to value themselves as women.

It's important to have women's cooperatives because men are more likely to be wastrels [*despilfarradores de plata*] and to misuse money than are women, who are more thrifty [*retenedoras*]. We are the ones who manage the home, who are economical, and know how to administer what funds we have. Having been both father and mother myself, I had to learn quickly. The majority of women in AMOC are single mothers too. We are a group of women who have suffered, and our experiences make us want to help each other advance. We don't want anyone to say of us, "there goes that poor woman with her little suitcase and three rags." No. We have decided to fight to our last breath to help women at least to earn their daily bread; when you can do that you can retain your dignity.

How it all started was like this. In 1994, I belonged to the *Secretaría de la Mujer* [Women's Secretariat] in La Cuz, here in Chinandega. I was the only woman, all the other directors were men, and I took the work seriously. The men stayed in town, but I went out and hitched rides to the most remote areas, going on horseback, foot, by cart, organizing the women. I would go to the campesinos' homes asking them for a fee of four *córdobas* and then I would give them a card saying that they were affiliates of the Secretaría of La Cuz.

Well, as you can imagine, after six months, I was physically worn out. I would come back and the men of the secretariat, who had just been sitting around doing nothing for the organization, would say to me, "Well, how much did you collect this month?" Those *cabrones* [bastards], did they think I was going to keep on slaving away just to bring home money to them? So one day I told them, "I'm out of here, I'm going to form my own association. I have all the affiliation cards, I travel and work with all the people in the area, and they are going with me, not with the Secratanía of La Cuz." That's exactly what happened.

We called an assembly, and we named ourselves AMOC, the Association of Rural Women Workers, although we have both male and female members. In 1995 we had 272 women. It was a tremendous amount of work and during the organizational period I neglected my children and my mother too much. In 1996, I first met Doña Eliett Heller who introduced me to the PMA [*Programa Mundial de Alimento*, World Food Program], after which I began to work even harder for the women because now there was real hope for our future. I memorized Doña Eliett's words so that I could transmit them throughout the countryside. Through her good offices we obtained funds from the PMA even though AMOC's legal status as a not-for-profit was still in process. Fortunately, this was followed by another disbursement from the milk project of the PMA. The *Asamblea* [National Congress] kept my documents for a year, only to tell me that they were not in order. So I had to submit everything all over again and, of course, pay another lawyer. There was much red tape and many fees, signatures, and trips involved. Finally our status was approved and published in *La Gaceta* [the government record]. Since then, I have to appear annually before the Asamblea for renewal of approval. The government does not like NGOs, and the process was discouraging and unnecessarily complicated, but I did it. I wasn't about to give up.

AMOC has a good administrative record. Currently we have four municipalities in our charge: El Viejo, Villa Nueva, San Pedro del Norte, and Realejo. We attend to small and medium producers who need credit for cattle and agriculture, and we are assisting 400 additional producers who are not affiliated with AMOC, but who receive funds from the NGOs Protierra and Inifom. We have 400 more in Villa Nueva, that makes 800. We also have 121 in San Pedro del Norte, in cattle only. And we have 104 more producers from Realejo. With regard to affiliates, we have not grown because I have not had time to go out to the communities to organize them, but with respect to beneficiaries, there are many.

We lost members after Hurricane Mitch in 1998 because 129 migrated to other departments, and four others perished, out of a total of 538. But we don't say, *No pue', vamo' a desequilibrarnos* [Well, we're going to collapse]. No. We have to maintain ourselves and keep on going, but it has been tough because many people lost everything. I felt very down then and would ask God to give me strength to encourage the women. I was having problems at home, with my children and their studies, and I would wonder how I could solve my own problems as well as those of the women.

But there are so many positive things too. I would like to take you to Realejo to show you how the women there are going forward with the chicken farm. They are working, their hands are scarred, but the spirit, the feeling they put into their work is wonderful, and they are seeing that they are capable of great things. They're now making *las galeras* [chicken houses] with funds from Protierra. In this case, the women have demonstrated a high administrative level, and I marvel at them. Last night I went there about 7:00 p.m., watching how they bustle about, they're like *zompopos* [ants] scurrying around. I took them 15,000 córdobas because one has to take out credits a bit at a time [*talonadamente*], according to how the construction is going on the galera. The better the construction proceeds, the more funds are released. So, I took them 15,000 córdobas because they are going to need an energy generator for the *pollitos* [chicks].

The funds come from Protierra for the chicken house, and AMOC is administering them. The women are required to make payments every six months. It's a good system. They have a three-year period for repayment; it's actually something that they could probably pay back in one year, but this program gives them time. I'm not going to be the one to tell the women to cancel their debt in less time. If it benefits them, that's what matters.

There are those who go broke or who do not pay; I am not going to say only marvellous things. For the most part the district leaders [*líderes comarcales*] are selecting reliable beneficiaries who, on the whole, are very clear that credit is credit and not a gift. The money they receive is seed money, which has to be paid back in order for them to borrow again; this is what is going to keep on giving them life, it is their future if they know how to administer it well. Then there are other district leaders who are not doing a good job in recommending people. They get carried away by *apasionamiento* [passion, friendship]; because so and so is their best friend, they recommend him, and in the end it is that person who defaults on the loan. As a result, some of the funding agency's technicians have called them to reflection so they can see some of the errors into which they are falling. As an administrator, I can make suggestions, and I tell the technicians to bring financial reports to the mayors so they can help choose responsible beneficiaries. Sometimes, a man is given funds who then leaves, and his wife is left there on the front lines. Typically, she has no experience in this sort of thing. We have to prepare her. We need training plans for leadership for women so they will not be left behind.

There are leadership training programs for men. In spite of that there still are problems, especially with regard to *el apasionamiento* and to viewing credit as another gift, not as seed money for the community. To those recipients we explain that they have to come up with leadership and payment plans.

You see, if people don't pay us back, then that hurts us [*se nos baja*], and we become a less reliable disburser of funds. And we need to keep our good record with Protierra and Inifom, for example.

Some communities are very responsible. In Realejo, for example, in addition to funds for the chicken house, they were also given credit for cattle raising, which they are paying back on schedule. The thing is, you have to go out there to the community, not stay behind your desk. You have to get to know the people, talk to them about their responsibilities, and show them that you care about them. That way the producers are very clear about what's expected of them, and they feel supported. Yesterday, for example, when I went out to take a look at the chicken house construction in Realejo, several concerned women asked me to postpone payment of their quota because they had not been able to sell their *chanchitos* [little pigs]. I had to be severe and tell them to start sooner trying to sell their pig or chicken so they will have the money when it is due. They wanted a three-week extension, but I could only give them one, or else the lawyer would be after me, asking, "Who's in charge here?" He comes to the office every Monday, so I told them they had to be there next Monday morning so that I could pay him when he arrived in the afternoon.

In San Pedro they paid up 100 per cent two weeks ago. Marvellous! I felt good because San Pedro is one of the municipalities in which it's very hard to collect. It is so difficult to travel there, it's practically inaccessible, very little assistance arrives there, and it's difficult for the people to travel here to make payments. To have them pay up on time means that they have learned the basic concept and have developed the leadership skills the community needs to begin raising pigs and chickens early enough in order to sell them before they have to pay up. They paid their debt and with what was leftover they bought more piglets, which will be ready to sell in six months when they need to make the next payment. They go to the market to sell, but if they don't find a buyer, they can always sell to a pig cooperative.

From AMOC's beginning, the land title question has been a major obstacle to our producers' receiving credit. In this, Technoserve, the NGO, has been of great service. There are a number of cooperatives that were part of the agrarian reform [under the Sandinistas] but were never officially accepted by later governments. Technoserve has helped measure and parcel the land out to each recipient. Soon they will receive official status.

In 1995, those very few whose titles were officialized were afraid to give me the original to take to the bank, but, of course, copies were useless. They were afraid that the bank would come and take their land away. As for the others, they had only a certificate of possession [*constancia de posesión*] from the agrarian reform, which is not considered official. It would've been very easy for the government to make these documents official, but they didn't, and very few of our members have had their agrarian reform certificates validated. Technoserve is facilitating that process now, helping to secure their plots [*parceliarlos*].

In the case of new cooperatives, Technoserve is helping inexperienced campesinos with their founding documents, *el Acta Constitutiva*, and with putting the land in the name of those who are working it. People feel secure and tranquil knowing they have their little piece of land in their name and knowing that is so stated in the *Acta Constitutiva*. It's very important because then they can sell, mortgage, borrow against it, facilitate credit, everything.

This is especially significant for women because traditionally everything has belonged to the man, first, second, last, and always. The woman has never owned anything, so the question was how to divide the *parcela* so that it becomes the property of both. This way, the women and children can't be thrown off their land. You see, in Nicaragua, if a man finds another woman, he can just bring her to live with him and *despachar* [throw out] his wife and children. It's the practice both in the countryside and the city. A fundamental objective of those who are working on legislation for women and children is for women to have patrimony because up to now they have had no protection.

Those who are getting their titles are holding on to their land; they have no intention of selling it. I know that in other areas they are being forced to sell out of necessity, but no, no, no, no, no—they are not selling here, they are clinging to it for dear life, and we are here to try to help them hold on. When I see the small producers on TV lamenting their impoverished situation, I say to myself, "That's where the NGO ought to be." We have to go to where the need is and help them get up, that's why we were created. But what happens? Some NGOs just sit there waiting for manna from heaven. But we have to get moving ourselves in order to help others. We can't just sit there with arms folded and say, "Too bad, those campesinos are too remote," or "It's too hard to get credit." If we sit around, we are not doing our job, and God helps those who help themselves.

There have been a number of positive changes already, just from hard work and example, material changes, like the chicken house, and also psychological changes. I'm not going to deny that the pace is very slow, but there are achievements. Take, for example, women's self-esteem. Although the men say, "NO, there have been no changes," you can see changes in the homes. I have been to homes where the woman is tending to the children and the man is trying to figure out how to iron his pants. Before, in this same sector, what you would see is the man lying in the hammock, saying "hand me my sandals, bring me my hat" [*pásame las chinelas, traeme el sombrero*]. Not now. Another example, a few years ago I would go out to those homes, and it was the poor woman who was out there with an axe or a machete cutting a tree trunk to make a fence. Now you go there, and the man is figuring out how to repair a fallen portion of the fence— slow, but sure, with regard to sharing domestic chores.

As for women's advances, they are going ahead by giant steps. Women are not interested in hearing that such and such a job is a man's job; no sir, women are repairing tractors. I go to the country, and in the cooperative the women are involved [*embrocadas*] as mechanics, doing tractor repair. I also see it in school construction—there are the women, even if they are only mixing concrete [*batiendo sus mezclas*], and the ones who are up above are the men, still, they are there working mixed in with the men. This kind of thing makes for better relations between men and women. They see that they are working side by side in groups, and they come to know each other better and to have fewer stereotypes and more respect.

Another thing that helps women is to talk about family planning. We don't do it directly as part of AMOC; there is another organization that comes to talk about women's themes, health, illness, pregnancy, abortion. They give good workshops, and the women are very interested in them. The husband of one of the members of AMOC asked me one day, "How come when the women have these workshops you don't invite us men? We too have something to offer." That's a sign that men are raising their consciousness with regard to the rights that women ought to have. So I asked the women, how would they like to have a new meeting and invite the men. Now the men are attending, they are agreeing with the need to improve women's health, and they too want birth control.

The women whom AMOC serves all live in the same communities. That's one of the requirements of the Association. The requirements are: 1) they have no criminal record; 2) that they be Nicaraguans; 3) that they be born in the countryside and work their lands; 4) that they receive technical training whenever the agronomist or other technician offers it, which is usually twice a month; 5) that they be affiliated with AMOC at least six months before being eligible to receive a credit package. The ordinary meetings are every month, while Assemblies are once a year.

What we really need are rural cooperative banks to replace these urban banks where it's nearly impossible for *los pequeños* [the little ones] to get financing for two or three *manzanas* [1 mz. = 0.7 hectares]. They close the door in their face, saying they have to have a minimum of 50 manzanas. The banks just make the rich richer and the poor poorer. So what we try to do is help those who have nothing become those who have one thing [*los de una*], so they can keep going.

Sometimes people just can't make their payments to AMOC. If a woman can't pay her debt, not because she doesn't want to but because she is unable to, then we have under rental contract 100 manzanas where we keep cattle. Say a woman cannot pay back her loan. We take her cattle to our site, and through the milk those very cows produce, we pay the lending agency back. The cattle stay on site until the woman recuperates economically enough to pay us back; then she can happily take her cattle back home. The thing is, we are not going to take away her land and leave her with nothing to sit on. We have to employ people to take care of the cattle, so on paying her debt, the woman has to assume the personal expenses with regard to the maintenance of the cattle. This is important because AMOC cannot afford that expense and because that way women learn that not everything is a gift. That's the legacy of assistentialism that we are still trying to overcome too.

That is important, how to educate people and to be very clear that everything doesn't come as a gift. We also try to teach people to maintain a little savings, even a tiny amount, and not think that if you go under the *patrón* will take care of everything. That is a deeply ingrained way of thinking among the poor. We have to help people learn to be responsible. They are beginning to learn the basic lesson: "If I pay, I have credit again for the next year," and so on successively, because ours is a revolving fund.

The normal procedure is for people to come asking for money to buy cattle. What we do is authorize the cash. Then they go out and buy the cattle themselves. Oh, if I went out and bought the cattle, they would say that I gave them the smallest or skinniest or whatever. So they choose themselves; it is always a milk cow. A cow that costs about 3,500 córdobas gives about five litres of milk. We give them one year and a half to pay the credit. That's a short period, they have to have some other source of income apart from the milk, such as their *chanchito* [little pig], or chickens.

As I think back, it's amazing that we are here talking today about AMOC, because not all that long ago, in 1990, I was a soldier in the army. Then from 1990-94 I was a businesswoman, working from one end of Managua to the other. That was when I discovered that in military life, I hadn't looked beyond my nose. I was closed to everything that wasn't the army.

I loved those years of my life, don't get me wrong, but I got tired of it. I had left my children and my mom. At that time I didn't work nearly as hard as I do now, but I was isolating myself from my kids, I didn't know anything about them, I was not seeing or sharing in their development. When I left in 1990, I went into business. That was when I saw the stagnancy in which I had enclosed myself. I was with "my eyelashes lowered," that is, completely ignorant of the outside world. You asked why AMOC focuses on women. I don't know why other entities do, but I do so because of my own personal experience.

I saw that women are mistreated, that they have fewer opportunities, that they are as capable as men, but that they always have lower salaries. In the military, I was in Communications; I worked from one border to the other, but who received the awards and praise were the men. It took me a while to clear my vision and realize that this happens to women all the time. I began vaguely to desire to form some kind of an association. I began to make contact with *Punto de Encuentro* [Point of Encounter], a women's group. Brother! When I attended the first meeting, I was a clinical case. I didn't have any idea what they were talking about, and I couldn't answer a single question. There women were holding debates, discussing important issues, and I was mute. I didn't know anything about anything. Gender, what's that? But in a short time one learns to advance. What I learned is that we have to organize if we are going to get anywhere. Since 1995, I don't say that I'm a professional or a specialist with regard to women's issues, but now I can defend the rights of another woman. I can put myself in front of a group and speak up. I feel proud of myself and grateful to those who gave me a hand.

I don't regret my time in the army. I joined up in 1978 because my brother was already a guerrilla. He was a guerrilla's guerrilla. He motivated me to enter the ranks of the Frente. I had never even voted. When the *repliegue* [retreat before the final victory] took place, we went to Honduras. My brother was taken prisoner, and later they sent him to Colombia, he entered through the southern front. He was totally committed, but I was always thinking about my mom and my kids, and from Honduras I came back here with the triumph in 1979. I stayed within the military structures. When they had to make the selection of who was going to the navy, who was going to the police, who to the army, I chose the police. But at once I saw that it was too bureaucratic. I have never liked to be behind a desk. So I requested a transfer to the army, which was more active. We were on the move a lot, from Matagalpa to Jinotega.

I had ample opportunity to see how women are mistreated, in and out of the army. The army mentality was so narrow. All they taught us was politics; we never had any workshops on women's rights, or how to value ourselves as women, nothing. Just politics, so much so that I don't ever want to hear about politics again. My flag is the need of the poorest people in my country; that's my symbol. I don't want to hear anything, anything, anything about politics! I don't even know the political affiliation of the campesinos or the women, or their religious affiliation either. I don't want to know. I am not interested.

Among themselves, they talk about politics, but they see it more as a business, that is, which party might give me something. Since they are needy, since hunger looms large, people are interested. But they are not deceived by all that empty talk [*habladuría*] of the politicians. They live in the moment and they vote for someone only if they are going to receive some benefit that will help them solve their economic needs.

With regard to religion, the evangelicals talk about it the most, but they are very respectful. I don't talk about religion because it's always a delicate subject, you just have to respect each person's beliefs, that's all. We all worship the same God. We all have the same goal. We all get along very well in that regard. There are a few people in the sector of La Villa 15 de junio who are "into miracles" [*maravichuchas*] so to speak, and there are some *pastores* who are opportunistic—you know, people want to give the pastor a little cup of soup or the best cut of the pig they've just slaughtered. This is common.

What is very clear is that in the countryside what you see is the activity of many evangelicals, some Jehovah's Witnesses, and, less numerous but still active, Mormons. Who is not active is the Catholic church, even though the majority of our communities are Catholic. The Catholic church needs to reach out to these remote and poor communities, but they do not. The evangelicals are more lively, they care about their message. Their pastors come and live with the people; maybe some of them take advantage of the people, but they also share their lives. They arrive and put up their humble dwelling [*ranchito*], and they build their church with a few boards. They are poor, but they come out here to the marginal communities.

I don't know why the Catholic church doesn't do this, but I tell you they are as far removed from the communities as the politicians are. They ought to reach out, but they don't. Nobody's asking for a big church, just a little house, and in that little house on Sundays a visit by a priest. There's a perfect opportunity in a little community about 20 or 30 kilometres into the interior. There the children have not been baptized, and there is a great need, but nothing.

In the same communities another problem is getting the kids to go to school. The parents definitely need to be sensitized, but the problem is basically economic necessities. For example, the school is there, but necessity means that the parents take their children to the parcela to look after the pigs. So, today Juan doesn't go to school, tomorrow he doesn't either, soon a week has gone by, and after two weeks he fails. In that regard, the best thing we have going right now is the *Vaso de Leche* [Glass of Milk] program of the PMA. That's of great value, because at times the parents have no food, and, as they have no income, they have no way to buy food for their children, but in school they get a glass of milk and a cookie. The parent knows at least he is guaranteed that for his child, and he sends the child to school. When there are children's feeding centers [*comedores infantiles*] in the schools themselves, they provide nourishment for infants to six years of age, so the parent is not going to keep that child from going to school. But where there is no Vaso de Leche program, there is lower attendance.

The parents definitely need the help of their children in the fields. They can't afford to buy insecticide to repel pests; they don't have anything to improve the soil; they don't have money for clearing and weeding once the weeds [*coyotlillos*] come. So that child is not going to go to school when it's time to clear the field for corn because, if they leave that crop and let the coyotl grow, the crops will be lost. While the parents are doing one thing, the children go along cutting the weeds. Our recipients need more financing so that they can at least hire adult hands to help them and not have to depend on their children. I would also say that it would be good for a community to have a pair of oxen to plow the earth so the kids can attend school. Without education they have no future.

Sometimes those who have opportunities don't take advantage of them, but then they have unrealistic expectations for themselves. You go and ask a country kid what they want to do when they grow up, and no one says, "I want to be a campesino." They all say, "I want to be a doctor, a professional."

I think that idea came with the health brigades. It's like when I was a girl in the city, we were very poor, and I remember that I saw a nurse dressed all in white and it fascinated me and I would tell my mom, "I'm going to be a nurse when I grow up." I even studied nursing. I think that's the kind of thing the country children are doing too; they see doctors, nurses, those from Profamilia, that's why they say they want to be doctors.

The health promoters come to teach; they have their base house in the communities, that's where they have meetings. Profamilia promoters go to the base houses and offer training to women and men in all aspects of family life. They go out to the people. You'll see their *casa base* everywhere you go in the communities. They give information about health, how to plan your family. The men are very interested too, as I mentioned earlier. I remember that years back the campesino saw his wife completely as an object and not as a subject. But today, the women have valued themselves and they say NO. Four kids, and I'm "canceling the account" [*cuatro hijos y yo me cancelo*]. Profamilia is their right arm, because when it's time to plan these cancellations, they are certain about not having more children. They want to have children according to their economic capacity to support them. The men agree because they also see that if they have too many children then they can't buy a television, a recorder, or other things.

The method most women use is the injection because it is very sure and it lasts three months. They have to remember, they have their little data [*control*] card with a stamp, and Profamilia has the other card with the days planned for their visits to the community. They check the woman's card to verify when she will need another injection. Of course, the injection costs, but not at pharmacy prices, at a comfortable price, it's accessible. Better to spend 680 pesos on an injection than to have a child I can't afford to maintain, who will just suffer. Planning also results in better health for the woman and for the other children that she already has.

Care for women is not what's lacking in the countryside. What's lacking is basic treatment and preventive medicine. Malaria is very common, but we have no medicine in the health posts. Not to mention the serious coughs and respiratory ailments which are chronic and untreated. We just have nurses who come every month, but no doctor and no medicine.

I want to tell you a shameful story about medicine. A week after Hurricane Mitch, when I asked for help, various doctors came and offered their services. But there was this one doctor who told the victims, "You have no medicines. Tell me what you most need, and I will get it for you." So the people told her, and she promised to send a helicopter with those medications. A week later, the helicopter came. Everyone was so excited. But what happened? There was the doctora selling the medicines and at a high price in the moment of greatest need for those poor people who had lost their crops and homes in the hurricane! She knew very well that those medicines were donated for the emergency. One of the founders of AMOC has chronic asthma, and she went to get medication. She was so excited because it was her salvation, but when she got there she couldn't pay for it. This is the sort of thing that poor people have to put up with.

The other big problem and the one that we are making progress in overcoming is *asistencialismo* in the cooperatives, that is, dependency, of waiting passively for someone to solve your problems or give you a handout. The education that is provided through the many workshops our women attend is very, very, very clear on this point. They indoctrinate the producers with the idea that they have to pay back loans, that it is the responsibility of the borrower. You can measure the success in changing attitudes by the number of *recuperaciones* [paid up accounts]. Also, it's hard for people to understand that the person standing there in front of them, the NGO member, is just the intermediary, the one who facilitates the credit from national or international organizations. Sometimes the producers think that I have the money, or that I can intercede for them to postpone loan payments.

We charge 6 per cent annual interest, 4 per cent on giving the loan and 2 per cent on payment. Why that 4 per cent? Well, because we have to spend money on paper, on legal procedures so that everything will be in order. Plus, if we didn't, people would say this is just another gift. So, to make it all very clear, people have to sign contracts, cards, the lawyer's signature has to be there too, and the lawyer charges me, and he doesn't give me a break. So for all these *trámites* [transactions] we charge 4 per cent when they take out the loan.

But with that 4 per cent I do great juggling tricks. I pay the two assistants a very precarious salary, 800 for the accountant, Norita, who has a very strong social conscience in order to accept such a salary, and the lawyer who charges me 400 córdobas per project. Since we are now tending to four municipalities, that's 1,600 pesos per month that this man takes away, but I have to pay it. With the little that remains I have to maintain the office and find a salary for myself because I am supporting my mother. The office staff is very responsible. If Norita can't do something, then Nilda, the other assistant, steps in. For example, tomorrow I have to go to Masatepe to learn how to put up a latrine. I'm leaving at 4:00 a.m., but they are both here to take care of things.

No one is indispensable. It is essential for us to create local leadership so there will be continuity. This is one thing we are really working on. Protierra is helping a great deal. The women have to learn how to organize, and they have to learn about cooperativism, what it is, what makes it work. They have to learn that leadership development also means going frequently to the communities to encourage the women and keeping in close contact with them so they do not feel isolated in their problems. We also need to establish more cooperatives, you need a minimum of ten members. The thing is that the NGOs are not always going to be around, and the women need to be trained so that they can administer their own funds. That's why we are trying so hard to teach them how to manage revolving funds, because if they don't learn that, then all our work and hopes will collapse. Eventually, the cooperatives must become self-sustaining if we are to survive.

El Viejo, 3 November 1997; 10 August 1999

Juanita Medina de Matus

The name of Juanita Medina de Matus is synonymous with cooperativism in the Malpaisillo area of León where she is highly respected and much beloved for her steadfast commitment to cooperativist principles. Where many others waver and eventually drop out of cooperative associations, Medina has never given up on the concept or lost hope, even when her San Francisco savings and credit cooperative was reduced to one member—herself. Medina's involvement with cooperatives dates back to 1972, during the Somoza years, when "a well-to-do gentleman" came to her village to explain the benefits of cooperativism for the rural poor. Medina has weathered dictatorship, revolutionary, and neoliberal governments; during most of the period, she says, "we were dead but still fighting" [estábamos muertas luchando]. In response to the desperate poverty of her own village, Medina more recently founded a second association, the Cooperative of Widows and the Retired, which assists the neediest community members with items such as burial expenses. For Medina, the key to sustaining, and resuscitating, a cooperative is not technical or scientific expertise, bookkeeping skills, or workshops on group process, though all these are important. The key, she maintains, is love, doing things for the good of the group.

I was born in 1938 and grew up about 10 kilometres from here. Later, when I married, I moved to a nearby *finca* [farm] where my husband and I ran a little store. Later we came here; I've been here for 32 years. When I first came to Malpaisillo, I raised pigs and I had a milk stand.

It's an interesting story how our San Francisco Cooperative got started, and it's amazing that we're still going because we have taken more steps backward than forward. In 1972, a well-to-do gentleman [*un señor platudo*] came to help the villages; at that time I was selling milk and soft cheese [*cuajada*]. The señor taught us how to begin a cooperative and said that we needed a subscription fee of 10 córdobas per person. At that time with 10 córdobas, you could buy a *quinta* [50 pounds] of frijoles and a bag of sugar, many things, a bag of rice, salt. He told us that, if we could save 40 pesos, he would give us 120, and with that we could go to the market and buy whatever we wanted. Everybody just walked away, because how were we going to save 40 córdobas? We didn't have enough to buy food, so how were we going to save? Most people were afraid they would lose their 10 córdobas. They didn't believe in the concept of saving now in order to receive later; they didn't see how that could ever work. But the señor kept coming back and giving talks.

It's strange how things happen. I have a daughter who was born in 1972. My husband was working in Managua at that time, and they gave him insurance that covered free milk for our baby. When the señor platudo came, my husband was not there to talk to him because he was in Managua and I had no money [*reales*]. But since our daughter was allergic to cow's milk, I began to sell the milk that they gave to my husband. With those funds, I was able to join the cooperative, but, unfortunately, most of the other women who wanted to join couldn't afford it. I am one of the original founders.

Those of us who remained said, "Well, let's give it a try." We didn't have the least idea of how to concretize the concept. We had meeting after meeting, but we just stumbled along. It was a struggle from 1972 to 1975 when our cooperative became officially legal through the efforts of a lawyer from the Ministerio del Trabajo. That was four years before the Revolution, when Don William Báez was executive director of FUNDE [*Fundación Nicaragüense de Desarrollo*]; he was very beloved by all of us. We started because of that señor platudo who came out to talk to us about cooperativism, saying that it was for the poor, that it would help us in our struggle to get by. From 1975 we have been struggling, and we will keep on, through all the changes of government, even when everything came crashing down during the blockade and no financing was coming and FUNDE couldn't support the cooperatives any longer. Before the change of government in 1990, Don William left the country for the US to try to obtain funds. FUNDE wasn't sponsored by the Somoza government, but Somoza didn't prohibit cooperatives of small businesses.

During the period of the blockade in the 1980s the cooperatives were dead but still fighting [*muertas luchando*]; I personally never gave up. During 1990, 1991, 1992, still dead, no funding. We couldn't even pay the rent on our small office. That's when the number of members dropped to zero from six in 1990. And to think we had 712 in the beginning! But one gentleman at FUNDE, Carlos Santamaría, told me, "Never say that the cooperative is closed. Say it is in search of funding." He kept inviting us to meetings where we would learn new things.

All the savings cooperatives date from when William Báez was with FUNDE. Through FUNDE, he helped set up cooperatives in Chinandega, El Viejo, El Sauce, and many other places in this region. All the savings and credit cooperatives that I know of were created in that period, during the 1970s. Anyway, our cooperative was failing, and we couldn't obtain financing. For most of those years, I had just been a member, never an officer. But in 1987 someone from FUNDE asked me to become a candidate for president. I said, "No, I can't. I'm no good at anything" [*no sirvo para nada*]. I felt bad because I don't know how to read or write. But he said, "No, don't worry about that, we'll help you with things like signing checks. Let's go over the duties of the president, and you'll see that you can do everything." I finally agreed because we needed to do whatever was necessary to go forward, and I have been president ever since.

We had a real crisis in 1987 looking for funds. We obtained 12,000 córdobas in an emergency loan [*empréstamo relámpago*]. We were 12 active members at that time, paying our monthly dues, but then came the change in currency, and inflation wiped us out [*nos remató*]. If you had 1,000 pesos, perhaps they gave you 100 for it. But there we were, still hopeful, with our sign out front and the office furniture we had bought, a filing cabinet, a desk, and a fan, waiting, waiting for things to change.

Well, then the government changed, and in 1990 Doña Violeta came in, and everybody thought that the dollars would come in with her. We thought that the cooperatives would begin to lift themselves up. But we were in for more disappointments. When Don William came back in 1993 to work with the government, he invited all the cooperatives that he had formed to try to revitalize themselves. He called us all together for a meeting with him in March of 1993. He promised that he would give all the cooperatives a *transferencia* so that we could get bank loans. That gave us a boost, but he wasn't able to bring it about.

However, I did have a voucher [*aval*] from FUNDE that recommended our cooperative as creditworthy, but, the thing is, by then I was the only one left in the cooperative! And there was no way I could even pay the rent on the little office. So, I brought the furniture home, and everyone said to me, "The cooperative is dead, it's broken up, let it go." I would answer, "Someday things will improve, I can't abandon it." My children said to me, " Mama, they've all left you alone, and here you are breaking your back" [*se anda quebrando la cabeza*]. I said, "No, children, the cooperative soon will have legal status" [*personaría jurídica*]. I had requested it, and everything was in process with the Ministry of Work. Those who had been in charge of the cooperative before me had neglected to apply for this status as required by Doña Violeta's government.

Those were hard times. But I loved the cooperative, and I was constantly trying to think of a way to keep it going. Two friends and I decided to mortgage our homes and to ask the bank for 70,000 pesos. They didn't accept my house as collateral because it wasn't officially registered in the proper books. The lawyer who had taken care of the documentation for me when I bought it didn't enter it officially. I felt bad that we couldn't use my house as collateral, since it had been my idea, but the bank manager said he would give us 50,000 for the other two. Unfortunately, shortly thereafter came the collapse of the banks; they closed, and nobody gave us anything.

Still, I had faith in the cooperative and in Don William. I knew that somehow he would help us as he had promised in 1993. Two years later, in 1995, the bank gave us our first loan. Don William put up the guarantee for that amount as *Ministro de Acción Social* [Minister of Social Action], and the bank disbursed 30,000 córdobas.

It was a lot, especially considering that we had nothing. It was Easter Monday when the bank called us to come for the funds. *La muchacha* [the bank employee] is *evangélica*, she doesn't believe in the saints, but I like her very much and we get along very well. We got there about 11:00 a.m. to see her, but she said that we would have to wait until the afternoon because the manager still had not signed the authorization. Well, I often went to visit San Benito in León on Mondays, but that day I didn't go because we had to pick up the money. So, my friend, la muchacha from the bank, and I decided to have lunch out—imagine that, with borrowed money!—and then visit San Benito church. La muchacha waited for us outside. Then we all went back to the bank where the order for the disbursal of funds was signed and ready. I exclaimed to everyone, *San Benito quería que lo visitara* [San Benito wanted me to visit him], and we all laughed.

I got home and asked everyone to come over, because they had already put in their proposals, hoping that we would receive the reales. So, one, two, three [*ra, ra, ra*], they came one after the other, and we gave out the loans, and everyone was so happy. The repayment period was one year. Each member received 1,000 or 2,000 pesos depending on their savings and the likelihood that their business enterprise would succeed. That was on April 10, 1995; on the 25th, MAS [*Ministerio de Acción Social*, Ministry of Social Action] called us and gave us 25,000 pesos more. With that additional sum we got moving. We paid off our loan at the bank on time, and we had good credit with them. The bank agreed to give us another loan, but as the guarantee was not only for us but also for other cooperatives, and they hadn't paid back their loans, the bank told us that they couldn't give us any money until the other coops had paid up. We were very disappointed, but in May they gave us 10,000 more. We are the only ones that they gave that sum to because our credit was good, and that is what we have been working with. It's for small businesses, and we are lending in bits of 500, 1,000, 2,000, 3,000 pesos. Some sell used clothing in the market, others have a milk stand, some make *cuajada* [soft cheese], another *palmea la tortilla* [pats out tortillas] to sell, another raises pigs. And now with the Proyecto Lechero [Milk Project] from the PMA [World Food Program] we will have milk for our children for a while at least. We have no agricultural production; ours are all micro businesses. A few make clay artefacts to sell, a few are seamstresses, almost all pay their monthly dues.

It has been over 25 years of struggle in the coop. When Don William was in FUNDE years ago it was better, we got a little financing even in 1982, 1983, at least we had enough to scrape by.

We also have the Cooperative of the Widows and the Retired here in Malpaisillo, which serves a very important function in our community. We united because we all share the same situation of necessity. These are the most humble people in our village; we have joined together to give each other moral support. We carry out activities, such as raffles of items like blenders, recorders, pitchers, and from the proceeds we pay a portion of cemetery maintenance, together with the mayor's office. We also pay the husbands or sons or brothers of the women members to carry out the raffle itself. The little bit that is left over helps us buy soap or coffee. We also have a small fund to help with burials, or to help out if the health center says the patient needs to go to León but they can't pay for the bus or ambulance. Right now, we have 50 pesos in that fund. In the Cooperative of the Widows and the Retired we are well organized, and when a family member dies we are able to provide 320 córdobas. We hope to raise the donation to 400 córdobas next year. Everyone pays a 10 córdoba monthly fee. I tell the women that we are not going to let anyone die for lack of a pill. The problem is that in the health center there is no medicine. Occasionally they may have medicine, but we can't pay even if the contribution is small.

We do not get discouraged because we are 15 women in that cooperative and 15 brains, and we are always thinking of ways to help each other in times of crisis. It was urgent to help the widows and retired, that is, those who have no work, I kept saying "let's put a little 'dirt' in our pockets" [*vamos a meter la tierra en la bolsita*] and that's how the coop was formed, out of common need and determination to help each other. For example, María's son was hospitalized and she doesn't work; she has four other children and a sick mother to care for and only one sister who has work. So, this fund has helped her son.

We have a member whose husband just died, and another whose daughter died, and we are assisting them a bit. It's a small amount, but enough to help with the funeral or to buy plastic flowers. All the women say that joining together makes everything less difficult, that they don't feel all alone. Together we can scrape up the money for treatment or burial, but by ourselves it's impossible. One of our members used to bake cakes, so we loaned her enough to buy flour and other ingredients, and now she is making a little money that she is putting into our fund. A number of women, like myself, are members of both cooperatives, San Francisco and the Cooperative of Widows and the Retired. The thing is that most women are both mother and father, and some of the daughters, although they may be very young, act as a parent too. Many times the men abandon the women [*los hombres lo dejan a uno sola*], and the women have to organize themselves to provide for their children.

As for the San Francisco cooperative, I have always kept alive the hope that it would move forward. I have a very deep love for it after all these years. I have dedicated myself to it with all my heart and energy. My husband, who passed away several years ago will forgive me, but sometimes husbands get jealous because you have to leave your home and go out working for the cooperative, and you don't earn anything by doing that, but I kept on anyway. You have to love others as well as yourself, because the cooperative does not serve me but all of us.

I am Catholic and the other leader of the coop is *Testigo de Jeová* [Jehovah's Witness], but we both serve our neighbor and receive them with love. Within San Francisco there are evangelicals and Catholics, perhaps more Catholics. I really don't get into religion in the cooperative, because what if I were to say, "Today is San Francisco Day, let's celebrate it with a mass?" Many members would not come. If we sit down to talk, the other doesn't talk to me about her religion and I don't talk about mine because each of us would tell the other only the most positive things. We both have our faith, that is what is important, and what we have had is respect. We have no pastor or priest as our advisor. That would cause a problem because if a *pastor evangélico* comes, well, I'm not evangélica, and I will not attend. If a priest comes, someone else will stay home for the same reason. But we know that each member has her political and religious views, and we are respectful of them.

The presidency is for three years, renewable. I'm tired of the responsibility and am ready to pass it on. I didn't want to leave the cooperative as I had found it, bankrupt [*en quiebra*], but now we know that we can walk, and I feel that things will continue if I step down.

Soon we will have our twenty-fifth anniversary party. The mayor of Malpaisillo will be part of the celebration. That's the same mayor who was treasurer before I was elected president and who turned over to me a dead cooperative, without funds. He just abandoned it. So, I asked him, smiling, to please tell the history of the cooperative to the assembled public for the dedication of the land for our office. We will have our own property for our office, but we are still waiting for the title. I remember when he was treasurer of the cooperative, I was selling bread in the street and thinking about dropping out because I couldn't afford to pay my monthly sum, but he begged me to stay in because if I left they would have even less capital. So I stayed and stuck with it, and poured love into the cooperative. Now, when someone withdraws, I ask them the reason. We turn in a monthly report to the *Ministerio del Financiamiento* [Ministry of Finance]. We say this member left and why. The main reason is that they are moving, sometimes they make up a reason because they can't pay.

The savings coops are the ones that continued functioning during the government of Alemán; to my knowledge they are all neutral politically. We have the whole spectrum of political beliefs in our cooperative. There's no tension because we don't talk about politics. If it looks like there will be problems, we avoid the topic. We have more a neutral than a *sandinista* or *arnoldista* tendency. Mostly our topics are our problems, how we are going to put shoes on our children's bare feet [*figúrate que a mi niño lo tengo descalzo*].

La capacitación [training] is a requirement for the coop but we have not been able to sponsor any because we have to pay for them and, as we are so poor, it is impossible. We are very interested in cooperativism and in learning more about it, many of us do not know what cooperativism is really. What I know is that we have to love the cooperative, to be united, to struggle together if we want to survive. You know before, during *Somicismo* [the Somoza dictatorship], if you had, you had, and if you didn't, you didn't [*si vos tenés, tenés, si yo no tengo, no tengo*]. But with sandinismo we learned to be united, to work together. We don't say that only one person is going to go forward, but rather all of us, and the cooperative is based on that spirit.

Plus, it just makes sense to work cooperatively. Before, one had to go to a bank, face those who wear ties [*los de corbata*] asking you, "What have you got?" Then you had to go to a lawyer, pay the lawyer, and at the end you were left with nothing. The best bet is to maintain the cooperative.

That's what I tell members who are having difficulties. I talk to those who are behind in their payments. Sometimes they are evasive [*hurañas*] because they feel bad that they haven't paid, and they say they want to drop out. But I ask them please to stay in, that the cooperative will go forward for all of us, not just for one or two.

I understand how they feel because I went through the same thing recently when we couldn't pay FUNDE because of Cerro Negro [site of mountain slide from Hurricane Mitch in 1998], and I told Don Bayardo that all our mini businesses had collapsed, every one of them. We barely had enough to eat, and people couldn't make their payments. I couldn't either, there's no better lesson than the one you live yourself [*no hay mejor lección que lo que uno vive en carne propia*].

The thing I keep telling the members over and over is, "You have to put love into the cooperative" [*Hay que ponerle amor a la cooperativa*]. You can't just say,

"Oh, I can't go because I have to be at home." No, the coop has to be your priority. You know, we have had educated people in the past as officers, but I don't know why they haven't done a good job. I guess education doesn't guarantee that you will love the cooperative.

I learned how to love when I was a young child. It has been the most valuable lesson of all. My father died when I was three years old and my mother sent me to live with my grandparents and an aunt. Then my mother took off, she was young and wanted to start over I guess. I was eight before I knew who my mother was. My grandparents couldn't give me an education, but they gave me lots of love. That's why I was able to love my husband so much, until God separated us, and why I love my 11 children. My husband has been dead for three years. but we always walked united as a family. It was my grandparents who taught me to love, and it is that quality that I have poured into the cooperative.

The problem is that most people look out only for their own interest, but we struggle for others. If we don't live that way, then the coop has no future. Those who are looking only for individual gain don't last very long.

We have 80 members now. We are doing a little better than the last time you visited us [two years earlier], but not much. What pains me is that the majority of those who founded it [the coop] didn't give it love or constant tending. Where there is no vigilance, there is no hope [donde no hay que velar no hay que esperar], and we have had to be vigilant all the time. First there was the mortgaging of the houses in 1990 or 1991, and the situation remained terrible through 1993. Then came the banking crisis, and the banks closed, and with inflation our money was worth nothing. All the cooperatives failed at that time, we didn't have anything except our account books. That's when Don William promised the cooperatives that he would help us, in 1993, but it wasn't until 1995 that we got our first loan, which he secured for us through the Banco Popular. That's when we got the 30,000 pesos on San Benito Day, which we paid off in the one year allotted. When we got the next 10,000 we bought a typewriter, calculator, telephone, and a fan. With the 35,000 plus the aportaciones [contributions] of the members we were managing, now we have 40,000 pesos.

Here in our village there is no source of work. One has to leave to find a job. It used to be agriculture; this was a major cotton producing area with large farms. Now that is all gone, it has disappeared, and Malpaisillo lives very poorly. There is no agriculture. People figure that the only way to survive is by raising cattle and tending their small plots. In 1998, [Hurricane] Mitch dealt us a serious blow because we lost all our corn and we donated most of the used clothing to those who had lost everything. We continue to hold raffles to keep going and to keep our spirits up. And we try never, ever to lose hope. That's why we have that sign over there above the door with our motto: "Hope doesn't satisfy, but it sustains" [La esperanza no llena, pero mantiene].

Malpaisillo, 4 November 1997; 4 August 1999

Olfania Medina

*This dynamic, enterprising young woman from Masaya cre-
ated the Multiple Services savings and credit cooperative
out of frustration and necessity: frustration with the unre-
sponsiveness of the Union of Farmers and Ranchers
[UNAG] to women's concerns, and the necessity brought
about by the daily struggle of Olfania Medina and women
like herself to feed their families. Olfania Medina, the
president of Multiple Services, describes the varied, creative
projects supported by the cooperative as well as the difficulties it faces as economic hardship forces members to emigrate
and/or sell their property. She discusses the psychological stress the campesino feels because
of the ongoing property disputes and the negative local effects of machismo and partisan politics, which she feels characterize the national UNAG leadership. Olfania Medina describes
for us with precision and clarity how the cooperative came into being, its accomplishments
and challenges, the burden of increasing government restrictions and paperwork, and the
continuing awakening of a feminist consciousness among the cooperative's members. Along
the way, she makes insightful observations on the role of NGOs, the consequences of neoliberalism in Nicaragua, the need for cooperatives to become self-sustaining, and the urgency
of creating new economic alternatives to offset the anticipated negative impact of the Free
Trade Agreement of the Americas [FTAA].*

We officially constituted ourselves as the Multiple Services Cooperative
(*Cooperativa de Servicios Múltiples*) in May, 1995. The two main obstacles to our
survival have been the machismo and partisan politics of the national leadership
of our unions, and the land title issue, which has intensified the campesinos' economic hardships. Supposedly, rural women's interests were represented by the agricultural union UNAG [*Unión Nacional de Agricultores y Ganaderos*, National Union
of Farmers and Ranchers] established in 1990, but the leadership was never
interested in women's advancement. During the 1980s we had begun to desire to
have our own cooperatives and structures. We were furthered in our desire to
develop rural women by our contacts with NORAD, a Norwegian funding agency
that encouraged us to set up a women's savings and credit cooperative, which finally
became a reality in 1995.

The principal objective of the Multiple Services cooperative is to try to solve
our problems together, collectively; that's why we're a cooperative. The problem
of one is the problem of all; by the same token, one tree with another gives more
shade. We began with 250 members in 1997, but we are now down to 150. Some
women raise sheep, others have the mill project or chicken, pigs, cattle, or dairy
projects. Masaya is a feminine city, known for its lovely crafts—embroidery,
flowers, little cornhusk dolls; we also support these arts, because not everyone wants
to raise pigs. We solicited all the hopes and ideas from the women about what

projects they wanted, and then asked the credit committee to see which ones were viable. All our credits are revolving funds, so we have to make sure that a project is likely to make a go of it. That was difficult because we come from a decade, during the revolution, when we were accustomed to everything being given or donated. It was really hard to get the women to understand that those days are over, that external help too will not last forever. We have to keep on surviving, so we have to learn what a loan means, and that it has to be paid back.

They say that every cloud has a silver lining [*no hay mal que por bien no venga*], and in one way the change from Sandinismo to a neoliberal government has been good for us. When the banks began saying that the campesinos are not good subjects for credit, especially the women, we began to study how we would use credit if we ever got any. That's how we came up with the poll of our women and the decision to finance small and medium agricultural production. This means producing basic grains, beans, and corn, and diversifying the rest of the parcel for marketing. The problem is that the economic situation and the threat of losing their lands because of the cloud over their titles has forced many campesinos to sell. We tell everyone, "If you sell that land, you are like a naked person, you have nothing. The land is the source of your life and you have to fight for it." They recognize that they depend on the land, but their immediate needs are great.

When people began selling off their land, many groups came, like the Jesuits from NITLAPAN [an organization promoting land reform], a project funded by the padres from the *Universidad Centroamericana* (UCA), telling people not to sell. What happened with the majority of campesinos who have unclear titles is that they have sold quite a bit among themselves. We have been telling the women to hold on and giving them technical workshops. It became clear right away that we also needed leadership training for our women and workshops on self-esteem. We had attended seminars on how to diversify, choose seeds, apply natural insecticides, but we hadn't taken up the delicate topic of each woman's valuing herself and believing that she is capable. We saw that we had to provide that in order to have integral training [*capacitación integral*].

We began to see that our labor is important when we worked with FIDEG [*Fundación Internacional para el Desafío Económico Global*, International Foundation for the Global Economic Challenge] on a study they conducted on the contribution of rural women to the gross domestic product [*producto interno bruto*]. We wanted women's domestic work and labor in the fields to be measured so people could see their importance nationally. Almost nothing had been written with regard to country women's economic contribution, even during Sandinismo. We helped FIDEG carry out the surveys, both of women who are organized and those who are not; organized women are a tiny minority. We were open-mouthed at the results of the study because the economic contribution of rural women is so significant. We have been reflecting on this national report, which details each department. It has figures like the income from the domestic work of women, the working hours, the day's work that they do in the home and in the field. We want to circulate this among the women so they will realize the importance of their contribution.

Some men are just never going to be in agreement with women leaving their hidden world [*mundo oculto*], going into the public world, and organizing their own cooperatives. They say that they want the women to succeed, but when they see that their wives begin to dream, to have new aspirations, it bothers them.

It was very difficult for the women to opt to form the cooperative because it's a declaration of independence, and they have told us of their husbands complaining, "You have abandoned the children because you're gone for two days to *capacitación* [workshops]." So we started inviting the husbands to the meetings and we told them that responsibility is shared, that the children belong to both of us. We have moved forward in this way. Before, where the women were so very quiet [*tan calladita*s], they are now talking about their rights, and they are talking about this with their husbands. Things are changing, and the husbands are becoming more supportive.

The biggest clashes are not with husbands, not at the family or community levels, but with the departmental municipal leaders. Such officials, who should have a clearer vision of the work of the women, sometimes put stumbling blocks in our path so that we fall. For example, women at the municipal level are often subject to the will of a particular leader who simply forbids them from carrying out their work. Now, however, we are learning to point to the guidelines and strategies of our organization, and say we don't have to obey his arbitrary will. Some men see us as a threat to their leadership positions. These are the same people who worked against us at the UNAG Congress in 1995 when they spoke fearfully about how large the women's sector had grown.

The heart of the matter is that many UNAG leaders don't accept that the women have their own structure, which they can manage by themselves according to their own judgment without the men instructing them. What we have tried to achieve in the Multiple Services cooperative is to comply with the strategy and philosophy that emanates from UNAG and adapt it to our conditions, but by no means abandon the space that we have conquered as women. We tell the young women that we have earned this space and we can't permit UNAG to put it aside.

When we were still a women's section within UNAG, we had a little corner in UNAG's offices. Soon we decided we needed a space of our own. We took out a loan and got a place of our own; we have paid back the loan, and this room here is all ours. We are currently sponsoring a series of activities in order to fix it up so that we can give better attention to the members of our cooperative. Here we feel confident and secure, but that still bothers many of the UNAG men. We are now completely independent of UNAG, but before we came to that point, we were under such stress with the UNAG leadership that at national meetings we would become depressed and cry.

The fundamental element in the awakening of women has been the revolution—above all, the right to organize, to mobilize, to defend our gains that we otherwise would've lost. Of course, it came with problems, machismo, the war, but we knew that the revolution was made for men and women and that women had played an important role in the triumph. The revolution brought women out of traditional roles; many went to other countries where they learned a lot, others joined the socialist camp; all that strengthened us. Also many international solidarity groups came here, and that relationship allowed us to move forward in defining ourselves.

My own experience is within the party, the Sandinista Front, which sponsored me to Cuba for organizational and leadership training. There I was fortunate to meet the Brazilian educator Paulo Freire, who spoke with us a number of times and who was a great influence. Later, during the Alemán government [1996-2002], I had the opportunity to go to Norway and more recently to Guatemala on a cooperative exchange. Both in Cuba and Norway the women were impressed that we had a separate cooperative for rural women.

I am now president of the Multiple Services savings and credit cooperative [*Cooperativa de Servicios Múltiples*] and also a member of the Women Producers of Guanacastillo agricultural cooperative [*Cooperativa de Productoras de Guanacastillo*]. I think it has helped that I studied sociology for two years. I couldn't continue because of financial problems, but it has helped me understand the situation of country women. My dream is to create a national network of women's cooperatives, one that would be democratic and representative and not torn by partisan politics.

For a while the Sandinistas had a very feminist line; after AMNLAE [*Asociación de Mujeres Nicaragüenses Luisa Amanda Espinosa*, Luisa Amanda Espinosa Nicaraguan Women's Association] there were created *Sí Mujer* [Yes, Woman] and the *Centro de la Mujer* [Women's Center], which have radical positions. They say that men can't come to the training workshops, and then clashes occur. I think that's wrong; we have to include both genders in our work. In our Multiple Services cooperative we are very careful to project a positive image of the woman leader: she shouldn't go to a meeting smelling of alcohol. That was a mistake of the revolution, such that with AMNLAE we always equated the term liberation with libertinism. We have to try to erase that image, above all in the countryside. Little by little the men are coming too, participating, giving their support.

In our Multiple Services cooperative we have women who are from the Liberal, Sandinista, Conservative, or no party. Also Catholics, Evangelicals, everything. They get along well. It helps to have the different religions; sometimes when we have an organizational problem, for example, we say, "Let's see what the Bible says." A big lesson that the revolution left us is that you have to share with everyone. That includes sharing power. Even in the National Assembly for example, the Evangelicals are represented by CEPAD [*Comité Evangélico por Ayuda al Desarrollo*, Evangelical Committee for Development Assistance]. There are more divisions in the Catholic church than among the Evangelicals. CEPAD has helped us considerably in the district with children's feeding centers and clothing for children. We are also working with Catholic organizations. For example, some campesinos from France recently came to visit us in solidarity; their group is called *Pan contra el Hambre* [Bread against Hunger]. We have also worked with a national organization called CESADE which is secular, and more recently, we have aid from Luxemburg.

CESADE gave us the assistance to form a small theater group. The women adapt their scripts to the reality they live in their cooperative or in their village. They play roles, such as in the home, which carry a moral or social message. Some compañeras have developed painting, others embroider, some make cornhusk flowers, still others work in porcelain, and others create sweets in the shape of little animals. We are doing what we can to get by.

The women of the cooperative have an ecological awareness; they know that they have to take care of the land. Many no longer use chemical fertilizers [*abonos*], just organic ones. One of our cooperativists have done a beautiful job with organic fertilizer. She uses weeds [*maleza*], turkey buzzard droppings [*gallinaza*], and she fumigates her crops with natural insecticides. She also reforests her parcel. She is out there from 4:00 to 11:00 a.m. every day, and she has so far defended her land from very powerful men, including former government officials, who want to take away her title, claiming that the land is theirs.

We work with UNAG on ecological matters and also with *Campesino a Campesino* [Country person to Country person], whose programs we participate in regularly. As a result, we have contributed to reforestation by planting windbreaks [*cortinas rompevientos*], putting up living barriers that maintain moisture. We have made retaining barriers [*cercas vivas*] to keep the earth from eroding, and we also use organic insecticide and organic beans such as *el mungo*. We work with nurseries of fruit trees, anything that might help us. Currently we are working with medicinal plants, *ruda*, cilantro, *hierbabuena* [mint] and with fruit trees, such as *granadilla* [passion flower] and orange. We have found a good market locally for *culantro* [coriander], *ruda*, *albahaca* [sweet basil]; there's a good demand. We also cultivate flowers to market.

The environmental challenge is a tremendous one. There is so much use of chemicals, especially in the region of León where they grow cotton. We are now receiving information from the *Centro de Salud* [Health Center] about people who all their lives have worked with agrochemicals. It is shocking to see the consequences; there is much cancer in the rural zone, especially among women, because of the use of insecticides. We are trying now to promote the use of silos for storing produce, because previously, so that it would not get moth-eaten, they would always use insecticides on their own corn. It's much better now with the new training.

With regard to the health of women and families, Multiple Services is working with two NGOs, Profamilia and Ixchen. Above all, we are interested in the pap test because of the incidence of uterine cancer. Family planning, including the proper use of contraceptives [*anticonceptivos*] is also very important. The idea of family planning has become very accepted in the countryside, and many women have had the operation [tubal ligation]. The husband or compañero accepts it because he has no job, no credit, and he cannot support a large family. With so much unemployment and so many men who have left for Costa Rica, who is left is the woman with a house full of kids. The men may or may not return, and many of them find new compañeras. It is strange, but the Catholic church allows Profamilia to operate. Profamilia gives talks [charlas] with the men and with the women. Sometimes it's difficult to approach the topic because there is timidity and because there are heart-rending testimonies of women who have been sexually abused.

Some men do not want their women to be checked. I asked Profamilia please to include a woman on their team, because there is this taboo that says that a woman can't be seen naked by another man. Along with the male doctor, the NGOs now send a woman gynecologist and a psychologist to attend the emotional problems of the women. The point is for women to begin to see that their health is important, that they must take care of their bodies.

Contraceptives, such as condoms and the pill, are given free, as are the charlas. What costs is the pap test; we have to pay 25 pesos, which is difficult for our members. If they don't have the money, we lend it through the cooperative and ask them to repay 10 pesos, regarding the other 15 as a service the cooperative provides. The problem is when the women have infections, then the medication is expensive. We need a pharmacy for members, that's something we'd like to establish in the future.

I am the recording secretary of the *Federación* [National Federation of Cooperatives], and I have also been representing the area of gender. Lately, I have been so involved in gender issues at the national federation level that my compañeras Juana and Gloria have done practically all the work here at the local level for both the Multiple Services and the Women Producers of Guanacastillo cooperatives. I am so glad that they have had such good workshops and training, because these have enabled them to assume leadership responsibilities.

I'm working with a compañero now on how to come up with a strategy for having men's and women's cooperatives collaborate at the business and marketing level, because the sad fact is that, with neoliberal politics, the cooperatives have been screwed [fregadas]. A great many in the department of Masaya alone have folded because the campesinos have sold their land. You see them now in the streets, some work collecting garbage, carrying baskets in the market, perhaps selling a little fruit.

There used to be 35 cooperatives within the Federación, now there are 25, and of these we are trying at the departmental level to help at least 11 to join together with others, because there are just one or two compañeros left in each of these cooperatives. So we are trying to consolidate them, take care of the base, organize from the perspective of the individual producer. We would like to organize them in a broader municipal structure in an effort to have civil society reach them all. There are some poor people who can get by [quien medio puede], but there are others who are being crucified, and we are trying to reach them. They've sold the most land in Region IV: Masaya, Carazo, Rivas and Granada. Most has been in Rivas, where Dr. Alemán has bought the zone for tourist development, especially along the water. Many sold because of their immediate financial needs, others because of the title question and the fear of losing their land.

In addition to the ownership problem, cooperatives also have to comply with the increasing paperwork required by the Ministry of Work. The requirements are very strict and they are expensive. You go to the Ministry of Work and they tell you this is going to cost you $3,000 dólares per cooperative. We have a lawyer in Matagalpa who advises the cooperative, and we took care of all the requirements that the Ministry of Work asked in order to legalize the property; we went through all the bureaucratic procedures [*trámites*]. But Dr. Alemán's government says they have not one single document as record of our having complied. It's a terrible lack of responsibility on the part of the government. But it's that sort of thing that convinces you to sell your land. So the campesino to whom they say they no longer have any record of his title, he says, "I better sell my land before I'm left with nothing."

Many of the lands that are being sold are in agrarian conflict, that is, the titles are being contested. The land is in conflict as long as the campesino has not given in, but as soon as he does, no more conflict. This has us very worried, we have lost a large part of the base of cooperativism that way. Some hang on because they know clearly that without land, they are naked, they have nothing. They hold on, but their resources are running out, and they can't get financing. Those who do have legal papers have no access to financing now that the state bank has disappeared completely and everything is private. They are being squeezed. We know there will not be another agrarian reform, there will be no more lands delivered, so we must cling to what we have. Not just here, this is going on nationally.

The Federation of Cooperatives has carried out a study to see just how many cooperatives remain. When we began the Federation, we had 950 associated cooperatives, but now there are perhaps 300 total. From 1990 to 1999 we lost about 40 per cent of the agricultural cooperatives. New cooperatives have sprung up, but they are of savings and credit.

We're trying to take some positive lessons from these experiences for the future of agricultural cooperatives. For one thing, we need to join together those two or three left in each cooperative and create a municipal cooperative that would have, say, 20-30 members. Where there are no political problems, they can work with the mayor's office. For example, in León the mayor is a clear-headed woman, and she supports the idea of linkages. Where the mayoralties belong to the Liberal party, there will be contradictions because we are not compatible with the model they wish to develop. But there are places where we can become stronger. So, now, let's gather together the few who remain and form a new structure and obtain credit in order to continue producing and see how we can enter into other programs. An organization from Denmark is helping us with the linkage modality and also with agricultural diversification. We need everything.

We also need to help the tiny cooperatives keep track of their records. Sometimes the *Libros de Actas* [official, government-approved record books] don't arrive. Or, the book is there, but they don't inscribe it properly. Some cooperatives don't have assemblies every year; some don't send a copy in to the government; some don't report if 20 members left and why. There's a law that says you have to report a change in membership numbers. So, there are all these requirements that we have to take care of, and you can see that we are just about disappearing. But the cooperatives have to keep their books in order, even if they are demoralized and just a few people are trying to do all the work. The financing organizations also want to see our books, our balances. We can't just say in our minutes "we talked about such and such a topic," you have to have the discussion and the agreements written down. The Assembly proceedings [*Memoria de la Asamblea*] have to be in writing. The agricultural cooperatives are the weakest in compliance. The linked ones are bigger and can contract a lawyer to go over things for them. The very small cooperatives are left to fend for themselves. The Federation is helping them update their documents.

Another initiative we are looking at to help agricultural cooperatives survive is direct marketing. The cooperatives of Matagalpa and Boaco are talking about selling their coffee directly to Italy and France. We have been discussing with various organizations how to sell our produce directly. In France and Italy there are groups that promote produce from cooperatives in Nicaragua, and we are pursuing possibilities with them. In Matagalpa they produce enough for agroexport; in the zone of Boaco we have been working on the milk cooperative with direct export in mind, such as an alternative Central American market. But we need to learn how to sell, how to market. The idea is to look for alternatives and suggest them to the campesinos. The problem with basic grain production is that it is subject to too much rain, or not enough rain, and this is terrible for the campesino without credit, without anything. So we are studying other solutions. For example, UESA, an agency of the European Union, has funds for storing production until market conditions are optimal for selling. We are asking them for assistance.

Another thing we are doing is that now we have a pre-membership status of about 50 people in our Multiple Services Cooperative. We say "pre" because they have not been accepted yet in the assembly but are in process. As you know, our membership in the women's cooperative has gone way down. Many of the women have gone to Costa Rica to work as domestic servants in order to survive. They leave their families here, sometimes with a grandmother, but other times they are left abandoned and helpless. So what happens? We have desperate women who want to join the cooperative. They know nothing about cooperativism, they only want help. Many think that a cooperative exists to give them something [*para que me dé*], but the cooperative must receive from them as well or else that's the end for all of us. There are duties and privileges, not just privileges.

Everyone wants someone to give them something, but that's not the way it works. That's a culture that developed during the revolution when we had a government that facilitated many things for us. If the revolution gave us the clarity and perspective to organize ourselves, it also gave us the idea that you can get things without much effort, no? We've been trying to change the conduct that results from that philosophy because subsequent governments have not at all favored cooperatives, nor do they pardon debts. Further, the whole world is in need, and we are no longer the center of attention: there are other places, other problems. We have to maintain our own household, our own cooperative.

To that end, we have been developing the habit of saving, a habit we've never had before. We always had the attitude of: we'll ask for help today, and who knows about tomorrow [*hoy lo pedimos y mañana no sabemos*]. So we have had to begin from zero to get people to accept the idea. Now we ask them for 2 per cent of each loan to be put into savings, and they're doing it. It's a very positive experience, but it requires constant follow-up and encouragement. It is very difficult to save, because it is a daily struggle to bring bread home to our children. My objective as a cooperative member is not to have to worry each day about putting food on the table.

We are in the process of affiliating with the Caja Rural in Managua. Caja Rural [CARUNA] is a Nicaraguan organization with funds from NORAD, Germany, OXFAM, and others, all organizations with a gender focus. They are offering credit, savings, capacitación [training], technical assistance, and legal advice, all of which we desperately need. The membership fee is $1,000, but we can pay in instalments. NORAD will help us with a computer and programs for accounting. Here at our Servicios Múltiples office, we just have three people—Gloria, Juana, and myself—where before we were 10, but so many members have left for Costa Rica or Managua. We can't remain on our own and survive. If we don't affiliate, we are dead. Caja Rural offers a good alternative to UNAG, because it allows us to retain our identity. I have faith that we will survive, because I believe that Christ has shown us the path in the past and is present with us today. He is the one who gave us the courage to chart our course independently of UNAG, and he gives us the strength to continue now. Yes, our women's cooperative is struggling, but we are still here.

UNAG is a trade organization, and as such it has political interests, but they need to talk more about what UNAG 's mission is as a labor organization. UNAG members contribute considerably to the gross domestic product [PIB, *producto interno bruto*] and they need to use that economic capacity as a political tool in order to obtain benefits for members. But UNAG isn't doing that, nor are they opening up to broader participation by women. They're all talk. We don't want speeches, we want deeds, we want to see more women on the board of UNAG. But they claim that it's not prudent yet. Gender equity? That's not gender equity.

One male compañero at the Federation told me that gender work is just another burden for the Federation. I say no, it means including women in each training program, not just men. We have to institutionalize gender policies and not fight over whether "María" is going to become more important than the man. That's the conflict: "María's not going to boss me around!" In such a situation, men look at women as enemies, not as allies. If a woman develops herself, she is an enemy. It's an issue they just can't stomach [*Es una cuestión que no la logran digerir*].

The base, that is the local communities, are the ones who suffer. The national leadership makes promises, but they have no economic project, no plan other than their own self-interest, they are opposed to gender equity, they don't listen to the people, and, deep down, the leaders don't even like the campesinos [*no quieren a estas personas*]. They just continue to name leaders from within their same small circle.

The future of national cooperative associations has to come from the local communities. In order to keep communication flowing between the communities and the regional or national leaders, local representatives have to be given funds for transportation so they can attend meetings. We also need to professionalize the leadership, because as it stands now, whether they do their job or not, they still collect their salary. The other thing is that you're always going to meetings, it takes you away from the community and it's tiring. Often, the purpose of the meeting is never made clear, and you can go to all the meetings in the world, but if you have no objective and no conclusions, you have nothing to bring back home to the base.

Another thing is that the leadership needs to realize that the Sandinista party and the cooperative are not the same thing; far from it. They can no longer go around asking people if they are Sandinistas or not, that is the least important thing [*estar diciendo en que si tú eres sandinista, eso es lo de menos*]. People can go to their political sessions, but please don't bring their party lines here. Here we respect only this hat, the cooperative; outside, you can wear any hat you like. Some national leaders accept that, others resist it. Sometimes I feel like we have to keep on trying to drag the organization along with us so they will not lose their vision. At other times, I think they have already lost it, and that we women were for too long the dupes [*tontos útiles*] of the leadership, allowing them to do as they wish.

If cooperativists are not united at the local level, either our own national UNAG leaders or the government will kill us. Unity and challenge: we hope that these will inject strength in order to help us parry all the assaults that are yet to come. Those who have dropped out, left the country, when they return they will see that we are organized, they will be impressed; some are returning already.

I mentioned earlier that our membership in Multiple Services dropped from 250 to 150 over a period of several years. Though these are the casualties of neoliberalism, that system is not altogether negative. Sometimes I would dream that, if Sandinismo had continued to triumph, we would all be comfortable and everything would be given to us. But Nicaragua has changed, and the world has changed. The Berlin wall fell. The two Germanies unified, who would've believed it? If all these things had occurred during the Sandinistas' reign, what would we have done? Foreign attention and assistance wouldn't have been focused on us.

I think that if Sandinismo ever returns, it will be different from before, because that particular moment was unique. If they gain power again, they would have to deal with the free trade war, it's another type of war. How do the little ones survive when the great powers are absorbing them? The large powers have defined what they want, and they don't consult the small. We have to learn how to fight this other war and survive. Whatever government is in power has to face that reality.

I don't think that the Frente [Sandinista Front] has evolved very much, nor do I believe that they would be able to handle this new global situation. They couldn't afford to commit the same errors as when they were in power. And they would never have the tremendous base of popular support that they had in those great moments such as the national literacy campaign or the giving of land to the poor. That was a one-time occurrence.

Beyond that, what we need to do is to open the eyes of the campesino, telling them to work hard and not sell out. I must emphasize, however, how hard it is to do that when you see children suffering and babies dying from malnutrition. But we can't all go to the US or Costa Rica; they are having their problems too. The campesinos have to understand that the only way out is to stay here and make their piece of land generate their own food.

How to get them to do it? I think it is a process of changing one's mentality. Skill-building and workshops help a great deal, but they aren't everything. Testimonies of personal experience help too. Some who have returned from Costa Rica, for example, converse with the campesinos who then learn that in Costa Rica the patrón treated them badly, or that they ate once a day because they had to work so hard to send money home. There are rich experiences at the grassroots level, we need to learn how to make them more widely known. One compañero in a cooperative meeting told us, "Brothers and sisters, don't sell your land; sell your little pig or chicken, but not your land." If a leader says these things, the people can say, "Sure, he has a salary." But if it comes from the mouth of the campesino, it is effective.

Things are very bad in Nicaragua, but that's also true for all of Central America. Even Costa Rica, because this invasion of nicas is hurting them, and the *ticos* [Costa Ricans] are jealous because the wage scale has been reduced by nicas who work for almost nothing because they are illegal. They have developed savings and credit cooperatives in Costa Rica, but very few agricultural cooperatives because they have almost all private production. Guatemala is the same, but the indigenous have some cooperatives; however, the government is hostile to them. Almost all the cooperatives in Guatemala are indigenous. The problems of Honduras and Nicaragua were made much worse by [Hurricane] Mitch in October 1998 because the infrastructure was destroyed, leaving many families with nothing and forcing them to move.

As a region, the Central American countries have much in common. For example, we are all very preoccupied about the agreement that will soon open all the ports to free trade [FTAA]. We are trying to develop a strategy for keeping our small production from disappearing with the impending invasion of commerce. We are looking hard for a way to market our production directly, as I mentioned before. We are not yet clear about what that free market will mean in practice.

I was in Canada in August of 1999 at a conference on free trade sponsored by a group called *Horizontes* [Horizons of Friendship]. I told them that Central Americans feel a growing anxiety that we will be flattened by the powerful countries. I feel great anguish because the Nicaraguan campesino is not prepared to deal with these big economies. Look at the example of Mexico, which has been absorbed by the US. What will happen to Nicaragua, which is so much smaller? How will our vulnerable Central American economies fare, say, if it rains too much, especially now that neoliberalism has done away with all that we had before in terms of a safety net and access to credit. So I asked them in Canada to please show me what were the benefits of the existing *Tratado de Libre Comercio* [Free Trade Agreement] and the projected Free Trade Agreement of the Americas [FTAA]. They couldn't come up with a single one. In the meantime, we can't just sit here and do nothing and hope that someone will give us the panacea that will solve the problem of the poor.

For us, neoliberalism has its positive and negative aspects. Life is constant movement and change, and neoliberalism makes us develop our abilities more. It forces us to be highly productive in terms of thought and work and not wait passively until someone gives us something. Now, there are many things about neoliberalism that affect us negatively. The economic and political policies continue to be extremely painful for us; they wear us down. At the same time, however, they make us more productive as human beings. There are times in peoples' lives when they are asleep and times when they are awake. Before, we were asleep, but now neoliberal policies have waked up the part that was asleep and pushed us to our outer limits. That elevates one's capacity for thought and personal development, but it does not equalize [*no iguala*]. The neoliberal and the Sandinista worlds are two different things. The very neoliberal policies that are stressing me so, giving me tension headaches and insomnia, are also pushing me to say, "I can do it, I want to do it, I am capable of doing it."

Masaya, 29 October 1997; 13 August 1999

Juanita Solórzano Gaitán, Bertha Rosa Rojas, Lorena Solórzano, Zoila María Rojas Calero, and William Vivas Soto

Juanita, the president of the cooperative, The Women Producers of Guanacastillo [Las Productoras de Guanacastillo], is a hearty, upbeat woman. She works nearly all the time, caring for her crops and animals at the farm, poring over forms and reports that she must file on behalf of the Women Producers, and helping out at the office of the other cooperative to which she belongs, Multiple Services, in nearby Masaya.

For Zoila, the oldest member of the five-woman agricultural cooperative, work in the fields is therapeutic, a way to escape the sorrow that pursues her as a result of the contra war's continuing corrosive effects on her family. Bertha and Lorena find that cooperative member-ship has taught them how to discuss personal disagreements openly, a lesson that has come hard for all the Women Producers.

The women, Catholic and evangelical alike, express their deep religious faith, their belief that Christ is present in their daily lives, and their conviction that only the grace of God enabled them to resurrect the cooperative. The group discusses what the cooperative means to them, and why, despite their tiny number, they are not eager to recruit new members at this time. As the con-versation begins, William, Bertha's husband and Zoila's son-in-law, stops by briefly to express his admiration for the hard work and determination the women have demonstrated.

JUANITA SOLÓRZANO GAITÁN

JUANITA: We organized this cooperative, the Women Producers of Guanacastillo [*Las Productoras de Guanacastillo*] out of necessity. Our experience has been one of constant effort, push-ing ourselves to continue and not give up. They say that one arrives at Christ through necessity, when you need to feel his presence with you. That's the kind of need we felt to form the cooperative and to ask God to be present, to find something here that was worth continuing. It was a risk, but from the beginning we trusted that Christ would accom-pany us. In these recent years of drought and more drought, we were in great need, we often went hungry, and we had no economic possibilities. It appeared that we had nowhere to turn. Then we heard about the *Cooperativa de Servicios Múltiples* in Masaya, and I went there with a small group of women to ask for help.

WILLIAM: We have to give the women credit for persisting in difficult times. My wife Bertha has never given up. They just needed a little help, like the Servicios Múltiples provided. The idiosyncracy of the Nicaraguan people is that we are always grateful. We have been through so much—a war that no one wanted, earthquakes, floods, droughts, hunger; we have experienced all these personally, in our own

WILLIAM VIVAS SOTO AND
BERTHA ROSA ROJAS

flesh. That's why we are so grateful when someone extends their hand to us. We are happy to work, not to be given things. It's very bad simply to receive and not work. These women work all the time for their cooperative [Women Producers of Guanacastillo]; one has to admire their strength and value them for what they have accomplished.

We cannot offer you food, only a chair to sit on, but we also extend our friendship. I am a Baptist pastor, and I believe that God is always showing us his favor. We have faith that we will get ahead with help and with hard work.

We are still suffering the effects of the [contra] war; it was a time of sadness, fear, and anxiety. I remember when Zoila, my mother-in-law, delivered her son to the military service, and I remember when they brought him home dead. Those are times we do not want to see return ever.

JUANITA: Despite this history, we try not to afflict ourselves with worry. We round up our problems, put them in a bag, tie it up, and throw it in the river. Like Lorena, the first thing I do every morning is give thanks to God for a new day.

ZOILA MARÍA ROJAS CALERO

ZOILA: We have a lot of problems and we have a lot of work. But whatever job we are doing, if there is a problem, we have to discuss it. Then we see how to resolve the situation and move on. Work is like a therapy for me, I forget my problems a bit. Many compañeras say that they want to come to our cooperative to do projects with us. But we see that mostly they want to come to be "owners" and to be in charge. I am here every day working, and people ask me how come I'm not in charge then, since I'm always here. I answer that we have an elected president, Juana, and she is in charge of our little army, just like the president is in charge of vice-presidents, deputies, and so on. If the president goes out of the country, then it's the vice-president, but it is the president who is charge. That's the way it is with us. We work together so that we will succeed. But I work here so much that I am practically forgetting my own house. I no longer have young children, just my granddaughter here, her papa, my son, died, and her mother some seven months ago became a "missing person." She left me with this little creature because she was running around [andaba por la calle] saying that she was leaving for Mexico, and I don't know what all else. Soon after that, she left her daughter at my house. She returned only long enough to bring me all her documents, birth certificate, and to say that she no longer wanted her daughter, that she wanted to be free. I bring her here with me to teach her how to work. I always work, no type of work bothers me, not even under the burning sun. You just have to say, go work over there, and there I go, without a hat, without anything, in order to work. I don't feel the sun, hunger, thirst, I don't feel anything. I just work. I arrive at work happy, content. I arrive home happy, satisfied from working.

My house is big for just myself and my granddaughter. For the last four months my son has been in bed. Thanks to God that he is now better and I don't have so many problems taking care of him, preparing his meals. He is separated from his wife, she just comes Saturday or Sunday and leaves on Monday. She never spends a weekday in my house. Sunday I chastised my son because he wanted me to bring him his breakfast, but I told him that his wife was there and that she could get up and prepare it for him.

My children have caused me much suffering. I have one son who was in jail four months ago. His wife had him thrown in jail three or four times previously, and I have gotten him out. He beats his wife, that's why they put him in jail. The lawyer charges me, and the next day she's back at the police station, and they come and arrest him again. I told my son to leave, work, and don't drink. The police even came and searched my house. I am so ashamed. I haven't stolen anything, I haven't done anything except work in the fields. What shame is mine! [¡Qué vergüenza, la mía!] I can't get it out of my mind. Thanks be to God that I have my work and my friends here.

I have a little land, about one manzana, where I have my house. I also have another ten manzanas that I have not been able to sell because they've gone to ruin because my sons don't work them, they don't do anything. They were totally corrupted by the war, so much violence, it has stayed with them. One son in particular is always angry and goes around drunk. He learned karate in the war and now he threatens everyone with it; he nearly broke my friend's hand at the bus stop the other day. I feel such shame! And his wife is a gold-digger [es platera]; she will go with whoever has money.

My property [terreno] is quite a ways from here; it is mountainous and very beautiful, but now it's all covered with wild vegetation, sticks, and stubborn weeds. I go there to clear what I can, but I can't do too much by myself. If I get the corn, the pesticide, if I can pay for a machine [tractor], then they will plant the seed, but that's all. The land has to be cared for regularly, but it has been abandoned. All that has aged me.

BERTHA: I have a little piece of land that we bought out where we have a little house. Each one of us has a little house somewhere else. I live near Los Altos.

JUANITA: I have two sons; they are both grown, but they live at home with me. I thank God that they have not fallen into these vices; they don't go out drinking. My daughters too live with me; all my children are studying. A good education will help them develop themselves. We worry because of Zoila's experience.

255

It pains us what Zoila has had to endure, especially because of her son Enrique, who is very violent. He is a product of the war [*es fruto de la guerra*]; he shows what he has lived [*muestra lo que ha vivido*]. He has no respect for anyone. He's not in his five senses and is always drunk.

BERTHA: I feel good working here. I haven't worked as much as I should lately because the property is far from my home and I have to pay bus fare, but I always come when I can. Now there is more work to do, which is the fruit of our progress.

JUANITA: I was recommending to Bertha a while back that she send my daughter Margarita to help her work, because when I can't come she comes in my place. She also brings me milk and guards the property.

My daughter wants to get her university degree and become a technician, she goes to UNA. I asked her, "Do you know how to castrate a pig?" Of course she said no, so I told her, "I hope you learn there, because I don't want you to practice on mine!"

In our cooperative, we have gone through the worst, I hope, and now we will be able to have some good times. I am working for all five members, not just for myself. We must be organized and work together, because I do not want to run things, I don't want to be a boss.

BERTHA: Juanita has organized us well, and we support her, and we have unity now. Before, we would argue, and there were hard feelings. Now, we all participate in everything, we support each other, and we coordinate our work more.

JUANITA: Care and support, these are the two things that we have that are helping us. We have to care about each person's work, and we have to support each other in a way that we did not before. We always communicate with each other now, we work and converse.

ZOILA: The main thing is not to sit in a wheelchair like a cripple! I have to work. I can't depend on my children. Here we are still working together, five women: Juanita, Lorena, Bertha, Olfania, and myself. There's an agreement among us, and we have to remember that. It gives me pleasure to come here. I come early in the morning to clear here; I don't stay at home because there are too many problems in my house. I come here with pleasure to work peacefully. It is work that has sustained our group and that has sustained me.

LORENA SOLÓRZANO

LORENA: We have had many low points, but steps forward too. We have gone forward because there has been more unity and harmony, because before there was much discord. The harmony that we have is a blessing from God. And we are beginning to make a go of it economically. The harmony began when we finally sat down together to dialog. It produced greater understanding.

JUANITA: During our low points there were many hard feelings. For example, doña Zoila thought that I was trying to boss her around, but the problem was that we lacked coordination. There was lots of gossip [*chismes*] because of lack of communication and trust; we didn't coordinate our activities well either. What Lorena says is right. We finally faced our problems because we were in danger of collapse and not just from lack of funds. The importance of unity and of doing away with malicious gossip was finally brought home to us. It has also been very difficult to stay together when we have had, until recently, nothing to show for all our efforts.

However, it is not financial assistance that has facilitated our unity. No, no, no. What has facilitated our union is God. We have loved God and believed in him. We believe that he exists and that he is here with us, in every moment he lives here with us. This belief has pushed us to recognize and confess the bad thoughts that we have each carried inside ourselves. Our faith in God has made us value ourselves and our common project. Later came the financial assistance, which helped bring more unity because God has wanted it to be thus. Since we have thrown out the bad, God has blessed us greatly. We have swept clean our house so that we would be blessed. Unity, God has given us that, that did not come from financial assistance.

It's also important that our cooperative is not Sandinista, Arnoldista, evangélico, or católico. We put political and religious divisions in that bag of troubles that we threw in the river. When we first organized ourselves, doña Norma Cantón, who was helping us, said that she would ask a priest to come out to inaugurate the cooperative. But we had a different idea; we wanted to have an inauguration of thanksgiving before the padre came. We wanted to ask for prayers from a reverend who is not a priest. We were going to do it Tuesday before the inauguration with the priest on Wednesday. Then doña Norma came to me and said, "How about Monday for the priest?" I told her what we had planned, and she said, "Then I won't bring the padre. The padre is cancelled." We appreciated that very much and were so happy to have the ceremony with the reverend. We invoked God's blessing on our enterprise from the beginning and in the way that we felt most comfortable.

But trying to work cooperatively was a constant quarrel from the beginning. We women were at each other's throats, I couldn't control the meetings, plus they were angry with me. One would cry, another would scream; they would say very "irregular" things to each other [*se decían cosas muy irregulares*]. This went on for a long time, and it was tearing us apart. Finally, I asked God to help me because my house, my family, and the women were all out of control. We put ourselves in God's hands and began to pray together again. That's when the glory of God became manifest, and there was unity and pardon among us. That's when we began the road to recovery. We are working for the honor and glory of God because that is the only thing that has saved us.

We are planning to hold a vigil for the next several nights that we think will help us to come to know God's will for our future direction, how to proceed. We will invite a pastor from Lorena's church. She is evangelical, but neither I, nor Bertha, nor doña Zoila are evangelical; some time ago, someone even criticized doña Zoila for going to a service with Lorena if you can imagine, but those times are gone along with our bad times of division and gossip.

We all five have the document saying that we are the owners of the cooperative, the Women Producers of Guanacastillo: Zoila, Juana, Lorena, Bertha, Olfania. It's all done properly. It was on February 2, 1999, that it was arranged officially.

We owe much to the Cooperativa de Servicios Múltiples because they helped us get started. Our compañera Olfania is the president of that cooperative and also a member of ours. I, too, am now a member of both. Olfania told me her problem, which is that often she cannot be here in the fields working because of her job in Masaya as president of Multiple Services. So, I'm keeping her work up for her.

Thank heavens we made it through our crisis and it has brought us closer to God and to each other. We have put behind us rancor, whining, lies, all the disasters that we have experienced; we have learned lessons from them in order to move ahead. We had to pick ourselves up from a complete collapse. We know that our situation is still precarious and that if we are not united we will destroy ourselves; but we also know that if we are united we can overcome our problems.

We began to organize unofficially as a cooperative on May 5, 1997. Our first big project was fencing the property, which we accomplished with many cuts and bruises. It was a huge job, and we did it all by ourselves; sometimes our hands would bleed, and our backs were sore, but we dug the postholes, set the posts, strung the wire, everything. We work like men, not women. The fence we put up is a good example. I had to get someone to look after my crops and animals, then we spent a whole week working on it, but we still didn't finish. We also have work to do at home, so we had to get people to take care of our domestic responsibilities in order to complete the fence.

Our association with INTA [*Instituto Tecnológico y Agropecuario*, Technological and Agrarian Institute] has helped us because they have given us technical training and they have taught us valuable things like where to plant, where to put the troughs for the animals, how to raise chickens. We needed to learn how to do these things ourselves because we can't be paying people to come and do them for us. But we don't mind paying someone to do the heavy work; why kill myself when I can pay someone.

INTA's assistance in teaching us how to raise chickens and pigs and care for our few cows has helped us to succeed, and this, too, has helped diminish the personal problems that were dividing us. We are managing our finances carefully in hopes that in the future we won't have to take our animals out for pasture, that we will have enough for them to eat here. Before, they didn't go out because we bought food and we fed them here. But with the economy the way it is, we can't buy feed, and we certainly can't buy another cow because we have no food for them. So they have to pasture here and there. We rent land where we take them to pasture, but it's too expensive. We have started pasturing in doña Zoila's terreno but it is far. I told her that we would pay just like anyone else, but she says no since her land is not occupied. That's a big help because we're not paying anything. We have rented that field that you see over there next to ours, and we are preparing to plant it; we still have to grade it, by ox and by hand.

We've thought about whether we should have more members now, but it would not be helpful because the more people, the more disorganization you have. Fewer people, better organization. Also, there's the fact that we are the only ones who have gone through the difficult experience of sweating, scraping, cutting our hands on the wire, having empty stomachs—no one else can value what that has meant for us. No one can appreciate the sweat that has poured from us since we started. They say things like, "I can't come today because I have too much to do. I have to look after the children, the kitchen, fix my husband his dinner, iron because my husband is going out." They give all these excuses because they don't understand, nor are they willing to make the cooperative their top priority. That's why we have to give them some help with a little project, so they can learn how to do something and prove to themselves that they can do something on their own and that it is important. So what we are thinking now is that in order for our cooperative to develop pig farming, or chicken farming, we should organize small groups of women who wish to work in each of these areas, each with a little pig or cow so that they can develop themselves with livestock. I'm talking about the women of the community, so that they can learn how to care for animals responsibly, and that will help the community.

Unlike the other women in the community, we left everything behind to try to make a go of it; sometimes I didn't even know where my children were, but I was here working. I left my little girl with friends, and I don't even know if they took good care of her, but I was here working. We had to do this, and we had to believe in what we were doing even though people criticized us. We know that who will ultimately benefit are our children, for which I am thankful because they have suffered while we have tried to get going. They have put up with a lot, many times I have left them without preparing a meal, perhaps just a glass of milk, in order to come here and lend a hand. So, you have to appreciate that history of personal sacrifice, and the people who come up to us and say they want to join the cooperative don't appreciate what all this has cost us. It's not egoism on our part, it's just that this is a job that we have carried out by the sweat of our brow, but willingly.

The project probably looks small, but it is large. We are going to continue to develop it so that some tomorrow people will see that the women of Nicaragua know how to work and do not waste what is entrusted to them. That is our hope, to go forward ourselves, to help the community, and to show everyone that we can do it. One purpose of our cooperative is to benefit the community. For example, we hire people to help us out because there is no work around here. We have milk which we sell, which is also a benefit to the community because we sell it at a low price and it is good milk. We also have a watchman who is from the village.

For us the word cooperative means people uniting to carry out the work that we have forged in organization. Cooperative for us expresses our belief that together we can get ahead [*unidas todas salimos adelante*]. Cooperative also means education because we have to learn how to care for what we have so that we can develop it; that is the future for our children and our community. My daughter Margarita is a teenager, and she is a member of the cooperative; she knows that this is her future. We are in a fragile period; even though we are hopeful, we are just emerging from a collapse. We think it prudent not to add more members at present, except in the way that I have described.

Lorena, will you please close with a prayer.

Guanacastillo, 30 October 1997; 8 August 1999

Gloria Siesar González

In her interview, Gloria Siesar relates with obvious pride her work as secretary of the Multiple Services cooperative, her active participation in a small mill cooperative, her past involvement in local workshops on nutrition, her political and feminist consciousness, and her family's role in the agrarian reform. She describes how cooperativism has broadened her worldview, opened her eyes to the pernicious effects of machismo, and motivated her to become more self-sufficient. In her comments, Siesar is careful to distinguish between the Frente Sandinista at the local and the national levels. At the former, she explains, the party is still responsive to the people, while at the latter, it has other priorities. Despite the country's stark political and economic realities, she has high hopes for her young daughter. She is convinced that, if she just works hard enough, she can achieve for her daughter the coveted education that she herself has thus far been unable to attain.

I am a founding member of the mill cooperative and the Multiple Services cooperative. The mill project began in 1991 when I belonged to the Women's Section of UNAG, which was created shortly after the agrarian reform. In my district of Piedra Menuda we had no mill for grinding our corn, and we are three kilometres from the highway. So we asked the Norwegian organization that was helping UNAG at the time, and they gave us the loan in 1990. Our group was one of the very first to be financed by the Norwegians. The mill is motorized, with a fairly large diesel-powered engine; you have to pull the cord to start it. We wanted a mill because it was dangerous in general in the countryside, and the mothers had to send small children out to do errands. They had to travel three kilometres, including walking along the edge of the highway without any safety precautions. Because of that problem, we decided to look for help.

The mill cooperative developed as follows. First, we had to find a place to house the mill because it is too big and heavy to carry from place to place. So we gathered contributions from all 11 members, and we built a little room where we keep the mill. Once it was installed, we had two women working there every day. We would spend all day there happily; it was a joy for the community because we had never had a mill before. The priest came to offer a prayer of thanksgiving, and all the community participated in the inauguration of the project.

Before we had a mill, everyone individually had to grind corn at home by hand; a few took their corn to Masaya for grinding. Previously I had given classes at a community preschool, and in talking with the mothers, I saw the need for a mill. So we began with a few mothers, my godmother, and a cousin and an aunt of mine, and we affiliated with a small UNAG group in our district because they were part of the agrarian reform. They helped us outline our proposal, we wrote it, and turned it in, and the Norwegians financed us directly. The mill is still functioning, though we each work only one day a week now. As we became more experienced, we became more efficient, but we also lost numbers; some of the women left to do other things. Currently, of the 11 original members, only five remain. The others either drifted away in search of work or because the mill requires a great deal of force to start it up, and some women aren't strong enough. But with five we can keep going. We now have a clientele, and we have made friendships in the district; people know us because of the mill. The project serves our personal needs and those of the community, and it allows us to meet people and talk with them while they are using our services.

The mill cost us $400 dollars; it was not a gift, but rather was sold to us at low cost. Thank God we were able to pay off our debt in one year. Since then we have been independent. First, we worked just to pay off the loan. Now the mill produces a very small income, but it has been decreasing because of the current economic situation. Each month we get together and turn in what we made during the month, but in addition to that we have a record of everything in an official notebook. We subtract the amount spent on fuel and maintenance. The room where the mill is housed is loaned to us rent-free, we only have to pay water. In a good month, we make 100-300 córdobas. It's not a large sum, but it is certainly more than we had before, which was nothing. We divide everything up equally. We have not had to make monthly contributions since we cancelled our debt. We've been doing this since 1991, six or so years before the Multiple Services cooperative was formed. I believe that there were another seven women's cooperatives that received mills at the same time we did.

Some of my most pleasurable experiences have been giving training workshops where I would talk about the Coprosa [Comisión Social de Promoción Arquidiocesana, Archdiocesan Social Promotion Commission], an infant survival project. In that project they trained people, like myself, to go out and teach other communities about the health benefits of breastfeeding, of adding natural herbs to the diet, and of making meals with soy and green leaves. We learned all about proper diet and how to make many things from soy. I became the leader of the group in our district. They would give us soy, and we would invite mothers to these sessions and chat with them about these topics. In the mornings I would give classes, and two afternoons a week I would work for the program. Besides teaching the mothers about nutrition for their children, we also taught them how to make a variety of meals. I loved that work and the opportunity to become acquainted with parents in our district.

As interesting as that activity was, it is the Multiple Services cooperative that has most broadened my world. It was begun by Olfania after she held a large assembly where the women gave suggestions about the kind of services they needed, and then they helped create the statutes. I participated too; we ourselves wrote the statutes. Now, I meet people from all over the department, not just the next village, and together we have learned to develop ourselves, to overcome our timidity as women, and to rise above those myths based on gender that are especially prevalent in the countryside. Myths, for example, that say that a little girl should only play with dolls, with kitchen things, and the little boy with guns. And if the girl touches the boy's toys, they call her a tomboy [*una hombrejona*]. If the boy touches the girl's toy, that child is a sissy [*un colchón*]. Let them play with whatever they want because that's how they learn to develop their self-esteem. There has been progress, for example, in my house, with my brothers and sisters. They say that cooking is only for women, but as a result of the workshops that I have received, I know that is not true. I told them, "No, you get hungry and I get hungry. When I get hungry, I look for a way to fix myself something to eat. That's what you should do too, and not be waiting for some woman to come along and make your dinner." In my family, my brothers have gradually accepted that idea, and they have learned to cook.

In our families and in the community, at first there was some negative reaction that the Multiple Services cooperative was just for women. It hurt the pride of some men to see that women could overcome their hardships and be responsible financial managers, because women generally pay back their debts more responsibly than do men.

In my own family we have an example of a financially responsible woman. Very early on, my mother received land under the agrarian reform. It was so early that at that time they were still giving credit to campesinos! They extended her credit year after year for a good while, beginning more or less in 1981, very early, no? She paid everything back every year, had perfect credit, and everything was in her name.

She had heard about the agrarian reform, that they were giving out land. At that time, we had only a tiny, very stony plot where it was almost impossible to plant. So, on hearing about the reform, my mother became involved and began participating in all the meetings. They told her that the meetings were just for men, but my father was working at a factory in Helotes at that time and couldn't attend, so he delegated that responsibility to my mother. She got involved in a big way and became a beneficiary in her own name. She was given four manzanas, which we all worked together. It was very hard labor, but we were proud of our efforts. My mother was one of the first two women to receive land in this area; the other was an older señora.

She held onto her land for a number of years, but she had only the agrarian reform certificate, she was never given any other official title. Things were fine until the pressure began to sell. You know, there are some men who don't value what is given to them and who also have the vice of alcohol. Well, there were people pressing the cooperativists to sell, and only my mother and two of her brothers opposed the deal. They held out as long as they could, and then they gave in too, since everyone else was selling; that was in 1998. The thing is that the men were in debt and they drank too much; they wanted to get out from under their debts, so they sold out at a low price to some people who had returned from Miami.

My mother was left in a bad situation, but later she was able to buy six and one-half manzanas in Nindirí; everything is now in both my mother's and my father's names, and they have secure title to it. It's their own private property, and that's where we now live, my parents, my brothers and sisters, my son, my daughter Viqui Francela, and myself. I work at the mill on Saturdays, and on weekdays I work here at the Multiple Services office. My mother takes care of my daughter. The property is very pretty with lots of trees. We have chickens, pigs, and a few cows. My father is an expert in planting. In the orchard he cultivates chayote, *pipián* [squash], watermelon, *pepino* [cucumber], *frijol* [beans], *maíz*, *yuca*, and banana. We don't have to buy anything in the market except for rice and oil.

I have high hopes for my daughter. My objective is to continue working so that I can give her the education that I did not have, prepare her so that she can become a professional. When I was a student, you had to leave the district if you wanted to continue past sixth grade. Most of the time, that was enough to discourage people. That was the case with my brothers and sisters, but then you end up laboring under the hot sun for the rest of your days. I told them that I wanted to continue studying even if they didn't. Now there is a school right here, so there's no reason to drop out. When I studied, I had to go to the Normal in Managua. I would travel by myself, and at that time there were no roads, so vehicles could not enter all the way. I had to walk four kilometres to get to the highway to wait for the bus to take me to class. Every day, I would get up at 4:00 a.m. and return about 6:00 p.m., study, and then get up at 4:00 the next day again. So, I tell my brothers and sisters that they must go to school because the secondary is so close, there is even a bus that takes you to the door. Oooooh! I would have been all smiles studying like that!

My mother was never against my studying, but it was my own idea. I always had the desire to study, to continue, ever since I was in fifth grade. In one class I was the *promotora*, that is, the best student, and the profesora would give me the assignments which I would then help her teach to the rest of the class, like an assistant. I enjoyed natural sciences and told my mother that was what I wanted to study and later teach. After fifth grade, I went on to *la normal* which lasts five years, but I finished only the *básico* because it was very difficult, and I was worn down by all the commuting. Even though I did not finish normal school, I could still teach here. But it's not too late to go back to school; I'm in my twenties, and I'm determined to graduate, even if it's through Saturday classes.

I also enjoy my office work here at Multiple Services. Even since I began studying accounting I have liked it more and more. I attended workshops at Multiple Services, but previous to that I had taken classes at the high school for a certificate in accounting. Here my responsibilities are the proposals, income, and expenses, although the cooperative has an official accountant who does the final reckoning; he balances everything, while I manage all the daily bookkeeping.

Cooperatives always have problems, and the biggest one for us is that a number of board members have left, creating a huge workload for three people, Olfania, Juana, and myself. In spite of that, we must keep on, we are determined not to let the cooperative fail. We will survive, even if it's only the three of us.

Four have left because of the economic situation. Of course, they receive no salary as board members, just transportation expenses [*un viático*] to enable them to attend meetings. The problem is that they can't afford not to be working when they are attending meetings. On the other hand, if you work as a domestic, you receive housing, food, and a salary, and that's why it is attractive to them because they have to support their children, and the situation we are in is really difficult. We understand that because it is hard for us too. That's what happened in three cases. The fourth one decided to try selling in the market, also out of necessity. These women all have husbands who work too, but it is not enough to maintain their kids [*chavalos*] and send them to school. It's really tough.

We need more people on the board because we need more suggestions, new thoughts, fresh ideas. We badly need the stimulus of other people for our own work too. We are 100 per cent autonomous, independent of UNAG for example, but we are too small to make it completely on our own. We are thinking of affiliating with the *Federación de Cooperativas de Mujeres* in Managua. I think it is a good idea to affiliate because it could help us develop ourselves more, and it would help lessen the impact of the economic crisis [*nos ayudaría un poco a bajar la crisis económica*].

I think that women's interests are different from those of men because, for the most part, all the responsibility for the home falls on us, that is the principal thing. That's not the case for the man; no, his interests are different. For example, when they have vices, there are few men who think about the economic development of their families, but we always have to think about the well-being of ours, and how to overcome our situation. The man comes home and expects to be served his dinner. He also has to have his clothes washed for him. He thinks that he can't do these things, but yes, he can; it's just that in our machista society all that responsibility is placed on the woman. If she were to say no, they would categorize her as incompetent, a bad woman. Liquor is the principal vice of men; it is a growing problem that is destroying homes. It is terrible because the kid sees his father's behavior and he imitates what he sees. If parents aren't careful, often at ten years of age the kids begin to drink. By age 15, they are beyond help. That's what I see in about 50 per cent of all homes. The man, when he is drunk, does not pay rent, he beats his wife, he leaves his children without food, and he lets the children go into the street begging and sniffing glue. It's destructive for everyone.

I don't know why men drink so much, maybe because it makes them feel more like men. It's the only release [*desahogo*] they have from the stress of unemployment. But I'd say 90 per cent of women do not have that mentality and they do not have that vice, because they have to be strong in order to take care of their children. Thank heavens at least there is an AA [Alcoholics Anonymous] here in Masaya.

In the Multiple Services cooperative, 95 per cent of the members are Sandinistas, and there are, as you can imagine, few political problems; however, in the district there are significant political conflicts. For example, where I live it is 50 per cent Sandinista and fewer than 40 per cent Liberal. In my small town of Nindirí I am a member of the executive board of the Sandinista party. Politics is the main topic of conversation because the candidates all want to tell people what their party does and why it's the best. The Liberal party so far has not put forward any alternatives, just pretty words. But those of us who have participated in cooperatives have learned so much from that experience and from the workshops, we have changed our mentality [*hemos aprendido tanto dentro de la cooperativa, de las capacitaciones, hemos cambiado de mentalidad*]. One major change is in our self-confidence as women. This has led us to advocate changes in education and family planning that will help our daughters and other women. For example, I think that from the time a child begins preschool they should begin to hear about women's equality. They speak very little of that in school. I think that there should also be sex education, but the mothers themselves reject this idea. Unfortunately, mothers often don't even talk with their daughters about menstruation, and when it happens, it is a shock. This is the sort of thing that should be part of the natural science curriculum.

With regard to family planning, some institutions such as Ixchen, the Centro de Mujeres, and Profamilia go into the schools and present videos on family planning and on sexually transmitted diseases; they do a very good job. In the past, it seems that women didn't want family planning because the idea was inculcated that a woman should bear as many children as God would send her and that planning was a sin. The husband was convinced that his wife was with another man if she wanted to practice birth control. But that's disappearing now, and women are saying, "No more than the three children I have. I'm not going to burden myself with too many children because the economic situation frightens me." Men feel the same way too. But it is always the woman who has to use a birth control method, the man does not use a condom. Everyone is practicing birth control, Catholic, evangelical, everyone because they don't want more children than they can support. The Catholic church doesn't say anything.

The problem with the Sandinista party is that the national leadership has abandoned the country [*han abandonado la patria*] in their anxious quest for power. As a party, we have popular support at the municipal and departmental levels. We are always meeting, discussing back and forth, setting out alternatives, maintaining contact with each local community. The Frente at the local level is uniting, this is not the problem. The problem is at the national level where they just don't care about us, and they don't visit us at all. I began working with the elections in 1996, but I've been politically aware since I was a young teenager. What I see is the complete isolation of the national Sandinista leaders from the people. They are only concerned about themselves. Meanwhile, at the local level, we are doing our best to keep body and soul together and feed our children.

Masaya, 9 August 1999

Nubia Boniche Calero

A beneficiary of the agrarian reform through Plan Masaya (1985), Nubia Boniche grows a variety of bountiful crops on her five lush, fertile manzanas in Nindirí, which could serve as a poster promoting the virtues of organic farming. It is clear from her calloused hands and sun-bronzed skin that Nubia Boniche spends a great deal of time working out-doors. She is well-known locally for her environmental consciousness, her efforts to promote sustainable agricultural practices, and her popular workshops on organic farming. In her interview, Boniche expresses with great conviction her views not only on the importance of conservation, but also on the value of the revolu-tion, the need to defend one's property, and the obligation of parents to sacrifice in order to educate their children. Though Boniche is a determined woman, confident in the legality of her title, still, one can sense the toll exacted by the constant tension of wondering how long she can hold out against powerful former owners who continue to dispute her title to the land.

This is a house of struggle. I say that because we women have to work constantly in order to raise up our home, work the land, and keep everything from dying. And thanks be to God and to all the NGOs that help us, because the organizations have played a great role here in Nicaragua, owing to the fact that we receive no assis-tance from any of our governments. Since the agrarian reform [Plan Masaya, 1985] gave us our land, no government has worried itself about the campesino at all.

I did not live here before the agrarian reform. I left my home to move here and cultivate this property. It has been difficult to pull up roots and start again, but we did it out of necessity. We tend this land, and that's how we make our living [*de eso vivimos*]. We know that we depend on the land; it is the only thing that enables us to maintain ourselves, so we conserve it the best we can.

It's no escape from poverty to sell your land and then be left with nothing. Some compañeras have sold, but it is a big mistake. People are tempted to sell because there are anxious times when you don't have the wherewithal for planting and you can't get bank financing to help you out. On top of that, in many areas, the crops have gone very badly for the past several years; the only thing that saves us are the organizations. The compañeras who sell out think they will start up a little business in the city, but then they find out that is not stable either, and they are unable to maintain themselves and their children. As difficult as things are, it's best to keep your land. That's the way I see it.

My children and my husband work here too, we all do. We have planted *plátanos* [plantains], corn, beans, yuca, *pipián* [squash], *chiltoma*, and papaya. We have also planted many trees since we've been here. They prevent erosion and provide shade. We've had the land for 12 years, but, because of all the difficulties with financing and with ownership status, we have only been able to plant for the past year or so.

I came here and took possession as soon as I received the *escritura pública* [document issued by the Sandinista government]. Now it is my property, but with my fingers crossed. That's because the highest political force is against us, the vice-president of the Republic, Enrique Bolaños, claims this is his property [Bolaños was elected president in November 2001]. The government could reject all our documents at any minute. That's why we have to organize; he who does not organize dies. One person alone can do nothing.

After the revolution, they began to work on the agrarian reform, and they came up with Plan Masaya, which is how I received my land. Here the revolution was made by everyone and when it triumphed, it was a triumph for everyone. [*Aquí la revolución fue de todos y cuando triunfó, fue un triunfo de todos.*] Now it's different, the governments have turned their back on the people. It is a situation that causes us sorrow.

At any rate, during the agrarian reform, I requested a little piece of land, two manzanas, but they gave me five, in my name. I remember that the official in Nindirí, René Membreño, told me that two manzanas were not enough because I was a hard-working woman, and why ask for two when I could work ten. I said that we couldn't afford to work so much land when we don't even have the seed for planting. He told me not to worry, that everything would be taken care of down the line, and that they would give me five now. I thought that was great, and I accepted.

Before moving here, I would come to keep watch over the property and to support the other campesinos who had been given land here. They pointed out to me that I was the first woman to join the cooperative, which they pretty much regarded as theirs. They were not welcoming at first, and I became discouraged for a while. Then I began looking for another woman to join, but no one wanted to follow me. After much pleading, I finally prevailed upon my good friend Conchita who reluctantly agreed, saying, "It scares me, but I'm with you, I'll accompany you." It frightened her because agrarian reform was very controversial; it was just the two of us women in the cooperative, and you have to be watchful in the midst of men.

At first, while we were camping out here in order to claim our land—because we had to do that as there was strong opposition—we had nothing to eat. Soon, assistance began to arrive from all those who supported us, food, coffee, *pinolillo* [a cornmeal beverage], oatmeal from various restaurants and from the mayor's office. We were 90 members of three cooperatives. Conchita and I did all the cooking. The men brought firewood down to us, they hauled water, and the meals were very festive because we had so much to eat. The two of us cooked like that for two weeks, and that's how we joined the cooperative. There are three women in the cooperative now; the other joined because her son had to leave to do his military service. We all agreed that now the land was no longer his, but hers. She's still here working that piece of land every day.

The training we have had through Casa Ave María [a US/Nicaraguan NGO] has helped us greatly. On topics like soil conservation, business administration, basic accounting, organic fertilizer, how to conserve through making terraces, how to grade the land [*nivelación*]. We've learned all these things from them. I developed my environmental consciousness at Casa Ave María.

We have also had workshops on gender through the *Sección de la Mujer* [Women's Section] of UNAG on topics such as sexual relations, women's rights, birth control, women's health. These have been very helpful; they're lovely workshops. All the women I know have faith that we are going to get ahead, even in the midst of our daily difficulties and the grave national economic situation. Things are always hard when you have children to support, but, as you know, we now have to pay for their schooling as even elementary education is no longer free; now, nothing is free. Before, when the revolution triumphed, it was wonderful. University students received scholarships, and many people from modest families studied abroad. Today, there is absolutely nothing. But I am determined to educate my children. Last week, my son defended his thesis in engineering at the university. The resources necessary to keep him in school all come from here, this property. While we work our land, the main thing we think about is how to pay for our children's studies. We struggle, we take food to the market to sell, we do whatever we can to keep them in school. I have three boys, two are agricultural engineers and one is studying medicine. Like all mothers, I want the best for my children, but the economic situation is almost too big an obstacle. Even in elementary school you have to pay a quota, a fee. A mother with four or five children, what can she do? If you can't pay, you can't go to school. It started to get bad under Doña Violeta, and it has become steadily worse ever since.

The 6 per cent you hear about is the percentage that the government pays for university expenses. If the government doesn't contribute the 6 per cent, then the student's situation becomes more critical. For example, I pay 250 córdobas a month, just to the university. If I don't pay those 250 they will take my son out of UNAN. They say that UNAN is free, but it costs 250 a month. It used to be free when my daughter studied there. She didn't graduate because she got married, but while she was a student, I didn't pay for her; that was during the revolution. If the government doesn't give the 6 per cent, then our monthly payment becomes more expensive. Everything is a struggle.

We are here on this land now because we have struggled. Whenever they threaten to throw us out, to take away our land, we have to go to the highways to pronounce, to demonstrate, because we are not going to allow them to remove us. We are the owners and these lands have been paid for [*nosotros somos dueños y estas tierras ya fueron pagadas*]. The former owners who were paid for these lands now say that they have not received any money. But these lands were indemnified, compensated [*estas tierras fueron indemnizadas*]. I know that Señor Bolaños has expensive lawyers and that they hope to recover the land either in the courts or by buying us all out. The Sandinista government paid them, but they deny it. In a meeting that the bank person in charge of finances held with us, they told us not to sell the lands. You see, we still had a small debt remaining, and some people who were fearful thought they'd better sell in order to be able to pay off their bank loans. But the bank representatives were emphatic in insisting that we not sell our lands. They said they would give us three years to pay off our debts and that we could pay in instalments. And that's how it happened; I paid off my debt, and they gave me my five manzanas. Then the people at the bank told me, "Don't sell your land because the previous owner has been paid, and now you have your own five manzanas." I thought the land might be worth about 50,000 córdobas, but they said it was worth much more, and that would be giving it away.

Like I said, leaving my home and moving here to start all over again was very sad, but, of course, it was the only way to make a living, and we were very fortunate to receive this property. But I was very sad and depressed for many months, and my husband would say to me, "Why don't you go back to the home we left in the other zone, and I'll take care of this property. I don't want you to get sick." I had been working so hard all day in the broiling sun and sleeping in the little straw shack, whereas in the place we left we had a real house of cinder block with a separate bedroom. But I said, "No, I have to be here, in this *ranchito.*" How else could my children go to school?

My husband has never resented the fact that the property is in my name. He sees it as all part of the family. He is very tranquil and comprehending. Nor does he mind the gender workshops; he knows that I have to attend and participate. It's like I was saying, the revolution taught us many things, and these workshops have been taking place ever since the revolution. Men have also been raising their consciousness, and they have seen the need for women to become organized and participate.

Before, women couldn't do anything. It was not allowed. If a woman wanted to fill out an application for a loan, that was unthinkable; she had absolutely no credibility. Now it's very different. In the Multiple Services women's cooperative we formed with Olfania, she has made it crystal clear that it is the woman who has the right to request credit and that the woman is the one who should work with the credit, because not all men are like my husband. Often the man tries to dominate the woman, and when they give her credit, he takes it away, beats her, insults her with profanities. squanders the money, and then it's all gone. There have been numerous cases like that. That's why different organizations speak with women about their rights and hold meetings about gender, to help us not be deceived.

But I have seen changes in the men as well. Many of those who started out wanting to dominate the woman now have a different view. Little by little, the man is gaining confidence in the woman, and is realizing that she has her rights too. Before, they just didn't believe that women were capable, we were considered incompetent, but the men also felt threatened. Everything comes at a cost and this is a slow process, but it is advancing.

Religion is very important in our cooperative. There is freedom of worship because there are many religions here. We all have friends who are of other religions and we work together well, there are no problems because of religion.

Here you will find evangélicos, Jehovah's witnesses, Mormons, Pentecostals. As I recall, the only group that we don't welcome are the Moonies because they were paying people to join their religion, which everyone thought was diabolical. You know that in Nicaragua now things are so desperate, that there are people who would join just for the money.

One thing the campesinos don't sell, however, is their votes. No. There has been too much consciousness raising about the importance of the vote for that to happen. What we have in our elections is fraud, not campesinos selling their votes, but, as in the election of Alemán [1996], sabotage. Do you remember that the votes for the Frente and those for the evangelical pastor were found dumped all over the place, still in the voting urns? That shows a terrible lack of respect for the public. The voting boxes turned up all over the place, abandoned along the highways, behind voting offices, in garbage bins. There is always corruption, even among some of the Sandinista leaders, but not Daniel Ortega. He has always wanted peace for Nicaragua. During the war, and in spite of the war, we lived better than we do now; at least there were jobs. When the mothers would go to visit our sons, they gave us food, and at times they even paid our passage, round trip. They did many things to help the mothers. The Sandinista Front during the contra war tried to give us assistance even with a war going on. All that has changed radically. Now, there is no war, but everything is worse.

The government wants to control all the assistance money that comes into the country from the NGOs. It is the campesinos who are the most affected by government restrictions on helping organizations. The government has made it more difficult for them to come and work here than in the past. That is terribly important to us because recently the organizations have focused their efforts here in the countryside; they have been wonderful for the campesinado. I don't know what we will do if the government gets rid of them. We have no credit in the bank, they no longer grant us loans, all that's left are helping organizations. Again, I say that we have to do everything possible to support ourselves from our land.

I am a dedicated ecologist. Many campesinos, both men and women, attend my classes on sound environmental practices. In my workshops, I tell everyone that we must care for the earth, that we depend on it, we must not burn trash, and we must use natural fertilizer. Organic fertilizer is very important. For one thing, chemical poisons cost money, and we have none. For another, organic fertilizer increases your yield. Sometimes people from the city come out to my land, and they say, "What've you got planted there?" They may come out of curiosity, but then they become interested and ask, "How does one do that?" They learn a little, go home and try it, and then they come back again with more questions. It's not the same thing at all to spray a chemical poison on your crops as it is to use an organic one. I tell people to use Nin, which comes from a local tree, because it's very healthful. We use it on the beans to kill the white fly and other insects; the Nin kills them but does not harm the plant. We dry the Nin, and then we also use it on the chayote plants as both fertilizer and pesticide. The INTA [National Agrarian Institute] sends technicians out to see me, and they hold their little meetings on my plot because they want to learn from the producer's experience. Then they go and teach others at other meetings. That's how the word spreads. When it's harvest time we see which produced more, this little parcel that was cultivated with cattle and turkey buzzard fertilizer, or others that used chemical fertilizer. The yield is always greater with my *parcelita* than it is on those that used chemicals.

It gives me great satisfaction to teach others the basic principles of organic farming. That's how we will survive.

Nindirí, 5 November 1997

Guilhermina Barrera Moncada and Edmundo González Matute

GUILHERMINA BARRERA MONCADA

Extroverted, gregarious, and not at all reluctant to express her opinions, Mina Barrera is well-known and warmly regarded in the local area of Las Pilas Orientales de Masaya. Her animated observations are punctuated by song and further enlivened by the contribution of her husband Edmundo "Mundo" González Matute. Barrera and González are both Pentecostal ministers who speak of the joy they find in their faith and who give witness to God's miracles in their own lives. The couple were ardent supporters of the Sandinista revolution, which benefitted González through the Literacy Crusade, Barrera through the feminism ushered in by the revolution, and both of them through legal recognition of the land occupation in which they participated. Barrera has created her own eclectic blending of Pentecostalism and feminism, as one observes in her campesino theater productions and her interpretations of scripture.

BARRERA: I'm from Somoto in the Department of Madriz. I still prepare the typical foods of Somoto, my little tortilla, beans, cream, milk, and cheese. Here people eat *plátano*, yucca, and rice, but in Somoto we use yucca only for soup, and rice is just for special occasions. I think it's important to prepare familiar foods; it helps keep you close to your place of origin and that makes you happier, no?

We have been very involved in theater out here in the countryside. We were supported by CESADE, a helping organization, but now, unfortunately, there are no more funds. Many of us have a certain flair for theater which we use to expose people to the reality that we live so they can see our problems and try to change them; for example, *machismo*. We also present our belief that as a gender women are capable and that we can contribute to creating a better world. Women are waking up, but some husbands don't realize this. They still come home and one, two, three, there he is in his hammock saying, "My socks, dear, bring me my coffee, my tortillas." We have just come in from the field too, but with our two hands we pat out the tortillas. Of course, there's also the washing, and then finally we go to bed exhausted, but there he is with his "come to me," and all that. That was the kind of attitude that we were used to, but women are changing and, thanks be to God, in this zone machismo is decreasing.

The change is because, well, I'll tell you straight out, it's because of the revolution, which was for us an awakening. Before, women too believed that we were good only for housework, bearing children, caring for them, and that we had no ability to do anything else. We were the most useless beings, and there were many times when I felt like, "*caramba*, why wasn't I born a man." Today, I am so happy and proud to be a woman because I know that God cares about us and doesn't want us to live as slaves. Often the wife was like a slave to her husband.

This is the sort of thing that I teach in church, I am an evangélica, and in church today it's my turn to preach. It is Women's Day, and I am taking advantage of the opportunity to speak from the pulpit and tell everyone that women are not just any old thing [*no somos cualquier cosa*]. I've done it many times and with great enthusiasm. I also ask them, "Why is it that in the Bible the woman hardly speaks? Why does it say that the woman should be quiet in the congregation?" Because it was all written by men and they all stick together! I try to joke so that people don't get too upset.

In one seminar we had a little dispute over the gender issue, and a man came up and said, "The thing is that women can't get along without men." I told him that God gave life to all and saw that it was good. But then God decided that it was not good for man to be alone, so He said, "I'll make him a helpmate" [*una 'ayudaiona'*]. So I told the man, "You see, it's men who can't get along by themselves, they have to have our help." I was joking, but you can see the negative attitude toward women. It all began with how people see the story of Adam and Eve. Adam was eyeing that tree in the garden, and God told him not to eat of its fruit, that he could taste anything else but that tree. Adam knew very well what God had told him. But he ate of the tree anyway, and said, "Mmmm, delicious." Since then, women have been blamed for everything. We have to stand up and say, "No! That's not right. I'm proud to be a woman."

My own feminist consciousness came from the revolution because there were women who went to the *montaña,* who fought in the front lines, who commanded battalions, women like Dora María Tellez [military commander and later Minister of Health under the Sandinistas] and Doris Tijerino [military commander and later Chief of Police in Managua under the Sandinistas] who were great examples. I worked clandestinely with other rural women to help the revolution triumph. There were also AMPRONAC and AMNLAE, two women's organizations that were very important during and after the revolution. I would give talks at their local meetings. That's how we raised consciousness, our own and that of other women; these organizations gave us skill training and consciousness raising. We learned that you can't go around telling other women to wake up if in your own home your own husband is still unaware. It's hard work to raise one's own husband's consciousness, but my husband and I respect each other very much.

There is a contradiction between being a feminist and being an evangelical. There is a long tradition of discrimination against women in our church, as in others, and there are still those denominations that don't permit women to go out to meetings because they fear they will become corrupted, and learn how to betray their husband. But I belong to the Church of God [*Iglesia de Dios*], which is based in love. Our missioner is brother Rodolfo Fonseca, he's a *nica,* as are most pastors by now. By chance, I'm going to talk about love this afternoon, about how the Samaritan woman was afraid to speak to Jesus because people would say, "and your husband?" I'm going to speak about how we women often have a low opinion of ourselves. But when we value ourselves, we have everything, peace, respect, unity.

I am a community leader in the district. It's hard work, and many times I've wanted to drop out, but I believe that Jesus showed us that the contradiction between feminism and evangelismo can be overcome. He didn't practice machismo, he loved men and women equally. In my church, I have seen discrimination in that all the privileges have been for men, but you have to work on that. You have to take advantage of every opportunity possible to teach. For example, during the revolution, after I had been here only two months, they named me president of the cooperative. There were Sandinistas, Somocistas, everything in our group, and I was president without any experience at all. But I told them I would try, and I wasn't just any old thing because I already knew God [tenía conocimiento de Dios]. I said, "Señor, you have called me to this post, now you have to help me out, give me the ability. I cannot do it without you." And with the help of God, everything turned out fine. I have never left God for last; I always put Him first.

I was president for four years, and then they re-elected me, but I declined so someone else could have a chance. I came from Somoto in 1982 and have been here ever since. Mundo is from this area, which is why I brought myself on down here.

I didn't simply arrive and join the cooperative. It wasn't as easy as that. First came the struggle for the land. It's an involved story, but let's sort it out. I came straight here from Somoto after they [Somocistas] had killed my son who was in military service. Since all my family was antisomocista, they [the National Guard] were after all of us. Just before he died, my son gave me a scrap of paper in which he had written "Mother, the cause that I have furthered today, please finish for me" [lo que yo continuo hoy, termínalo tú]. That's when I gave myself completely to the revolution.

Well, turns out that this land here was idle because the owner had sent his sons to Costa Rica. He had everything marked out; there were 70 manzanas that belonged to him. Our community had sent 12 fathers and sons to military service, but he who had land was able to send his sons to Costa Rica. Our husbands were in the monte and we had nothing for our families, not even a little pinol [drink made from ground toasted corn with water and sugar]. We needed land to cultivate so that we could eat and take tortillas and pinol to the montaña. This land was just sitting here unused and abandoned, and we were in desperate need, so we got to work. We managed to find four men with shovels to help us prepare the earth for planting, and we put up a big banner at the entrance of the property saying, "These lands are taken by the Patriotic Front." When a group of angry men showed up to fight with us, we told them to come on and fight, that we were ready for them, but they left and didn't return.

Then we sent a representative to UNAG and one to the police telling them what we had done. We put banners up everywhere on the property, and we made a pact among ourselves to stick together, saying that whoever broke ranks would be disgraced. UNAG sent out Carlitos Bravo to talk with us. He wanted to move us to the north, to Chinandega, but we told him that the lands there are not arable, that's a cattle zone, and to send ranchers there. We wanted to stay here. Don

Carlitos told us that the police could come and throw us off at any moment, but we responded that, if we weren't afraid of the guardia, then we certainly weren't going to be frightened by the police. Don Carlitos replied that he was just testing our fighting spirit. UNAG supported our cause and we became the José Martín Useda Cooperative, named after the fallen compañero of one of our women.

You understand that it was out of our need to feed our families that we took over the land. Our men were in the montañas, others were in the reserve, and we were left on our own, abandoned, and we had to care for our children. We were ten women; later four men joined. The cooperative still exists; we have a mill, some sheep, pigs, and chickens. They haven't broken us yet, we are still struggling [*no nos han podido doblegar todavía, estamos luchando*].

Here in our community we have differing religious beliefs, but we get along very well. If they invite me to do some special Catholic celebration, I'm there. And vice versa. I think there is so much brotherhood because we are united and practically the whole district [*comarca*] is still Sandinista. This reduces conflict, and we have learned to love and support each other. Like the proverb says, "Better a plate of weeds given in love than a fatted ox in bitterness" [*Mejor un plato de hierbas con amor que un buey bien cebado con amargura*].

We are all brothers and sisters. That's why I especially like the story of the Good Samaritan, which says that we should love our brother, that is, whoever we come into contact with. In the parable, a priest passed by, not wanting to come near, but the Samaritan got down off his mount and saw that the man was badly wounded. He gave him from the precious oil he had, placed him on the mount, and took him to the inn. Then he paid the innkeeper to care for the man and said that, if necessary, he would pay more when he returned. Hallelujah for that, no? The lesson for us is to go outside of our houses, open our eyes, and see how we can help others with their problems. In other words, we can't isolate ourselves from the world, just because there is sin and evil. How can I preach if I don't face the world? We do not set ourselves apart from it.

EDMUNDO GONZÁLEZ MATUTE

GONZÁLEZ: Not all denominations are like ours. Some believe that evil is libertinism, and they don't want to be contaminated by it, they are very puritanical. We are not like that. We try to prepare people as they grow and mature in contact with the world, strengthening their armor so to speak. When the armor, their Christian faith, is solid enough, then the person is capable of surviving in the world without losing his values.

Some politicians say that I am too interested in politics to possibly be an evangélico. But, why not? God wasn't against politics. On the contrary, he lets each person think as he wishes, freely. Jesus was with the Pharisees, with the Sadducees, with the doctors in law, with the poor, with the Zealots, with all those who rebelled against the Roman empire. And he taught all these people to love. That really is what we try to do. For example, I am a Sandinista. It doesn't bother me if someone else is an Arnoldista because I have my own principles. I just try to live a moral live and deepen my understanding of the Bible. Here is a certificate of recognition that I will always treasure. It is from where I used to work with three priests up in the north, along with UNAG, CEPAD [a Protestant development organization], and other organizations. We all worked together ecumenically, and they recognize me for that in this certificate. On our departure, they honored us at the priests' home, and members of the Frente participated too.

Some of the Frente leaders have behaved very badly, and you have to say so when it's the truth. For example, we had here a leader who went around disparaging the people in his district. He even came and accused us of being contras, just because we were criticizing some of his directives. That sort of thing happens in organizations, you get some bad officials.

BARRERA: I would like to tell you about the dramas we present; the theme is exploitation. In one, I dressed up as a *finquero* [owner of a landed estate] who was fumigating everything with pesticides, and the women workers became ill. You know pesticides have caused serious health problems here, especially among women. We did another drama about a man who was against family planning. He would go out drinking and running around to all the cantinas, getting women pregnant. Meanwhile, his pregnant wife had all these kids, and they were constantly clamoring, "Mamá where's my bottle, mamá, I want a dress to go to school." The woman couldn't provide for her children, and she was very weak when it came time for her to have her baby. Death was encircling her house and called to her, "I'm coming to get you." She responded, "I'm coming" and died right after childbirth. This is the sort of thing we see here in the district. We create the script, learn it, and then we practice it. We have no costumes or props or anything, just our imagination. Now that we have no more funding, we practice and present our dramas in our church. These are situations that we live daily. The public cries, at least they did in Tisma when we presented a drama there. In one part, one son, who was always a fighter, becomes a gang member. His mother tries to break up a fight her son is in, and he accidentally kills her. As she lies there dying, she calls all her other children to her, Pedrito, Chonita, and so on, and tells them that they will all see each other soon. She calls the gang member son, who had always refused to obey her, and says, "Goodbye, son." He says, "Mamá, why do you tell them that you will see them soon, but you say goodbye to me?" "Dear son, you cannot go where I'm going because you never obeyed and you never accepted Jesus Christ." Then he cries, "Mamá I accept Christ." She prays for her son, they both cry and embrace, and the mother dies. All the mothers and children who viewed this wept bitterly, because many mothers are desperately searching for alternatives, ways to guide their children who face powerful temptations with drugs and gangs. We sometimes think that with rice and beans in our kids' stomachs everything is fine. But children need attention to their problems, and even if we are tired and poor that's no excuse. We have to protect the family because today society is more corrupted than before. The mother is the key because where there is no mother, there is no moral development.

GONZÁLEZ: That's right. What we have to do is be actively involved in our community to help families stay together. Some Pentecostals are *verticalistas*, that is, they only look up to heaven, they don't see the world down here where we live. We look at both things, heaven and earth, because God wouldn't have come down here if there hadn't been a need, and if He hadn't loved the world. We are not very puritanical, what we are is doers, we believe that what is saintly are good works, that is, justice [*obras de santidad, es decir, la justicia*].

We believe in divine healing [*sanidad divina*] in our church, but not as a formal doctrinal imposition, rather as something evidential; that is, you believe it because you experience it or you see it. For example, there was a girl who was paralyzed for ten years, and you would always see her dragging herself around. One day, while I was in a group praying, there was a movement in the room, and we all looked up, and there was that child jumping over the rows of seats. It can't be her, I thought, but it was. I saw it with my own eyes and that's why I testify. If someone says it is not true, that is their problem, because my eyes have seen the marvels of God. Today that child is a mother with children of her own.

There are three ways to become a minister in our church: through preparation, at the Institute for Ministry [*Instituto para el Ministerio*] here in the region or in Managua, because we need capable people centered in the doctrine; through a call, God calls them and if they listen to God, then they understand; and through compassion, that is, having such love for others that you identify totally with what they are feeling.

God chose me very easily. I had been pretty lost ever since I was a child. I live here in the mountains now, but I wasn't raised here, my family is from Masaya and Monimbó. I learned at the age of seven to play the guitar. There were some popular trios, like the Llaneros and the Gocipolca in Granada; they were a famous trio, and I played with them. We made a recording, we played at various festivals. But I gave myself over to liquor from about the age of 11. I was completely corrupted and not in control of my thoughts or emotions. Then I got cirrhosis. At that time we still had the old hospital, so I went to see Doctora Alvarado, she had been my grandmother's doctor. I had no friends, no mother, no father, just my grandmother. The doctor told me, "Your illness has no cure." I was about 17 by then, and I had a girl friend who liked a song by Los Panchos called "Un siglo de ausencia," and I sang it to her and recorded it on one of those big cassettes as a remembrance. The Sister began to cry, saying, "What a shame that you are going to die."

My grandmother would come to see me, and one day she read to me the miracle of Jairo, about a woman whose only daughter had died and at that instant Jesus had healed her. If Jesus healed her, why not me? I had no idea how to approach

God, how to pray, anything. I just said, "I don't want to die, Señor. If you heal me, I will preach your word." I was like Jairo. I'll never forget that. I don't know how to explain it, but I felt something, and then a voice said, "Don't die." My feet began to feel warm, and I could move them again. I knelt down right there and dedicated myself to God. The doctor arrived, and she said, "So, you love life, eh?" She examined me, said my illness was "erased," consulted with another doctor who agreed that I was no longer ill. I left the hospital to give witness.

The problem is that there was a small evangelical church where some compañeros and I used to go and make trouble for the pastor. Going back there would be a problem, but I had to do it. The pastor, I saw he was afraid when he saw me, because I had been part of a group of troublemakers. But there I went, like the black sheep, to ask his forgiveness because I wasn't allowed to enter. What I decided to do was to wait until they had all closed their eyes and then go in. That's what I did. When the brother said, "Close your eyes and pray because the enemy can come among us at any time," that's when I entered. When he saw me, he exclaimed in fear, "That man, here!" But I said, "Don't be afraid, I have come to accept Christ." I began to give witness, and I preached in Masaya for eight days straight. That was about 40 years ago; I have had some very difficult times since then, but I keep on serving God.

Here we built our church, the Iglesia de Dios. It has the emblem of the cross on it, and we have communion every six months. Some have it every month, others every 14 days. We sing, dance, and we believe that God acts through the Spirit. That's why we are evidential Pentecostals, because we experience the Spirit. One person will dance, another will cry, another will sing, another will speak in tongues. That's the evidential part. We baptize in water. We believe that baptism should only be for people who are aware, who have recognized that they are sinners, and who want a new life in Jesus. I agree with the reformed Catholics, the charismatics, who no longer believe in infant baptism. The charismatics are also leaving behind the images, which no longer have value for them. Many charismatics are very like evangelicals.

I have almost no formal education. In school, I didn't continue past the first grade. Of course, as an adult, I had problems reading the Bible, but as God has taken me out of that world [*me ha sacado de ese mundo*] so too has he given me the words to speak. I am grateful to the revolution above all because the revolution taught me in the adult Literacy Crusade. When the Crusade came along, I began to study right here. When I reached the third level, I gave my compañero instruction at the second level, and so on up to the sixth grade. I wanted to go on to secondary school but I couldn't, because you had to go to Masaya for that. So I enrolled in a theological program at the *Comunidad Obrera Teológica* [COT, the Workers' Community Theological School]. It was open, interdenominational, and I studied there for three years. They taught us psychology, how to manage grammar, how to write a letter, a telegram, how to do a greeting, how to help people. For example, on seeing that someone has a problem, sometimes we don't know what to do, that's where psychology comes in. We would stop and talk about those points as we read Scripture. If the Literacy Crusade had not stopped, all Nicaragua would now know how to read. Revolution is progress and development; if there is ever another revolution, Nicaragua would overcome its problems, because I saw the difference in villages where everyone was illiterate, and afterwards, when I would go back to these places to set up churches, more than 40 per cent of those people could read and write and do accounts. I also met an old gentleman of about 70 years who did not know how to read but who reached the fifth level during the Crusade. He later went to COT with me for three years, and now he is a pastor in the north. There are many such cases.

BARRERA: Education is different now, they've changed it. My daughter came home one day telling me that Christopher Columbus was a hero. I told her, "No, he was a thief who came to Nicaragua to steal its treasures and deceive the people with little mirrors," and to tell that to her teacher. Her teacher admitted, "Yes, it's true, but they want us to tell it this way."

GONZÁLEZ: Have you ever seen any newspapers from 1979, the time of the insurrection against Somoza? I am saving these for my children, for the future, so they will know what actually happened because they don't teach the truth in the schools.

BARRERA: The new books are a disgrace; they've burned all the old ones and changed the curriculum. There's not a trace left. We too are left with nothing. No one has anything. We fought for so long and so many sacrificed their lives, but today we have nothing.

GONZÁLEZ: I'd like to sing for you a verse from "You Found Me" [*Tú me encontraste a mí*]. Do you know that one? It's one of our favorites because it lifts your spirits, it talks of God's love: "I was not looking for you/you found me/you gave me consolation/ you filled my soul with your holy power/thank you for the strength you give me/to love you each day more.

BARRERA: Now I'd like to sing for you "Something Different" [*Algo diferente*]. It's about how through Christ we can overcome everything: "I'll sing for you something different/ so that people will know there is a God/ he conquered the devil and now I no longer worry/ that the devil will come close to me/with his lies he once had me dazzled/ but Christ has defeated him/ although I seem small/ I have Christ by my side. Ay, ay, ay, ay ..."

That's the way we feel. We are small, we are poor, we don't know what will happen to us or our land; but we have faith and that makes us strong.

Las Pilas Orientales de Masaya, 30 October 1997; Masaya, 6 August 1999

Conclusion

The campesinos included here have given us first-hand accounts of their own efforts to survive poverty, hardship, and the neoliberal policies that reduce them to landless laborers once again. What can we learn from these stories? We have seen that chief among their survival strategies are cooperative membership, the support of NGOs, and the strength of personal religious beliefs. The cooperative endeavor has only sporadically brought monetary benefits, but it has brought rich rewards of a personal, social, and cultural nature. The women in our study have developed organizational, technical, social, problem-solving, and negotiating skills, which have improved their productivity, contributed to the creation of alternatives to ease their plight, and strengthened their tenacity and determination to succeed. Benigna Mendiola, a leader of the women's section of UNAG, reported in a 1992 interview with the newspaper Barricada that what rural women want is very simple—land, titles, and loans. Whatever progress they have made toward that end, she says bluntly, has been due to their own "stubbornness" because the government "has not given them one cent."[1]

Women cooperativists, like Gloria Siesar of Masaya, have spoken of the self-confidence that they now feel, for they have proved to themselves and others that they are capable workers and that they play an important social and economic role. Similarly, Rosario Flores commented that AMOC members in Chinandega today are likely to be found working alongside men in non-traditional activities such as cement-mixing or tractor repair. In Guanacastillo, Don William's praise of his wife Bertha's efforts and those of her four compañeras in their minuscule agricultural cooperative attests to the change that is taking place in traditional and machista attitudes regarding women's innate capabilities and culturally conditioned gender roles. It has not been easy, nor is it easy today. Traditional machismo is still very much alive, but things are changing.

Despite the "double day" and the countless invisible adjustments made by women (mothers, grandmothers, adult female relatives) and their daughters, women cooperativists join, rejoin, or remain in cooperatives because they hope through collaboration to survive and, ultimately, to improve their economic situation and that of their children. Thus, they see membership as a way to live with dignity, one of the stated objectives of the Women Producers of Guanacastillo and of the initial Agrarian Reform Law of 1981.

The women who have shared their histories with us have been assisted in their struggle for survival by numerous NGOs, both domestic and foreign. NGOs in Nicaragua, unlike those in Brazil, Bolivia, or the rest of Latin America, until recently have been very closely associated with the Nicaraguan government. Though the line between government and nongovernment agendas has always been blurry, in the case of NGOs and the Sandinistas it was practically nonexistent, as many NGOs found that their objectives and those of the revolutionary government for the most part coincided. Some NGOs, like Oxfam, have always steered an independent course. Many of the older NGOs in Nicaragua have links to progressive Catholic or Protestant churches and are Christian in orientation. CEPAD, the Protestant NGO, began by providing relief to earthquake victims in 1972; other international NGOs began to cooperate with the Nicaraguan government in the early 1980s when the contra war began to heat up.[2] One of the most important NGOs for the women cooperativists is the Norwegian Agency of Cooperation for Development [Agencia Noruega de Cooperación para el Desarrollo, NORAD], one of the first to provide technical and financial assistance to campesinos during the Sandinista period, and one which, like Oxfam, has a strong gender focus.

During the 1990s, the association of NGOs with the former Sandinista government made things more difficult for Nicaragua's poor. In Brazil and Bolivia NGOs have operated freely and, in the case of Bolivia, with the enthusiastic welcome of a government only too eager to relinquish its public responsibilities. But in Nicaragua, the Alemán government is suspicious of many NGOs, and increasingly complicated bureaucratic red tape regarding eligibility status, bookkeeping, and disbursement of funds has resulted in the reduction or delay of badly needed assistance to the poor.

Another source of support for the women cooperativists is their strong religious faith. Though we noted the crucial part that religion has played in the seringueiro and Guaraní communities, in Nicaragua it plays a somewhat different, but equally important, role. There has been no protection or leadership training offered, such as the seringueiros received, and no accompaniment or community development, such as have benefitted the Guaraní. In fact, there have been no concerted efforts by the official Nicaraguan Catholic church on behalf of the poor. The post-Sandinista church, like the post-Sandinista governments, has pursued a laissez-faire policy in regard to the economic standing of the people. Religious support for the poor women included here has in no way been institutional. Rather, it has emanated from the well-spring of their own personal faith and spirituality. One observes this religiosity in references in the actas, or minutes, of the San Francisco cooperative meetings, for example. They contain statements such as the importance of always "giving love to our work and to God above all."[3] References, such as "with the help of God," dot conversations with the Guanacastillo producers as they recount the collapse and reconstitution of their fledgling cooperative. These are not just colorful figures of speech, but expressions of core religious beliefs. The women's lived spirituality gives them resilience and strength, for which they frequently express their gratitude.

Further, one can observe a fairly widespread ecumenism at the grassroots (not official) level among cooperative members, something not so evident in the Brazilian and Bolivian examples for reasons of their different histories. This, too, is a legacy of the Nicaraguan revolution, for progressive Catholic and Protestant clergy and laypersons worked together from the 1960s to concretize their dream of social equality and their belief in the inherent worth of each individual, much as the Brazilian Catholic base communities did to such great effect in the Amazon. The combination of personal religious faith, grassroots ecumenism, feminism, and national and international NGO assistance has not only helped women cooperativists to survive, it has also fostered their sense of personal dignity, their ability to solve problems, to envision a different future, and to connect with others beyond their borders.

As Richard Barnet and John Cavanagh observe in *Global Dreams*, "More and more people who are bypassed by the new world order are crafting their own strategies for survival and development, and in the process are spinning their own transnational webs to embrace and connect people across the world."[4] Nowhere is this more true than among the campesinos of Nicaragua, among the poorest nations in the Western Hemisphere.

NOTES

1. Benigna Mendiola, "We Have More Serious Problems," *Barricada Internacional* (March 1992): 25-26.
2. For more on NGOs in Nicaragua, see Laura Macdonald, "The Political Role of Non-Governmental Organizations in Nicaragua," *Supporting Civil Society: The Politics of Non-Governmental Organizations in Central America* (New York: St. Martin's Press, 1997) 97-139.
3. Acta s/n (25 junio 1999).
4. Quoted in Macdonald 153.

CONCLUSION

The Brazilian rubber tappers, the Bolivian Guaraní, and the Nicaraguan women cooperativists all are displaying agency and consciousness in their struggle for cultural and economic survival. We have seen that the seringueiros of Acre faced violent evictions from their traditional lands by immigrants from the south of Brazil who came to raise cattle and engage in logging for export. The seringueiros responded by organizing themselves—creating a union, a national council, and a cooperative and joining the Workers Party. They were prepared for and assisted in these activities first and foremost by the Catholic church, then by national and international environmental groups and other NGOs. Although they are still locked in a struggle for economic survival, the seringueiros have embraced economic diversification to an impressive extent, and they have benefitted significantly from the acclaimed forest-based educational program, Projeto Seringueiro.

The Guaraní of O'Connor Province in the Chaco of Bolivia faced the challenge of defying the unjust system represented by the patrón. They, too, responded by organizing, joining with other groups, such as the campesinos' union, starting a school for their children and holding up education as the way to preserve their language and their past and to secure their children's future. They have revived the cultural tradition of assembly, participated in the national Guaraní organization, and welcomed the women's basket-weaving initiative. The Sisters of the Presentation have been instrumental in helping the Guaraní in their struggle and in strengthening the bonds of community. The Guaraní have also been assisted by national and international NGOs, which provide technical assistance and training; however, despite such assistance, they, like the rubber tappers, remain extremely poor.

The Nicaraguan campesinas have faced and continue to face eviction, the threat of eviction, forced land sales, and credit restrictions so severe as to have starved both agricultural and savings and credit cooperatives. The women have responded by organizing, forming more cooperatives, and seeking educational, technical, and financial assistance from NGOs everywhere; however, they are being squeezed relentlessly. In Nicaragua, ecumenical Christian groups have worked in solidarity with the poor from the 1960s and collaborated with the Sandinistas when their social goals coincided. With the advent of neoliberal government in 1990, official support from church and state ceased abruptly, exacting a continuing heavy toll.

We have observed that the seringueiros of Acre, the Guaraní of the Chaco, and the campesinas of Nicaragua have been profoundly affected by the negative features of globalization, as represented by the logger, the rancher, or the neoliberal policy-maker, in ways that have caused them to lose control over their own lives. Their stories tell of their efforts to regain that control. There is much that separates these communities from each other—geography, language, culture, ethnicity—but what they have in common is far more important.

We have seen that seringueiros, Guaraní, and campesinas alike live in conditions of acute poverty, rendering them vulnerable to abuse by those who are more powerful. As a result, they have experienced forced evictions, or the threat of eviction, from their lands or the threat of legal action, often by those whose only "title" is the barrel of a gun or familiarity with the world of courts, lawyers, and the closed circle of the elite.

The rural poor in these communities have been systematically excluded from basic health and educational services, especially since the wave of privatizations in the 1980s. If their lack of access to these basic necessities continues, it will seriously affect future generations. As the communities have become more destitute, they have been hit hard by severe cultural erosion and destabilization. Symptoms include migration as a way of life, increased alcoholism, and the threatened and real disintegration of families. Their poverty and social exclusion are compounded by the absence even of rudimentary infrastructure to market their products and improve their lot. Finally, members of all three communities have been subject to one form or another of soul-destroying debt peonage, through the figure of the patrão/patrón. In sum, the people whose voices we have heard tell a common story of poverty, injustice, social destabilization, and cultural disintegration.

Globalization, in the form of corporations and international financial institutions, has been involved in the pressure on these communities, but it is not a dark, monolithic force that set out to annihilate the poor, or the environment, or national sovereignty, or cultural diversity, or to increase the misery of women. How have the individuals and communities addressed the aspects of globalization that imperil their continued existence? As we have seen, they have not given up, they have not despaired, and they have not become passive victims—far from it.

Their responses have much in common. The communities have come up with creative alternatives born of necessity. These amount to a reconfiguration of, and a challenge to, the values underlying globalization. For example, the communities have put forward an ethic of sufficiency over "economics without ethics," as Bishop Dom Moacyr describes the quest for unlimited capital accumulation. The villagers have demonstrated that local control over local resources is vital for economic and cultural survival, and they have proposed a localist value to replace the centralized control exercised by remote, foreign experts or self-interested and often corrupt national elites.

The people who have shared their stories here have organized their communities and their cooperatives to an astonishing degree. As Facundo Galeán of Ñaurenda exhorted residents of his former village who were afraid to stand up to the patron, "Organize, organize, organize!" Doña Nubia Boniche of Nindirí put it in starker terms, "Organize or die." Members of these communities have chosen the difficult road of building community solidarity as a defense against the unchecked individualism of the prevailing system. They believe that there is strength in numbers. "Two trees give more shade than one," explains Olfania Medina. The people of these communities have organized and raised political, gender, and environmental consciousness and expressed their heightened awareness, with varying emphases, in the statutes and founding documents of their cooperatives and associations.

These people welcomed technical training programs and workshops in personal and community development. Indeed, they have eagerly sought them out as a means to help them increase production and to build self-esteem and family and community values. Every community has expressed its conviction that education for its children is the hope for a better future. The benefits of both formal education and the many *capacitación* [training] efforts extend deep into each community, enabling families and assemblies to confront and discuss issues such as alcoholism, domestic abuse, and machismo. For all three communities, education makes empowerment possible. As Valerio Muñoz of Agua Buena expresses it, when Guaraní children are educated, "they can stand up for themselves."

Largely as a result of consistent exposure to consciousness-raising workshops and technical training sessions, these traditional groups have embraced economic diversification, calling into question the notion that peasants are inherently conservative and resistant to change. The seringueiros have been the most savvy in this regard, moving from traditional gathering activities to the cultivation of vegetables, pupunha, palmito [heart of palm], and similar products for the market, but the Guaraní women were quick to take up the basket-weaving initiative, and their villages are also beginning to cultivate vegetables, while the nicas are cultivating nontraditional crops as well as engaging in countless micro-enterprises in order to increase income. All are changing in order to survive.

In many ways, these communities have transformed themselves from the ground up. Crucial to this process is the development of a political consciousness that ultimately produces local leaders. In this, the seringueiros have been quite advanced, for their leadership has been remarkable, and Senator Marina Silva continues that tradition today. The Guaraní of O'Connor province are not as far along, but they are developing a political consciousness and becoming more active in indigenous organizations. The nicas experienced the consciousness-raising of the Sandinista revolution and, thus, are perhaps the most politically articulate and astute of the three; they are keenly aware of their own rights.

In their efforts to raise consciousness, the seringueiros, the Guaraní, and the nicas have received essential assistance for several decades from members of religious groups and secular NGOs who have helped them develop leadership skills and technical expertise. These are, ironically enough, agencies of globalization. Compared to the other communities, the Nicaraguan women excel in the areas of organization, verbal prowess, and feminist awareness because these were nurtured not only by NGOs but, above all, by the Sandinista revolution. Over the long haul, the raising of consciousness in all three communities promotes autonomy by simultaneously cultivating a sense of individual worth and group responsibility. The individuals interviewed for this study are choosing autonomy and empowerment over "assistentialism" and paternalism. The latter are particularly insidious, for the passivity they breed plays into the negative features of globalization by leaving all decision-making to the market, the powerful new patrón. Community members like Dom Sebastião Mendes of the Cachoeira Reserve, though extremely poor, feel that they are empowered. In contrasting life under the patrão with life in the cooperative, he says simply, "Now, we are our own masters."

The organizing of associations, cooperatives, and communities and the emphasis on education and consciousness-raising has not come easily. The fact that cooperatives and projects fail, begin again, and are always undertaken against the current indicates the deep reservoir of faith and hope that continues to motivate and sustain members of these communities. As Doña Juanita of Malpaisillo says, "Hope sustains, but it does not satisfy"; thus, the cooperativists are continually pushed to think of new alternatives that will satisfy their basic needs.

These three communities are working toward autonomy and empowerment. The worrisome irony is that they are pursuing these goals within a broader framework of dependency, that of their own national governments. They could serve as models for the direction their governments might take. What the national elites do not realize is that it is not just the poor people's end of the boat that is sinking. They are in the same boat, and the poor are the only ones who are bailing. Rather than viewing the alternatives advanced by these communities as last gasp efforts of a few impoverished villages, the elites could regard them as bold heralds of a new age in which people relate to each other and to the earth in more inclusive and sustainable ways.[1]

The special twist to the story is that, in putting forth alternative values and models, the communities have worked in close collaboration with global helping institutions—religious, environmental, feminist, educational, health, development, technical, and communications—making highly eclectic use of the positive features for human development that are also part of globalization. These embattled communities are not alone. Not only do they represent countless similar communities all across Latin America, but they are connected also to organizations throughout the world dedicated to finding alternatives to "progress" as it has been narrowly defined. These communities and their international supporters believe that the economy should be at the service of human beings and not the other way around.

Unfortunately, a human-centered system cannot simply be willed into existence. It has to be built on a base of respect for the dignity of each person and the right of each community to choice. This presupposes a commitment to justice and equality. This commitment has motivated the Catholic church in the Amazon and the missionary sisters in the Chaco to live in solidarity with the seringueiros and the Guaraní, and it has inspired the important work of ecumenical Christian groups in Nicaragua for decades.

Thus, we see that the people who have given voice to their grassroots experiences of globalization are engaged with dignity in a struggle for survival whose outcome is uncertain. The increasing hardships they have had to endure have impelled them to raise their consciousness, and now they are raising ours.

NOTE
1. See Bill McKibben, "An Alternative to Progress," *Mother Jones* (June 2001): 78-83.

BIBLIOGRAPHY

Acebey, David. *Quereimba, apuntes sobre los ava-guaraní en Bolivia*. Bolivia: Ediciones Gráficas, 1992.

Actas (community assembly reports). *Libro de Actas*. Ñaurenda, Tarija, Boliva: n.p., various dates.

Actas (San Francisco de Asisi cooperative). *Libro de Actas*. Malpaisillo, León, Nicaragua: n.p., various dates.

Adriance, Madeleine Cousineau. *Promised Land: Base Christian Communities and the Struggle for the Amazon*. New York: State University of New York Press, 1995.

Aguirre, Lucia, and Martha Luz Padilla, with Carmen Diana Moore. *Tough Row to Hoe: Women in Nicaragua's Agricultural Cooperatives*. Trans. Paola Pérez Alemán and Phil Martínez. Managua: Rural Women's Research Team, CIERA, and San Francisco: Food First, 1985.

Albó, Xavier. *La comunidad de hoy*. Volume 3 of *Los Guaraní-Chiriguano*. La Paz: Centro de investigación y promoción del campesinado, 1990.

Allegretti, Maria Helena, and Stephan Schwartzman. "Extractive Production in the Amazon and the Rubber Tappers' Movement." Washington, DC: Environmental Defense Fund, 1987.

Allegretti, Maria Helena. "Reservas Extrativis-tas: Parâmetros para uma Política de Desenvolvimento Sustentável na Amazônia." *O Destino da Floresta, Reservas Extrativistas e Desenvolvimento Sustentável na Amazônia*. Ed. Ricardo Arnt. Rio de Janeiro: Dumará Distribuidora de Publicações Ltda. and Instituto de Estudos Amazônicos e Ambientais, Fundação Konrad Adenauer, 1994. 17-47.

Almeida, Barbosa de, and Mauro William "Rubber Tappers of the Upper Jurúa River, Brazil." Diss. University of Cambridge, 1992.

Anderson, Sarah, and John Cavanagh, with Thea Lee. *Field Guide to the Global Economy*. New York: The New Press, 2000.

Arancibia, Dr. Guillermo. Personal interview. Sucre, Bolivia. 16, 17 December 2000.

Arebayo, Pascuala, Rosario Mendoza, Gregoria Catuire, and Santos Arebayo. Personal interview. Ñaurenda, Bolivia. 3 August 1998.

Baldassari, Padre Paolino. Personal interview. Sena Madureira, Brazil. 31 July 1996; 4 August 1996.

Barbosa Júlio. Personal interview. Xapuri, Brazil. 2 August 1996.

Barrera Moncada, Guilhermina, and Edmundo González Matute. Personal interview. Las Pilas Orientales de Masaya, Nicaragua. 30 October 1997; Masaya, 6 August 1999.

Barros, Raimundo de. Personal interview. Xapuri, Brazil. 30 July 1996; 31 August 1997.

Blanco, Ligia, "Mujer, trabajo y pobreza."*Barricada* (Managua). 24 septiem-bre, 1997: sección 6A.

Boff, Clodovis. *Teologia Pé no Chão*. Petrópolis: Editôra Vozes, 1984.

Bourgois, Philippe."Nicaragua's Ethnic Minorities in the Revolution." Rosset and Vandermeer 459-72.

Calero, Nubia Boniche. Personal interview. Nindirí, Nicaragua. 5 November 1997.

Campbell, Connie, with the Women's Group of Xapuri. "Out on the Front Lines but Still Struggling for a Voice." *Feminist Political Ecology: Global Issues and Local Experiences.* Ed. Dianne Rocheleau, Barbara Thomas-Slayter, and Esther Wangari. New York: Routledge, 1996. 27-61.

Carta alimentaria nicaragüense (Managua). 1,5 (setiembre/octubre 1997): 1.

Castells, Manuel. *The Power of Identity.* Volume II of *The Information Age: Economy, Society and Culture.* Malden, MA and Oxford, England: Blackwell Publishers, 1997.

Ceppi, Padre Luiz. Personal interview. Xapuri, Brazil. 1 August 1996.

Chagas, Francisco das. Personal interview. Rio Branco, Brazil. 30 July 1996. Manaus, Brazil. 8 September 1997.

Chávez, Susana de. Personal interview. Yukimbia, Bolivia. 7 August 1998.

Chumiray, Guido. "La Asamblea del Pueblo Guaraní: sus 10 años." *Ñee Jeroata* (Bolivia) 61 (enero/febrero, 1997): 12-18.

Clay, Jason. *Indigenous Peoples and Tropical Rainforests: Models of Land Use and Management from Latin America.* Cultural Survival Report 27. Cambridge, MA: Cultural Survival, Ind., 1988.

Close, David. *Nicaragua: the Chamorro Years.* Boulder: Lynne Rienner Publishers, 1999.

Cobb, John B. Jr. *Sustainability: Economics, Ecology, and Justice.* Maryknoll, NY: Orbis Books, 1992.

Collins, Joseph, with Frances Moore Lappé, Nick Allen, and Paul Rice. *Nicaragua: What Difference Could a Revolution Make?* New York: Grove Press, A Food First Book, 1986.

Cunha, Euclides da. "Impressões Gerais." *Um Paraíso Perdido. Reunião dos Ensaios Amazônicos.* Petrópolis: Editôra Vozes, 1976.

Cunha, Manoel Estébio Cavalcante da. Personal interview. Rio Branco, Brazil. 10 June 1999.

Daly, Herman E. *Beyond Growth: the Economics of Sustainable Growth.* Boston: Beacon Press, 1996.

Daly, Herman E., and John B. Cobb, Jr. *For the Common Good: Redirecting the Economy toward Community, the Environment, and a Sustainable Future.* 2nd ed. Boston: Beacon Press, 1994.

Davis, Shelton. *Victims of the Miracle: Development and the Indians of Brazil.* Cambridge: Cambridge University Press, 1977.

El Catequista. Entre Ríos, Tarija, Bolivia: Academia of the Sisters of the Presentation, various dates.

Enríquez, Laura J. *Agrarian Reform and Class Consciousness in Nicaragua.* Gainesville, FL: University Press of Florida, 1997.

——. *Harvesting Change: Labor and Agrarian Reform in Nicaragua, 1979-1990.* Chapel Hill, NC: University of North Carolina Press, 1991.

Escobar, Arturo. *Encountering Development: the Making and Unmaking of the Third World.* Princeton, NJ: Princeton University Press, 1995.

Estado de la población nacional, 1998, Las nuevas generaciones: Nicaragua. Managua: Fondo de Población de las Naciones Unidas, 1998.

Estatutos de la Asociación de Mujeres Obreras y Campesinas, 1997. El Viejo, Chinandega, Nicaragua: n.p., 1997.

Estatutos de la Cooperativa Agropecuaria de Producción, Productoras de Guanacastillo, 1997. Masaya, Nicaragua: n.p., 1997.

Estatutos de la Cooperativa de Ahorro y Crédito "San Francisco de Asis" R.L. 1993. Malpaisillo, León, Nicaragua: n.p., 1993.

Fisher, Julie. *The Road from Rio: Sustainable Development and the Nongovernmental Movement in the Third World.* Westport, CT and London: Praeger, 1993.

Flores Neira, Maria del Rosario. Personal interview. El Viejo, Nicaragua. 3 November 1997; 10 August 1999.

Galeán, Facundo. Personal interview. Timboy, Bolivia. 13 May 1997.

Gallardo Jorge (Machirope). Personal interview. Timboy, Bolivia. 2 August 1998.

Gallardo, Jorge (Machirope), and Feliciano Tárraga. Personal interview. Timboy, Bolivia. 4 May 1997.

Gareca, Mario. Personal interview. Sella Cercado, Bolivia. 9 August 1998.

Ghai, Dharam, and Jessica M. Vivian, eds. *Grassroots Environmental Action: People's Participation in Sustainable Development.* London and New York: Routledge, 1992.

Gilbert, Dennis. *Sandinistas: the Party and the Revolution*. New York: Basil Blackwell, 1988.

Gill, Lesley. *Teetering on the Rim: Global Restructuring, Daily Life, and the Armed Retreat of the Bolivian State*. New York: Columbia University Press, 2000.

Gonçalves, Maria Ronizia Pereira. A Fala Sagrada e Social do "Todos Somos Irmãos" de 1976 a 1982. BA thesis. Universidade Federal do Acre, 1997.

González, Gloria Siesar. Personal interview. Masaya, Nicaragua. 9 August 1999.

Goodland, Robert. *Race to Save the Tropics: Ecology and Economics for a Sustainable Future*. Washington, DC and Covelo, CA: Island Press, 1990.

Grabowski, Cândido, ed. *Chico Mendes. Fight for the Forest: Chico Mendes in His Own Words*. Trans. Chris Whitehouse. Additional material Tony Gross. Ed. Duncan Green. London: Latin American Bureau, 1989. Adapted from *O Testamento da Floresta*. Ed. Cândido Grabowski. Rio de Janeiro: FASE, 1989.

Grechi, Dom Moacyr. Personal interview. Rio Branco, Brazil. 7 August 1996; 26 August 1997; 1 September 1997; 31 May 1999.

Gutiérrez, Justina, and Capitán Sambo Gutiérrez. Personal interview. Potrerillos, Bolivia. 4 May 1997.

Heyck, Denis L. "Baptism among the Guaraní of Bolivia." N.p.: 1998.

—. *Life Stories of the Nicaraguan Revolution*. New York: Routledge, 1990.

Heyck-Williams, Shannon D. "The UNDP's Human Development Index: An Incomplete Measurement of Human Well-Being." MA thesis. Yale University, 2000.

Hirshon, Sheryl L., and Judy Butler. *And Also Teach Them to Read*. Westport, CT: Lawrence Hill, 1983.

Hostetler, Sharon, JoAnn Lynen, and Leia Raphaelidis. *A High Price to Pay: Structural Adjustment and Women in Nicaragua*. Washington, DC: Witness for Peace, 1995.

Hostetler, Sharon, JoAnn Lynen, Tim Welsh, and Hyward Wilkirson. *Bitter Medicine: Structural Adjustment in Nicaragua*. Washington, DC: Witness for Peace, 1995.

Hoyt, Katherine. *The Many Faces of Sandinista Democracy*. Athens, OH: Center for International Studies, Ohio University, 1997.

Instituto Brasileiro de Geografia e Estatística, IBGE. Web site: http://www.ibge.gov.br

Kaimowitz, David. "Nicaragua's Agrarian Reform: Six Years Later." Rosset and Vandermeer 390-93.

Karliner, Joshua, Daniel Faber, and Robert Rice. "An Environmental Perspective." Rosset and Vandermeer 393-408.

Klein, Herbert S. *Bolivia: the Evolution of a Multi-Ethnic Society*. 2nd ed. New York and Oxford: Oxford University Press, 1992.

Kleymeyer, Charles David, ed. *La expresión cultural y el desarrollo de base*. Arlington, VA.: Fundación Interamericana, 1993.

Korten, David C. *Getting to the 21st Century: Voluntary Action and the Global Agenda*. West Hartford, CT.: Kumarian Press, 1990.

—. *When Corporations Rule the World*. West Hartford, CT: Kumarian Press; San Francisco: Berrett-Koehler Publishers, 1995.

La Gaceta (Managua) 8 (13 enero 1986).

—.188 (21 agosto 1981).

Leiken, Robert S., and Barry Rubin. *The Central American Crisis Reader*. New York: Summit Books, 1987.

Libermann, Kitula, and Armando Godínez, eds. *Territorio y dignidad: pueblos indígenas y medio abiente en Bolivia*. Caracas: Editorial Torino; Bolivia: Instituto Latinoamericano de Investigaciones Sociales and Editorial Nueva Sociedad, 1992.

Lima, Cláudio Araújo. *Coronel de Barranco*. São Paulo: Gráfica Urupês, 1970.

López, Guísela, and Roberto Navia. "Boom: Tarija despierta y asume el liderazgo petrolero de Bolivia." *El Deber* (Santa Cruz de la Sierra) 22 abril 2001.

Lunes Socio-Económico de Barricada. Managua: CIERA, 1984.

Macdonald, Laura. *Supporting Civil Society: the Politics of Non-Governmental Organizations in Central America*. New York: St. Martin's Press, 1997.

McCarthy, Sr. Maura PBVM. Personal interview. Evanston, IL. 5, 6 June 2000.

—. "Estatutos, Zona Guaraní de Itika Guasu, Departamento de Tarija." Appendix. "Hacia la tierra sin mal: proyecto de promoción social." N.p.: n.p., 1989.

——. "God and the Lice," *Oak Leaves* 23, 1/2 (27 June, 1997).

McKibben, Bill. "An Alternative to Progress." *Mother Jones* (June 2001): 78-83.

Medina, Olfania. Personal interview. Masaya, Nicaragua. 29 October 1997; 13 August 1999.

Medina de Matus, Juanita. Personal interview. Malpaisillo, Nicaragua. 4 November 1997; 4 August 1999.

Meléndez, Miranda, René Chavarría Balmaceda, and Leonardo Chavarría Balmaceda. *Legislación cooperativa*. Managua: Fundación para el Desarrollo, 1995.

Meliá, Bartolomé. *Ñande Reko: Nuestro modo de ser*. Volume I of *Los Guaraní-Chiriguano*. La Paz: Centro de investigación y promoción del campesinado, 1988.

Mendes, Chico. Letter to Bishop Dom Moacyr Grechi. 29 July 1987. Courtesy of Dom Moacyr Grechi.

Mendes, Sebastião Teixeira de. Personal interview. Assentamento Extrativista Chico Mendes, Brazil. 2 August 1996.

Mendiola, Benigna. "We Have More Serious Problems." *Barricada Internacional* (March, 1992): 25-26.

Menezes, Valdir and Ivonilde. Personal interview. Rio Branco, Brazil. 31 May 1999.

Ministerio de Acción Social. "Compendio para la preparación de multiplicadores de desarrollo humano." Managua: Programa de las Naciones Unidas para el Desarrollo, 1995.

Ministerio de Cultura, Juventud y Deportes. *Para que el grupo permanezca unido*. San José, Costa Rica: Centro Nacional para el Desarrollo de la Mujer y la Familia, 1989.

Molyneux, Maxime. "Women: Activism without Liberation?" Rosset and Vandermeer 478-81.

Mota, Aldenir Rodrigues, Alzenite de Araújo Verçosa, Cosmo Araújo e Araújo, Maria Mavy Dourado de Souza, Rosineide Rodrigues Lopes, Zairnéia Soares de Lima, and Zilah Carvalho Mastub de Oliveira. "A Formação do Partido dos Trabalhadores em Xapuri: os 15 Anos do PT." *Xapurys* 1 (1995): 18-29.

Mota, Aldenir Rodrigues, Alzenite de Araújo Verçosa, Cosmo Araújo e Araújo, Rosineide Rodrigues Lopes, Zairinéia Soares de Lima, and Zilah Carvalho Mastub de Oliveira. "Empate pela Vida e Defesa da Floresta em Xapuri." *Xapurys* 2 (1996): 5-18.

Muñoz, Paulina. Personal interview. Potrerillos, Bolivia. 11 May 1997.

Muñoz, Valerio. Personal interview. Ñaurenda, Bolivia. 7 May 1997.

NACLA Report on the Americas. Vol. 12. New York: North American Congress on Latin America, November-December 1978.

Norberg-Hodge, Helena. "Buddhism in the Global Economy." *Resurgence* 181 (March/April 1997): 18-22.

Novillo, Porfirio. Personal interview. Saladito, Bolivia. 13 May 1997.

Núñez, David. "Talar los grandes árboles." *Pensamiento Propio*. Managua: CIERA, 1986. 31-36.

Oliveira, Luiz Antônio Pinto de. "O Sertanejo, o Brabo e o Posseiro (Os cem anos de andanças da população acreana)." MA thesis. Universidade Federal do Acre, 1985.

Paulo, Amós D'Avila de, Angela Maria Gomes Alves, Caticilene Rodrigues, Rosilene da Silva, and Valcidene Soares Menezes. "Soldados da Borracha de Xapuri: Memórias de um Viver." *Xapurys* 1 (1995).

Pereira, Assis. *Versos Amazônicos*. Rio Branco: Fundação Garibaldi, 1996.

Pifarré, Francisco. *Historia de un pueblo*. Volume II of *Los Guaraní-Chiriguano*. La Paz: CIPCA, 1989.

Polanco, Roland. Personal interview. Rio Branco, Brazil. 28 August 1996.

Prevost, Gary, and Harry E. Vanden, eds. *The Undermining of the Sandinista Revolution*. 2nd ed. London: Macmillan Press; New York: St. Martin's Press, 1999.

Prevost, Gary, and Harry E. Vanden. "Introduction." Prevost and Vanden 1-8.

Ramos, Ana, and Josenira Oliveira. "O Seringueiro Conta a sua História." BA thesis. Universidade Federal do Acre, 1996.

Renzi, María Rosa, and Sonia Agueto. *La mujer y los hogares rurales nicaragüenses: indicadores económicos y sociales*. Managua: Fundación Internacional para el Desafío Económico Global, 1997.

Resistencia campesina: efectos de la política económica neoliberal del Decreto Supremo 21060. La Paz: Centro de Estudios para el Desarrollo Laboral y Agrario, 1989.

"Resumo do Programa." Rio Branco CTA office (29 July 29, 1997). N.p.

Revkin, Andrew. *The Burning Season: the Murder of Chico Mendes and the Fight for the Amazon Rain Forest*. New York: Penguin, 1990.

Rich, Bruce. *Mortgaging the Earth: the World Bank, Environmental Impoverishment, and the Crisis of Development*. Boston: Beacon Press, 1994.

Riester, Jürgen. *Textos sagrados de los guaraníes en Bolivia*. La Paz and Cochabamba: Editorial "Los amigos del libro," 1984.

Rosset, Peter and John Vandermeer, eds. *Nicaragua: Unfinished Revolution*. New York: Grove Press, 1986.

Sánchez, Renán. Personal interview. Entre Ríos, Bolivia. 11 December 2000.

Saravia, Capitán. Personal interview. Saladito, Bolivia. May 2, 1997.

Schuchard, Barbara. "La conquista de la tierra: relatos guaraníes de Bolivia acerca de experiencias guerreras y pacíficas recientes." *Chiriguano*. Ed. Jürgen Riester. Volume III of *Pueblos Indígenas de las tierras bajas de Bolivia*. Santa Cruz: Apoyo para el Campesino-Indígena del Oriente Boliviano, 1994. 421-71.

Schumacher, E.F. *Small is Beautiful: Economics as if People Mattered*. New York: Harper and Row, 1973.

Schwartzman, Stephan. "Seringueiros Defend the Rainforest in Amazônia." *Cultural Survival Quarterly* 10,2 (1986): 41-43.

Shibata, Ricardo Hiroyuki. Personal interview. Rio Branco, Brazil. 1 June 1999.

Silva, Bernardinho Ribeiro da. Personal interview. Terra Alta and Xapuri, Brazil. 8, 9 June 1999.

Silva, Maria do Perpétuo Socorro, José Rodrigues Arimatéia, and Franckinato da Silva Batista *Seringueiros, Memória, História e Identidade*. Vol 1. Rio Branco: UFAC, Centro de Documentação e Informação Histórica, 1997.

Silva, Matilde and Eliana Ribeiro da. Personal interview. Terra Alta, Brazil. 8 June, 1999.

Silva, Senadora Marina. Personal interview. Rio Branco, Brazil. 7 August 1996.

Sobrinho, Pedro Vicente Costa. *Capital e Trabalho na Amazônia Ocidental*. São Paulo: Cortez Editôra; Rio Branco: UFAC, 1997.

Solórzano Gaitán, Juanita, Bertha Rosa Rojas, Lorena Solórzano, Zoila María Rojas Calero, and William Vivas Soto. Personal interview. Guanacastillo, Nicaragua. 30 October 1997; 8 August 1999.

Spalding, Rose. *Capitalists and Revolution in Nicaragua: Opposition and Accommodation, 1979-1993*. Chapel Hill, NC: University of North Carolina Press, 1994.

Stahler-Sholk, Richard. "Structural Adjustment and Resistance: The Political Economy of Nicaragua Under Chamorro." Prevost and Vanden 74-113.

Stein, Andrew J. "The Church." *Nicaragua Without Illusions*. Ed. Thomas W. Walker. Wilmington, DE: Scholarly Resources, 1997. 235-47.

Stephenson, Marcia. *Gender and Modernity in Andean Bolivia*. Austin, TX: University of Texas Press, 1999.

Tagüe, Angela. Personal interview. Ñaurenda, Bolivia. 6 May 1997.

Tárraga, Feliciano. Personal interview. Timboy, Bolivia. 3 August 1998.

Tárraga, Paulina. Personal interview. Ñaurenda, Bolivia. 12 May 1997.

United Nations Development Program. *Human Development Report 1997*. New York and Oxford: Oxford University Press, 1997.

Vaca de Vásquez, Elvira. Personal interview. Entre Ríos, Bolivia. 11 December 2000.

Weinstein, Barbara. *The Amazon Rubber Boom 1850-1920*. Stanford: Stanford University Press, 1983.

Willman, Alys, with Sharon Hostetler and Steve Bennett. *A Bankrupt Future: the Human Cost of Nicaragua's Debt*. Washington, DC: Witness for Peace, 2000.

Young, Mariana, "Las mujeres son mejores pagadoras que los hombres?" *El cooperativista* (Managua) 3,17 (1999): 11.

INDEX

AGMV Marquis

MEMBER OF SCABRINI MEDIA

Quebec, Canada
2002